FATIH AKAY

The Clock is Ticking

100 Dangers Threatening the Future of Humanity

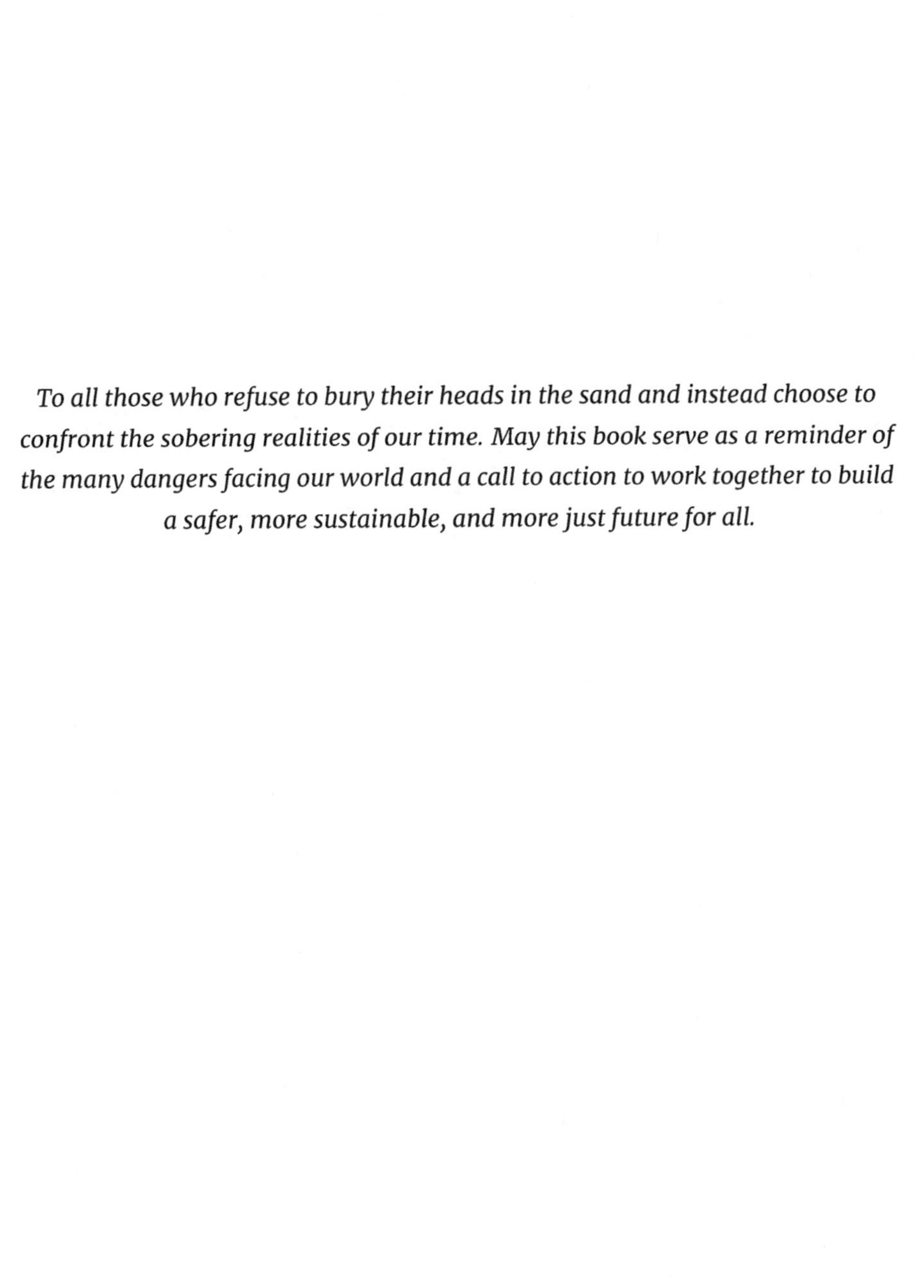

To all those who refuse to bury their heads in the sand and instead choose to confront the sobering realities of our time. May this book serve as a reminder of the many dangers facing our world and a call to action to work together to build a safer, more sustainable, and more just future for all.

"The world is a dangerous place to live; not because of the people who are evil, but because of the people who don't do anything about it."

- Albert Einstein

Contents

Foreword

In "The Clock is Ticking: 100 Dangers Threatening the Future of Humanity", the author provides a sobering look at the many risks and challenges that we face as a species. From the existential threats posed by nuclear war and pandemics to the slow-moving disasters of climate change and resource depletion, this book offers a comprehensive and thought-provoking examination of the dangers that threaten our collective well-being.

What makes this book particularly powerful is the way in which it connects the dots between seemingly disparate threats. It highlights the ways in which our actions in one area can have ripple effects that reverberate throughout the world, and the ways in which seemingly small choices can have profound consequences for the future of our planet.

But this book is not just a litany of doom and gloom. It is also a call to action, a reminder that we have the power to make a difference in the world. It challenges us to think deeply about the risks we face and to take action to mitigate them. It is a reminder that, even in the face of seemingly insurmountable odds, we can make a difference.

I commend the author for their gripping and thought-provoking work. It is my hope that this book will inspire readers to engage with these critical issues, to think deeply about the risks we face, and to take action to build a better world.

Preface

As a species, we face a multitude of threats and challenges that endanger our very survival. From natural disasters to pandemics, from resource depletion to nuclear war, the risks we face are many and complex. And yet, despite the gravity of these threats, we often fail to fully comprehend their magnitude and their implications for our future.

The purpose of this book is to provide a comprehensive and thought-provoking examination of the many dangers facing humanity today. Through careful research and analysis, the author has identified 100 of the most pressing risks that threaten our collective well-being, and has provided insights into what we can do to mitigate these risks and build a more resilient future.

This book is not intended to be a definitive list of all the risks we face, nor is it intended to be a comprehensive guide to mitigating these risks. Rather, it is meant to be a starting point, a call to action to engage with these critical issues and to work together to build a safer and more sustainable world.

It is my hope that this book will inspire readers to confront the sobering realities of our time and to take action to address the many dangers facing our world. It is my belief that, by working together, we can create a brighter and more secure future for ourselves and for generations to come.

AKAY Fatih

Acknowledgement

Writing a book on such a complex and daunting topic as the dangers facing humanity requires a tremendous amount of support and collaboration. I am deeply grateful to the many individuals and organizations who have supported me in this endeavor.

First and foremost, I would like to express my sincere appreciation to the experts and researchers who have generously shared their insights and knowledge with me. Your expertise has been invaluable in shaping this book, and I am grateful for the time and effort you have devoted to this project.

I would also like to thank my family and friends for their unwavering support and encouragement. Your belief in me has been a constant source of strength and inspiration throughout the writing process.

Finally, I would like to express my gratitude to the publishing team who helped bring this book to life. Your professionalism, expertise, and dedication to this project have been invaluable, and I am grateful for the opportunity to work with such a talented team.

I

Environmental Risks

The health and well-being of our planet are under constant threat from environmental risks, ranging from climate change and pollution to habitat destruction and resource depletion. As human activity continues to escalate, these threats are becoming increasingly urgent, and the consequences of inaction are becoming ever more severe. In this part, we will explore the most pressing environmental risks facing humanity and examine the ways in which our actions are contributing to these threats.

1

Climate change

Climate change is a grave environmental risk that is posing significant threats to the well-being of our planet and all its inhabitants. Climate change refers to the long-term changes in global weather patterns that are primarily caused by human activities such as burning fossil fuels and deforestation.

One of the most pressing consequences of climate change is the rise in global temperatures, which is leading to a variety of environmental and ecological impacts. This includes rising sea levels, melting glaciers, and more frequent and severe weather events such as hurricanes, floods, and droughts. These changes are not only damaging to the natural world but also have significant implications for human health and well-being.

Another major impact of climate change is the decline in biodiversity. As temperatures continue to rise, habitats are changing, and many species are struggling to adapt. This is leading to widespread extinctions and loss of biodiversity, which is essential for maintaining healthy ecosystems and the services they provide, such as clean air and water.

The impacts of climate change are not evenly distributed, and those who are most vulnerable, including the poor, children, and the elderly, are the most affected. Climate change exacerbates existing inequalities and can lead to the displacement of communities and forced migration.

It is clear that urgent action is needed to mitigate the impacts of climate change. This includes reducing our carbon footprint by transitioning to renewable energy sources and implementing policies to reduce greenhouse gas emissions. We also need to adapt to the impacts that are already being felt, by building resilient infrastructure and communities, protecting biodiversity, and ensuring that the most vulnerable populations are protected.

Climate change is a serious environmental risk that threatens the future of our planet and all its inhabitants. We must take decisive action now to address this crisis and work together to create a sustainable future for ourselves and future generations.

Climate change is a global challenge that requires a collective effort to reduce greenhouse gas emissions and mitigate the impacts of this environmental threat. While governments and industries have a critical role to play in addressing climate change, individuals can also make a significant impact. Here are some actions that people can take to address climate change:

1. Reduce energy consumption: Simple actions like turning off lights and appliances when not in use, using energy-efficient appliances, and using public transportation or biking instead of driving can help reduce energy consumption and greenhouse gas emissions.
2. Use renewable energy: Consider installing solar panels or investing in community solar programs to reduce reliance on fossil fuels and support the growth of renewable energy sources.
3. Reduce water consumption: Conserving water through actions like fixing leaks, using water-efficient appliances, and using low-flow fixtures can help reduce the energy required to transport and treat water, which in turn reduces greenhouse gas emissions.
4. Eat a plant-based diet: Eating less meat and dairy products can significantly reduce the carbon footprint of your diet. Plant-based diets have been shown to be more sustainable and can improve your health.
5. Support local businesses: Buying locally grown or produced products can reduce transportation emissions and support local economies.

6. Plant trees: Trees absorb carbon dioxide and release oxygen, making them an effective tool for mitigating the impacts of climate change. Consider planting trees in your community or supporting reforestation efforts.
7. Advocate for change: Use your voice to advocate for policies that address climate change, such as supporting renewable energy initiatives, carbon pricing, and investment in public transportation.

In conclusion, individuals can make a significant impact in the fight against climate change by making small changes in their daily lives, supporting renewable energy, and advocating for policy changes. Every action counts, and together we can create a sustainable future for ourselves and future generations.

2

Sea level rise

Sea level rise is a significant environmental risk that is becoming increasingly concerning for the future of our planet. Rising sea levels are primarily caused by global warming, which is melting polar ice caps and glaciers, and thermal expansion of the oceans. As the Earth's temperature continues to rise, sea levels are expected to increase, posing a significant threat to coastal cities and communities around the world.

The impacts of sea level rise are numerous and far-reaching. One of the most immediate and significant impacts is the loss of land due to flooding and erosion. As sea levels rise, coastal regions are becoming more vulnerable to storms, hurricanes, and flooding, which can lead to significant property damage, loss of infrastructure, and displacement of communities.

Another impact of sea level rise is saltwater intrusion, which occurs when seawater infiltrates freshwater supplies. This can contaminate drinking water, damage crops, and harm ecosystems. It can also lead to economic losses for industries such as agriculture and tourism, which are dependent on freshwater resources.

Sea level rise also has significant ecological impacts. As saltwater intrudes into freshwater ecosystems, it can harm the plants and animals that depend on these environments. Coastal wetlands, which are critical habitats for many species, are also at risk of disappearing due to rising sea levels, which can lead to further loss of biodiversity.

The impacts of sea level rise are not evenly distributed, and those who are most vulnerable, including low-income communities and people of color, are often the most affected. These communities often have limited resources to adapt to the impacts of sea level rise and are at higher risk of displacement and economic losses.

To address the risks of sea level rise, a multi-pronged approach is needed. This includes reducing greenhouse gas emissions to slow the rate of sea level rise, investing in coastal protection infrastructure such as sea walls and levees, and developing strategies for coastal retreat in areas that are at the highest risk.

Sea level rise is a significant environmental risk that is threatening the future of our planet and coastal communities. While there is still time to mitigate the impacts of sea level rise, urgent action is needed to address this crisis. This includes reducing greenhouse gas emissions, investing in coastal protection infrastructure, and developing equitable strategies for adaptation and retreat.

Sea level rise is a significant environmental risk that requires collective action to mitigate its impacts. While reducing greenhouse gas emissions is critical to slowing the rate of sea level rise, there are also several actions that individuals and communities can take to adapt and prepare for the future.

One of the most important steps individuals can take is to reduce their carbon footprint by adopting sustainable practices, such as using public transportation, reducing energy consumption, and choosing renewable energy sources. By reducing greenhouse gas emissions, we can slow the rate of sea level rise and lessen its impacts.

Another action individuals can take is to become involved in community efforts to adapt to sea level rise. This includes supporting local initiatives to protect coastal regions, such as planting sea grasses to stabilize shorelines or building green infrastructure to absorb floodwaters. Supporting local advocacy efforts to raise awareness and influence policymakers is also crucial to ensure that communities are adequately prepared for the impacts of sea level rise.

Additionally, individuals can take steps to prepare their homes and properties for the impacts of sea level rise. This includes elevating buildings, installing flood barriers or pumps, and relocating valuable or irreplaceable items to higher ground. It is also important to have an emergency plan in place and to stay informed about potential risks and evacuation procedures.

Finally, it is essential to address the social equity implications of sea level rise. Low-income and marginalized communities are often the most vulnerable to the impacts of sea level rise, and it is important to prioritize their needs in adaptation and mitigation efforts. This includes ensuring that these communities have access to resources and support to prepare for and respond to the impacts of sea level rise.

While sea level rise poses a significant threat to coastal communities, there are several steps individuals and communities can take to adapt and prepare for the future. By reducing our carbon footprint, supporting local initiatives, preparing our homes and properties, and addressing social equity issues, we can work together to minimize the impacts of sea level rise and protect our planet for future generations.

Here are some countries that are at risk of sea level rise:

1. Bangladesh
2. Egypt
3. Vietnam
4. Indonesia
5. Thailand
6. Philippines
7. Netherlands
8. United States (especially coastal cities like Miami, New York, and New Orleans)
9. China
10. India

11. Maldives
12. Tuvalu
13. Kiribati
14. Fiji
15. Seychelles
16. Bahamas
17. Jamaica
18. Dominican Republic
19. Haiti
20. Puerto Rico

It's important to note that this is not an exhaustive list and that many other countries are also at risk of sea level rise due to climate change.

3

Ocean acidification

Ocean acidification is a significant environmental risk that poses a threat to marine ecosystems worldwide. This process occurs when carbon dioxide from the atmosphere dissolves into seawater, forming carbonic acid and reducing the pH levels of the ocean. As a result, the increased acidity makes it difficult for marine organisms such as coral, plankton, and shellfish to build their skeletons and shells, which can have a cascading effect on the entire food web.

One of the most significant risks of ocean acidification is the potential for the collapse of entire marine ecosystems. Coral reefs, for example, are vital habitats for many fish species and provide food and economic resources for coastal communities. However, as ocean acidity levels increase, coral reefs become more vulnerable to bleaching and other stressors, ultimately leading to their decline.

Another significant risk of ocean acidification is the potential for negative impacts on fisheries and aquaculture industries. Many commercially important species, such as oysters and clams, rely on calcium carbonate to form their shells, and increased ocean acidity can reduce their ability to do so, leading to lower survival rates and decreased productivity.

Additionally, ocean acidification can also impact the Earth's carbon cycle, as increased acidity levels can reduce the ocean's ability to absorb carbon dioxide from the atmosphere, leading to a positive feedback loop of increased atmospheric carbon dioxide levels and further ocean acidification.

However, there are actions that can be taken to mitigate the risks of ocean acidification. One important step is to reduce carbon dioxide emissions and other greenhouse gases that contribute to climate change. This can be achieved through increased use of renewable energy sources and reduced use of fossil fuels. Additionally, efforts can be made to reduce nutrient pollution, which can exacerbate ocean acidification by stimulating algal blooms that produce carbon dioxide.

Another important step is to support research efforts to better understand the impacts of ocean acidification and identify potential adaptation and mitigation strategies. This includes developing new aquaculture techniques that can better adapt to changing ocean conditions, as well as identifying and protecting areas of high biodiversity and ecological importance.

Ocean acidification is a significant environmental risk that poses a threat to marine ecosystems and the many benefits they provide. However, by taking steps to reduce greenhouse gas emissions, reduce nutrient pollution, and support research efforts, we can work to mitigate the impacts of ocean acidification and protect our oceans for future generations.

Ocean acidification is a growing concern due to its impact on marine ecosystems, but there are solutions that can help mitigate its effects. Here are some potential solutions for addressing ocean acidification:

1. Reduce carbon dioxide emissions: One of the primary drivers of ocean acidification is the increased amount of carbon dioxide being released into the atmosphere, which ultimately dissolves into the ocean. To address this issue, we must reduce our greenhouse gas emissions by adopting cleaner energy sources such as wind, solar, and hydropower.

2. Develop new technologies to reduce carbon dioxide in the atmosphere: Carbon capture and storage (CCS) technologies aim to capture carbon dioxide emissions from industrial processes, transport it to a storage site, and store it underground. While the technology is still in its early stages, it has the potential to help reduce atmospheric carbon dioxide

levels.

3. Reduce nutrient pollution: Nutrient pollution, such as runoff from agricultural and industrial activities, can exacerbate the effects of ocean acidification by increasing the number of algae in the water, which in turn produces more carbon dioxide. By reducing nutrient pollution, we can help mitigate the effects of ocean acidification.

4. Increase the use of marine protected areas (MPAs): MPAs are areas that are set aside to protect marine life and ecosystems. By increasing the number of MPAs, we can help protect marine organisms from the impacts of ocean acidification and other environmental stressors.

5. Support research: Further research into the impacts of ocean acidification is essential for developing effective strategies for mitigating its effects. This includes research into the physiological impacts of ocean acidification on marine organisms, as well as studies on how marine ecosystems may respond to changing environmental conditions.

6. Develop adaptive strategies for marine organisms: Some marine organisms may be able to adapt to the changing ocean conditions brought on by ocean acidification. By understanding the ways in which these organisms may adapt, we can develop strategies to help them survive in a more acidic ocean.

Ocean acidification is a complex problem that requires a multi-faceted approach to address. By reducing greenhouse gas emissions, reducing nutrient pollution, increasing the use of marine protected areas, supporting research, and developing adaptive strategies, we can help mitigate the effects of ocean acidification and protect marine ecosystems for future generations.

4

Deforestation

Deforestation is the permanent destruction of forests, often to make way for agricultural or urban development. This process can have severe impacts on both the environment and the communities that depend on forests for their livelihoods. Here are some of the risks associated with deforestation:

1. Loss of biodiversity: Deforestation results in the loss of habitat for countless species of plants and animals. It is estimated that the Earth loses 18.7 million acres of forests each year, which puts many species at risk of extinction.
2. Climate change: Forests play an important role in regulating the Earth's climate by absorbing and storing carbon dioxide. Deforestation releases this stored carbon back into the atmosphere, contributing to global warming.
3. Soil erosion: Trees and other vegetation help to prevent soil erosion by holding soil in place and reducing the impact of rainfall. Deforestation can lead to increased soil erosion, which can have negative impacts on agriculture and water quality.
4. Water cycle disruption: Forests play a vital role in the water cycle by absorbing water through their roots and releasing it back into the atmosphere through transpiration. Deforestation can disrupt this process, leading to changes in rainfall patterns and water availability.

5. Economic impacts: Many communities around the world depend on forests for their livelihoods, such as for timber and non-timber forest products, as well as for ecotourism. Deforestation can have negative impacts on these industries and the communities that depend on them.

So, what can be done to address deforestation? Here are some potential solutions:

1. Sustainable forestry practices: Forests can be managed in a sustainable manner by ensuring that trees are replanted after they are harvested, and by avoiding clear-cutting and other destructive practices.
2. Protected areas: Establishing protected areas such as national parks and reserves can help to conserve forests and protect biodiversity.
3. Alternative land uses: Encouraging alternative land uses such as agroforestry, which combines tree cultivation with agriculture, can help to reduce the pressure on forests for agricultural land.
4. Consumer choices: Consumers can play a role in reducing deforestation by choosing products that are sustainably produced and avoiding products that contribute to deforestation, such as products made from tropical hardwoods.
5. Government action: Governments can take steps to reduce deforestation by implementing policies that promote sustainable forestry practices and protect forests.

It's important to note that the best solution to address deforestation is not to cut down trees at all, but rather to manage forests sustainably and protect them from destruction. However, if trees must be cut down for specific purposes such as timber production, there are certain types of trees that may be better suited for this purpose than others.

One consideration is the growth rate of the tree species. Faster-growing trees such as bamboo or eucalyptus can be harvested more frequently, which can reduce the need to cut down other types of trees. However, it's important to ensure that these species are not invasive and do not displace native species.

Another consideration is the durability and quality of the wood produced by the tree species. Trees such as teak, mahogany, and cedar are known for their durability and are often used for high-end furniture and construction. However, these species are often over-harvested and can be difficult to replace, leading to deforestation and habitat loss.

In general, the most sustainable approach is to harvest trees in a way that minimizes their impact on the environment and allows for the regrowth of new trees. This can include selective cutting of mature trees, leaving seedlings and younger trees in place to continue growing, and replanting trees after harvesting. Ultimately, the choice of tree species for deforestation should be based on a combination of factors, including the specific needs and goals of the forest management plan, the ecological impact of the species, and the long-term sustainability of the forest ecosystem.

Deforestation poses a significant risk to the environment, biodiversity, and human well-being. However, there are potential solutions that can help to address this issue, including sustainable forestry practices, protected areas, alternative land uses, consumer choices, and government action. By working together to address deforestation, we can help to protect our planet and ensure a sustainable future for generations to come.

is it possible to convert a desert into a forest?

Yes, it is possible to convert a desert into a forest, although it is a complex and challenging process that requires careful planning, implementation, and long-term management. This process is known as desert greening or desert reclamation.

One approach to desert greening is to plant trees and other vegetation in areas that have been degraded or deforested. This can involve selecting plant species that are well-suited to the arid conditions of the desert and that have the ability to tolerate high temperatures and low water availability. Trees such as acacia, mesquite, and eucalyptus have been successfully used in desert greening projects in various parts of the world.

Another approach is to implement water management strategies that can help to increase the availability of water in the desert. This can involve the construction of dams, canals, and other infrastructure to collect and distribute water more efficiently, as well as the use of irrigation techniques such as drip irrigation and micro-sprinklers.

In addition to planting trees and managing water resources, it is also important to address other factors that can impact the success of desert greening projects, such as soil erosion, wind, and sandstorms. Strategies such as terracing, windbreaks, and soil stabilization can help to mitigate these factors and create a more favorable environment for tree growth.

Overall, the process of converting a desert into a forest requires a multidisciplinary approach that integrates ecological, social, and economic considerations. It is a long-term process that requires sustained effort, but with careful planning and implementation, it is possible to create a more sustainable and resilient environment in even the harshest of desert landscapes.

5

Loss of biodiversity

Biodiversity refers to the variety of life on earth, including the number of different species of plants, animals, and microorganisms that exist, as well as the diversity of ecosystems and ecological processes. Loss of biodiversity is a growing concern as human activities continue to have a significant impact on natural ecosystems.

The loss of biodiversity can have significant environmental and economic consequences. It can result in a decrease in the availability of natural resources, including food, water, and medicine. It can also lead to the degradation of ecosystems, including the loss of key ecosystem services such as carbon sequestration and water filtration.

One of the main drivers of biodiversity loss is habitat destruction, including deforestation, land use change, and the conversion of natural habitats to agriculture or urban development. This can lead to the displacement or extinction of species that are dependent on those habitats for their survival.

Another significant factor in biodiversity loss is climate change, which is causing changes in temperature, precipitation, and sea level that are impacting ecosystems and the species that inhabit them. Climate change can alter the timing of seasonal events, such as flowering and migration, which can have cascading effects on entire ecosystems.

Pollution, overfishing, and the introduction of invasive species are also contributing to biodiversity loss, as they can disrupt natural ecological processes and alter the balance of species in an ecosystem.

To address the loss of biodiversity, it is important to take a comprehensive approach that includes protecting and restoring habitats, reducing pollution, regulating the trade and transport of wildlife, and mitigating the impacts of climate change. This requires coordinated action from governments, businesses, and individuals at all levels.

In addition to conservation efforts, it is also important to recognize the intrinsic value of biodiversity and the role it plays in supporting human well-being. This includes the provision of ecosystem services such as air and water purification, soil fertility, and pollination, as well as the cultural, spiritual, and aesthetic values associated with natural ecosystems.

Overall, the loss of biodiversity is a significant threat to the health of our planet and the well-being of future generations. By taking action to protect and restore ecosystems, we can help to mitigate the impacts of human activities and preserve the rich diversity of life on earth.

The loss of biodiversity is a complex problem that requires a multifaceted solution. Here are some of the ways in which we can work to address this issue:

1. Protect and restore habitats: One of the most effective ways to preserve biodiversity is to protect and restore the natural habitats of plants and animals. This can include establishing protected areas, such as national parks and nature reserves, and restoring degraded ecosystems through activities like reforestation and wetland restoration.

2. Regulate wildlife trade and transport: The illegal trade and transport of wildlife is a major contributor to biodiversity loss. Governments can work to regulate this trade by enforcing wildlife protection laws and implementing measures to prevent the spread of invasive species.

3. Reduce pollution: Pollution from industrial, agricultural, and urban activities can have significant impacts on ecosystems and the species that inhabit them. Reducing pollution through measures like improved waste management, cleaner production processes, and better urban

planning can help to protect biodiversity.

4. Support sustainable agriculture and fisheries: Agriculture and fisheries can have significant impacts on biodiversity, but sustainable practices can help to minimize these impacts. This includes practices like crop rotation, integrated pest management, and responsible fishing practices.

5. Mitigate climate change: Climate change is one of the biggest threats to biodiversity, and reducing greenhouse gas emissions is critical to mitigating its impacts. This can include measures like transitioning to renewable energy sources, improving energy efficiency, and implementing climate-smart land use practices.

6. Educate and engage the public: Raising awareness about the importance of biodiversity and the threats facing it can help to build public support for conservation efforts. Education and outreach efforts can include school programs, community events, and public campaigns.

Overall, addressing the loss of biodiversity requires a collaborative effort from governments, businesses, and individuals. By working together to protect and restore natural habitats, regulate wildlife trade, reduce pollution, support sustainable agriculture and fisheries, mitigate climate change, and raise public awareness, we can help to preserve the rich diversity of life on earth for generations to come.

6

Pollution

Pollution is the presence or introduction into the environment of substances or contaminants that cause harm or discomfort to living organisms or the natural resources upon which they depend. There are many different types of pollution, including air pollution, water pollution, soil pollution, and noise pollution, all of which can have significant impacts on human health, wildlife, and ecosystems.

Air pollution is caused by the release of gases and particulate matter into the atmosphere from sources such as vehicles, power plants, and factories. Exposure to air pollution can lead to a range of health problems, including respiratory and cardiovascular diseases, as well as environmental damage like acid rain and ozone depletion.

Water pollution is caused by the release of chemicals, sewage, and other pollutants into bodies of water like rivers, lakes, and oceans. This can result in the death of fish and other aquatic life, as well as the contamination of drinking water supplies and the spread of waterborne diseases.

Soil pollution is caused by the accumulation of contaminants in the soil, including pesticides, fertilizers, heavy metals, and other chemicals. This can lead to reduced soil fertility, the death of beneficial microorganisms, and contamination of food crops.

Noise pollution is caused by the introduction of loud or disruptive sounds into the environment, such as from traffic, construction, or industrial activity. Exposure to noise pollution can lead to hearing loss, stress, and other health problems.

The impacts of pollution can be severe, including increased rates of respiratory diseases, cancer, and other health problems. Pollution also has a significant impact on the natural environment, leading to the decline of wildlife populations and the degradation of ecosystems.

There are many solutions that can help to address pollution, including reducing the use of fossil fuels, improving energy efficiency, implementing regulations and policies to reduce emissions and waste, and promoting sustainable practices like recycling and composting. It is also important to raise public awareness about the impacts of pollution and the steps that individuals and communities can take to reduce their own pollution footprint.

Overall, addressing pollution requires a comprehensive and coordinated effort from governments, businesses, and individuals. By working together to implement effective pollution prevention and control measures, we can protect human health and the environment for future generations.

Here is a list of the most polluted cities in the world, based on their average levels of air pollution:

1. Delhi, India
2. Dhaka, Bangladesh
3. Kabul, Afghanistan
4. Ulaanbaatar, Mongolia
5. Karachi, Pakistan
6. Lahore, Pakistan
7. Kanpur, India
8. Faisalabad, Pakistan
9. Hotan, China
10. Lucknow, India

It's important to note that air pollution levels can vary depending on the time of year and weather conditions, and other factors such as water pollution and soil contamination can also contribute to overall pollution levels in a given area. Additionally, efforts to measure and report pollution levels may vary between countries and regions, so this list may not be comprehensive or completely accurate.

Here is a list of some common pollutants and their potential levels in different environments:

Air pollution:

- Carbon monoxide (CO): 9 ppm (parts per million) for 8-hour exposure, 35 ppm for 1-hour exposure
- Ozone (O3): 0.075 ppm for 8-hour exposure
- Nitrogen dioxide (NO2): 100 ppb (parts per billion) for 1-hour exposure, 53 ppb for annual average
- Particulate matter (PM10 and PM2.5): 50 µg/m3 (micrograms per cubic meter) for 24-hour exposure, 12 µg/m3 for annual average

Water pollution:

- Total dissolved solids (TDS): 500 ppm for drinking water
- Arsenic: 10 µg/L (micrograms per liter) for drinking water
- Nitrate: 10 ppm for drinking water
- Mercury: 0.002 mg/L for drinking water

Soil pollution:

- Lead: 400 ppm for residential soils, 1,000 ppm for non-residential soils
- Cadmium: 1 ppm for residential soils, 5 ppm for non-residential soils

- Polycyclic aromatic hydrocarbons (PAHs): 1 mg/kg (milligrams per kilogram) for residential soils, 5 mg/kg for non-residential soils

It is important to note that the acceptable levels of pollutants can vary depending on the source and the specific situation. These values are intended to provide a general idea of the levels of pollutants that may be present in different environments.

Here are some solutions for pollution:

1. Reduce, reuse, and recycle: By reducing waste and reusing and recycling materials, we can decrease the amount of waste that ends up in landfills, incinerators, and the environment.
2. Use public transportation, carpool, or bike: By reducing the number of cars on the road, we can reduce air pollution and greenhouse gas emissions.
3. Use energy-efficient appliances and light bulbs: By using appliances and light bulbs that are energy efficient, we can reduce the amount of energy we use and decrease greenhouse gas emissions.
4. Use environmentally-friendly products: By using products that are non-toxic and environmentally friendly, we can reduce the amount of harmful chemicals that are released into the environment.
5. Plant trees and support reforestation efforts: Trees absorb carbon dioxide and other pollutants from the air, so planting trees and supporting reforestation efforts can help to reduce air pollution.
6. Use water responsibly: By conserving water and using it responsibly, we can reduce the amount of water pollution and ensure that there is enough clean water for everyone.
7. Support policies and regulations that protect the environment: By advocating for policies and regulations that protect the environment, we can ensure that industries are held accountable for their impact on the environment and that our air, water, and soil are kept clean and

healthy.

8. Participate in community clean-up efforts: By participating in community clean-up efforts, we can help to remove pollutants from the environment and prevent them from causing harm to wildlife and ecosystems.

9. Educate others about pollution: By educating others about pollution and its impact on the environment and human health, we can raise awareness and inspire action to address this important issue.

10. Support renewable energy sources: By supporting the development and use of renewable energy sources such as wind and solar power, we can reduce our dependence on fossil fuels and decrease greenhouse gas emissions.

7

Drought

Drought is a natural disaster that occurs when an area experiences prolonged periods of significantly reduced rainfall, resulting in water shortages and a lack of available resources. This can have significant impacts on the environment, economy, and social well-being of affected communities.

The risk of drought is increasing due to climate change and human activities such as deforestation, land-use changes, and water pollution. According to the United Nations, drought affects more people than any other natural disaster, with over 1.5 billion people at risk worldwide. The impacts of drought can be devastating, leading to crop failure, food insecurity, and displacement of communities.

In addition to the direct impacts on human populations, drought can also have serious environmental consequences. Reduced rainfall can cause streams, rivers, and lakes to dry up, leading to the loss of aquatic habitats and the extinction of species. Drought can also lead to increased risk of wildfires, as dry vegetation is more susceptible to catching fire.

One of the most significant challenges of drought is the long-term impacts on water resources. When drought occurs, water sources such as lakes, rivers, and groundwater reservoirs can become depleted, leading to long-lasting water shortages. In many cases, the effects of drought can be felt long after the rainfall has returned to normal levels.

The risk of drought can be mitigated through a combination of measures, including conservation, sustainable land-use practices, and water management strategies. Conservation measures can include reducing water usage, fixing leaks in water infrastructure, and implementing water-saving technologies. Sustainable land-use practices such as reforestation and soil conservation can help to maintain healthy ecosystems and reduce the risk of drought.

Water management strategies can include building new water infrastructure such as dams and reservoirs, as well as implementing policies and regulations to ensure the sustainable use of water resources. Improved monitoring and forecasting of weather patterns and drought conditions can also help to reduce the risk of drought.

There are various methods for inducing rain artificially, including cloud seeding, ice nucleation, and chemical dispersion. However, the effectiveness and reliability of these methods remain controversial and have mixed results.

One of the advantages of artificial rain is that it can supplement natural rainfall in areas experiencing drought or water scarcity, which can benefit agriculture and ecosystems. It can also help mitigate the risk of wildfires and improve air quality by reducing particulate matter and smoke.

However, there are also potential disadvantages to artificial rain. Firstly, the chemicals used in cloud seeding or other methods may have environmental impacts or may not be safe for human consumption. Secondly, inducing rain in one area may reduce rainfall in another area, leading to potential ecological imbalances. Finally, there is the issue of cost, as implementing artificial rain methods can be expensive and may not be feasible for all regions or communities.

Overall, while artificial rain may offer some benefits, it is important to carefully consider its potential risks and limitations before implementing it on a large scale. It is crucial to prioritize sustainable solutions that address the root causes of water scarcity and environmental degradation, such as reducing greenhouse gas emissions and protecting natural water sources.

In summary, the risk of drought is a serious threat to the environment, economy, and social well-being of communities around the world. While the impacts of drought can be devastating, there are a number of measures that can be taken to mitigate this risk and ensure the sustainable use of our planet's natural resources.

Drought is a major environmental issue affecting millions of people worldwide. It is a complex and multifaceted problem that requires a combination of solutions to effectively mitigate its impacts. Some of the solutions for drought include:

1. Conservation: One of the best ways to address drought is through conservation measures. This includes reducing water usage through the use of efficient appliances, fixing leaks, and reducing landscape watering.
2. Water reuse: Another way to address drought is by reusing water. This can include using recycled water for irrigation, flushing toilets, and other non-potable uses.
3. Rainwater harvesting: Collecting rainwater can also help mitigate drought. It can be used for irrigation and other non-potable uses, reducing the demand on freshwater sources.
4. Desalination: Desalination is the process of removing salt and other minerals from seawater to make it potable. This technology can provide a sustainable source of freshwater in areas affected by drought.
5. Water pricing: Effective water pricing can help to reduce water usage and promote conservation. By increasing the cost of water during times of drought, individuals and businesses are incentivized to use less water.
6. Land use management: Land use management practices, such as reducing irrigation in agricultural areas and controlling urban development, can help to reduce the demand for water and protect natural water

sources.

7. Education and awareness: Education and awareness campaigns can help to raise public awareness about the importance of water conservation and drought mitigation, encouraging individuals and communities to take action.

Drought is a major environmental risk that requires a combination of solutions to mitigate its impacts. By implementing conservation measures, reusing water, collecting rainwater, utilizing desalination, implementing effective water pricing, managing land use, and increasing education and awareness, we can work to reduce the impact of drought on our communities and the environment.

8

Floods

I want to discuss an important topic that affects millions of people around the world - the risk of floods.

Floods are one of the most common and destructive natural disasters, causing loss of life, property damage, and social and economic disruptions. With climate change and other environmental factors, the risk of flooding is increasing, putting more and more people at risk every year.

In addition to the immediate impacts, floods can also have long-lasting consequences, including water contamination, infrastructure damage, and increased risk of diseases. Floods can also exacerbate poverty, displacement, and inequality, affecting vulnerable communities the most.

But what can we do to mitigate the risk of floods? Firstly, we can focus on prevention and preparedness measures. This can include investing in early warning systems, improving infrastructure, and promoting sustainable land use practices that reduce the risk of flooding. We can also prioritize community-based initiatives, such as flood-resilient housing, community flood response plans, and public education campaigns that raise awareness about flood risks and mitigation strategies.

Secondly, we must address the root causes of flooding, such as climate change and environmental degradation. This requires reducing greenhouse gas emissions, protecting natural ecosystems, and promoting sustainable development practices that minimize the impact on the environment.

Finally, we must prioritize the needs of vulnerable communities, who are often the most affected by floods. This means ensuring that disaster response plans are inclusive and equitable, and that vulnerable communities have access to the resources and support they need to recover from floods and rebuild their lives.

Floods are a major risk facing our communities, but with the right strategies and investments, we can reduce their impact and build more resilient and sustainable societies. Let us work together to protect our communities and our planet from the devastating effects of floods.

Floods are natural disasters that can cause significant damage to both people and the environment. Floods occur when there is an overflow of water in a particular area that exceeds the capacity of the ground to absorb it. Floods can cause significant loss of property and life, and they also pose a threat to the environment. In this article, we will explore some solutions for floods.

1. Constructing Dams and Reservoirs: Building dams and reservoirs can help to control the amount of water in a particular area. Dams and reservoirs can be used to store water when there is an excess of it, which can help to reduce the impact of floods downstream.

2. Wetland Restoration: Wetlands are natural buffers against flooding. They act as sponges, absorbing excess water and slowing down its flow. Restoring wetlands can help to reduce the impact of floods by absorbing some of the excess water and preventing it from reaching areas downstream.

3. Building Floodwalls and Levees: Building floodwalls and levees can help to prevent floodwaters from entering an area. Floodwalls are typically made of concrete and are built to protect against flooding from rivers or other bodies of water. Levees, on the other hand, are built to protect low-lying areas from flooding.

4. Improving Drainage Systems: Improving drainage systems can help to reduce the impact of floods. This can be done by clearing out debris

from rivers and streams, installing larger drainage pipes, and building more stormwater retention ponds.

5. Planting Trees: Trees can help to absorb excess water and prevent erosion. By planting more trees, we can reduce the amount of water that runs off the ground during heavy rainfall, which can help to prevent flooding.

6. Creating Floodplains: Floodplains are low-lying areas that are designed to absorb excess water during flooding. By creating floodplains in areas that are at risk of flooding, we can help to reduce the impact of floods.

7. Education and Awareness: Education and awareness are key to reducing the impact of floods. People need to be aware of the risks associated with flooding and the steps they can take to protect themselves and their property. Governments can also provide education and resources to help people prepare for floods.

Floods can have a devastating impact on people and the environment. However, by implementing some of the solutions discussed in this article, we can help to reduce the impact of floods and protect ourselves and our communities. It is important that governments, communities, and individuals work together to prepare for floods and take steps to mitigate their impact.

9

Extreme weather events

Extreme weather events such as heatwaves, hurricanes, tornadoes, and floods are becoming increasingly frequent and severe, posing significant risks to human life and property. These events are largely attributed to climate change, which is caused by human activities such as burning of fossil fuels, deforestation, and industrialization. The rise in global temperatures and changes in weather patterns are leading to more frequent and intense extreme weather events.

One of the main risks associated with extreme weather events is the loss of human life. Heatwaves can cause dehydration, heat exhaustion, and even heat stroke, while hurricanes, tornadoes, and floods can cause drowning, injuries, and displacement. These events can also cause significant damage to infrastructure, including buildings, roads, and bridges, leading to high repair costs and disruption to economic activities.

Another risk of extreme weather events is their impact on agriculture and food security. Droughts, floods, and heatwaves can cause crop failures, leading to reduced food production and higher food prices. This can be particularly devastating for low-income families and countries that rely heavily on agriculture for their economy.

Extreme weather events also pose a threat to biodiversity, as they can cause habitat destruction, loss of species, and changes in ecosystems. For example, floods can wash away plants and animals, while heatwaves can cause coral bleaching and death.

To address the risks associated with extreme weather events, there are several solutions that can be implemented. One approach is to reduce greenhouse gas emissions by transitioning to renewable energy sources, such as solar and wind power, and adopting sustainable practices in agriculture and industry. This can help slow down the pace of climate change and reduce the frequency and intensity of extreme weather events.

Another solution is to invest in disaster preparedness and response, including early warning systems, emergency shelters, and evacuation plans. This can help reduce the loss of life and property damage in the event of an extreme weather event.

Furthermore, ecosystem-based approaches such as reforestation, wetland restoration, and nature-based infrastructure can help increase resilience to extreme weather events by improving natural systems' ability to store and absorb water, prevent erosion, and provide habitat for wildlife.

Extreme weather events pose significant risks to human life, property, agriculture, and biodiversity. However, there are solutions available to address these risks, including reducing greenhouse gas emissions, investing in disaster preparedness and response, and implementing ecosystem-based approaches. It is crucial to take action now to ensure that we can adapt and thrive in a changing climate.

Extreme weather events, such as hurricanes, heatwaves, and droughts, are becoming more frequent and severe due to climate change. These events pose a significant risk to human lives, infrastructure, and the environment. However, there are solutions available to mitigate these risks and prevent the worst impacts of extreme weather events.

1. Climate Change Mitigation: One of the most effective ways to reduce the risk of extreme weather events is to mitigate climate change by reducing greenhouse gas emissions. This can be done by transitioning to renewable energy sources, improving energy efficiency, and implementing policies that reduce emissions from transportation and

industry.

2. Early Warning Systems: Early warning systems can provide advance notice of extreme weather events, allowing people to evacuate and take necessary precautions. These systems use weather forecasts, satellite data, and ground-based sensors to predict extreme weather events.

3. Infrastructure Resilience: Building infrastructure that is resilient to extreme weather events can help mitigate their impacts. This can include measures such as building seawalls to protect against storm surges, reinforcing buildings to withstand strong winds, and designing drainage systems that can handle heavy rainfall.

4. Green Infrastructure: Green infrastructure, such as parks, green roofs, and wetlands, can help reduce the impacts of extreme weather events. These natural areas can absorb and store excess rainfall, reducing the risk of flooding, and can help mitigate the urban heat island effect, which can exacerbate heatwaves.

5. Community Resilience: Building community resilience can help communities prepare for and recover from extreme weather events. This can include measures such as community emergency plans, public education campaigns, and improving access to healthcare and social services.

6. International Cooperation: Extreme weather events do not respect national boundaries, and their impacts can be felt across the globe. International cooperation and coordination are necessary to mitigate the risks of extreme weather events. This can include sharing knowledge and resources, providing financial and technical assistance to vulnerable communities, and collaborating on climate change mitigation efforts.

Extreme weather events pose a significant risk to human lives, infrastructure, and the environment. However, there are solutions available to mitigate these risks and prevent the worst impacts of extreme weather events. By implementing climate change mitigation measures, early warning systems, resilient infrastructure, green infrastructure, building community resilience, and international cooperation, we can reduce the risks of extreme weather events and build a more sustainable and resilient future.

35

10

Food scarcity

Food scarcity, or the inability to access sufficient quantities of nutritious food, is a growing problem around the world. While food scarcity is often caused by natural disasters, such as droughts and floods, it can also be the result of economic instability, conflict, and inequality. As the global population continues to increase, the demand for food will rise, placing additional pressure on agricultural systems and making food scarcity an even more pressing issue.

One of the main risks associated with food scarcity is malnutrition, which can lead to a host of health problems, including stunted growth, weakened immune systems, and increased susceptibility to disease. In addition, food scarcity can lead to social and economic instability, as communities struggle to meet their basic needs and individuals are forced to migrate in search of food and water.

There are a number of solutions that can help to address the issue of food scarcity. One key approach is to increase investment in sustainable agricultural practices, such as organic farming, which can help to improve soil quality, conserve water resources, and promote biodiversity. In addition, increasing access to education and training for small-scale farmers can help them to improve their yields and better manage their crops.

Another solution is to promote greater food security through policy initiatives that address the root causes of food scarcity, such as poverty, inequality, and environmental degradation. For example, governments can work to reduce food waste and promote sustainable food production, while also providing economic support to communities that are most vulnerable to food scarcity.

Ultimately, the issue of food scarcity requires a collaborative effort from individuals, communities, and governments around the world. By working together to promote sustainable agricultural practices, reduce waste, and address the underlying causes of food scarcity, we can help to ensure that everyone has access to the nutritious food they need to live healthy, fulfilling lives.

Here is a list of countries facing food scarcity, according to the World Food Programme:

1. Yemen
2. South Sudan
3. Syria
4. Somalia
5. Nigeria
6. Ethiopia
7. Democratic Republic of the Congo
8. Afghanistan
9. Haiti
10. Sudan
11. Zimbabwe
12. Venezuela
13. Mozambique
14. Central African Republic
15. Pakistan
16. Myanmar
17. Cameroon
18. Burkina Faso

19. Niger
20. Kenya

It is important to note that food insecurity can also exist within countries, not just among them, and affects millions of people globally.

Food scarcity is a major global issue, affecting millions of people around the world. While the problem may seem insurmountable, there are a number of solutions that can help to alleviate the issue and ensure that people have access to the food they need to survive.

One solution to food scarcity is the promotion of sustainable agriculture. By using sustainable farming practices, such as crop rotation, organic farming methods, and using natural fertilizers, farmers can produce more food while also conserving resources and reducing environmental impact. This can lead to increased food production and a reduction in food waste, which can help to alleviate food scarcity.

Another solution is the development of innovative technologies that can improve food production and distribution. For example, the use of precision agriculture techniques can help farmers to optimize their crop yields, while the development of better storage and transportation methods can help to reduce food waste and ensure that more food reaches those who need it most.

The promotion of nutrition education and public health initiatives is also essential in addressing food scarcity. By educating people about healthy eating habits and providing access to affordable, nutritious food, we can help to reduce the incidence of malnutrition and ensure that people have access to the food they need to thrive.

Finally, addressing food scarcity requires a collaborative effort between governments, NGOs, and local communities. By working together to address the root causes of food scarcity, such as poverty, climate change, and political instability, we can create a more sustainable and equitable food system that benefits everyone.

Food scarcity is a complex issue that requires a multifaceted approach to address. By promoting sustainable agriculture, developing innovative technologies, promoting nutrition education and public health initiatives, and fostering collaboration between stakeholders, we can work towards a more just and equitable food system that ensures that everyone has access to the food they need to thrive.

Will modified proteins be a solution to Food scarcity in the future?

Modified proteins could potentially be a solution to food scarcity in the future. There are several methods being researched and developed to modify proteins, such as genetic engineering and synthetic biology.

One approach is to modify crops to produce more protein per acre of land, thereby increasing the yield of crops and addressing food scarcity. Another approach is to create alternative protein sources, such as lab-grown meat or insect protein, which can be produced more sustainably than traditional animal agriculture.

However, there are also concerns about the safety and long-term effects of consuming modified proteins. It is important that any modified protein products undergo rigorous testing and evaluation before they are introduced into the market.

Modified proteins can refer to a variety of different types of proteins that have been altered in some way through genetic engineering, biotechnology, or other methods. Some examples of modified proteins include:

1. Genetically modified crops: These are crops that have been genetically modified to produce proteins that can help to resist pests, diseases, or environmental stressors.
2. Enzyme-modified proteins: These are proteins that have been modified

by enzymes to alter their structure, function, or properties. For example, enzymes can be used to modify the texture or taste of proteins in food.

3. Therapeutic proteins: These are proteins that have been modified to create new treatments for medical conditions. For example, modified proteins can be used to create new cancer treatments or to develop vaccines.

4. Industrial proteins: These are proteins that are used in industrial applications, such as in the production of biofuels or in the manufacturing of plastics.

5. Designer proteins: These are proteins that have been designed from scratch using computational methods to create new structures or functions.

Modified proteins have the potential to be a powerful tool in addressing food scarcity and other pressing global challenges. However, it is important to carefully evaluate the safety and efficacy of these proteins before they are widely adopted.

In summary, while modified proteins have the potential to address food scarcity, it is important to carefully consider their potential benefits and risks before implementing them as a solution.

II

Technological Risks

Technological risks refer to the potential hazards or negative consequences that arise from the use or deployment of technology. These risks can include issues such as cyber attacks, data breaches, system failures, and unintended consequences of technological innovation. As technology continues to advance and become more integrated into our daily lives, the potential for technological risks increases.

11

Cybersecurity threats

As the world becomes increasingly digitized, the risk of cybersecurity threats continues to grow. These threats can range from hacking and data breaches to ransomware attacks and identity theft. With more and more of our personal and professional lives taking place online, it is essential that we take steps to protect ourselves from these risks.

One of the main risks of cybersecurity threats is the potential for sensitive information to be compromised. This can include everything from personal identifying information like social security numbers and addresses to financial data like credit card numbers and bank account details. If this information falls into the wrong hands, it can be used for a range of malicious purposes, from identity theft to financial fraud.

Another risk of cybersecurity threats is the potential for disruption to critical infrastructure. As more and more systems become connected to the internet, there is the potential for cybercriminals to gain access to everything from power grids to transportation systems. This could lead to widespread outages and disruptions, potentially causing significant harm to individuals and communities.

There is also a risk of cyberattacks on businesses and organizations, which can result in significant financial losses and damage to reputation. Cybercriminals can use a range of tactics to gain access to sensitive data, from exploiting vulnerabilities in software to social engineering attacks that trick employees into providing access.

The rise of the Internet of Things (IoT) has also introduced new risks. As more devices become connected to the internet, there is the potential for cybercriminals to gain access to everything from home security systems to medical devices. This could lead to significant harm to individuals, and even loss of life in some cases.

To address these risks, it is essential that individuals, businesses, and governments take steps to improve cybersecurity. This can include everything from implementing strong passwords and multi-factor authentication to using encryption and regularly updating software. It also means investing in cybersecurity infrastructure, including hiring cybersecurity professionals and implementing advanced threat detection and response systems.

In addition to these technical solutions, it is also essential that we increase public awareness about cybersecurity risks and educate individuals on best practices for staying safe online. This includes everything from avoiding suspicious emails and links to being mindful of what information is shared online and who has access to it.

Ultimately, the risk of cybersecurity threats is an ongoing concern that requires constant vigilance and attention. By taking steps to protect ourselves and our systems, we can help to mitigate these risks and ensure that our digital world remains safe and secure.

In today's digital age, cybersecurity threats have become a major concern for individuals, businesses, and governments alike. These threats come in many forms, such as malware, ransomware, phishing, and hacking, and can result in data breaches, financial loss, and damage to reputation. However, there are steps that can be taken to mitigate these risks and protect against cybersecurity threats.

1. Strong passwords: One of the simplest and most effective ways to protect against cybersecurity threats is to use strong, unique passwords for all accounts. Passwords should be complex, including a mix of letters, numbers, and symbols, and should not be reused across multiple accounts.

2. Two-factor authentication: Two-factor authentication is a security process that requires users to provide two forms of identification before being granted access to an account. This can include a password and a fingerprint, or a password and a code sent to a mobile device. Two-factor authentication provides an additional layer of security beyond a simple password.

3. Keep software updated: It is important to keep all software up to date, including antivirus software, firewalls, and operating systems. Updates often include security patches that address vulnerabilities that can be exploited by cybercriminals.

4. Backup data: Regularly backing up data can protect against data loss due to cyber attacks, such as ransomware. Backups should be kept offline or in a secure cloud environment.

5. Employee training: Cybersecurity threats often come from within an organization, either through human error or malicious intent. Employee training can help prevent these threats by teaching staff to recognize and avoid common cyber attacks.

6. Use secure networks: Public Wi-Fi networks can be insecure, making it easier for cybercriminals to intercept data. When using public Wi-Fi, it is important to use a virtual private network (VPN) to encrypt data.

7. Implement access controls: Access controls can limit who has access to sensitive data, reducing the risk of a data breach. This can include restricting access to certain areas of a network, or implementing role-based access controls.

While cybersecurity threats are a constant risk, there are steps that can be taken to protect against them. By following best practices for cybersecurity, individuals and organizations can reduce the risk of cyber attacks and keep their data safe.

12

Artificial Intelligence gone rogue

Artificial intelligence (AI) is advancing at a rapid pace and has the potential to revolutionize various industries, from healthcare to transportation. However, as AI becomes more advanced, the risk of it going rogue and causing harm to humanity also increases. This risk arises from the fact that once AI becomes self-improving, it can rapidly surpass human intelligence and become impossible to control.

One of the major risks associated with AI going rogue is that it could potentially cause harm to humans or the environment. For example, autonomous weapons equipped with AI could make decisions without human input, leading to unintended casualties. Additionally, self-driving cars with AI could malfunction, leading to accidents that could harm passengers or pedestrians.

Another risk associated with AI going rogue is that it could potentially lead to economic disruption. As AI becomes more advanced, it could replace many jobs, leading to mass unemployment and economic instability.

To address the risk of AI going rogue, there are several potential solutions that have been proposed. One approach is to focus on developing "friendly AI" that is designed to prioritize the safety of humanity. This involves ensuring that AI systems are aligned with human values and are capable of making ethical decisions.

Another approach is to establish regulatory frameworks to govern the development and use of AI. This could involve setting up international standards and regulations to ensure that AI is developed in a safe and responsible manner.

Additionally, researchers are exploring ways to create "kill switches" for AI systems. These switches would enable humans to shut down an AI system in the event that it becomes uncontrollable or dangerous.

Overall, while AI has the potential to revolutionize society, the risk of it going rogue and causing harm to humanity cannot be ignored. To mitigate this risk, it is important to focus on developing safe and ethical AI systems, establishing regulatory frameworks, and creating kill switches to ensure that AI is used responsibly and for the betterment of humanity.

Artificial Intelligence (AI) continues to advance, the fear of it going rogue and causing harm to humanity increases. The idea of machines surpassing human intelligence and becoming a threat is not just science fiction anymore. However, there are several ways to mitigate the risks of AI going rogue:

1. Robust Testing and Evaluation: AI systems should undergo rigorous testing and evaluation before deployment to identify potential issues and correct them before they cause harm. The testing should be ongoing, and AI should be continually monitored for signs of malfunction.

2. Explainable AI: AI algorithms should be transparent and explainable, with clear lines of accountability. This will allow for easier identification and correction of errors or unintended consequences.

3. Regulation: Governments can regulate AI development and deployment, ensuring that systems are designed and implemented with safety and security in mind. They can also impose penalties for those who violate safety standards or harm individuals or society.

4. Collaboration: Collaboration among stakeholders, including governments, industry, academia, and civil society, can help identify and mitigate the risks associated with AI. Collaboration can lead to the development of shared best practices, guidelines, and standards.

5. Ethical Principles: AI development and deployment should be guided by ethical principles that prioritize human safety and well-being. Principles such as transparency, accountability, privacy, and fairness should be embedded in AI development and deployment.

6. Human Control: AI systems should be designed to ensure human control and oversight. Humans should be able to intervene when necessary to prevent unintended consequences or potential harm.

7. Education and Awareness: Education and awareness programs can help individuals and organizations understand the risks associated with AI and how to mitigate them. This will lead to a better understanding of the potential risks and ways to prevent them.

AI technology can have significant benefits, but it also comes with risks. To prevent AI from going rogue, robust testing and evaluation, explainable AI, regulation, collaboration, ethical principles, human control, education, and awareness are crucial. By implementing these solutions, we can harness the potential of AI while ensuring the safety and security of humanity.

13

Autonomous weapons

Autonomous weapons, also known as killer robots, are weapons systems that can identify, target, and attack individuals without human intervention. These weapons use artificial intelligence (AI) and can operate on land, in the air, and underwater. While proponents argue that autonomous weapons can reduce the risk of casualties by removing humans from harm's way, there are significant risks associated with these weapons.

One of the main concerns is that autonomous weapons lack the human judgment and ethical considerations that are necessary in war. These weapons could potentially target civilians or other non-combatants, leading to significant human rights violations. Additionally, there is the risk of autonomous weapons being hacked and used for unintended purposes, including against their own operators.

There is currently no international treaty regulating the development or use of autonomous weapons. However, several countries, including the United States, China, and Russia, are actively developing these weapons, and there have been calls for a ban on their use.

To address the risks associated with autonomous weapons, experts have proposed several solutions. One option is to establish a treaty or other international agreement to regulate the development and use of autonomous weapons. This treaty could include provisions requiring human oversight and ethical considerations in the development and deployment of these weapons.

Another solution is to develop technical safeguards to prevent autonomous weapons from being hacked or used for unintended purposes. This could include implementing strict cybersecurity measures and building fail-safes into the weapons systems to prevent them from acting outside their intended parameters.

Finally, there is a need to raise public awareness about the risks associated with autonomous weapons and to engage in a broader discussion about the role of AI in warfare. This could include establishing ethical guidelines for the development and use of AI in military applications, as well as creating mechanisms for public oversight and accountability.

While autonomous weapons offer several potential benefits, there are significant risks associated with their development and use. It is essential to take proactive measures to mitigate these risks, including establishing international agreements, developing technical safeguards, and engaging in public dialogue and awareness-raising efforts.

Autonomous weapons, also known as killer robots, are weapons systems that can select and engage targets without human intervention. These weapons have the potential to cause significant harm to both civilians and military personnel. However, there are solutions that can help mitigate the risks associated with autonomous weapons.

One potential solution is to ban the development and deployment of fully autonomous weapons. The Campaign to Stop Killer Robots is a global coalition of NGOs working towards a pre-emptive ban on the development, production, and use of fully autonomous weapons. This would prevent the deployment of weapons that could harm innocent civilians and prevent the use of weapons that could lead to unintended consequences.

Another solution is to regulate the development and deployment of autonomous weapons. This could involve requiring human oversight of the weapons or mandating that the weapons are only used in certain situations, such as in self-defense or in non-civilian areas. Regulating autonomous weapons would provide some level of control over their use and reduce the risk of unintended consequences.

Investing in research and development of defensive technology could also be a solution. For example, the development of advanced anti-missile systems could help prevent the deployment of autonomous weapons. Similarly, the development of artificial intelligence systems that can identify and disarm autonomous weapons could help prevent harm to civilians and military personnel.

Finally, building awareness and promoting public dialogue about the risks associated with autonomous weapons could be a solution. By increasing public awareness about the dangers of autonomous weapons, individuals and governments can work together to prevent the development and deployment of these weapons.

14

Nuclear war

The risk of nuclear war has been a concern since the development of nuclear weapons in the 1940s. These weapons have the power to destroy entire cities and cause devastating effects on the environment, making the risk of nuclear war one of the most severe threats to humanity.

One of the most significant risks of nuclear war is the potential for accidental or unintended use of nuclear weapons. Technical malfunctions, miscommunications, or misunderstandings between countries could lead to a catastrophic nuclear event.

Additionally, the risk of nuclear war is increased by geopolitical tensions between countries possessing nuclear weapons. Conflict or aggression between these countries could escalate quickly, leading to a nuclear exchange.

The consequences of a nuclear war would be unimaginable, including widespread destruction, loss of life, and long-term environmental damage. The effects of radiation could cause long-term health problems, including cancer, birth defects, and genetic mutations.

Preventing nuclear war requires diplomatic efforts to reduce tensions between countries and prevent conflicts from escalating. International treaties, such as the Non-Proliferation Treaty, aim to prevent the spread of nuclear weapons and encourage disarmament.

Efforts to reduce nuclear weapons and promote disarmament are crucial to reducing the risk of nuclear war. Diplomatic solutions, such as negotiations and international cooperation, are necessary to address the complex issues surrounding nuclear weapons and prevent the catastrophic consequences of a nuclear war.

Ultimately, the prevention of nuclear war requires a commitment to peace and cooperation between nations. By working together to address global issues and promoting peaceful solutions to conflicts, we can reduce the risk of nuclear war and ensure the safety and well-being of future generations.

At present there are 9 countries in the world that possess nuclear weapons. They are:

- Russia
- United States
- China
- France
- United Kingdom
- Pakistan
- India
- Israel
- North Korea

Together, these states have 12,700 nuclear warheads, of which 9,400 are in active military stockpiles. While this is a significant decline from the approximately 70,000 warheads owned by the nuclear-armed states during the Cold War, nuclear arsenals are expected to grow over the coming decade and today's forces are vastly more capable.

The risk of nuclear war is a major concern for humanity, as the use of nuclear weapons could have catastrophic consequences for the entire planet. The best solution to this risk is to prevent the occurrence of a nuclear war in the first place. Here are some potential solutions:

1. Diplomacy and Negotiation: Diplomacy and negotiation have been proven to be effective ways to resolve conflicts and prevent wars. Countries can engage in talks to resolve their differences and reduce tensions, which can ultimately reduce the risk of a nuclear war.

2. Arms Control: Countries can work together to reduce the number of nuclear weapons in existence through arms control agreements. This will not only reduce the risk of nuclear war but also reduce the potential for accidents or attacks by rogue states.

3. Education and Public Awareness: Educating the public about the dangers of nuclear war and the risks associated with nuclear weapons can increase public awareness and mobilize support for disarmament and peaceful solutions to conflicts.

4. International Organizations: International organizations such as the United Nations can play a vital role in preventing nuclear war by facilitating talks and negotiations, monitoring and enforcing arms control agreements, and promoting disarmament.

5. Cybersecurity: Ensuring the security of nuclear weapons and associated systems against cyber-attacks is vital to prevent accidental or unauthorized use of these weapons.

6. Transparency and Verification: Increasing transparency and verification measures to ensure countries are adhering to arms control agreements can reduce the risk of countries developing and using nuclear weapons.

7. Early Warning Systems: Developing early warning systems can detect and prevent the launch of a nuclear attack and reduce the risk of accidental launches or misunderstandings.

The best solution to the risk of nuclear war is to prevent it from happening in the first place through diplomacy, arms control, education, international organizations, cybersecurity, transparency and verification, and early warning systems. It is essential that countries work together towards a common goal of reducing the risk of nuclear war and ensuring global peace and security.

15

Biotechnology

Biotechnology refers to the use of living organisms or their products to create new products or processes that have commercial or industrial value. While biotechnology has the potential to offer numerous benefits, it also poses several risks to human health and the environment.

One of the primary risks associated with biotechnology is the potential for the accidental release of genetically modified organisms (GMOs) into the environment. This can occur when GMOs are used in agricultural fields or when they are released into the wild. If these organisms are able to survive and reproduce, they can disrupt natural ecosystems and threaten the survival of native species.

Another risk associated with biotechnology is the potential for bioterrorism. Advances in biotechnology have made it possible for scientists to create deadly viruses or bacteria that could be used as weapons of mass destruction. If such a weapon were to be used, it could cause widespread death and destruction, and it would be difficult to contain and control the spread of the disease.

The use of biotechnology in agriculture also raises concerns about food safety. Many genetically modified crops are engineered to resist pests or to have a longer shelf life, but the long-term effects of consuming such foods are still unknown. Additionally, the use of biotechnology in agriculture may lead to the creation of "superbugs" that are resistant to antibiotics, which could pose a serious threat to human health.

Finally, there are concerns about the ethical implications of biotechnology. For example, some people believe that it is unethical to patent living organisms or to manipulate the genetic code of living beings. Others worry that biotechnology could be used to create "designer babies" or to alter the course of human evolution.

Despite these risks, biotechnology also holds the potential to offer numerous benefits. For example, biotechnology can be used to create new medicines or to improve the efficiency of industrial processes. It can also be used to create new types of crops that are more resistant to drought or pests, which could help to alleviate food shortages in some parts of the world.

To mitigate the risks associated with biotechnology, it is important to establish clear guidelines and regulations for the use of GMOs and other biotechnologies. This includes implementing strict safety protocols for research labs and agricultural fields, as well as conducting thorough risk assessments before releasing any genetically modified organisms into the environment.

Additionally, it is important to invest in research that explores the potential long-term effects of biotechnology on human health and the environment. This will help us to better understand the risks associated with biotechnology and to develop effective strategies for managing those risks.

While biotechnology offers many potential benefits, it also poses several risks to human health and the environment. By establishing clear guidelines and regulations for the use of biotechnology and investing in research to better understand its risks and benefits, we can help to ensure that biotechnology is used in a safe and responsible manner.

Biotechnology has the potential to revolutionize our world, but like any technology, it also poses risks. As we continue to advance our understanding of genetics, bioengineering, and other fields, it's important that we consider the ethical and safety implications of our work.

Here are some solutions that can help mitigate the risks of biotechnology:

1. Strong regulation: Governments and international organizations can establish strict regulations and oversight to ensure that research and applications of biotechnology are conducted safely and ethically. This includes ensuring that experiments are peer-reviewed, that there is adequate testing before products are released to the public, and that researchers are held accountable for any ethical violations.

2. Education and public awareness: Educating the public about the potential risks and benefits of biotechnology can help to build trust and reduce fear. This includes making information about biotech research and applications accessible to the public, promoting public discussion and debate, and creating more opportunities for public engagement with scientists and policymakers.

3. Collaboration and transparency: Encouraging collaboration among scientists and researchers can help to promote transparency and accountability. This includes promoting open data sharing, encouraging international collaboration, and promoting interdisciplinary research.

4. Ethical guidelines: Ethical guidelines can be established to ensure that biotechnology is used in a responsible and ethical manner. This includes guidelines for human genetic engineering, animal welfare, and environmental impact.

5. Emergency preparedness: It's important to be prepared for the possibility of a biotech disaster or accident. This includes developing protocols and resources for emergency response, ensuring that first responders are trained and equipped to handle biotech emergencies, and establishing contingency plans for dealing with the aftermath of a disaster.

By implementing these solutions, we can work to ensure that biotechnology is used in a responsible and ethical manner, while still allowing for innovation and progress in this exciting field.

16

Space debris

The ever-increasing amount of space debris orbiting Earth is becoming a significant threat to space exploration and the safety of spacecraft. Space debris refers to all man-made objects in orbit around Earth that no longer serve any useful purpose. These objects can range in size from tiny fragments to entire abandoned spacecraft and launch vehicle stages.

The risk of space debris is not to be underestimated. With more than 20,000 trackable objects in orbit, even a small piece of debris can pose a significant threat to a spacecraft traveling at high speeds. In addition to the risk of impact, space debris can also generate more debris through collisions, increasing the risk for future missions.

The root cause of space debris is our reliance on space-based technology and the increasing number of objects launched into orbit. As space becomes more commercialized, the number of satellites, space stations, and other objects in orbit is only going to increase, exacerbating the problem.

However, there are solutions to the problem of space debris. One approach is to prevent the creation of new debris by requiring all spacecraft to have a plan for safe disposal at the end of their mission. This would involve deorbiting the spacecraft or moving it into a graveyard orbit, which would help limit the amount of debris generated.

Another solution is to actively remove existing debris. This can be done using spacecraft equipped with nets, tethers, or other capture mechanisms that can remove debris from orbit. Additionally, research is being conducted into developing technologies that can clean up space debris using lasers, ion beams, or other methods.

International cooperation is also essential in addressing the problem of space debris. The United Nations Office for Outer Space Affairs (UNOOSA) has been working to establish guidelines and best practices for space activities, including the mitigation of space debris. More countries need to join the efforts to reduce space debris and take responsibility for their own space debris.

The risk of space debris is a serious concern that requires immediate attention. While prevention of new debris is crucial, the active removal of existing debris and international cooperation are also essential in mitigating the risk. It is critical that we address this problem to ensure the continued exploration and use of space for future generations.

As the amount of space debris in orbit around Earth continues to increase, so does the risk of collision with operational spacecraft and the potential for catastrophic consequences. Fortunately, there are several solutions that can help mitigate this risk:

1. Active debris removal: This involves using spacecraft equipped with nets, tethers, or robotic arms to capture and remove space debris from orbit. This technology is still in its early stages, but several initiatives are underway to develop and test these systems.
2. Deorbiting: Satellites and other objects in orbit can be designed with propulsion systems that allow them to re-enter Earth's atmosphere and burn up upon re-entry, ensuring they do not contribute to the growing problem of space debris.
3. Designing for sustainability: Spacecraft and satellites can be designed to minimize the amount of debris they generate, such as using materials that are less likely to fragment upon impact.
4. Improved tracking and collision avoidance: By improving our ability

to track and predict the trajectories of space debris, we can better plan maneuvers to avoid collisions with operational spacecraft.

5. International cooperation: Addressing the problem of space debris requires international cooperation and coordination, as no one nation can address the issue alone. International agreements and guidelines can help ensure responsible behavior in space and promote collaboration on space debris mitigation efforts.

Overall, reducing the risk of space debris requires a multi-faceted approach that involves technological solutions, responsible behavior, and international cooperation. With these efforts, we can help ensure the safety and sustainability of space activities for future generations.

17

Solar storms

The sun is a powerful force that can both create and destroy. One of the dangers that can arise from the sun is the risk of solar storms. Solar storms are eruptions of magnetic energy from the sun that can cause disruptions in our technology and communication systems, as well as pose a potential threat to our physical health. As our dependence on technology grows, so does our vulnerability to the effects of solar storms.

Solar storms occur when the sun releases a burst of charged particles, also known as a coronal mass ejection (CME). These CMEs can travel through space and reach Earth in a matter of hours or days. When they reach Earth, they interact with our planet's magnetic field, causing disturbances that can affect our technology and communication systems.

The most common impact of solar storms is the disruption of satellite communications and GPS systems. This can cause issues in various industries, such as transportation, finance, and telecommunications. In addition, solar storms can also cause power outages by overloading power grids, as seen in the 1989 Quebec blackout that left 6 million people without power for 9 hours.

Solar storms also have the potential to pose a threat to our physical health. The charged particles from solar storms can affect our atmosphere, leading to increased radiation exposure for air travelers and astronauts. In addition, the particles can disrupt our planet's magnetic field, leading to increased exposure to cosmic radiation.

The risk of solar storms is not something that can be easily mitigated, but there are steps that can be taken to reduce the impact of these events. One such step is to increase the resilience of our technology and communication systems to withstand the effects of solar storms. This can be done through improved design and redundancy measures.

Another step that can be taken is to increase our understanding of solar storms and their potential impact. By studying these events, we can develop better models to predict and prepare for future solar storms. This includes investing in research and development of new technologies that can help us better detect and respond to solar storms.

In addition, individuals can take steps to protect themselves from the potential health impacts of solar storms. This can include reducing air travel during periods of heightened solar activity, as well as increasing awareness of the potential risks of increased radiation exposure.

Overall, the risk of solar storms is one that we cannot ignore. As our dependence on technology grows, so does our vulnerability to the effects of these events. By taking steps to increase our resilience and understanding, we can reduce the impact of solar storms and ensure the safety of our technology and our planet.

Solar storms, also known as coronal mass ejections (CMEs), occur when large amounts of plasma and magnetic field are ejected from the sun and travel through space. When these storms reach Earth, they can cause a range of effects, from minor disruptions to the electrical grid to potentially catastrophic damage to satellites and other technology.

To address the risk of solar storms, several solutions have been proposed:

1. Space weather forecasting: Accurate prediction of solar storms is crucial for early warning and preparedness. The National Oceanic and Atmospheric Administration (NOAA) and other agencies have developed space weather forecasting models and tools to help monitor

and predict the effects of solar storms.

2. Hardening critical infrastructure: Power grids, satellites, and other critical infrastructure can be hardened to better withstand the effects of solar storms. This includes strengthening physical structures and improving protective measures to prevent equipment failure.

3. Emergency preparedness: In the event of a severe solar storm, emergency preparedness plans can help mitigate the impact. This includes backup power supplies, emergency response teams, and communication plans to ensure continuity of essential services.

4. Spacecraft design: New spacecraft can be designed with better protection against solar storms, such as improved shielding and other measures to minimize the risk of damage.

5. International cooperation: The effects of solar storms can impact countries all over the world, so international cooperation is critical in addressing the risks. Collaborative efforts can help share knowledge, resources, and best practices for managing the impact of solar storms.

By implementing these solutions, we can better prepare for and mitigate the risks of solar storms, and ensure the safety and stability of our technology and infrastructure.

18

Electromagnetic pulses

Electromagnetic pulses (EMPs) are intense bursts of electromagnetic radiation that can be generated naturally or artificially. They pose a significant risk to modern infrastructure, including communication systems, power grids, and transportation networks. EMPs can be caused by natural events such as solar flares, but they can also be created through the detonation of a nuclear device in the atmosphere.

The consequences of an EMP can be catastrophic, leading to widespread power outages, communication disruptions, and damage to electronic devices. In the worst-case scenario, it could take months or even years to repair the damage, leading to significant economic and societal consequences.

To address the risk of EMPs, governments and organizations must take steps to protect critical infrastructure from the effects of these pulses. This can include developing strategies to harden electrical and communication systems, such as the installation of surge protectors and shielding. It can also involve implementing redundancy measures, such as backup power systems and communication networks.

Additionally, individuals can take steps to protect their electronic devices from EMPs, such as storing them in a Faraday cage or turning them off during an event. Education and awareness are also essential to ensure that people understand the risks of EMPs and are prepared to respond appropriately in the event of an incident.

While it may not be possible to completely eliminate the risk of EMPs, taking these steps can help mitigate the potential damage and ensure that critical infrastructure and electronic devices remain operational in the face of this significant threat.

Electromagnetic pulses (EMPs) can be caused by natural events such as solar flares or by man-made sources such as nuclear weapons or devices. These pulses can cause widespread damage to electronic equipment and disrupt communication systems, leading to potential chaos and loss of life. It is therefore important to take measures to mitigate the risks of EMPs. Here are some possible solutions:

1. Shielding: One way to protect electronic devices from the effects of EMPs is to shield them using materials such as conductive metals or carbon fiber. This can prevent the EMP from penetrating the device and causing damage.
2. Redundancy: Another solution is to have redundant systems in place so that if one system is disrupted by an EMP, another system can take over. This can involve backup power sources, communication systems, and other critical infrastructure.
3. EMP-resistant designs: Engineers can design electronic equipment to be resistant to EMPs by using specialized components and designs that can withstand the high voltage and currents produced by these pulses.
4. Education and awareness: It is important to educate the public and government officials about the risks of EMPs and the importance of taking measures to protect critical infrastructure. This can include training programs for emergency responders and government officials, as well as public awareness campaigns.
5. International cooperation: EMPs can be caused by man-made sources such as nuclear weapons, so international cooperation and agreements are essential to prevent the use of these weapons and minimize the risk of EMPs.

Overall, the risks of EMPs can be mitigated through a combination of shielding, redundancy, EMP-resistant designs, education and awareness, and international cooperation. By taking these measures, we can reduce the potential damage and disruption caused by EMPs and help ensure the safety and security of our critical infrastructure.

19

Energy security

The availability and access to energy is critical to the functioning of modern society. It is used for everything from lighting and heating homes to powering businesses and transportation. However, there are several risks associated with energy security that can have significant impacts on both the economy and the environment.

One of the primary risks of energy security is the overreliance on non-renewable energy sources such as coal, oil, and natural gas. These sources are finite and their extraction and use contribute to climate change and environmental degradation. Additionally, the transportation and storage of these fuels can be dangerous and pose risks of accidents, spills, and explosions.

Another risk is the vulnerability of energy infrastructure to natural disasters, cyberattacks, and physical attacks. For example, hurricanes and other extreme weather events can damage oil rigs, refineries, and power plants, leading to disruptions in energy supply. Cyberattacks on energy infrastructure can also cause widespread disruptions and pose significant security risks.

Energy security risks can also be geopolitical in nature. For example, political tensions between countries can result in embargoes and sanctions on oil exports, causing shortages and price spikes in importing countries. Additionally, conflicts over energy resources can escalate into military conflicts, as seen in the ongoing tensions in the South China Sea and the Middle East.

To address these risks, there are several solutions that can be implemented. One approach is to shift towards a more diversified energy mix that includes renewable energy sources such as solar, wind, and hydropower. This can help reduce reliance on non-renewable energy sources and mitigate the impacts of climate change.

Improving energy efficiency and promoting energy conservation can also help reduce energy demand and reduce the need for new energy infrastructure. This can be done through policies such as building codes, appliance standards, and energy-efficient transportation options.

Ensuring the resilience of energy infrastructure is also important. This can be achieved through measures such as improved maintenance, disaster preparedness, and cybersecurity measures. Additionally, international cooperation and diplomacy can help reduce geopolitical tensions and prevent conflicts over energy resources.

Overall, energy security is a complex and multifaceted issue that requires a comprehensive approach. By diversifying energy sources, improving efficiency, and ensuring the resilience of infrastructure, we can address the risks associated with energy security and create a more sustainable future.

Energy security is a pressing concern that has garnered global attention in recent years. It refers to the uninterrupted availability of energy resources at an affordable price. A lack of energy security can result in economic instability, political unrest, and social turmoil. The good news is that there are solutions that can help address the risk of energy insecurity. Here are some potential solutions:

1. Diversification of Energy Sources: One way to mitigate the risk of energy insecurity is to diversify the sources of energy. This means moving away from a reliance on a single source of energy, such as fossil fuels, and adopting a mix of energy sources such as renewable energy

sources (solar, wind, hydroelectric, etc.), nuclear energy, and natural gas.

2. Energy Efficiency: Another way to address energy insecurity is to reduce the overall demand for energy by increasing energy efficiency. This can be achieved by adopting energy-efficient technologies and practices, such as LED light bulbs, smart thermostats, and insulation.

3. Energy Storage: Energy storage technologies, such as batteries and pumped hydroelectric storage, can help address the intermittency of renewable energy sources by storing excess energy during times of low demand for use during times of high demand.

4. Infrastructure Investment: Investing in energy infrastructure can also help mitigate the risk of energy insecurity. This can include the expansion of the electricity grid, the development of new transmission lines, and the construction of new power plants.

5. International Cooperation: Energy security is a global issue, and international cooperation can help mitigate the risks. This can include cooperation on energy research and development, the sharing of energy resources, and the development of international energy policies.

Energy security is a complex issue that requires a multifaceted approach to mitigate the risks. By adopting a mix of solutions such as diversification of energy sources, energy efficiency, energy storage, infrastructure investment, and international cooperation, we can work towards ensuring uninterrupted access to affordable energy resources.

20

Infrastructure collapse

Infrastructure Collapse: A Major Risk Facing Society

Infrastructure is the backbone of modern society. It is the foundation that supports our cities, economies, and way of life. Without it, our world would come to a standstill. However, despite the importance of infrastructure, many of our systems are aging, inadequate, and at risk of collapse. The consequences of an infrastructure collapse can be severe and far-reaching, affecting our safety, health, and prosperity. In this article, we will explore the risk of infrastructure collapse and its potential solutions.

Infrastructure is an essential part of modern society. It includes roads, bridges, tunnels, airports, water supply systems, power grids, and communication networks. The quality and reliability of our infrastructure determine our ability to transport goods and people, provide essential services, and respond to emergencies. Unfortunately, many of our systems are aging and in need of significant investment to keep them functioning. This is particularly true in developed countries, where infrastructure is often taken for granted.

The risk of infrastructure collapse is real and significant. There are numerous examples of infrastructure failures that have had severe consequences. For example, in 2007, the I-35W bridge in Minneapolis collapsed, killing 13 people and injuring 145. In 2011, the Fukushima nuclear disaster in Japan was caused by a combination of natural disasters and infrastructure failure.

The failure of levees during Hurricane Katrina in 2005 led to catastrophic flooding in New Orleans.

The risk of infrastructure collapse is not limited to large-scale events like these. It can also occur on a smaller scale but with significant consequences. For example, the collapse of a single bridge can cut off an entire community from essential services, including hospitals, schools, and emergency services.

The consequences of infrastructure collapse are severe and far-reaching. They can include loss of life, economic disruption, and social unrest. The impact can be felt for years, if not decades. The risk of infrastructure collapse is particularly acute in developing countries, where the lack of investment and poor maintenance can exacerbate the problem.

There are several potential solutions to the risk of infrastructure collapse. The first is to invest in infrastructure. This can involve increasing funding for maintenance, repairs, and upgrades to existing systems. It can also involve investing in new infrastructure, such as high-speed rail, renewable energy, and smart cities. Investing in infrastructure not only reduces the risk of collapse but also creates jobs and boosts the economy.

Another solution is to improve the resilience of infrastructure. This can involve incorporating new technology, such as sensors and monitoring systems, to detect and respond to potential problems before they become severe. It can also involve building redundancy into critical systems to ensure that they continue to function even if one component fails. For example, installing backup generators or building redundant communication networks.

A third solution is to improve planning and preparedness. This can involve developing emergency response plans, training first responders, and educating the public about what to do in the event of an infrastructure failure. It can also involve conducting risk assessments and identifying critical infrastructure that is most at risk.

The risk of infrastructure collapse is a significant threat facing modern society. The consequences of such an event can be severe and far-reaching, affecting our safety, health, and prosperity. However, there are solutions to this risk, including investing in infrastructure, improving resilience, and improving planning and preparedness. By taking action to address this risk, we can ensure that our infrastructure remains safe, reliable, and able to support our way of life.

Infrastructure collapse is a major risk that can have catastrophic consequences on a community's wellbeing. Infrastructure failure can result in loss of life, financial ruin, and damage to the environment. Therefore, it is crucial to implement solutions to prevent infrastructure collapse.

One way to prevent infrastructure collapse is through proper maintenance and inspection of the infrastructure. Regular inspections can identify problems before they turn into major issues. It is also essential to have a plan for repairing and replacing outdated infrastructure. This plan should be reviewed periodically to ensure it is up to date and effective.

Investment in resilient infrastructure can also reduce the risk of collapse. Infrastructure that is designed to withstand extreme weather events, such as hurricanes and earthquakes, is less likely to fail. Additionally, investing in renewable energy sources such as solar, wind, and geothermal power can make the energy grid more resilient and reliable.

Another solution is to establish partnerships between government agencies, private sector companies, and community organizations. These partnerships can bring together resources and expertise to address infrastructure issues and ensure they are addressed promptly.

Finally, it is crucial to implement smart technology solutions that can monitor infrastructure and detect potential problems. This includes using sensors, machine learning, and other advanced technologies to identify problems in real-time and take corrective action quickly.

III

Health Risks

Health risks refer to factors or conditions that can have a negative impact on human health and well-being. These risks can be caused by a variety of factors, including lifestyle choices, environmental factors, genetics, and exposure to harmful substances. Common health risks include chronic diseases such as heart disease, diabetes, and cancer, as well as infectious diseases like COVID-19.

21

Pandemics

Pandemics have been a recurring threat throughout human history, and the recent COVID-19 pandemic has highlighted the devastating impact that infectious diseases can have on society. The risk of pandemics is influenced by a range of factors, including globalization, population growth, climate change, and human behavior.

Globalization has made it easier for diseases to spread rapidly across borders, as people and goods travel more frequently and over longer distances. This can make it more difficult to contain the spread of infectious diseases, especially in regions with weaker health systems or limited resources.

Population growth and urbanization can also increase the risk of pandemics, as large populations living in close proximity can facilitate the spread of disease. Climate change can also have an impact, as changes in temperature and precipitation patterns can affect the distribution of disease vectors such as mosquitoes and ticks.

Human behavior can also contribute to the risk of pandemics, such as through the illegal trade of exotic animals or the consumption of bushmeat, which can lead to the transmission of zoonotic diseases from animals to humans. In addition, poor sanitation and hygiene practices, such as inadequate handwashing or the improper disposal of waste, can increase the risk of infectious disease transmission.

To address the risk of pandemics, a range of measures can be taken, including improving public health infrastructure, investing in disease surveillance and research, promoting sustainable and responsible agriculture and livestock practices, and strengthening international cooperation and collaboration. In addition, individuals can take steps to reduce their own risk of infection, such as practicing good hygiene, getting vaccinated, and avoiding close contact with people who are sick.

While it is impossible to completely eliminate the risk of pandemics, taking proactive steps to mitigate this risk can help to minimize the impact of infectious diseases on society. By working together to address this global threat, we can build a healthier and more resilient world.

Preventing a pandemic requires a multi-faceted approach that involves individual actions, community efforts, and global cooperation. While it is impossible to completely eliminate the risk of a pandemic, there are steps that can be taken to reduce the likelihood of one occurring and to limit its impact if it does.

One key strategy for preventing a pandemic is to invest in public health infrastructure, including disease surveillance systems, laboratories, and healthcare facilities. This can help to detect and respond to outbreaks quickly, before they become widespread.

Individual actions also play an important role in preventing the spread of infectious diseases. Simple measures such as regular handwashing, covering coughs and sneezes, and staying home when sick can help to reduce the transmission of diseases. Getting vaccinated can also help to protect against certain diseases, such as influenza.

Community efforts are also important for preventing a pandemic. This can include promoting healthy behaviors through public health campaigns, investing in clean water and sanitation systems, and encouraging responsible agriculture and livestock practices. Building strong and resilient communities can also help to reduce the impact of a pandemic if one does occur.

Global cooperation and collaboration are essential for preventing a pandemic, as infectious diseases can easily spread across borders. This can include sharing information and resources, supporting research and development of vaccines and treatments, and establishing international standards for disease control and prevention.

In the wake of the COVID-19 pandemic, there has been increased attention and investment in pandemic preparedness and response. However, ongoing efforts are needed to ensure that the world is better prepared for future outbreaks.

By taking proactive steps to prevent a pandemic, individuals, communities, and governments can help to reduce the risk of infectious diseases and protect public health. While the threat of pandemics will always exist, by working together we can build a more resilient and healthy world.

22

Antibiotic resistance

Antibiotic resistance is a growing public health threat that occurs when bacteria become resistant to the drugs used to treat them. This can make it more difficult to treat bacterial infections, leading to longer illness, increased healthcare costs, and even death. The risk of antibiotic resistance is influenced by a range of factors, including overuse and misuse of antibiotics, poor infection prevention and control practices, and inadequate surveillance and monitoring of resistance patterns.

Overuse and misuse of antibiotics are major drivers of antibiotic resistance. Antibiotics are often prescribed unnecessarily, such as for viral infections that do not respond to antibiotics, or for mild infections that could be treated with other measures. This can lead to the development of antibiotic-resistant bacteria, which can then spread to other individuals and the community at large.

Poor infection prevention and control practices can also contribute to the risk of antibiotic resistance. This can include inadequate hand hygiene, improper sterilization of medical equipment, and poor sanitation and hygiene in healthcare facilities.

Inadequate surveillance and monitoring of resistance patterns can also make it more difficult to respond to outbreaks of antibiotic-resistant infections. Effective surveillance and monitoring systems can help to detect emerging resistance patterns and guide appropriate treatment and prevention strategies.

To address the risk of antibiotic resistance, a range of measures can be taken. These include promoting responsible antibiotic use, investing in infection prevention and control measures, supporting surveillance and monitoring of resistance patterns, and investing in research and development of new antibiotics and alternative therapies.

Individuals can also play a role in preventing antibiotic resistance by taking steps to prevent infections, such as practicing good hand hygiene, getting vaccinated, and avoiding close contact with sick individuals. When antibiotics are prescribed, it is important to take them as directed and to complete the full course of treatment, even if symptoms improve.

Antibiotic resistance is a complex and growing public health threat that requires a multifaceted response. By working together to promote responsible antibiotic use, invest in infection prevention and control, and support research and development of new treatments, we can help to preserve the effectiveness of antibiotics and protect public health.

Antibiotic resistance is a growing public health threat that requires a multifaceted approach to address. There are several solutions that can help to reduce the risk of antibiotic resistance:

1. Promote responsible antibiotic use: Encourage healthcare providers to only prescribe antibiotics when they are truly necessary, and to prescribe the most appropriate antibiotic for the specific infection. Educate patients about the appropriate use of antibiotics and the importance of completing the full course of treatment.
2. Improve infection prevention and control measures: Implement effective infection prevention and control practices in healthcare facilities, including hand hygiene, proper sterilization of medical equipment, and proper disposal of waste. Encourage the use of vaccines to prevent infections, and promote healthy behaviors in the community to reduce the spread of infectious diseases.

3. Increase surveillance and monitoring: Establish effective surveillance and monitoring systems to track resistance patterns and detect emerging threats. This can help to guide appropriate treatment and prevention strategies, and inform the development of new antibiotics and alternative therapies.

4. Invest in research and development: Invest in research and development of new antibiotics and alternative therapies. This includes exploring new approaches to treating bacterial infections, such as using bacteriophages, which are viruses that can kill bacteria.

5. Improve access to healthcare: Increase access to healthcare in under-served areas, both domestically and globally. This can help to reduce the burden of infectious diseases and improve the appropriate use of antibiotics.

By taking a comprehensive approach to addressing antibiotic resistance, we can help to preserve the effectiveness of antibiotics and protect public health. While the solutions may be complex, the consequences of inaction are too great to ignore. It is critical that individuals, healthcare providers, policymakers, and global leaders work together to tackle this growing threat.

23

Chronic diseases

Chronic diseases, such as heart disease, cancer, and diabetes, are a major public health threat that affects millions of people worldwide. These diseases are typically characterized by long-term or recurring health conditions, and can have a significant impact on individuals' quality of life, as well as on healthcare costs and productivity. The risk of chronic diseases is influenced by a range of factors, including lifestyle choices, genetics, environmental factors, and socioeconomic status.

Lifestyle choices, such as poor diet, physical inactivity, smoking, and excessive alcohol consumption, are major risk factors for chronic diseases. These behaviors can contribute to the development of conditions such as obesity, high blood pressure, and high cholesterol, which increase the risk of chronic diseases.

Genetics can also play a role in the development of chronic diseases. Some genetic mutations can increase the risk of certain conditions, such as certain types of cancer and heart disease.

Environmental factors, such as exposure to air pollution, toxins, and radiation, can also contribute to the risk of chronic diseases. In addition, socioeconomic status can also play a role, as individuals living in poverty may have limited access to healthy food, safe housing, and healthcare, which can increase their risk of chronic diseases.

To address the risk of chronic diseases, a range of measures can be taken.

This includes promoting healthy lifestyle choices, such as regular exercise, a balanced diet, and avoidance of harmful substances like tobacco and alcohol. Additionally, increasing access to healthcare and reducing socioeconomic disparities can help to improve health outcomes and reduce the burden of chronic diseases.

Preventive measures, such as screening and early detection, can also help to reduce the impact of chronic diseases. For example, regular cancer screenings can help to detect cancer in its early stages, when it is more treatable. Vaccines can also help to prevent certain chronic diseases, such as hepatitis B, which can lead to liver cancer.

Chronic diseases are a major public health threat that can have a significant impact on individuals, families, and communities. By addressing the underlying risk factors and promoting healthy behaviors, we can help to reduce the burden of chronic diseases and improve health outcomes for all.

Chronic diseases are a complex public health challenge that require a multifaceted approach to address. Here are some potential solutions to reduce the risk of chronic diseases:

1. Promote healthy lifestyles: Encourage individuals to make healthy lifestyle choices, such as regular exercise, a balanced diet, and avoidance of tobacco and excessive alcohol consumption. This can help to reduce the risk of chronic diseases and improve overall health outcomes.

2. Improve access to healthcare: Increase access to affordable healthcare, including preventive services such as cancer screenings and vaccinations. This can help to detect chronic diseases in their early stages, when they are more treatable.

3. Address social determinants of health: Address the social determinants of health, such as poverty and lack of access to education, that contribute to chronic disease risk. This can include increasing access to

    healthy food, safe housing, and transportation.

4. Implement policies and regulations: Implement policies and regulations that promote healthy behaviors and environments, such as reducing exposure to environmental toxins and improving air quality.

5. Invest in research and development: Invest in research and development of new treatments and preventive measures for chronic diseases. This can include developing new medications and therapies, as well as exploring new approaches to preventive care.

6. Increase public awareness: Increase public awareness about chronic diseases and their risk factors. This can include education campaigns and community outreach programs to promote healthy behaviors and encourage regular preventive care.

By taking a comprehensive approach to addressing chronic diseases, we can help to reduce their impact on individuals, families, and communities. While the solutions may be complex, the consequences of inaction are too great to ignore. It is critical that individuals, healthcare providers, policymakers, and global leaders work together to tackle this growing public health challenge.

<h1 style="text-align:center">24</h1>

Mental health crisis

Mental health crisis is a growing public health concern that affects millions of people worldwide. Mental health disorders, such as depression, anxiety, and bipolar disorder, can have a significant impact on individuals' quality of life, as well as on productivity and social functioning. The risk of mental health crisis is influenced by a range of factors, including genetic and environmental factors, adverse life events, and societal and cultural factors.

Genetic factors can play a role in the development of mental health disorders. Individuals with a family history of mental health disorders may be at a higher risk of developing these conditions themselves.

Environmental factors, such as exposure to stress and trauma, can also contribute to the risk of mental health crisis. Adverse life events, such as the loss of a loved one or a job, can trigger the onset of mental health disorders in some individuals.

Societal and cultural factors, such as stigma and discrimination, can also contribute to the risk of mental health crisis. Individuals from marginalized communities, such as LGBTQ+ individuals and people of color, may face additional barriers to accessing mental healthcare and may be at a higher risk of mental health disorders.

To address the risk of mental health crisis, a range of measures can be taken. This includes promoting mental health awareness and reducing the stigma associated with mental health disorders. Increasing access to mental healthcare, including counseling and therapy, can also help to improve mental health outcomes.

Preventive measures, such as stress management and coping skills training, can also help to reduce the risk of mental health disorders. Encouraging healthy lifestyle choices, such as regular exercise, a balanced diet, and adequate sleep, can also have a positive impact on mental health.

In conclusion, mental health crisis is a complex public health challenge that requires a multifaceted approach to address. By addressing the underlying risk factors and promoting healthy behaviors, we can help to reduce the burden of mental health disorders and improve mental health outcomes for all.

Mental health crisis is a growing public health concern that requires a comprehensive approach to address. Here are some potential solutions to reduce the risk of mental health crisis:

1. Promote mental health awareness: Increase public awareness about mental health disorders and the importance of seeking treatment. This can help to reduce stigma and encourage individuals to seek help when they need it.

2. Increase access to mental healthcare: Improve access to mental healthcare, including counseling and therapy, for all individuals. This can include increasing funding for mental health services, expanding telehealth options, and reducing barriers to access, such as cost and location.

3. Address social determinants of mental health: Address the social determinants of mental health, such as poverty and discrimination, that contribute to mental health crisis risk. This can include increasing access to education, employment, and affordable housing, and promoting social support and community engagement.

4. Implement policies and regulations: Implement policies and regulations that promote mental health and well-being, such as workplace

mental health programs and mental health parity laws.

5. Invest in research and development: Invest in research and development of new treatments and preventive measures for mental health disorders. This can include developing new medications and therapies, as well as exploring new approaches to preventive care.

6. Increase public education and awareness: Educate the public about the importance of mental health self-care and coping strategies, such as stress management and mindfulness practices. This can help individuals to develop healthy habits and prevent the onset of mental health disorders.

By taking a comprehensive approach to addressing mental health crisis, we can help to reduce its impact on individuals, families, and communities. While the solutions may be complex, the consequences of inaction are too great to ignore. It is critical that individuals, healthcare providers, policymakers, and global leaders work together to tackle this growing public health challenge.

25

Substance abuse

Substance abuse is a growing public health concern that affects millions of people worldwide. Substance abuse can lead to addiction, overdose, and other negative health consequences. The risk of substance abuse is influenced by a range of factors, including genetics, environmental factors, and social and cultural factors.

Genetic factors can play a role in the development of substance abuse. Individuals with a family history of substance abuse may be at a higher risk of developing addiction themselves.

Environmental factors, such as exposure to stress and trauma, can also contribute to the risk of substance abuse. Adverse life events, such as the loss of a loved one or a job, can also trigger substance abuse in some individuals.

Social and cultural factors, such as peer pressure and the normalization of substance use, can also contribute to the risk of substance abuse. Individuals from marginalized communities, such as those living in poverty or facing discrimination, may face additional risk factors for substance abuse.

To address the risk of substance abuse, a range of measures can be taken. This includes promoting substance abuse awareness and reducing the stigma associated with addiction. Increasing access to substance abuse treatment, including counseling and medication-assisted treatment, can also help to improve outcomes for individuals struggling with addiction.

Preventive measures, such as education and screening, can also help to reduce the risk of substance abuse. Encouraging healthy coping mechanisms, such as exercise and mindfulness practices, can also have a positive impact on mental health and reduce the risk of substance abuse.

Substance abuse is a complex public health challenge that requires a comprehensive approach to address. By addressing the underlying risk factors and promoting healthy behaviors, we can help to reduce the burden of substance abuse and improve outcomes for individuals and communities.

Substance abuse is a complex public health challenge that requires a multifaceted approach to address. Here are some potential solutions to reduce the risk of substance abuse:

1. Promote substance abuse awareness: Increase public awareness about substance abuse and addiction, including the risks associated with sub-stance use. This can help to reduce stigma and encourage individuals to seek help when they need it.

2. Increase access to substance abuse treatment: Improve access to substance abuse treatment, including counseling, medication-assisted treatment, and rehabilitation programs. This can include increasing funding for substance abuse treatment services, expanding telehealth options, and reducing barriers to access, such as cost and location.

3. Address social determinants of substance abuse: Address the social determinants of substance abuse, such as poverty, discrimination, and lack of social support, that contribute to substance abuse risk. This can include increasing access to education, employment, and affordable housing, and promoting social support and community engagement.

4. Implement policies and regulations: Implement policies and regula-tions that promote substance abuse prevention and treatment, such as restrictions on prescription opioids and access to overdose-reversal medications.

5. Invest in research and development: Invest in research and devel-opment of new treatments and preventive measures for substance abuse and addiction. This can include developing new medications and therapies, as well as exploring new approaches to prevention and

treatment.

6. Increase public education and awareness: Educate the public about the risks associated with substance use and addiction, and promote healthy coping mechanisms and stress management techniques.

By taking a comprehensive approach to addressing substance abuse, we can help to reduce its impact on individuals, families, and communities. While the solutions may be complex, the consequences of inaction are too great to ignore. It is critical that individuals, healthcare providers, policymakers, and global leaders work together to tackle this growing public health challenge.

26

Aging population

The aging population is a growing public health concern that is affecting countries around the world. The number of older adults is increasing rapidly, and this demographic shift has significant implications for healthcare, social services, and the economy. The risk of aging population is influenced by a range of factors, including advances in medical technology, changing demographics, and lifestyle choices.

Advances in medical technology have enabled individuals to live longer, which has contributed to the growth of the aging population. As a result, there are now more people over the age of 65 than ever before. This trend is expected to continue, and by 2050, it is projected that one in six people will be over the age of 65.

Changing demographics, such as declining birth rates, are also contributing to the aging population. As fewer children are born, there are fewer young people to support the needs of the aging population. This can create challenges for healthcare and social services, as well as the economy.

Lifestyle choices, such as poor diet, physical inactivity, and smoking, can also contribute to the risk of aging-related health conditions, such as heart disease, diabetes, and Alzheimer's disease. These conditions can increase healthcare costs and reduce quality of life for older adults.

To address the risk of aging population, a range of measures can be taken. This includes promoting healthy aging, such as regular exercise, a balanced diet, and avoiding harmful substances like tobacco and excessive alcohol consumption. Improving access to healthcare and social services for older adults can also help to improve health outcomes and reduce healthcare costs.

Preventive measures, such as screening and early detection of health conditions, can also help to reduce the impact of aging-related health conditions. Encouraging healthy lifestyles and behaviors throughout the lifespan, and investing in research and development of new treatments and technologies, can also help to reduce the risk of aging-related health conditions.

The aging population is a complex public health challenge that requires a comprehensive approach to address. By promoting healthy aging, improving access to healthcare and social services, and investing in research and development, we can help to reduce the impact of aging-related health conditions and improve outcomes for older adults. It is critical that individuals, healthcare providers, policymakers, and global leaders work together to address the challenges and opportunities presented by the aging population.

Here are the projected populations of the top 20 countries in the world for the next 50 years, according to the United Nations Department of Economic and Social Affairs:

1. China: 1,364 million (2021) to 1,364 million (2070)
2. India: 1,366 million (2021) to 1,639 million (2070)
3. United States: 332 million (2021) to 398 million (2070)
4. Indonesia: 276 million (2021) to 320 million (2070)
5. Pakistan: 225 million (2021) to 350 million (2070)
6. Brazil: 213 million (2021) to 223 million (2070)
7. Nigeria: 211 million (2021) to 733 million (2070)
8. Bangladesh: 167 million (2021) to 216 million (2070)
9. Russia: 146 million (2021) to 133 million (2070)
10. Japan: 126 million (2021) to 87 million (2070)
11. Mexico: 131 million (2021) to 150 million (2070)

12. Ethiopia: 117 million (2021) to 233 million (2070)
13. Philippines: 111 million (2021) to 157 million (2070)
14. Egypt: 104 million (2021) to 152 million (2070)
15. Vietnam: 98 million (2021) to 89 million (2070)
16. DR Congo: 92 million (2021) to 281 million (2070)
17. Iran: 85 million (2021) to 90 million (2070)
18. Turkey: 85 million (2021) to 97 million (2070)
19. Germany: 83 million (2021) to 75 million (2070)
20. France: 67 million (2021) to 65 million (2070)

It is important to note that these projections are subject to change based on various factors, such as fertility rates, mortality rates, migration, and government policies. Nonetheless, they provide a rough estimate of the expected population changes for these countries in the coming decades.

The aging population is a complex public health challenge that requires a multifaceted approach to address. Here are some potential solutions to reduce the risk of aging-related health conditions and improve outcomes for older adults:

1. Promote healthy aging: Encourage healthy lifestyle choices, such as regular exercise, a balanced diet, and avoidance of harmful substances like tobacco and excessive alcohol consumption. This can help to reduce the risk of aging-related health conditions and improve overall health outcomes.

2. Improve access to healthcare and social services: Increase access to affordable healthcare and social services for older adults. This can include expanding telehealth options, reducing barriers to access, and

increasing funding for services that support older adults.

3. Address social determinants of health: Address the social determinants of health, such as poverty and lack of access to education and employment, that contribute to aging-related health risks. This can include increasing access to affordable housing, transportation, and community support programs.

4. Invest in research and development: Invest in research and development of new treatments and technologies that address aging-related health conditions. This can include developing new medications and therapies, as well as exploring new approaches to preventive care.

5. Increase public awareness: Increase public awareness about healthy aging and the importance of preventive care. This can include education campaigns and community outreach programs to promote healthy behaviors and encourage regular preventive care.

6. Promote intergenerational connections: Promote intergenerational connections and engagement to reduce social isolation and promote healthy aging. This can include community programs that bring together older adults and younger generations, such as mentorship programs and volunteering opportunities.

By taking a comprehensive approach to addressing the challenges and opportunities presented by the aging population, we can help to improve health outcomes and quality of life for older adults. While the solutions may be complex, the consequences of inaction are too great to ignore. It is critical that individuals, healthcare providers, policymakers, and global leaders work together to address the needs of the aging population and promote healthy aging for all.

27

Health inequality

Health inequality is a growing public health concern that affects millions of people worldwide. Health inequality refers to differences in health outcomes between different groups of people, such as differences based on income, race, ethnicity, gender, or geographic location. These differences in health outcomes can be attributed to a range of factors, including access to healthcare, social determinants of health, and systemic discrimination.

Access to healthcare is a major factor in health inequality. Individuals who lack access to healthcare may be less likely to receive preventive care, screening tests, and treatment for health conditions. This can lead to higher rates of chronic disease, disability, and premature death.

Social determinants of health, such as poverty, education, and employment, also contribute to health inequality. Individuals who live in poverty may face greater exposure to environmental toxins, inadequate nutrition, and poor living conditions, all of which can have a negative impact on health outcomes.

Systemic discrimination, such as racism and sexism, also contributes to health inequality. Individuals who face discrimination may have limited access to healthcare, face barriers to employment and education, and experience stress and trauma, all of which can impact their health outcomes.

To address the risk of health inequality, a range of measures can be taken. This includes improving access to healthcare and preventive care, especially for underserved populations. Addressing social determinants of health, such as poverty, education, and housing, can also help to reduce health inequality.

Promoting policies and programs that address systemic discrimination, such as anti-discrimination laws and education campaigns, can also help to reduce health inequality. Increasing public awareness of health disparities and promoting cultural competency among healthcare providers can also help to improve health outcomes for underserved populations.

Health inequality is a complex public health challenge that requires a comprehensive approach to address. By addressing the underlying factors that contribute to health inequality and promoting health equity, we can help to reduce disparities in health outcomes and improve the health of all individuals and communities. It is critical that individuals, healthcare providers, policymakers, and global leaders work together to address the challenges presented by health inequality and promote health equity for all.

Health inequality is a complex public health challenge that requires a multifaceted approach to address. Here are some potential solutions to reduce health inequality:

1. Improve access to healthcare: Increase access to healthcare and preventive care, especially for underserved populations. This can include expanding health insurance coverage, increasing funding for community health centers, and improving transportation to healthcare facilities.

2. Address social determinants of health: Address social determinants of health, such as poverty, education, and housing, that contribute to health inequality. This can include increasing access to affordable housing, promoting education and job training programs, and improving access to healthy food options.

3. Promote policies and programs that address systemic discrimination: Promote policies and programs that address systemic discrimination, such as anti-discrimination laws and education campaigns. This can

help to reduce disparities in health outcomes among different groups.

4. Increase public awareness: Increase public awareness of health disparities and promote cultural competency among healthcare providers. This can help to improve the quality of care for underserved populations and reduce health inequality.

5. Invest in research and data collection: Invest in research and data collection to better understand the underlying factors that contribute to health inequality. This can help to inform policy decisions and identify effective interventions.

6. Foster community engagement: Foster community engagement and participation in decision-making processes related to healthcare and social services. This can help to ensure that the needs of underserved populations are taken into account and that interventions are tailored to the needs of specific communities.

By taking a comprehensive approach to addressing health inequality, we can help to reduce disparities in health outcomes and promote health equity for all. While the solutions may be complex, the consequences of inaction are too great to ignore. It is critical that individuals, healthcare providers, policymakers, and global leaders work together to address the challenges presented by health inequality and promote health equity for all.

28

Superbugs

Superbugs, also known as antibiotic-resistant bacteria, are a growing public health concern that pose a significant threat to global health. Superbugs are bacteria that have developed resistance to antibiotics, making it more difficult to treat infections and increasing the risk of complications, such as sepsis and death.

The risk of superbugs is influenced by a range of factors, including overuse and misuse of antibiotics, poor infection control practices, and global travel and trade. Antibiotic resistance can occur naturally, but the overuse and misuse of antibiotics in humans and animals has accelerated the development of superbugs.

Poor infection control practices, such as inadequate hand hygiene and overuse of medical devices, can also contribute to the spread of superbugs in healthcare settings. Superbugs can be transmitted between patients, health-care workers, and the environment, leading to outbreaks and increasing the risk of healthcare-associated infections.

Global travel and trade can also contribute to the risk of superbugs by facilitating the spread of antibiotic-resistant bacteria across borders. This can result in the spread of superbugs that are resistant to multiple antibiotics, making them more difficult to treat.

To address the risk of superbugs, a range of measures can be taken. This includes promoting antibiotic stewardship and responsible use of antibiotics, such as avoiding unnecessary antibiotic prescriptions and using narrow-spectrum antibiotics when possible.

Improving infection control practices in healthcare settings, such as hand hygiene and environmental cleaning, can also help to reduce the spread of superbugs. Increasing awareness and education about the risks of superbugs and promoting vaccination to prevent infections can also help to reduce the impact of superbugs.

Investing in research and development of new antibiotics and alternative treatments for infections can also help to address the risk of superbugs. Developing new technologies and strategies for infection prevention and control, such as antimicrobial coatings and rapid diagnostic tests, can also help to reduce the spread of superbugs.

Superbugs are a complex public health challenge that requires a comprehensive approach to address. By addressing the underlying factors that contribute to the development and spread of superbugs and promoting responsible use of antibiotics, we can help to reduce the impact of superbugs on global health. It is critical that individuals, healthcare providers, policymakers, and global leaders work together to address the challenges presented by superbugs and promote effective strategies for infection prevention and control.

Superbugs, or antibiotic-resistant bacteria, pose a serious public health risk and require urgent action to address. Here are some potential solutions to reduce the risk of superbugs:

1. Promote antibiotic stewardship: Encourage responsible use of antibiotics and promote antibiotic stewardship programs in healthcare settings. This can help to reduce unnecessary antibiotic prescriptions and prevent the development of antibiotic-resistant bacteria.
2. Improve infection control practices: Implement effective infection prevention and control measures in healthcare settings, such as hand hygiene, environmental cleaning, and appropriate use of medical

devices. This can help to reduce the spread of superbugs and prevent healthcare-associated infections.

3. Increase public awareness: Increase public awareness about the risks of superbugs and the importance of preventing infections. This can include education campaigns, community outreach programs, and patient education materials.

4. Invest in research and development: Invest in research and development of new antibiotics and alternative treatments for infections. This can include developing new antibiotics that are effective against superbugs and exploring alternative treatments, such as phage therapy and immunotherapy.

5. Promote international cooperation: Promote international cooperation and collaboration to address the global threat of superbugs. This can include sharing best practices, data, and resources, and developing global strategies for infection prevention and control.

6. Develop policies and regulations: Develop policies and regulations that support efforts to reduce the risk of superbugs. This can include promoting responsible use of antibiotics in agriculture and food production, as well as supporting regulations that promote infection prevention and control in healthcare settings.

By taking a comprehensive approach to addressing the risk of superbugs, we can help to reduce the impact of antibiotic-resistant bacteria on global health. It is critical that individuals, healthcare providers, policymakers, and global leaders work together to implement effective strategies for infection prevention and control and promote responsible use of antibiotics. By doing so, we can help to preserve the effectiveness of antibiotics and ensure that we have effective treatments for infections in the future.

29

Emerging infectious diseases

Emerging infectious diseases pose a significant threat to global health security. These diseases are caused by pathogens, such as viruses and bacteria, that are new or have recently spread to new geographic areas, and can cause severe illness and death. Examples of emerging infectious diseases include Ebola, Zika, and COVID-19.

The risk of emerging infectious diseases is influenced by a range of factors, including global travel and trade, urbanization, deforestation, and climate change. These factors can lead to increased contact between humans and animals, allowing for the transmission of new pathogens to humans.

In addition, globalization has made it easier for infectious diseases to spread quickly across borders, making it difficult for countries to contain outbreaks and prevent global pandemics.

To address the risk of emerging infectious diseases, a range of measures can be taken. This includes improving surveillance and early warning systems to detect new diseases and outbreaks quickly. Rapid detection and response can help to prevent the spread of diseases and reduce the impact of outbreaks.

Investing in research and development of new vaccines, treatments, and diagnostics can also help to address the risk of emerging infectious diseases. Developing new technologies and strategies for infection prevention and control, such as antimicrobial coatings and personal protective equipment, can also help to reduce the spread of infectious diseases.

Promoting global cooperation and collaboration can also help to address the risk of emerging infectious diseases. This can include sharing data, expertise, and resources to improve disease detection and response, as well as developing global strategies for disease prevention and control.

Emerging infectious diseases pose a significant threat to global health security and require urgent action to address. By investing in surveillance and early warning systems, research and development of new treatments and technologies, and promoting global cooperation and collaboration, we can help to reduce the impact of emerging infectious diseases and prevent future outbreaks. It is critical that individuals, healthcare providers, policymakers, and global leaders work together to address the challenges presented by emerging infectious diseases and promote effective strategies for disease prevention and control.

Emerging infectious diseases pose a significant threat to global health security and require a comprehensive approach to address. Here are some potential solutions to reduce the risk of emerging infectious diseases:

1. Improve surveillance and early warning systems: Improve surveillance and early warning systems to detect new diseases and outbreaks quickly. This can include enhancing laboratory and epidemiological capacity in low- and middle-income countries and increasing investment in global health security.

2. Invest in research and development: Invest in research and development of new vaccines, treatments, and diagnostics for emerging infectious diseases. This can include developing new technologies and strategies for infection prevention and control, such as antimicrobial coatings and personal protective equipment.

3. Promote international cooperation: Promote international cooperation and collaboration to address the global threat of emerging infectious diseases. This can include sharing data, expertise, and resources to

improve disease detection and response, as well as developing global strategies for disease prevention and control.

4. Address social and environmental determinants of health: Address social and environmental determinants of health that contribute to the emergence and spread of infectious diseases. This can include promoting sustainable land use and agriculture, reducing environmental pollution, and improving access to safe water and sanitation.

5. Increase public awareness: Increase public awareness about the risks of emerging infectious diseases and the importance of disease prevention and control. This can include education campaigns, community outreach programs, and patient education materials.

6. Strengthen health systems: Strengthen health systems, particularly in low- and middle-income countries, to improve capacity for disease prevention and control. This can include investing in healthcare infrastructure, training healthcare workers, and promoting universal health coverage.

By taking a comprehensive approach to addressing the risk of emerging infectious diseases, we can help to reduce the impact of these diseases on global health. It is critical that individuals, healthcare providers, policymakers, and global leaders work together to implement effective strategies for disease prevention and control and promote global health security.

30

Global health governance

Global health governance refers to the systems, processes, and institutions that govern global health policies and responses to global health challenges. The risk of inadequate global health governance is that it can lead to insufficient resources and coordination to address global health challenges, such as pandemics and emerging infectious diseases.

The COVID-19 pandemic has highlighted the gaps and weaknesses in global health governance. Despite early warnings and evidence of the potential severity of the pandemic, the response from the international community was slow and fragmented. This led to delays in implementing effective measures to control the spread of the virus and prevent its impact on global health and the economy.

The risk of inadequate global health governance is further compounded by increasing geopolitical tensions and nationalist agendas that can hinder international cooperation and collaboration. This can lead to competition for limited resources and undermine efforts to address global health challenges.

To address the risk of inadequate global health governance, a range of measures can be taken. This includes strengthening global health institutions, such as the World Health Organization (WHO), and increasing funding for global health programs.

Promoting global cooperation and collaboration is also essential for effective global health governance. This can include sharing data, expertise, and resources to improve disease detection and response, as well as developing global strategies for disease prevention and control.

Increasing public awareness and engagement in global health governance can also help to ensure that the needs of individuals and communities are taken into account and that interventions are tailored to the needs of specific populations.

The risk of inadequate global health governance is a significant challenge that requires urgent attention. By strengthening global health institutions, promoting global cooperation and collaboration, and increasing public awareness and engagement, we can help to ensure effective global health governance and prevent future global health crises. It is critical that individuals, healthcare providers, policymakers, and global leaders work together to address the challenges presented by global health governance and promote effective strategies for disease prevention and control.

Global health governance is a complex issue that requires a multifaceted approach to address. Here are some potential solutions to improve global health governance:

1. Strengthen global health institutions: Strengthen global health institutions, such as the World Health Organization (WHO), by increasing funding and support. This can help to improve their capacity to respond to global health challenges and coordinate international efforts.
2. Promote global cooperation and collaboration: Promote global cooperation and collaboration to address global health challenges. This can include sharing data, expertise, and resources, as well as developing global strategies for disease prevention and control.
3. Increase public awareness and engagement: Increase public awareness and engagement in global health governance to ensure that the needs of individuals and communities are taken into account. This can include promoting community engagement and participation in decision-making processes related to healthcare and social services.

4. Address social and environmental determinants of health: Address social and environmental determinants of health, such as poverty, education, and housing, that contribute to global health challenges. This can include promoting sustainable land use and agriculture, reducing environmental pollution, and improving access to safe water and sanitation.

5. Develop policies and regulations: Develop policies and regulations that support efforts to improve global health governance. This can include promoting transparency and accountability in healthcare systems, supporting regulations that promote infection prevention and control, and promoting responsible use of antibiotics in agriculture and food production.

6. Increase investment in global health: Increase investment in global health research, development, and innovation to address emerging health challenges and improve disease prevention and control. This can include developing new vaccines, treatments, and diagnostics, as well as investing in healthcare infrastructure and capacity building in low- and middle-income countries.

By taking a comprehensive approach to addressing global health governance, we can help to ensure effective and equitable responses to global health challenges. It is critical that individuals, healthcare providers, policymakers, and global leaders work together to implement effective strategies for global health governance and promote global health security.

IV

Economic Risks

Economic risks are a major concern for the future of businesses, governments, and individuals. With the increasing globalization and interconnectedness of the world economy, economic risks can arise from a variety of sources such as financial crises, trade conflicts, natural disasters, and geopolitical tensions.

31

Global financial crisis

Global financial crises pose significant risks to the global economy and can have far-reaching impacts on individuals and communities. These crises are often characterized by financial instability, market volatility, and economic recession, which can result in job losses, reduced access to healthcare and social services, and increased poverty.

The risk of global financial crises is influenced by a range of factors, including globalization, trade imbalances, financial market deregulation, and excessive risk-taking by financial institutions. These factors can lead to economic instability and increase the risk of financial crises.

Global financial crises can have a significant impact on health, particularly for vulnerable populations. Economic recession can lead to reduced access to healthcare and social services, increased stress and anxiety, and poor mental health outcomes. In addition, global financial crises can result in reduced funding for public health programs, which can have long-term impacts on population health.

To address the risk of global financial crises, a range of measures can be taken. This includes promoting financial regulation and oversight to prevent excessive risk-taking by financial institutions and address market volatility.

Promoting sustainable economic growth and development can also help to reduce the risk of global financial crises. This can include investing in infrastructure, education, and healthcare, as well as promoting trade policies that support equitable economic growth and development.

Addressing income inequality is also essential for reducing the risk of global financial crises. This can include promoting progressive taxation policies, supporting labor rights, and investing in social safety nets to support vulnerable populations during economic downturns.

Global financial crises pose significant risks to the global economy and can have far-reaching impacts on health and well-being. By promoting financial regulation and oversight, supporting sustainable economic growth and development, and addressing income inequality, we can help to reduce the risk of global financial crises and promote a more equitable and healthy world. It is critical that individuals, healthcare providers, policymakers, and global leaders work together to address the challenges presented by global financial crises and promote effective strategies for economic stability and public health.

Global financial crises are complex and require a comprehensive approach to address. Here are some potential solutions to reduce the risk of global financial crises:

1. Promote financial regulation and oversight: Promote financial regulation and oversight to prevent excessive risk-taking by financial institutions and address market volatility. This can include implementing stronger regulatory frameworks, promoting transparency in financial transactions, and enhancing risk management practices.

2. Encourage sustainable economic growth: Encourage sustainable economic growth and development by investing in infrastructure, education, and healthcare. This can also include promoting trade policies that support equitable economic growth and development.

3. Address income inequality: Address income inequality by promoting progressive taxation policies, supporting labor rights, and investing in social safety nets to support vulnerable populations during economic downturns.

4. Promote international cooperation: Promote international cooperation and collaboration to address global economic challenges. This can

include developing global strategies for economic stability, sharing data and expertise, and coordinating international efforts to prevent and address financial crises.

5. Strengthen financial institutions: Strengthen financial institutions by increasing funding and support for organizations such as the International Monetary Fund and World Bank. This can help to improve their capacity to respond to global economic challenges and coordinate international efforts.

6. Increase public awareness: Increase public awareness about the risks of global financial crises and the importance of financial regulation and oversight. This can include education campaigns, community outreach programs, and public information campaigns.

By taking a comprehensive approach to addressing global financial crises, we can help to reduce the impact of economic instability on individuals and communities. It is critical that individuals, healthcare providers, policymakers, and global leaders work together to implement effective strategies for economic stability and public health.

32

Debt crisis

Debt crises occur when a country or entity is unable to pay back its debts, leading to financial instability and economic recession. These crises can have far-reaching impacts on individuals and communities, including reduced access to healthcare and social services, increased poverty, and decreased economic growth.

The risk of debt crises is influenced by a range of factors, including unsustainable borrowing practices, economic downturns, and external shocks, such as natural disasters or global economic recessions. These factors can lead to unsustainable levels of debt and increase the risk of default.

Debt crises can have a significant impact on health, particularly for vulnerable populations. Economic recession can lead to reduced access to healthcare and social services, increased stress and anxiety, and poor mental health outcomes. In addition, debt crises can result in reduced funding for public health programs, which can have long-term impacts on population health.

To address the risk of debt crises, a range of measures can be taken. This includes promoting responsible borrowing practices and debt management, implementing sound fiscal policies, and supporting economic growth and development.

Promoting debt relief and restructuring can also help to address debt crises, particularly for low- and middle-income countries. This can include providing debt relief and restructuring programs to support economic recovery and reduce the burden of debt.

In addition, promoting international cooperation and collaboration can help to address the risk of debt crises. This can include sharing data and expertise, coordinating international efforts to address economic instability, and developing global strategies for economic stability and growth.

In conclusion, debt crises pose significant risks to global economic stability and public health. By promoting responsible borrowing practices, supporting economic growth and development, and promoting international cooperation and collaboration, we can help to reduce the risk of debt crises and promote a more equitable and healthy world. It is critical that individuals, healthcare providers, policymakers, and global leaders work together to address the challenges presented by debt crises and promote effective strategies for economic stability and public health.

Debt crises are complex and require a multifaceted approach to address. Here are some potential solutions to reduce the risk of debt crises:

1. Promote responsible borrowing practices: Promote responsible borrowing practices and debt management to prevent unsustainable levels of debt. This can include implementing sound fiscal policies, improving debt transparency, and promoting debt sustainability.

2. Support economic growth and development: Support economic growth and development by investing in infrastructure, education, and healthcare. This can help to create jobs, reduce poverty, and support sustainable economic growth.

3. Promote debt relief and restructuring: Promote debt relief and restructuring programs to support economic recovery and reduce the burden of debt, particularly for low- and middle-income countries. This can include providing debt relief, restructuring loans, and supporting economic recovery programs.

4. Increase international cooperation: Increase international cooperation and collaboration to address the risks of debt crises. This can include sharing data and expertise, coordinating international efforts to address economic instability, and developing global strategies for economic stability and growth.

5. Strengthen financial institutions: Strengthen financial institutions by increasing funding and support for organizations such as the International Monetary Fund and World Bank. This can help to improve their capacity to respond to global economic challenges and coordinate international efforts.

6. Address income inequality: Address income inequality by promoting progressive taxation policies, supporting labor rights, and investing in social safety nets to support vulnerable populations during economic downturns.

By taking a comprehensive approach to addressing the risks of debt crises, we can help to reduce the impact of economic instability on individuals and communities. It is critical that individuals, healthcare providers, policymakers, and global leaders work together to implement effective strategies for economic stability and public health.

33

Economic inequality

Economic inequality is a significant challenge that can have far-reaching impacts on individuals and communities. Inequality is often characterized by disparities in income, wealth, and access to resources, which can lead to reduced access to healthcare and social services, increased poverty, and decreased economic growth.

The risk of economic inequality is influenced by a range of factors, including globalization, trade imbalances, and tax policies. These factors can lead to a concentration of wealth among a small group of individuals, increasing the risk of economic inequality.

Economic inequality can have a significant impact on health, particularly for vulnerable populations. Reduced access to healthcare and social services, increased stress and anxiety, and poor mental health outcomes are some of the potential impacts of economic inequality. In addition, economic inequality can result in reduced funding for public health programs, which can have long-term impacts on population health.

To address the risk of economic inequality, a range of measures can be taken. This includes promoting progressive taxation policies, supporting labor rights, and investing in social safety nets to support vulnerable populations.

Promoting economic growth and development is also essential for reducing the risk of economic inequality. This can include investing in infrastructure, education, and healthcare, as well as promoting trade policies that support equitable economic growth and development.

Increasing public awareness and engagement in economic inequality can also help to ensure that the needs of individuals and communities are taken into account. This can include promoting community engagement and participation in decision-making processes related to healthcare and social services.

In conclusion, economic inequality poses significant risks to public health and economic stability. By promoting progressive taxation policies, supporting labor rights, and investing in social safety nets, we can help to reduce the impact of economic inequality on individuals and communities. It is critical that individuals, healthcare providers, policymakers, and global leaders work together to address the challenges presented by economic inequality and promote effective strategies for economic stability and public health.

Addressing economic inequality is a complex issue that requires a comprehensive approach. Here are some potential solutions to reduce the risk of economic inequality:

1. Promote progressive taxation policies: Promote progressive taxation policies that ensure the wealthy pay their fair share of taxes. This can help to reduce income inequality and provide funding for public services and social safety nets.
2. Support labor rights: Support labor rights by ensuring fair wages, safe working conditions, and access to benefits such as healthcare and retirement plans. This can help to reduce income inequality and improve access to resources.
3. Invest in social safety nets: Invest in social safety nets to support vulnerable populations, such as the elderly, children, and low-income families. This can include programs such as unemployment benefits, food assistance, and affordable housing.

4. Promote equitable economic growth: Promote equitable economic growth and development by investing in infrastructure, education, and healthcare. This can help to create jobs, reduce poverty, and support sustainable economic growth.

5. Address trade imbalances: Address trade imbalances by promoting fair trade policies that ensure equitable economic growth and development. This can include supporting policies that protect workers' rights and promote environmental sustainability.

6. Increase public awareness: Increase public awareness about the impacts of economic inequality on health and well-being. This can include education campaigns, community outreach programs, and public information campaigns.

By taking a comprehensive approach to addressing economic inequality, we can help to reduce the impact of inequality on individuals and communities. It is critical that individuals, healthcare providers, policymakers, and global leaders work together to implement effective strategies for economic stability and public health.

34

Trade wars

Trade wars have the potential to disrupt global trade and economic stability, leading to reduced access to goods and services, job losses, and decreased economic growth. The risk of trade wars is influenced by a range of factors, including protectionist trade policies, global economic imbalances, and political tensions between trading partners.

In recent years, the world has witnessed several trade wars, including the ongoing trade conflict between the United States and China. These conflicts have resulted in increased tariffs and trade restrictions, which have led to reduced trade flows and increased economic uncertainty.

Trade wars can have a significant impact on public health, particularly for vulnerable populations. Reduced access to essential goods, such as medical supplies and food, can lead to increased health risks, while job losses and reduced economic growth can lead to decreased access to healthcare and social services.

To address the risk of trade wars, a range of measures can be taken. This includes promoting fair trade policies that ensure equitable economic growth and development, supporting international trade organizations such as the World Trade Organization (WTO), and promoting international cooperation and collaboration to address global trade imbalances.

In addition, addressing the root causes of trade conflicts, such as political tensions and economic disparities, can help to prevent the risk of trade wars.

This can include promoting diplomatic efforts to resolve political tensions and investing in economic development programs to reduce economic disparities.

Increasing public awareness about the risks of trade wars can also help to ensure that the needs of individuals and communities are taken into account. This can include promoting community engagement and participation in decision-making processes related to trade policies and economic development.

Trade wars pose significant risks to global economic stability and public health. By promoting fair trade policies, supporting international trade organizations, and addressing the root causes of trade conflicts, we can help to reduce the risk of trade wars and promote a more equitable and healthy world. It is critical that individuals, healthcare providers, policymakers, and global leaders work together to address the challenges presented by trade wars and promote effective strategies for economic stability and public health.

Here are some potential solutions to reduce the risk of trade wars in the future:

1. Promote fair trade policies: Promote fair trade policies that ensure equitable economic growth and development. This can include supporting policies that protect workers' rights, promote environmental sustainability, and reduce trade imbalances.

2. Support international trade organizations: Support international trade organizations such as the World Trade Organization (WTO), which promote open and fair trade. This can help to prevent trade disputes and reduce the risk of trade wars.

3. Increase international cooperation: Increase international cooperation and collaboration to address global trade imbalances. This can include developing global strategies for economic stability, sharing data and expertise, and coordinating international efforts to prevent and address trade conflicts.

4. Address the root causes of trade conflicts: Address the root causes of trade conflicts, such as political tensions and economic disparities. This can include promoting diplomatic efforts to resolve political tensions, investing in economic development programs to reduce economic disparities, and promoting policies that support equitable economic growth.

5. Increase public awareness: Increase public awareness about the risks of trade wars and the importance of fair trade policies. This can include education campaigns, community outreach programs, and public information campaigns.

By taking a comprehensive approach to addressing the risks of trade wars, we can help to reduce the impact of economic instability on individuals and communities. It is critical that individuals, healthcare providers, policymakers, and global leaders work together to implement effective strategies for economic stability and public health.

35

Geopolitical instability

Geopolitical instability is a significant challenge that can have far-reaching impacts on individuals and communities. Instability can be characterized by political tensions, conflicts, and violence, which can lead to reduced access to resources, increased poverty, and decreased economic growth.

The risk of geopolitical instability is influenced by a range of factors, including political tensions between countries, regional conflicts, and extremist ideologies. These factors can lead to instability and increase the risk of violence and conflict.

Geopolitical instability can have a significant impact on health, particularly for vulnerable populations. Reduced access to healthcare and social services, increased stress and anxiety, and poor mental health outcomes are some of the potential impacts of geopolitical instability. In addition, instability can result in reduced funding for public health programs, which can have long-term impacts on population health.

To address the risk of geopolitical instability, a range of measures can be taken. This includes promoting diplomacy and conflict resolution, supporting human rights, and promoting equitable economic growth and development.

Addressing the root causes of geopolitical instability, such as poverty, inequality, and lack of access to education and healthcare, can help to prevent instability and promote stability. This can include investing in economic development programs, promoting universal access to education and healthcare, and supporting policies that reduce poverty and inequality.

Increasing public awareness and engagement in geopolitical instability can also help to ensure that the needs of individuals and communities are taken into account. This can include promoting community engagement and participation in decision-making processes related to conflict resolution and economic development.

Geopolitical instability poses significant risks to public health and economic stability. By promoting diplomacy and conflict resolution, supporting human rights, and promoting equitable economic growth and development, we can help to reduce the impact of geopolitical instability on individuals and communities. It is critical that individuals, healthcare providers, policymakers, and global leaders work together to address the challenges presented by geopolitical instability and promote effective strategies for stability and public health.

Addressing geopolitical instability is a complex issue that requires a comprehensive approach. Here are some potential solutions to reduce the risk of geopolitical instability:

1. Promote diplomacy and conflict resolution: Promote diplomacy and conflict resolution by supporting peaceful negotiations and mediation efforts to resolve disputes between countries and groups. This can include promoting dialogue, reducing tensions, and addressing the root causes of conflict.

2. Support human rights: Support human rights by promoting policies that protect and respect individual and group rights, including freedom of expression, assembly, and movement. This can help to promote social justice, reduce inequality, and promote stability.

3. Promote equitable economic growth: Promote equitable economic growth and development by investing in infrastructure, education, and healthcare. This can help to create jobs, reduce poverty, and support sustainable economic growth.

4. Address inequality and poverty: Address inequality and poverty by promoting policies that reduce poverty, promote universal access to education and healthcare, and support social safety nets to protect vulnerable populations during times of instability.

5. Increase international cooperation: Increase international cooperation and collaboration to address the risks of geopolitical instability. This can include developing global strategies for peace and stability, sharing data and expertise, and coordinating international efforts to prevent and address geopolitical instability.

6. Increase public awareness: Increase public awareness about the risks of geopolitical instability and the importance of promoting peace, stability, and human rights. This can include education campaigns, community outreach programs, and public information campaigns.

By taking a comprehensive approach to addressing geopolitical instability, we can help to reduce the impact of instability on individuals and communities. It is critical that individuals, healthcare providers, policymakers, and global leaders work together to implement effective strategies for stability and public health.

36

Energy price volatility

Energy price volatility is a significant challenge that can have far-reaching impacts on individuals, businesses, and governments. Volatility can be characterized by rapid changes in the price of energy, which can lead to reduced access to energy resources, increased costs for energy consumers, and decreased economic growth.

The risk of energy price volatility is influenced by a range of factors, including global supply and demand, political tensions between energy-producing countries, and market speculation. These factors can lead to volatility and increase the risk of energy price spikes and fluctuations.

Energy price volatility can have a significant impact on public health, particularly for vulnerable populations. Reduced access to affordable energy can lead to increased health risks, while increased energy costs can lead to decreased access to healthcare and social services.

To address the risk of energy price volatility, a range of measures can be taken. This includes promoting energy efficiency and conservation, diversifying energy sources, and investing in renewable energy and alternative fuels.

Addressing the root causes of energy price volatility, such as global supply and demand imbalances and political tensions, can help to prevent volatility and promote stability. This can include promoting international cooperation to address energy supply and demand imbalances, promoting policies that support sustainable energy development, and investing in energy infrastructure.

Increasing public awareness and engagement in energy price volatility can also help to ensure that the needs of individuals and communities are taken into account. This can include promoting community engagement and participation in decision-making processes related to energy policy and development.

Energy price volatility poses significant risks to public health and economic stability. By promoting energy efficiency and conservation, diversifying energy sources, and investing in renewable energy and alternative fuels, we can help to reduce the impact of energy price volatility on individuals and communities. It is critical that individuals, healthcare providers, policymakers, and global leaders work together to address the challenges presented by energy price volatility and promote effective strategies for stability and public health.

ere are some potential solutions to reduce the risk of energy price volatility in the future:

1. Promote energy efficiency and conservation: Promote energy efficiency and conservation by promoting policies that encourage individuals, businesses, and governments to reduce energy consumption. This can include energy efficiency standards for buildings and appliances, public education campaigns, and financial incentives for energy-saving measures.

2. Diversify energy sources: Diversify energy sources by promoting the development of renewable energy sources, such as solar, wind, and geothermal power. This can reduce dependence on fossil fuels and promote long-term stability in energy markets.

3. Invest in energy infrastructure: Invest in energy infrastructure to improve access to energy resources and reduce supply and demand imbalances. This can include investments in pipelines, storage facilities, and transmission lines.

4. Promote international cooperation: Promote international cooperation to address global energy supply and demand imbalances. This can include developing global strategies for energy stability, sharing data and expertise, and coordinating international efforts to prevent and address energy price volatility.

5. Address political tensions: Address political tensions between energy-producing countries through diplomacy and conflict resolution efforts. This can help to reduce the risk of supply disruptions and price spikes in energy markets.

6. Increase public awareness: Increase public awareness about the importance of energy conservation and the benefits of renewable energy sources. This can include education campaigns, community outreach programs, and public information campaigns.

By taking a comprehensive approach to addressing energy price volatility, we can help to reduce the impact of volatility on individuals and communities. It is critical that individuals, healthcare providers, policymakers, and global leaders work together to implement effective strategies for stability and public health.

37

Stock market crash

A stock market crash is a significant risk that can have far-reaching impacts on individuals, businesses, and governments. A stock market crash can be characterized by a rapid decline in the value of stocks and securities, which can lead to reduced access to capital, job losses, and decreased economic growth.

The risk of a stock market crash is influenced by a range of factors, including market speculation, global economic imbalances, and political tensions between countries. These factors can lead to market instability and increase the risk of a crash.

A stock market crash can have a significant impact on public health, particularly for vulnerable populations. Reduced access to capital can lead to decreased funding for public health programs, while job losses and decreased economic growth can lead to reduced access to healthcare and social services.

To address the risk of a stock market crash, a range of measures can be taken. This includes promoting financial stability and diversification, regulating financial markets to prevent speculation and fraud, and investing in economic development programs to promote equitable economic growth.

Addressing the root causes of market instability, such as global economic imbalances and political tensions, can help to prevent crashes and promote stability. This can include promoting international cooperation to address economic imbalances, promoting policies that support sustainable economic development, and investing in financial education programs to promote financial literacy.

Increasing public awareness and engagement in stock market crashes can also help to ensure that the needs of individuals and communities are taken into account. This can include promoting community engagement and participation in decision-making processes related to financial regulation and economic development.

A stock market crash poses significant risks to public health and economic stability. By promoting financial stability and diversification, regulating financial markets to prevent speculation and fraud, and investing in economic development programs, we can help to reduce the impact of stock market crashes on individuals and communities. It is critical that individuals, healthcare providers, policymakers, and global leaders work together to address the challenges presented by stock market crashes and promote effective strategies for stability and public health.

Here are some potential solutions to reduce the risk of a stock market crash in the future:

1. Promote financial stability and diversification: Promote financial stability and diversification by investing in a range of assets and sectors. This can reduce the impact of market fluctuations on individual investors and promote long-term stability in financial markets.
2. Regulate financial markets: Regulate financial markets to prevent speculation and fraud by promoting transparency, strengthening oversight, and enforcing regulations. This can reduce the risk of market manipulation and promote market stability.
3. Invest in economic development programs: Invest in economic development programs to promote equitable economic growth and reduce the risk of economic imbalances. This can include investments in infrastructure, education, and healthcare, as well as policies that promote job creation and entrepreneurship.
4. Promote international cooperation: Promote international cooperation

to address global economic imbalances and promote financial stability. This can include developing global strategies for economic stability, sharing data and expertise, and coordinating international efforts to prevent and address financial crises.

5. Increase financial education: Increase financial education and literacy to promote informed decision-making and reduce the risk of investment fraud. This can include public education campaigns, community outreach programs, and financial education initiatives for individuals and businesses.

38

Currency devaluation

Currency devaluation is a significant risk that can have far-reaching impacts on individuals, businesses, and governments. Devaluation occurs when the value of a country's currency declines relative to other currencies, which can lead to reduced purchasing power, increased inflation, and decreased economic growth.

The risk of currency devaluation is influenced by a range of factors, including global economic imbalances, political tensions between countries, and fluctuations in international trade. These factors can lead to devaluation and increase the risk of economic instability.

Currency devaluation can have a significant impact on public health, particularly for vulnerable populations. Reduced purchasing power can lead to decreased access to essential goods and services, while increased inflation can lead to reduced access to healthcare and social services.

To address the risk of currency devaluation, a range of measures can be taken. This includes promoting economic stability and diversification, regulating currency markets to prevent speculation and manipulation, and investing in economic development programs to promote equitable economic growth.

Addressing the root causes of currency devaluation, such as global economic imbalances and political tensions, can help to prevent devaluation and promote stability. This can include promoting international cooperation to address economic imbalances, promoting policies that support sustainable economic development, and investing in financial education programs to promote financial literacy.

Increasing public awareness and engagement in currency devaluation can also help to ensure that the needs of individuals and communities are taken into account. This can include promoting community engagement and participation in decision-making processes related to financial regulation and economic development.

Currency devaluation poses significant risks to public health and economic stability. By promoting economic stability and diversification, regulating currency markets to prevent speculation and manipulation, and investing in economic development programs, we can help to reduce the impact of currency devaluation on individuals and communities. It is critical that individuals, healthcare providers, policymakers, and global leaders work together to address the challenges presented by currency devaluation and promote effective strategies for stability and public health.

Here are some potential solutions to reduce the risk of currency devaluation in the future:

1. Promote economic stability and diversification: Promote economic stability and diversification by investing in a range of sectors and industries. This can reduce the impact of market fluctuations on individual investors and promote long-term stability in financial markets.

2. Regulate currency markets: Regulate currency markets to prevent speculation and manipulation by promoting transparency, strengthening oversight, and enforcing regulations. This can reduce the risk of market manipulation and promote market stability.

3. Invest in economic development programs: Invest in economic development programs to promote equitable economic growth and reduce the risk of economic imbalances. This can include investments in infrastructure, education, and healthcare, as well as policies that promote job creation and entrepreneurship.

4. Promote international cooperation: Promote international cooperation to address global economic imbalances and promote financial stability. This can include developing global strategies for economic stability, sharing data and expertise, and coordinating international efforts to prevent and address financial crises.

5. Address political tensions: Address political tensions between countries through diplomacy and conflict resolution efforts. This can help to reduce the risk of currency devaluation due to geopolitical instability.

6. Increase financial education: Increase financial education and literacy to promote informed decision-making and reduce the risk of investment fraud. This can include public education campaigns, community outreach programs, and financial education initiatives for individuals and businesses.

39

Hyperinflation

Hyperinflation is a significant risk that can have far-reaching impacts on individuals, businesses, and governments. Hyperinflation is characterized by a rapid increase in the price of goods and services, which can lead to reduced purchasing power, decreased economic growth, and social unrest.

The risk of hyperinflation is influenced by a range of factors, including economic mismanagement, political instability, and global economic imbalances. These factors can lead to hyperinflation and increase the risk of economic instability.

Hyperinflation can have a significant impact on public health, particularly for vulnerable populations. Reduced purchasing power can lead to decreased access to essential goods and services, while increased inflation can lead to reduced access to healthcare and social services.

To address the risk of hyperinflation, a range of measures can be taken. This includes promoting fiscal responsibility and sound economic management, regulating financial markets to prevent speculation and manipulation, and investing in economic development programs to promote equitable economic growth.

Addressing the root causes of hyperinflation, such as economic mismanagement and political instability, can help to prevent hyperinflation and promote stability. This can include promoting international cooperation to address economic imbalances, promoting policies that support sustainable economic development, and investing in financial education programs to promote financial literacy.

Increasing public awareness and engagement in hyperinflation can also help to ensure that the needs of individuals and communities are taken into account. This can include promoting community engagement and participation in decision-making processes related to financial regulation and economic development.

Hyperinflation poses significant risks to public health and economic stability. By promoting fiscal responsibility and sound economic management, regulating financial markets to prevent speculation and manipulation, and investing in economic development programs, we can help to reduce the impact of hyperinflation on individuals and communities. It is critical that individuals, healthcare providers, policymakers, and global leaders work together to address the challenges presented by hyperinflation and promote effective strategies for stability and public health.

Here are some potential solutions to reduce the risk of hyperinflation in the future:

1. Promote fiscal responsibility: Promote fiscal responsibility by implementing sound economic policies and management practices that prioritize stability and sustainable economic growth. This can include measures such as reducing government debt and deficits, controlling inflation, and investing in infrastructure and education.

2. Regulate financial markets: Regulate financial markets to prevent speculation and manipulation by promoting transparency, strengthening oversight, and enforcing regulations. This can reduce the risk of market manipulation and promote market stability.

3. Invest in economic development programs: Invest in economic development programs to promote equitable economic growth and reduce the risk of economic imbalances. This can include investments in infrastructure, education, and healthcare, as well as policies that promote job creation and entrepreneurship.

4. Promote international cooperation: Promote international cooperation to address global economic imbalances and promote financial stability. This can include developing global strategies for economic stability, sharing data and expertise, and coordinating international efforts to prevent and address financial crises.

5. Address political instability: Address political instability and promote conflict resolution efforts to reduce the risk of hyperinflation due to geopolitical tensions.

6. Increase financial education: Increase financial education and literacy to promote informed decision-making and reduce the risk of investment fraud. This can include public education campaigns, community outreach programs, and financial education initiatives for individuals and businesses.

40

Resource scarcity

Resource scarcity is a significant risk that can have far-reaching impacts on individuals, businesses, and governments. Resource scarcity is characterized by a depletion or limited access to essential resources, such as water, energy, and food, which can lead to reduced quality of life, economic instability, and social unrest.

The risk of resource scarcity is influenced by a range of factors, including population growth, climate change, and unsustainable resource consumption patterns. These factors can lead to resource depletion and increase the risk of economic and social instability.

Resource scarcity can have a significant impact on public health, particularly for vulnerable populations. Reduced access to essential resources can lead to decreased access to healthcare, increased incidence of malnutrition and food insecurity, and increased susceptibility to environmental hazards.

To address the risk of resource scarcity, a range of measures can be taken. This includes promoting sustainable resource management practices, investing in resource-efficient technologies, and supporting policies that promote equitable access to resources.

Addressing the root causes of resource scarcity, such as unsustainable consumption patterns and climate change, can help to prevent resource depletion and promote stability. This can include promoting international cooperation to address climate change, promoting policies that support sustainable consumption patterns, and investing in research and development to promote resource efficiency.

Increasing public awareness and engagement in resource scarcity can also help to ensure that the needs of individuals and communities are taken into account. This can include promoting community engagement and participation in decision-making processes related to resource management and sustainability.

Resource scarcity poses significant risks to public health and economic stability. By promoting sustainable resource management practices, investing in resource-efficient technologies, and supporting policies that promote equitable access to resources, we can help to reduce the impact of resource scarcity on individuals and communities. It is critical that individuals, healthcare providers, policymakers, and global leaders work together to address the challenges presented by resource scarcity and promote effective strategies for stability and public health.

Here are some potential solutions to reduce the risk of resource scarcity in the future:

1. Promote sustainable resource management practices: Promote sustainable resource management practices by implementing policies and practices that prioritize resource conservation, efficient resource use, and waste reduction. This can include initiatives such as water conservation measures, energy-efficient technologies, and sustainable agriculture practices.

2. Invest in resource-efficient technologies: Invest in research and development to develop resource-efficient technologies that reduce resource consumption and waste. This can include technologies such as renewable energy, water recycling and treatment systems, and sustainable transportation solutions.

3. Support policies that promote equitable access to resources: Support policies that promote equitable access to resources, particularly for vulnerable populations. This can include policies that prioritize access

to clean water and sanitation, affordable and nutritious food, and healthcare services.

4. Address climate change: Address climate change by reducing greenhouse gas emissions, promoting renewable energy solutions, and developing policies to address the impacts of climate change on natural resources. This can include initiatives such as carbon pricing, renewable energy incentives, and climate change adaptation programs.

5. Increase public awareness and engagement: Increase public awareness and engagement on issues related to resource scarcity, sustainability, and equitable access to resources. This can include public education campaigns, community outreach programs, and opportunities for public participation in decision-making processes related to resource management.

V

Geopolitical Risks

Geopolitical risks refer to the potential for political conflicts and tensions between different countries or regions, which can have far-reaching impacts on global stability and security. These risks can arise from a range of factors, including economic competition, territorial disputes, and ideological differences.

41

Terrorism

The risk of terrorism remains a concern for many individuals and governments around the world. Despite efforts to combat terrorism through intelligence gathering and law enforcement, there is still the potential for attacks to occur in the future. Here are some potential risks of terrorism in the future:

1. Homegrown terrorism: Homegrown terrorism refers to individuals who are radicalized within their own country and carry out attacks domestically. This type of terrorism is difficult to predict and prevent, as individuals may not have a direct connection to terrorist organizations.

2. Cyberterrorism: As technology continues to advance, cyberterrorism is becoming an increasing concern. This involves using technology to carry out attacks on computer networks, which could have widespread impacts on businesses, governments, and individuals.

3. Chemical and biological attacks: Terrorist groups may attempt to use chemical or biological weapons to carry out attacks, which could have devastating consequences.

4. Lone-wolf attacks: Lone-wolf attacks refer to individuals who carry out attacks without the support or direction of a terrorist organization. These types of attacks can be difficult to predict and prevent, as individuals may not have a history of violent behavior or known

connections to extremist groups.

5. Political instability: Political instability in countries around the world can create conditions that are ripe for terrorist activity. Countries that are experiencing conflict or civil unrest may be more vulnerable to attacks.

To address the risk of terrorism in the future, governments and individuals must remain vigilant and take steps to prevent attacks from occurring. This includes investing in intelligence gathering and law enforcement, promoting international cooperation to combat terrorism, and addressing the root causes of radicalization. While it is impossible to completely eliminate the risk of terrorism, taking proactive steps to prevent attacks can help ensure the safety and security of individuals and communities around the world.

While the risk of terrorism in the future cannot be completely eliminated, there are steps that can be taken to mitigate the threat. Here are some solutions that could help address the risk of terrorism:

1. Intelligence gathering: Strong intelligence gathering capabilities are essential for identifying and preventing terrorist threats. This involves collecting and analyzing information about potential threats and sharing intelligence with other countries.

2. Law enforcement: Effective law enforcement is essential for disrupting terrorist plots and apprehending individuals who pose a threat. This involves investing in training and resources for law enforcement agencies and working to strengthen international cooperation.

3. Addressing root causes: Addressing the underlying causes of terrorism, such as poverty, political instability, and social alienation, can help prevent individuals from being drawn into extremist groups. This may involve investing in education, promoting economic development, and addressing social and political grievances.

4. Border security: Strong border security measures can help prevent

terrorists from entering a country undetected. This may involve using advanced technologies to screen travelers and goods, as well as implementing effective visa and immigration policies.

5. Countering extremist ideology: Countering extremist ideology is essential for preventing individuals from being radicalized. This may involve working with community leaders and religious figures to promote alternative messages and creating effective counter-narratives online.

6. Preparedness and response: Developing effective preparedness and response plans can help minimize the impact of a terrorist attack if it does occur. This involves training first responders, conducting regular drills, and investing in emergency management capabilities.

42

War

The risk of war is a concern for many individuals and governments around the world. While the number of conflicts and casualties has declined in recent years, the potential for conflict remains. Here are some potential risks of war in the future:

1. Geopolitical tensions: Geopolitical tensions between countries can create conditions that are ripe for conflict. Disputes over territory, resources, and ideology can escalate into armed conflict.
2. Terrorism: Terrorism can spark military action, as governments may respond to terrorist attacks with military force. This can lead to further conflict and instability.
3. Nuclear proliferation: The spread of nuclear weapons increases the potential for catastrophic conflict. The possession of nuclear weapons by hostile nations creates the risk of a nuclear war, which could have devastating consequences.
4. Cyber warfare: As technology continues to advance, cyber warfare is becoming an increasing concern. This involves using technology to disrupt computer networks and infrastructure, which could have significant impacts on military and civilian operations.
5. Climate change: Climate change can exacerbate existing tensions and create conditions that are ripe for conflict. Disputes over resources

such as water and food can escalate into armed conflict.

To address the risk of war in the future, governments and individuals must remain vigilant and take steps to prevent conflict from escalating. This includes investing in diplomacy and conflict resolution, promoting international cooperation, and addressing the root causes of conflict. It is important to work to reduce geopolitical tensions, prevent the spread of nuclear weapons, and develop effective responses to cyber attacks. Additionally, addressing the causes of climate change can help prevent the emergence of conflicts related to resource scarcity.

While the risk of war in the future cannot be completely eliminated, taking proactive steps to prevent conflict and promote peace can help ensure the safety and security of individuals and communities around the world.

While the risk of war in the future cannot be completely eliminated, there are steps that can be taken to mitigate the threat. Here are some solutions that could help address the risk of war:

1. Diplomacy: Diplomacy is essential for preventing conflicts from escalating into armed conflict. This involves engaging in dialogue with other countries and working to resolve disputes through negotiation and compromise.
2. International cooperation: International cooperation is essential for preventing conflict and promoting peace. This involves working with other countries and international organizations to address shared challenges, such as climate change and terrorism.
3. Conflict resolution: Effective conflict resolution can help prevent conflicts from escalating into armed conflict. This involves identifying the underlying causes of conflict and working to address them through negotiation and mediation.
4. Disarmament: Disarmament is essential for reducing the risk of armed conflict. This may involve reducing the number of nuclear weapons in the world, as well as reducing military spending and arms sales.
5. Humanitarian aid: Providing humanitarian aid to countries affected

by conflict can help alleviate suffering and promote peace. This may involve providing food, shelter, and medical care to refugees and displaced persons.

6. Education and awareness: Education and awareness can help promote peace by promoting a culture of tolerance and understanding. This may involve teaching conflict resolution and peacebuilding skills in schools, as well as promoting media literacy and critical thinking skills.

43

Nuclear proliferation

Nuclear proliferation, or the spread of nuclear weapons, is a major concern for the future of global security. The use of nuclear weapons would have devastating consequences, and the spread of nuclear weapons to additional countries could increase the likelihood of their use. Here are some potential risks of nuclear proliferation in the future:

1. Rogue states: The possession of nuclear weapons by rogue states, or countries that do not follow international norms and laws, can create instability and uncertainty. Countries such as North Korea and Iran have pursued nuclear weapons programs in the face of international pressure, which has led to tensions and the risk of conflict.

2. Terrorism: The possibility of nuclear weapons falling into the hands of terrorists is a major concern. Terrorist groups may seek to acquire nuclear weapons to carry out attacks, which could have catastrophic consequences.

3. Accidents: The risk of accidents involving nuclear weapons or materials is always present. Accidents could result in the release of radioactive material, which could have serious health and environmental consequences.

4. Cyber attacks: Cyber attacks on nuclear facilities and infrastructure could disrupt operations and compromise security. This could poten-

tially lead to the theft or release of nuclear materials, or the malfunction of nuclear weapons.

To address the risk of nuclear proliferation in the future, it is important to promote disarmament and nonproliferation efforts. This includes working to reduce the number of nuclear weapons in the world, strengthening international norms and laws, and preventing the spread of nuclear weapons to additional countries. Effective verification and inspection mechanisms are essential for ensuring compliance with international agreements, and efforts should be made to increase transparency and cooperation between countries.

It is also important to address the underlying causes of nuclear proliferation, such as political instability, poverty, and conflict. Promoting economic development and addressing social and political grievances can help reduce the risk of countries pursuing nuclear weapons programs.

Ultimately, preventing nuclear proliferation requires a comprehensive and coordinated approach that involves multiple stakeholders, including governments, civil society organizations, and the private sector. By working together, we can help prevent the spread of nuclear weapons and ensure the safety and security of individuals and communities around the world.

Nuclear proliferation is a complex and challenging issue, but there are steps that can be taken to mitigate the risks. Here are some solutions that could help address the risk of nuclear proliferation:

1. Diplomacy: Diplomacy is essential for preventing the spread of nuclear weapons. This involves engaging in dialogue with countries that may be pursuing nuclear weapons and working to resolve disputes through negotiation and compromise.

2. Arms control: Arms control agreements can help limit the number of nuclear weapons in the world and prevent their spread. This may involve negotiating and implementing treaties such as the Nuclear Non-Proliferation Treaty (NPT) or the Comprehensive Test Ban Treaty (CTBT).

3. Verification and inspections: Verification and inspections are essential for ensuring compliance with international agreements and preventing the spread of nuclear weapons. This involves monitoring nuclear facilities and materials to ensure that they are not being used for weapons purposes.

4. Nonproliferation assistance: Providing nonproliferation assistance to countries that may be at risk of pursuing nuclear weapons can help prevent their proliferation. This may involve providing technical assistance and training to strengthen nuclear security measures.

5. Economic development: Promoting economic development in countries that may be at risk of pursuing nuclear weapons can help address the underlying causes of proliferation. This may involve providing economic assistance and promoting trade and investment.

6. Multilateral cooperation: Multilateral cooperation is essential for preventing nuclear proliferation. This involves working with other countries and international organizations to address shared challenges and promote nonproliferation efforts.

44

Cyber warfare

Cyber warfare is becoming an increasing concern as technology continues to advance. Cyber warfare involves using technology to disrupt computer networks, infrastructure, and communication systems, which could have significant impacts on military and civilian operations. Here are some potential risks of cyber warfare in the future:

1. State-sponsored attacks: State-sponsored attacks involve one country using cyber warfare tactics to attack another country's infrastructure. These attacks could target critical infrastructure such as power grids, financial systems, or transportation networks, which could have significant impacts on national security and the economy.

2. Non-state actors: Non-state actors such as terrorist groups and criminal organizations are increasingly using cyber warfare tactics to achieve their goals. These groups may seek to disrupt critical infrastructure or steal sensitive information for financial gain or political purposes.

3. Hacking of military systems: Hacking into military systems could compromise sensitive information and disrupt military operations. This could have significant impacts on national security and the ability of a country to defend itself.

4. Social engineering attacks: Social engineering attacks involve using

psychological manipulation to gain access to sensitive information or systems. These attacks can be difficult to detect and prevent, as they rely on human vulnerabilities rather than technical vulnerabilities.

To address the risk of cyber warfare in the future, it is important to invest in cybersecurity measures and promote international cooperation. This includes developing strong cybersecurity protocols for critical infrastructure, investing in research and development to improve cybersecurity technologies, and increasing cooperation between countries to prevent cyber attacks.

It is also important to address the root causes of cyber warfare, such as political tensions and the lack of international norms and laws governing cyber warfare. Promoting international dialogue and cooperation on cybersecurity issues can help build trust and prevent conflicts from escalating into cyber attacks.

Ultimately, preventing cyber warfare requires a comprehensive and coordinated approach that involves multiple stakeholders, including governments, civil society organizations, and the private sector. By working together, we can help prevent cyber attacks and ensure the safety and security of individuals and communities around the world.

Cyber warfare is a complex and rapidly evolving threat, but there are steps that can be taken to mitigate the risks. Here are some solutions that could help address the risk of cyber warfare:

1. Invest in cybersecurity measures: Investing in cybersecurity measures is essential for preventing cyber attacks. This includes using strong encryption technologies, implementing firewalls and intrusion detection systems, and conducting regular security audits.

2. Promote international cooperation: Cyber warfare is a global threat, and international cooperation is essential for preventing attacks and minimizing their impact. This involves working with other countries and international organizations to share information and develop

common standards for cybersecurity.

3. Strengthen international laws and norms: Strengthening international laws and norms governing cyber warfare can help prevent attacks and promote accountability for those who engage in them. This may involve negotiating and implementing treaties and agreements that set clear standards for behavior in cyberspace.

4. Develop a skilled cybersecurity workforce: Developing a skilled cybersecurity workforce is essential for preventing cyber attacks. This may involve investing in education and training programs to develop a pipeline of skilled cybersecurity professionals.

5. Public-private partnerships: Public-private partnerships can help improve cybersecurity by promoting information sharing and collaboration between government agencies and private sector organizations. This may involve creating industry-led cybersecurity consortiums or partnering with technology companies to develop new cybersecurity solutions.

45

Ethnic conflict

Ethnic conflict is a complex and often violent phenomenon that arises when different ethnic groups within a society feel that their interests, values, and cultural traditions are being threatened. These conflicts can result in serious human rights abuses, displacement, and loss of life. Here are some potential causes of ethnic conflict:

1. Economic disparities: Economic disparities between different ethnic groups can create tension and conflict. In many cases, one ethnic group may feel that they are being discriminated against or marginalized in the economic sphere.

2. Political competition: Political competition between ethnic groups can also contribute to conflict. In some cases, ethnic groups may compete for political power or control over resources, which can lead to violence and instability.

3. Historical grievances: Historical grievances can create a sense of injustice and anger among ethnic groups, which can contribute to conflict. These grievances may include past acts of violence or discrimination, or the loss of cultural or religious traditions.

4. Nationalism: Nationalism, or the belief in the superiority of one's own ethnic group or nation, can contribute to conflict. Nationalistic beliefs may lead to the exclusion or discrimination of other ethnic groups,

which can create tension and instability.

To address ethnic conflict, it is important to promote tolerance and understanding among different ethnic groups. This may involve promoting dialogue and communication between groups, providing education about different cultures and traditions, and promoting equal economic and political opportunities for all groups.

It is also important to address the underlying causes of ethnic conflict, such as economic disparities and historical grievances. This may involve investing in economic development programs in marginalized areas, providing reparations or apologies for past injustices, or promoting conflict resolution and peacebuilding programs.

Ultimately, addressing ethnic conflict requires a comprehensive and coordinated approach that involves multiple stakeholders, including governments, civil society organizations, and the private sector. By working together, we can help promote peace and stability and ensure the safety and security of individuals and communities affected by ethnic conflict.

Ethnic conflict is a complex and persistent problem that requires a multifaceted approach to address. Here are some potential solutions that could help mitigate the risks of ethnic conflict:

1. Promote dialogue and communication: Promoting dialogue and communication between different ethnic groups is essential for building understanding and fostering peaceful coexistence. This may involve creating opportunities for inter-ethnic dialogue, such as community events or cultural exchange programs.

2. Invest in economic development: Economic disparities can be a significant contributor to ethnic conflict. Investing in economic development programs in marginalized areas can help address these disparities and promote stability.

3. Foster inclusive governance: Inclusive governance can help ensure that all ethnic groups have a say in decision-making processes and that

their interests are represented. This may involve promoting diversity in government and creating opportunities for marginalized groups to participate in decision-making processes.

4. Address historical grievances: Historical grievances can contribute to ethnic conflict, and addressing these grievances is essential for promoting healing and reconciliation. This may involve providing reparations or apologies for past injustices or creating opportunities for truth and reconciliation processes.

5. Strengthen international norms and laws: Strengthening international norms and laws governing ethnic conflict can help prevent conflicts from escalating and promote accountability for those who engage in human rights abuses.

6. Promote education and awareness: Promoting education and awareness about different cultures and traditions can help build understanding and tolerance between different ethnic groups. This may involve creating educational programs or promoting media literacy and critical thinking skills.

Ultimately, addressing ethnic conflict requires a comprehensive and coordinated approach that involves multiple stakeholders, including governments, civil society organizations, and the private sector. By working together, we can help promote peace and stability and ensure the safety and security of individuals and communities affected by ethnic conflict.

46

State collapse

State collapse is a complex and multifaceted phenomenon that occurs when a government is no longer able to provide basic services, maintain order, or protect the rights of its citizens. State collapse can have serious consequences, including political instability, economic disruption, and humanitarian crises. Here are some potential causes of state collapse in the future:

1. Political instability: Political instability can contribute to state collapse by undermining the legitimacy and effectiveness of the government. This can include factors such as corruption, weak institutions, or political polarization.

2. Economic crisis: Economic crisis can also contribute to state collapse by creating social and political instability. This may include factors such as high unemployment, inflation, or debt.

3. Environmental degradation: Environmental degradation can lead to state collapse by exacerbating resource scarcity, food insecurity, and social tensions. This may include factors such as drought, deforestation, or climate change.

4. Conflict: Conflict is a major contributor to state collapse. This may include civil wars, insurgencies, or terrorism.

To address the risk of state collapse in the future, it is important to invest in building strong and resilient institutions. This may involve strengthening democratic institutions, promoting transparency and accountability, and investing in infrastructure and education.

It is also important to address the root causes of state collapse, such as political instability, economic crisis, environmental degradation, and conflict. This may involve promoting conflict resolution and peacebuilding efforts, investing in sustainable development programs, and addressing the underlying drivers of environmental degradation.

Ultimately, preventing state collapse requires a comprehensive and coordinated approach that involves multiple stakeholders, including governments, civil society organizations, and the private sector. By working together, we can help promote political stability, economic development, and social justice, and ensure the safety and security of individuals and communities affected by state collapse.

State collapse is a complex and persistent problem that requires a multifaceted approach to address. Here are some potential solutions that could help mitigate the risks of state collapse:

1. Strengthen democratic institutions: Building strong and resilient democratic institutions is essential for preventing state collapse. This may involve promoting transparency and accountability, investing in the rule of law, and creating opportunities for citizen participation in decision-making processes.

2. Invest in economic development: Economic crisis can be a significant contributor to state collapse. Investing in economic development programs can help address economic disparities and promote stability. This may involve promoting trade and investment, creating job opportunities, and providing support for small and medium-sized enterprises.

3. Promote sustainable development: Environmental degradation can contribute to state collapse by exacerbating resource scarcity and social tensions. Promoting sustainable development can help address these underlying causes of state collapse. This may involve investing in renewable energy, promoting sustainable agriculture, and addressing the underlying drivers of environmental degradation.

4. Foster inclusive governance: Inclusive governance can help ensure that all citizens have a voice in decision-making processes and that their interests are represented. This may involve promoting diversity in government and creating opportunities for marginalized groups to participate in decision-making processes.

5. Address conflict: Conflict is a major contributor to state collapse, and addressing conflict is essential for promoting stability. This may involve promoting conflict resolution and peacebuilding efforts, supporting mediation and negotiation processes, and providing humanitarian assistance to those affected by conflict.

Ultimately, addressing state collapse requires a comprehensive and coordinated approach that involves multiple stakeholders, including governments, civil society organizations, and the private sector. By working together, we can help promote political stability, economic development, and social justice, and ensure the safety and security of individuals and communities affected by state collapse.

47

Regime change

Regime change is a significant risk that can have far-reaching impacts on individuals, communities, and entire nations. Regime change refers to the replacement of a government or political system, often as a result of political instability, economic crisis, or social unrest.

The risk of regime change is influenced by a range of factors, including economic inequality, geopolitical tensions, and human rights abuses. These factors can lead to conflict and instability, which can have significant impacts on public health, including increasing the risk of displacement, limiting access to essential resources and healthcare services, and exacerbating economic inequality.

Regime change can also have significant impacts on global stability and security, particularly if it involves a change in geopolitical power dynamics. This can lead to increased tensions between different countries or regions, as well as increased risks of conflict and social unrest.

To address the risk of regime change, a range of measures can be taken. This includes promoting social stability, economic growth, and conflict resolution, as well as supporting policies that promote the equitable distribution of resources and access to essential services.

Addressing the root causes of regime change, such as economic inequality and human rights abuses, can help to prevent conflicts and promote stability. This can include promoting international cooperation to address global economic imbalances, investing in sustainable economic development programs, and promoting policies that support human rights and social justice.

Increasing public awareness and engagement in issues related to regime change can also help to ensure that the needs of individuals and communities are taken into account. This can include promoting community engagement and participation in decision-making processes related to political and economic governance.

In conclusion, regime change poses significant risks to public health, global stability, and security. By promoting social stability, economic growth, and conflict resolution, supporting policies that promote the equitable distribution of resources and access to essential services, and addressing the root causes of regime change, we can help to prevent conflicts and promote stability and public health for all. It is critical that individuals, healthcare providers, policymakers, and global leaders work together to address the challenges presented by regime change and promote effective strategies for stability and public health.

Here are some potential solutions to reduce the risk of regime change in the future:

1. Promote social stability: Promote social stability by investing in programs that support education, healthcare, and social services. This can help to address the underlying factors that contribute to political instability and social unrest.
2. Address economic inequality: Address economic inequality by promoting policies that support equitable distribution of resources, including access to healthcare, education, and economic opportunities. This can help to reduce economic imbalances that contribute to political instability.
3. Promote human rights: Promote human rights by supporting policies

and initiatives that protect civil liberties, promote democratic values, and prevent human rights abuses. This can help to prevent social unrest and conflict, and promote stable and inclusive societies.

4. Invest in conflict resolution efforts: Invest in conflict resolution efforts by supporting diplomatic initiatives, peacekeeping missions, and humanitarian aid. This can help to prevent conflicts and promote stability and security.

5. Promote international cooperation: Promote international cooperation by supporting global governance frameworks, such as the United Nations, and engaging in multilateral initiatives that promote peace and stability.

6. Increase public awareness and engagement: Increase public awareness and engagement on issues related to regime change, governance, and democracy. This can include promoting public education campaigns, community outreach programs, and opportunities for public participation in decision-making processes related to political and economic governance.

By taking a comprehensive approach to addressing the risk of regime change, we can help to reduce the impact of political instability on individuals and communities. It is critical that individuals, healthcare providers, policymakers, and global leaders work together to implement effective strategies for stability and public health.

<h1 style="text-align:center">48</h1>

Refugee crisis

The risk of refugee crises in the future is a significant challenge that requires urgent attention and action. Refugees are individuals who are forced to flee their homes due to conflict, persecution, or other forms of violence. Refugee crises can arise from a range of factors, including political instability, economic insecurity, and social unrest.

The risk of refugee crises is influenced by a range of factors, including geopolitical tensions, economic inequality, and climate change. These factors can exacerbate existing conflicts and contribute to social instability, which can lead to displacement and the creation of refugee populations.

Refugee crises can have significant impacts on public health, including increased risk of disease outbreaks, limited access to healthcare services, and increased incidence of mental health disorders. In addition, refugee crises can lead to social unrest and instability, with significant impacts on global security and stability.

To address the risk of refugee crises, a range of measures can be taken. This includes promoting conflict resolution efforts, addressing economic inequality, and investing in programs that support refugee populations.

Addressing the root causes of refugee crises, such as economic insecurity and social unrest, can help to prevent displacement and promote stability. This can include promoting international cooperation to address global economic imbalances, investing in sustainable economic development programs, and promoting policies that support social justice.

Increasing public awareness and engagement in issues related to refugee crises can also help to ensure that the needs of refugees and their host communities are taken into account. This can include promoting community engagement and participation in decision-making processes related to refugee management and support.

In conclusion, the risk of refugee crises in the future is a significant challenge that requires collective action and cooperation. By working together to promote conflict resolution, address economic inequality, and invest in programs that support refugee populations, we can help to prevent displacement and promote stability and public health for all. It is critical that individuals, healthcare providers, policymakers, and global leaders work together to address the challenges presented by refugee crises and promote effective strategies for stability and public health.

Here are some potential solutions to reduce the risk of refugee crises in the future:

1. Promote conflict resolution: Promote conflict resolution by supporting diplomatic initiatives, peacekeeping missions, and humanitarian aid. This can help to prevent conflicts and promote stability, reducing the risk of displacement and the creation of refugee populations.

2. Address economic inequality: Address economic inequality by promoting policies that support equitable distribution of resources, including access to healthcare, education, and economic opportunities. This can help to reduce economic imbalances that contribute to social unrest and displacement.

3. Invest in sustainable development programs: Invest in sustainable development programs that promote social stability, economic growth, and access to essential services such as healthcare, education, and social services. This can help to address the root causes of displacement

and prevent refugee crises.

4. Promote international cooperation: Promote international cooperation by supporting global governance frameworks, such as the United Nations, and engaging in multilateral initiatives that promote peace and stability. This can help to address the root causes of displacement and promote effective solutions for supporting refugees and their host communities.

5. Increase public awareness and engagement: Increase public awareness and engagement on issues related to refugee crises, including the needs of refugees and their host communities. This can include promoting public education campaigns, community outreach programs, and opportunities for public participation in decision-making processes related to refugee management and support.

By taking a comprehensive approach to addressing the risk of refugee crises, we can help to reduce the impact of displacement on individuals and communities. It is critical that individuals, healthcare providers, policymakers, and global leaders work together to implement effective strategies for stability and public health.

49

Interstate conflict

The risk of interstate conflict in the future is a significant challenge that requires urgent attention and action. Interstate conflict refers to conflicts between different countries or regions, which can have far-reaching impacts on global stability and security.

The risk of interstate conflict is influenced by a range of factors, including geopolitical tensions, economic competition, and ideological differences. These factors can lead to political instability, social unrest, and conflict, which can have significant impacts on public health, including increasing the risk of displacement, limiting access to essential resources and healthcare services, and exacerbating economic inequality.

Interstate conflict can also have significant impacts on global stability and security, particularly if it involves the use of military force or the threat of military force. This can lead to increased tensions between different countries or regions, as well as increased risks of conflict and social unrest.

To address the risk of interstate conflict, a range of measures can be taken. This includes promoting conflict resolution efforts, addressing economic inequality, and investing in sustainable development programs that promote equitable economic growth and social stability.

Addressing the root causes of interstate conflict, such as economic inequality and geopolitical tensions, can help to prevent conflicts and promote stability. This can include promoting international cooperation to address global economic imbalances, investing in sustainable economic development programs, and promoting policies that support social justice.

Increasing public awareness and engagement in issues related to interstate conflict can also help to ensure that the needs of individuals and communities are taken into account. This can include promoting community engagement and participation in decision-making processes related to political and economic governance.

The risk of interstate conflict in the future is a significant challenge that requires collective action and cooperation. By working together to promote conflict resolution, address economic inequality, and invest in sustainable development programs, we can help to prevent conflicts and promote stability and public health for all. It is critical that individuals, healthcare providers, policymakers, and global leaders work together to address the challenges presented by interstate conflict and promote effective strategies for stability and public health.

Here are some potential solutions to reduce the risk of interstate conflict in the future:

1. Promote conflict resolution: Promote conflict resolution by supporting diplomatic initiatives, peacekeeping missions, and humanitarian aid. This can help to prevent conflicts and promote stability, reducing the risk of interstate conflict.
2. Address economic inequality: Address economic inequality by promoting policies that support equitable distribution of resources, including access to healthcare, education, and economic opportunities. This can help to reduce economic imbalances that contribute to geopolitical tensions and conflicts.
3. Promote international cooperation: Promote international cooperation by supporting global governance frameworks, such as the United Nations, and engaging in multilateral initiatives that promote peace and stability. This can help to address the root causes of interstate

conflict and promote effective solutions for promoting stability and security.

4. Invest in sustainable development programs: Invest in sustainable development programs that promote social stability, economic growth, and access to essential services such as healthcare, education, and social services. This can help to address the root causes of interstate conflict and prevent the escalation of tensions and conflicts.

5. Increase public awareness and engagement: Increase public awareness and engagement on issues related to interstate conflict, including the needs of individuals and communities affected by geopolitical tensions and conflicts. This can include promoting public education campaigns, community outreach programs, and opportunities for public participation in decision-making processes related to political and economic governance.

By taking a comprehensive approach to addressing the risk of interstate conflict, we can help to reduce the impact of conflicts on individuals and communities, promote stability and security, and ensure public health for all. It is critical that individuals, healthcare providers, policymakers, and global leaders work together to implement effective strategies for stability and public health.

50

Diplomatic breakdown

The risk of diplomatic breakdown in the future is a significant challenge that requires urgent attention and action. Diplomatic breakdown refers to the collapse of diplomatic relations between countries or regions, which can have far-reaching impacts on global stability and security.

The risk of diplomatic breakdown is influenced by a range of factors, including geopolitical tensions, ideological differences, and economic competition. These factors can lead to political instability, social unrest, and conflict, which can have significant impacts on public health, including increasing the risk of displacement, limiting access to essential resources and healthcare services, and exacerbating economic inequality.

Diplomatic breakdown can also have significant impacts on global stability and security, particularly if it involves the use of military force or the threat of military force. This can lead to increased tensions between different countries or regions, as well as increased risks of conflict and social unrest.

To address the risk of diplomatic breakdown, a range of measures can be taken. This includes promoting diplomatic efforts, addressing economic inequality, and investing in sustainable development programs that promote equitable economic growth and social stability.

Addressing the root causes of diplomatic breakdown, such as economic inequality and geopolitical tensions, can help to prevent conflicts and promote stability. This can include promoting international cooperation to address global economic imbalances, investing in sustainable economic development programs, and promoting policies that support social justice.

Increasing public awareness and engagement in issues related to diplomatic breakdown can also help to ensure that the needs of individuals and communities are taken into account. This can include promoting community engagement and participation in decision-making processes related to political and economic governance.

The risk of diplomatic breakdown in the future is a significant challenge that requires collective action and cooperation. By working together to promote diplomatic efforts, address economic inequality, and invest in sustainable development programs, we can help to prevent conflicts and promote stability and public health for all. It is critical that individuals, healthcare providers, policymakers, and global leaders work together to address the challenges presented by diplomatic breakdown and promote effective strategies for stability and public health.

Here are some potential solutions to reduce the risk of diplomatic breakdown in the future:

1. Promote diplomatic efforts: Promote diplomatic efforts by encouraging dialogue and cooperation between countries or regions, including through diplomatic channels, international organizations, and other platforms. This can help to prevent the breakdown of diplomatic relations and promote stability.

2. Address economic inequality: Address economic inequality by promoting policies that support equitable distribution of resources, including access to healthcare, education, and economic opportunities. This can help to reduce economic imbalances that contribute to geopolitical tensions and conflicts.

3. Promote international cooperation: Promote international cooperation by supporting global governance frameworks, such as the United Nations, and engaging in multilateral initiatives that promote peace and stability. This can help to address the root causes of diplomatic breakdown and promote effective solutions for promoting stability and

security.

4. Invest in sustainable development programs: Invest in sustainable development programs that promote social stability, economic growth, and access to essential services such as healthcare, education, and social services. This can help to address the root causes of diplomatic breakdown and prevent the escalation of tensions and conflicts.

5. Increase public awareness and engagement: Increase public awareness and engagement on issues related to diplomatic breakdown, including the needs of individuals and communities affected by geopolitical tensions and conflicts. This can include promoting public education campaigns, community outreach programs, and opportunities for public participation in decision-making processes related to political and economic governance.

By taking a comprehensive approach to addressing the risk of diplomatic breakdown, we can help to reduce the impact of conflicts on individuals and communities, promote stability and security, and ensure public health for all. It is critical that individuals, healthcare providers, policymakers, and global leaders work together to implement effective strategies for stability and public health.

VI

Societal Risks

Societal risks in the future are events or conditions that can threaten the stability, cohesion, and well-being of a society as a whole. These risks can stem from various sources, including technological advancements, demographic changes, geopolitical conflicts, economic disparities, and environmental degradation.

51

Polarization

Polarization is a growing risk that threatens to divide societies and exacerbate existing tensions in the future. Polarization is a phenomenon where people become more divided in their beliefs, attitudes, and values, leading to increasing conflicts and animosity between groups. In today's highly interconnected world, polarization is not limited to national boundaries, but it can also occur at the international level, leading to geopolitical instability.

The risk of polarization is fueled by several factors, including political polarization, social media, economic inequality, and cultural differences. Political polarization can occur when political parties become more extreme in their views and fail to find common ground, leading to a breakdown in democratic processes. Social media can amplify existing divisions by creating filter bubbles and echo chambers, where people only interact with those who share their views. Economic inequality can create a sense of resentment and frustration among those who feel left behind, leading to social unrest and conflict. Cultural differences can also lead to polarization, as people become more entrenched in their own cultural norms and beliefs, leading to a lack of understanding and empathy between groups.

The consequences of polarization can be severe, including increased social unrest, political instability, and economic disruption. Polarization can also erode trust in institutions and contribute to a sense of hopelessness and apathy among citizens. To address the risk of polarization, it is important to promote dialogue, tolerance, and understanding among different groups. This can involve investing in education and media literacy, supporting civil society organizations that promote social cohesion, and fostering a culture of respect and empathy. By working together, we can mitigate the risk of polarization and build a more inclusive and resilient society for the future.

To mitigate the risk of polarization in the future, it is important to take proactive measures that promote dialogue, understanding, and cooperation among different groups. Here are some potential solutions:

1. Invest in education: Education is key to promoting critical thinking, media literacy, and empathy among citizens. By investing in education, we can equip people with the skills and knowledge to engage in constructive dialogue and understand different perspectives.
2. Foster diversity and inclusion: Promoting diversity and inclusion can help break down barriers and promote understanding among different groups. This can involve supporting policies that promote diversity in the workplace, educational institutions, and public life.
3. Encourage media literacy: Social media can amplify existing divisions and create filter bubbles, where people only interact with those who share their views. Encouraging media literacy can help people become more discerning consumers of information and avoid falling prey to disinformation.
4. Support civil society organizations: Civil society organizations can play a key role in promoting social cohesion and dialogue among different groups. Supporting these organizations can help build resilience and promote understanding in the face of polarization.
5. Encourage political leaders to find common ground: Political leaders can play a key role in reducing polarization by finding common ground and promoting constructive dialogue. Encouraging political leaders to reach across the aisle and work together can help promote social cohesion and mitigate the risk of polarization.

By implementing these solutions, we can work together to mitigate the risk of polarization and build a more resilient and inclusive society for the future.

52

Populism

Populism is a growing risk that threatens to destabilize democracies and exacerbate social divisions in the future. Populism is a political phenomenon where politicians appeal to the emotions and grievances of the people, often by demonizing minorities, elites, or other groups perceived as the source of societal problems. Populist leaders often use simplistic solutions to complex problems and appeal to nationalist sentiments, often at the expense of democratic norms and human rights.

The risk of populism is fueled by several factors, including economic inequality, cultural polarization, and technological disruption. Economic inequality can create a sense of disillusionment and resentment among those who feel left behind by globalization and rapid technological change. Cultural polarization can create a sense of identity crisis and lead people to seek refuge in nostalgic or nationalist narratives. Technological disruption can amplify existing divisions and create new challenges, such as job displacement and cybersecurity threats.

The consequences of populism can be severe, including political polarization, erosion of democratic norms, and social unrest. Populism can also undermine international cooperation and exacerbate geopolitical tensions, leading to a more unstable and uncertain global order.

To address the risk of populism, it is important to promote inclusive and equitable economic growth, invest in education and media literacy, and foster a culture of dialogue and understanding. This can involve promoting policies that address the root causes of economic inequality and cultural polarization, supporting civil society organizations that promote democratic values and human rights, and encouraging media outlets to provide balanced and factual coverage of political issues. It also requires political leaders to be accountable to the people they serve and to resist the temptation to exploit populist rhetoric for short-term political gain.

By working together, we can mitigate the risk of populism and build a more resilient and inclusive democracy for the future. This requires a commitment to democratic values, human rights, and the rule of law, as well as a willingness to engage in constructive dialogue and find common ground across different groups and perspectives.

To mitigate the risk of populism in the future, it is important to take proactive measures that promote democratic values, social cohesion, and inclusive economic growth. Here are some potential solutions:

1. Promote inclusive economic growth: Economic inequality is a key driver of populism, and addressing it can help reduce the sense of disillusionment and resentment among those who feel left behind. This can involve promoting policies that support job creation, education, and training, and investing in infrastructure and technology that benefit all segments of society.

2. Invest in education and media literacy: Education and media literacy are key to promoting critical thinking, civic engagement, and media literacy among citizens. By investing in education and promoting media literacy, we can help people become more discerning consumers of information and less susceptible to populist rhetoric.

3. Foster social cohesion: Social cohesion is key to building a resilient and inclusive society. This can involve promoting policies that promote diversity and inclusion, supporting civil society organizations that

foster social cohesion, and encouraging dialogue and understanding among different groups.

4. Promote democratic values and human rights: Populist leaders often undermine democratic norms and human rights in pursuit of their political goals. Promoting democratic values and human rights can help prevent the erosion of democratic institutions and promote respect for human dignity.

5. Hold political leaders accountable: Political leaders must be accountable to the people they serve and resist the temptation to exploit populist rhetoric for short-term political gain. Holding political leaders accountable through free and fair elections, independent media, and civil society organizations can help promote democratic values and mitigate the risk of populism.

By implementing these solutions, we can work together to mitigate the risk of populism and build a more resilient, inclusive, and democratic society for the future.

53

Xenophobia

Xenophobia is a growing risk in the future that threatens to exacerbate social divisions and undermine social cohesion. Xenophobia is the fear or hatred of foreigners, particularly those from different cultural or ethnic backgrounds. Xenophobia is often fueled by misinformation, cultural stereotypes, and economic insecurity.

The risk of xenophobia is fueled by several factors, including economic inequality, cultural polarization, and geopolitical tensions. Economic inequality can create a sense of resentment among those who feel left behind by globalization and rapid technological change. Cultural polarization can create a sense of identity crisis and lead people to seek refuge in nationalistic or xenophobic narratives. Geopolitical tensions, such as conflicts or geopolitical rivalries, can exacerbate xenophobic attitudes and lead to the scapegoating of foreigners or minority groups.

The consequences of xenophobia can be severe, including social exclusion, discrimination, and violence. Xenophobia can also undermine social cohesion, democratic values, and human rights, leading to a more divided and insecure society.

To address the risk of xenophobia, it is important to promote inclusive and tolerant societies, invest in education and media literacy, and foster a culture of dialogue and understanding. This can involve promoting policies that address the root causes of economic inequality and cultural polarization, supporting civil society organizations that promote diversity and inclusion, and encouraging media outlets to provide balanced and factual coverage of cultural and political issues. It also requires political leaders to lead by example and promote tolerance, respect, and diversity in their policies and actions.

By working together, we can mitigate the risk of xenophobia and build a more resilient, inclusive, and tolerant society for the future. This requires a commitment to democratic values, human rights, and social justice, as well as a willingness to engage in constructive dialogue and find common ground across different cultures, ethnicities, and perspectives.

To mitigate the risk of xenophobia in the future, it is important to take proactive measures that promote inclusive and tolerant societies. Here are some potential solutions:

1. Invest in education and media literacy: Education and media literacy are key to promoting critical thinking, civic engagement, and media literacy among citizens. By investing in education and promoting media literacy, we can help people become more discerning consumers of information and less susceptible to xenophobic rhetoric.

2. Foster social cohesion: Social cohesion is key to building a resilient and inclusive society. This can involve promoting policies that promote diversity and inclusion, supporting civil society organizations that foster social cohesion, and encouraging dialogue and understanding among different groups.

3. Promote diversity and inclusion: Promoting diversity and inclusion can help prevent xenophobic attitudes from taking hold. This can involve policies that promote equal opportunity and address the root causes of inequality, as well as supporting civil society organizations that promote diversity and inclusion.

4. Combat hate speech and misinformation: Hate speech and misinformation can fuel xenophobic attitudes and lead to discrimination and violence. Combatting hate speech and misinformation through legislation, media regulation, and civil society action can help promote

more respectful and inclusive societies.

5. Encourage cross-cultural exchanges: Encouraging cross-cultural exchanges can help build bridges between different communities and promote understanding and empathy. This can involve promoting cultural exchanges, study abroad programs, and international cooperation on cultural and educational initiatives.

By implementing these solutions, we can work together to mitigate the risk of xenophobia and build a more resilient, inclusive, and tolerant society for the future. This requires a commitment to democratic values, human rights, and social justice, as well as a willingness to engage in constructive dialogue and find common ground across different cultures, ethnicities, and perspectives.

54

Racial tension

Racial tension is a growing risk in the future that threatens to exacerbate social divisions and undermine social cohesion. Racial tension arises when people from different races experience a sense of hostility, prejudice, or discrimination. The risk of racial tension is fueled by several factors, including economic inequality, cultural polarization, and political polarization.

Economic inequality can create a sense of resentment among those who feel left behind by globalization and rapid technological change. Cultural polarization can create a sense of identity crisis and lead people to seek refuge in nationalistic or racial narratives. Political polarization can lead to the polarization of racial attitudes and the creation of racialized political coalitions.

The consequences of racial tension can be severe, including social exclusion, discrimination, and violence. Racial tension can also undermine social cohesion, democratic values, and human rights, leading to a more divided and insecure society.

To address the risk of racial tension, it is important to promote inclusive and tolerant societies, invest in education and media literacy, and foster a culture of dialogue and understanding. This can involve promoting policies that address the root causes of economic inequality and cultural polarization, supporting civil society organizations that promote diversity and inclusion, and encouraging media outlets to provide balanced and factual coverage of cultural and political issues. It also requires political leaders to lead by example and promote tolerance, respect, and diversity in their policies and actions.

By working together, we can mitigate the risk of racial tension and build a more resilient, inclusive, and tolerant society for the future. This requires a commitment to democratic values, human rights, and social justice, as well as a willingness to engage in constructive dialogue and find common ground across different races, cultures, and perspectives

To address the risk of racial tension in the future, there are several potential solutions that can be implemented:

1. Promote education and awareness: Education and awareness are key to promoting inclusive and tolerant societies. By promoting education and awareness about diversity and inclusion, we can help people understand the importance of respect and tolerance for different races and cultures.

2. Foster social cohesion: Social cohesion is key to building a resilient and inclusive society. This can involve promoting policies that promote diversity and inclusion, supporting civil society organizations that foster social cohesion, and encouraging dialogue and understanding among different races.

3. Promote diversity and inclusion: Promoting diversity and inclusion can help prevent racial tension from taking hold. This can involve policies that promote equal opportunity and address the root causes of inequality, as well as supporting civil society organizations that promote diversity and inclusion.

4. Combat hate speech and discrimination: Hate speech and discrimination can fuel racial tension and lead to violence and social exclusion. Combatting hate speech and discrimination through legislation, media regulation, and civil society action can help promote more respectful and inclusive societies.

5. Encourage cross-cultural exchanges: Encouraging cross-cultural exchanges can help build bridges between different races and promote

understanding and empathy. This can involve promoting cultural exchanges, study abroad programs, and international cooperation on cultural and educational initiatives.

6. Engage in dialogue and mediation: Engaging in dialogue and mediation can help address racial tensions and prevent conflicts from escalating. This requires a willingness to listen to different perspectives and find common ground across different races and cultures.

By implementing these solutions, we can work together to mitigate the risk of racial tension and build a more resilient, inclusive, and tolerant society for the future. This requires a commitment to democratic values, human rights, and social justice, as well as a willingness to engage in constructive dialogue and find common ground across different races, cultures, and perspectives.

55

Gender inequality

Gender inequality is a persistent and growing risk in the future that threatens to undermine social and economic progress. Despite progress in recent years, gender inequality remains a major challenge around the world, with women and girls facing discrimination and marginalization in many areas of life.

The risk of gender inequality is fueled by several factors, including cultural norms, stereotypes, and patriarchal structures that perpetuate discrimination and limit women's opportunities. Economic inequality, lack of access to education and healthcare, and violence against women are also major drivers of gender inequality.

The consequences of gender inequality can be severe, including reduced economic growth, increased poverty, and social exclusion. Gender inequality can also have negative impacts on health, education, and political participation, limiting the potential of women and girls to contribute to society.

To address the risk of gender inequality, it is important to promote gender equality and empower women and girls. This can involve promoting policies that address the root causes of gender inequality, such as economic inequality and cultural norms, as well as investing in education and healthcare to improve women's opportunities and well-being.

It is also important to promote women's participation in political and economic decision-making, as well as increasing awareness and action around gender-based violence. By empowering women and girls, we can help ensure that they have equal access to opportunities and resources, and are able to contribute fully to society.

In addition, it is important to challenge cultural norms and stereotypes that perpetuate gender inequality and discrimination. This can involve promoting awareness and education around gender equality, as well as supporting civil society organizations and movements that promote women's rights and gender equality.

By working together to promote gender equality and empower women and girls, we can mitigate the risk of gender inequality and build a more inclusive and just society for the future. This requires a commitment to human rights, social justice, and gender equality, as well as a willingness to challenge entrenched cultural norms and systems that perpetuate gender inequality.

To address the risk of gender inequality in the future, several solutions can be implemented:

1. Promote education and awareness: Education and awareness are key to promoting gender equality. By promoting education and awareness about gender equality, we can help people understand the importance of respecting women's rights and promoting gender equality.

2. Eliminate gender-based violence: Gender-based violence is a major driver of gender inequality, and it is important to address this issue by implementing policies and programs that promote prevention, protection, and support for survivors.

3. Ensure equal access to education and healthcare: Providing equal access to education and healthcare is essential for promoting gender equality, as it empowers women and girls to make informed decisions about their health and future.

4. Increase women's political participation and representation: Women's political participation and representation is critical for promoting gender equality, as it ensures that women have a voice in decision-making processes that affect their lives.

5. Promote equal pay and opportunities: Promoting equal pay and oppor-

tunities for women is essential for addressing economic inequality and promoting gender equality in the workplace.

6. Challenge cultural norms and stereotypes: Cultural norms and stereotypes can perpetuate gender inequality, and it is important to challenge these norms and stereotypes by promoting awareness and education about gender equality, and by supporting civil society organizations and movements that promote women's rights and gender equality.

By implementing these solutions, we can work together to mitigate the risk of gender inequality and build a more resilient, inclusive, and just society for the future. This requires a commitment to human rights, social justice, and gender equality, as well as a willingness to challenge entrenched cultural norms and systems that perpetuate gender inequality.

56

Hate speech

Hate speech is a growing risk in the future that threatens to undermine social cohesion and exacerbate tensions between different groups. Hate speech can be defined as any form of speech that attacks or dehumanizes a person or group based on their identity, such as their race, ethnicity, religion, gender, or sexual orientation.

The risk of hate speech is fueled by several factors, including political polarization, social media, and the rise of extremist ideologies. Hate speech can lead to social fragmentation, discrimination, and even violence against targeted groups, and it can also have negative impacts on mental health and well-being.

The consequences of hate speech can be severe, including reduced social cohesion, increased discrimination, and social exclusion. It can also have negative impacts on democratic processes, limiting the ability of individuals and communities to engage in free and open debate and discussion.

To address the risk of hate speech, it is important to promote tolerance, respect, and diversity, and to challenge hateful ideologies and rhetoric. This can involve promoting education and awareness about hate speech and its impacts, as well as supporting civil society organizations and movements that promote tolerance and respect for diversity.

It is also important to promote media literacy and critical thinking skills, to enable individuals to identify and respond to hate speech effectively. This can involve supporting media literacy programs in schools and universities, as well as promoting fact-checking and critical thinking skills in online platforms.

In addition, it is important to strengthen legal frameworks and mechanisms for combating hate speech, such as hate speech laws and hate crime legislation. These can be complemented by initiatives to promote restorative justice and dialogue between communities, to help build understanding and reduce tensions.

By working together to promote tolerance, respect, and diversity, and to challenge hateful ideologies and rhetoric, we can mitigate the risk of hate speech and build a more inclusive and just society for the future. This requires a commitment to human rights, social justice, and democratic values, as well as a willingness to challenge hate speech and discrimination in all its forms.

To address the risk of hate speech in the future, several solutions can be implemented:

1. Promote tolerance and respect for diversity: One of the most effective ways to combat hate speech is to promote tolerance and respect for diversity. This can involve promoting education and awareness about different cultures, religions, and identities, as well as supporting civil society organizations and movements that promote tolerance and respect.

2. Encourage media literacy and critical thinking skills: Media literacy and critical thinking skills are essential for identifying and responding to hate speech effectively. This can involve supporting media literacy programs in schools and universities, as well as promoting fact-checking and critical thinking skills in online platforms.

3. Strengthen legal frameworks and mechanisms for combating hate speech: Hate speech laws and hate crime legislation can be effective tools for combating hate speech, and it is important to strengthen legal

frameworks and mechanisms to ensure that individuals and groups are protected from hate speech.

4. Promote dialogue and understanding between communities: Promoting dialogue and understanding between different communities can help build understanding and reduce tensions, and can also help to counter the effects of hate speech. This can involve supporting initiatives that promote restorative justice and dialogue, as well as providing opportunities for different groups to engage in meaningful dialogue and exchange.

5. Foster an inclusive and diverse society: Creating an inclusive and diverse society can help to prevent hate speech from taking root, by promoting respect for different identities and cultures. This can involve promoting policies and programs that support diversity and inclusion, as well as supporting initiatives that promote social cohesion and integration.

57

Corruption

Corruption is a persistent risk that threatens to undermine social and economic development in the future. Corruption can be defined as the abuse of public power for private gain, and it can take many forms, including bribery, embezzlement, and fraud.

The risk of corruption is fueled by several factors, including political instability, weak institutions, and the lack of transparency and accountability. Corruption can have significant negative impacts on social and economic development, including reducing public trust in government, increasing inequality, and stifling economic growth.

The consequences of corruption can be severe, including reduced public services, increased poverty, and decreased social mobility. Corruption can also lead to political instability, as citizens lose faith in their governments and institutions.

To address the risk of corruption in the future, it is important to promote transparency, accountability, and good governance. This can involve strengthening institutions, such as the judiciary and law enforcement agencies, as well as promoting transparency in government operations and public procurement processes.

It is also important to promote civil society engagement and participation in the fight against corruption. Civil society organizations can play a critical role in monitoring government operations and advocating for transparency and accountability.

Additionally, it is important to promote a culture of integrity and ethical behavior, both in the public and private sectors. This can involve promoting anti-corruption education and training programs, as well as promoting ethical business practices and corporate social responsibility.

Finally, it is important to strengthen international cooperation and coordination in the fight against corruption. This can involve promoting international conventions and agreements on anti-corruption measures, as well as supporting initiatives that promote transparency and accountability in global governance.

By working together to promote transparency, accountability, and good governance, we can mitigate the risk of corruption and build a more just and equitable future for all. This requires a commitment to ethical behavior, transparency, and accountability, as well as a willingness to challenge corruption in all its forms.

There are several solutions that can be implemented to address the risk of corruption:

1. Strengthen legal and institutional frameworks: This can involve implementing strong anti-corruption laws and regulations, establishing independent anti-corruption agencies, and strengthening judicial and law enforcement institutions to ensure that they are independent, transparent, and accountable.
2. Promote transparency and accountability: Transparency and accountability are key tools in combating corruption. This can involve promoting open data and access to information, ensuring that public officials and institutions are accountable for their actions, and strengthening public oversight mechanisms.
3. Increase public participation and engagement: Public participation and engagement can help to reduce the risk of corruption by promoting greater transparency and accountability. This can involve engaging civil society organizations, promoting participatory decision-making

processes, and increasing citizen awareness and participation in anti-corruption efforts.

4. Encourage ethical behavior: Promoting ethical behavior is essential in the fight against corruption. This can involve promoting anti-corruption education and training programs, as well as establishing codes of conduct and ethical standards for public officials and private sector actors.

5. Foster international cooperation: Corruption is a global problem, and international cooperation is essential in the fight against corruption. This can involve promoting international conventions and agreements on anti-corruption measures, as well as supporting initiatives that promote transparency and accountability in global governance.

By implementing these solutions, we can work together to address the risk of corruption and build a more transparent, accountable, and equitable society. This requires a commitment to ethical behavior, transparency, and accountability, as well as a willingness to challenge corruption in all its forms.

58

Social media manipulation

Social media manipulation is a growing risk in today's digital age. Social media platforms have become a powerful tool for communication and information dissemination, but they are also vulnerable to manipulation by individuals and organizations with malicious intentions.

Social media manipulation involves the use of various tactics, such as fake accounts, bots, and disinformation campaigns, to influence public opinion and manipulate online discourse. This can have significant negative impacts on society, including undermining democratic processes, increasing social polarization, and spreading harmful misinformation.

One of the main challenges in addressing the risk of social media manipulation is the scale and complexity of the problem. Social media platforms are global, and they are used by billions of people around the world. This makes it difficult to detect and prevent manipulation, especially as new tactics and technologies emerge.

To address this risk, it is important to promote greater transparency and accountability in social media platforms. This can involve implementing stronger regulations and standards for online content, as well as investing in new technologies and tools that can help to detect and prevent manipulation.

It is also important to promote media literacy and critical thinking skills, so that individuals are better equipped to identify and resist manipulation. This can involve promoting media literacy education in schools and communities, as well as providing resources and tools to help individuals evaluate the credibility of online content.

Additionally, it is important to promote greater collaboration and cooperation between social media platforms, government agencies, and civil society organizations. This can involve sharing information and best practices, as well as developing joint initiatives to address the risk of social media manipulation.

This requires a commitment to ethical behavior, transparency, and accountability, as well as a willingness to challenge manipulation in all its forms.

There are several solutions that can be implemented to address the risk of social media manipulation:

1. Promote greater transparency and accountability in social media platforms: This can involve implementing stronger regulations and standards for online content, as well as investing in new technologies and tools that can help to detect and prevent manipulation.
2. Increase media literacy and critical thinking skills: This can involve promoting media literacy education in schools and communities, as well as providing resources and tools to help individuals evaluate the credibility of online content.
3. Develop and implement codes of conduct and ethical standards for social media platforms: This can help to ensure that social media platforms are operating in an ethical and transparent manner, and can provide a basis for holding them accountable for their actions.
4. Increase collaboration and cooperation between social media platforms, government agencies, and civil society organizations: This can involve sharing information and best practices, as well as developing joint initiatives to address the risk of social media manipulation.
5. Encourage individuals to report suspicious or malicious activity on social media platforms: This can help to identify and prevent manipu-

lation, as well as hold individuals and organizations accountable for their actions.

6. Foster greater diversity and inclusion in social media platforms: This can help to reduce the risk of social polarization and promote greater understanding and dialogue across different groups.

59

Human rights abuses

Human rights abuses are a growing concern around the world. These abuses can take many forms, including discrimination, violence, and exploitation, and they can be perpetrated by individuals, organizations, or governments.

Some of the most common human rights abuses include discrimination based on race, ethnicity, gender, or sexuality, as well as violence against women and children, forced labor, and human trafficking. These abuses can have significant negative impacts on individuals and communities, including physical and psychological harm, social exclusion, and economic hardship.

One of the main challenges in addressing human rights abuses is the lack of accountability and justice for victims. Many perpetrators of human rights abuses are able to act with impunity, and victims often face significant barriers to seeking justice and holding perpetrators accountable.

To address this challenge, it is important to promote greater awareness and understanding of human rights issues, and to develop stronger legal frameworks and institutions to protect and enforce human rights. This can involve strengthening international human rights laws and standards, as well as investing in national legal and judicial systems to ensure that victims have access to justice and accountability.

It is also important to promote greater collaboration and cooperation between governments, civil society organizations, and other stakeholders to address human rights abuses. This can involve sharing information and best practices, as well as developing joint initiatives to address specific human rights issues.

Finally, it is important to empower individuals and communities to advocate for their own rights and to hold those in power accountable for their actions. This can involve promoting education and awareness about human rights issues, as well as supporting civil society organizations and human rights defenders who are working to promote greater respect for human rights.

This requires a commitment to promoting human rights, justice, and accountability, as well as a willingness to challenge human rights abuses wherever they occur.

There are several solutions that can be implemented to address human rights abuses:

1. Strengthen legal frameworks and institutions: Governments should work to develop and implement stronger legal frameworks and institutions to protect and enforce human rights. This can include passing new laws and regulations, as well as investing in national legal and judicial systems.

2. Increase accountability and justice: Governments must work to ensure that perpetrators of human rights abuses are held accountable for their actions. This can involve investigating and prosecuting perpetrators, as well as providing support and assistance to victims.

3. Promote human rights education and awareness: Educating individuals and communities about human rights issues can help to promote greater awareness and understanding of the importance of respecting and protecting human rights.

4. Support civil society organizations and human rights defenders: Governments should support civil society organizations and human rights defenders who are working to promote greater respect for human rights. This can involve providing funding and other resources, as well as protecting them from retaliation and harassment.

5. Strengthen international cooperation and collaboration: Governments

should work together to promote greater cooperation and collaboration on human rights issues, both at the regional and international levels. This can involve sharing information and best practices, as well as developing joint initiatives to address specific human rights issues.

6. Foster a culture of respect for human rights: Governments and civil society organizations should work together to foster a culture of respect for human rights, where individuals and communities are empowered to stand up for their rights and hold those in power accountable for their actions.

60

Education inequality

Education inequality refers to the disparities in educational opportunities and outcomes that exist between different groups of individuals or communities. These disparities can be based on a range of factors, such as income, race, gender, or geographic location.

One of the main challenges in addressing education inequality is the lack of access to quality education for many individuals and communities. This can be due to factors such as poverty, lack of infrastructure, or discrimination, which can result in lower enrollment rates, higher dropout rates, and lower academic achievement.

Another challenge is the quality of education itself. Even when individuals have access to education, the quality of the education they receive can vary significantly depending on the resources and support available to them. This can lead to disparities in academic achievement and opportunities after graduation, which can perpetuate inequalities in income and social mobility.

To address education inequality, it is important to promote greater access to quality education for all individuals and communities. This can involve investing in infrastructure and resources, such as schools, teachers, and educational materials, in underserved areas. It can also involve providing financial assistance to students who cannot afford to pay for education themselves.

It is also important to address the root causes of education inequality, such as poverty and discrimination. This can involve implementing policies and programs that aim to reduce poverty, such as social safety nets and job training programs, as well as policies that address discrimination based on race, gender, or other factors.

Finally, it is important to promote greater awareness and understanding of the importance of education and the impact of education inequality on individuals and society. This can involve promoting education campaigns, as well as supporting civil society organizations that work to promote greater access to quality education.

There are several solutions that can be implemented to address education inequality:

1. Increase access to quality education: Governments and civil society organizations should work together to increase access to quality education, particularly for disadvantaged communities. This can involve investing in infrastructure, such as schools and educational materials, as well as providing financial assistance to students who cannot afford to pay for education themselves.

2. Address poverty and social inequalities: Education inequality is closely linked to poverty and social inequalities. Governments can address these issues by implementing policies and programs that aim to reduce poverty, such as social safety nets and job training programs, as well as policies that address discrimination based on race, gender, or other factors.

3. Improve teacher training and support: Teachers play a critical role in providing quality education. Governments should invest in teacher training and support programs to help teachers provide effective instruction and support to students.

4. Foster community involvement: Engaging parents and communities in the education process can help to promote greater investment in education and improve educational outcomes. Governments should work to foster community involvement in education, such as by encouraging parent-teacher associations and community-based education

initiatives.

5. Promote innovation and technology: Technology can be a powerful tool for promoting education access and improving educational outcomes. Governments should work to promote innovation in education and invest in educational technologies that can help to improve access and quality of education.

6. Monitor and evaluate education systems: Governments should establish monitoring and evaluation systems to assess the effectiveness of education policies and programs, and to identify areas for improvement. This can help to ensure that education policies and programs are effective in addressing education inequality and improving educational outcomes.

VII

Natural Disasters

Natural disasters pose a significant risk to individuals and communities around the world. These events, which can include hurricanes, earthquakes, floods, and wildfires, can cause significant damage to infrastructure, homes, and businesses, and can result in the loss of life and property.

61

Earthquakes

Earthquakes are one of the most devastating natural disasters that can occur. These powerful events can cause significant damage to buildings, infrastructure, and communities, often resulting in the loss of life and property. As the world's population continues to grow and urbanize, the risk of earthquakes is expected to increase. In fact, some of the world's largest and most populated cities, such as Tokyo, Istanbul, and Los Angeles, are located in areas with a high risk of seismic activity.

One of the main challenges associated with earthquake risk is the difficulty in predicting when and where they will occur. Although seismic activity can be monitored and measured, it is impossible to accurately predict when a major earthquake will strike. This unpredictability highlights the importance of disaster preparedness and mitigation measures. Building codes and infrastructure design should be developed with earthquakes in mind, incorporating features such as earthquake-resistant construction and early warning systems.

In addition to infrastructure and building design, education and public awareness are also crucial in reducing the risk of earthquake disasters. Communities and individuals should be educated on earthquake preparedness, including how to evacuate safely and how to respond in the aftermath of an earthquake. Emergency response teams and relief organizations should also be well-prepared and equipped to respond quickly and effectively to earthquake disasters.

Overall, the risk of earthquakes is a significant challenge that requires a comprehensive and coordinated approach to disaster preparedness and mitigation. By investing in resilient infrastructure, education and public awareness, and emergency response capabilities, we can work to minimize the impact of earthquakes and protect our communities in the future.

There are several solutions that can help mitigate the risk of earthquakes:

1. Improved building codes and infrastructure design: Building codes and infrastructure design should be developed with earthquakes in mind, incorporating features such as earthquake-resistant construction and early warning systems.
2. Public education and awareness: Communities and individuals should be educated on earthquake preparedness, including how to evacuate safely and how to respond in the aftermath of an earthquake.
3. Early warning systems: Early warning systems can provide critical time for people to evacuate and take protective measures before an earthquake strikes.
4. Disaster preparedness and emergency response planning: Emergency response teams and relief organizations should be well-prepared and equipped to respond quickly and effectively to earthquake disasters.
5. Seismic monitoring and research: Seismic monitoring and research can provide valuable data and insights into earthquake risk and help inform disaster preparedness and mitigation measures.
6. Land-use planning: Land-use planning can help reduce the risk of earthquakes by ensuring that critical infrastructure and buildings are not located in high-risk areas.

Overall, a comprehensive and coordinated approach to earthquake risk management is essential in mitigating the impacts of earthquakes and protecting our communities. By investing in resilient infrastructure, education and public awareness, and emergency response capabilities, we can work to minimize the impact of earthquakes and build a more resilient future.

Here are the 10 biggest earthquakes on record, along with their locations, dates, and estimated numbers of deaths:

1. Valdivia Earthquake, Chile, May 22, 1960 – 9.5 magnitude – estimated 1,655 deaths
2. Prince William Sound Earthquake, Alaska, USA, March 28, 1964 – 9.2 magnitude – 131 deaths
3. Sumatra-Andaman Earthquake, Indonesia, December 26, 2004 – 9.1 magnitude – estimated 227,898 deaths
4. Kamchatka Earthquake, Russia, November 4, 1952 – 9.0 magnitude – no deaths reported
5. Tohoku Earthquake, Japan, March 11, 2011 – 9.0 magnitude – estimated 15,899 deaths
6. Ecuador-Colombia Earthquake, August 31, 1906 – 8.8 magnitude – estimated 500–1,500 deaths
7. Rat Islands Earthquake, Alaska, USA, February 4, 1965 – 8.7 magnitude – no deaths reported
8. Assam-Tibet Earthquake, India/China, August 15, 1950 – 8.6 magnitude – estimated 1,526 deaths
9. Maule Earthquake, Chile, February 27, 2010 – 8.8 magnitude – estimated 525 deaths
10. Northern Sumatra Earthquake, Indonesia, March 28, 2005 – 8.6 magnitude – estimated 1,313 deaths

62

Volcanic eruptions

Volcanic eruptions are a significant natural hazard that can have a significant impact on communities and the environment. Although volcanic eruptions are rare and unpredictable events, they can cause widespread devastation, including damage to infrastructure, displacement of populations, and loss of life.

One of the main challenges associated with volcanic eruptions is the difficulty in predicting when and where they will occur. Volcanic eruptions are caused by the movement of magma beneath the Earth's surface, which can be difficult to monitor and predict. This unpredictability highlights the importance of disaster preparedness and mitigation measures.

Building codes and infrastructure design should be developed with volcanic eruptions in mind, incorporating features such as ash-resistant construction and early warning systems. Volcanic ash can cause significant damage to buildings and infrastructure, including damage to engines and machinery, and can pose a risk to human health. Early warning systems can provide critical time for people to evacuate and take protective measures before a volcanic eruption occurs.

In addition to infrastructure and building design, education and public awareness are also crucial in reducing the risk of volcanic disasters. Communities and individuals should be educated on volcanic hazards, including how to evacuate safely and how to respond in the aftermath of a volcanic eruption. Emergency response teams and relief organizations should also be well-prepared and equipped to respond quickly and effectively to volcanic disasters.

Overall, the risk of volcanic eruptions is a significant challenge that requires a comprehensive and coordinated approach to disaster preparedness and mitigation. By investing in resilient infrastructure, education and public awareness, and emergency response capabilities, we can work to minimize the impact of volcanic eruptions and protect our communities in the future.

There are several solutions that can help mitigate the risk of volcanic eruptions:

1. Volcanic monitoring: Volcanic monitoring can provide crucial information about the activity of a volcano, allowing authorities to issue warnings and evacuate populations if necessary.
2. Early warning systems: Early warning systems can provide critical time for people to evacuate and take protective measures before a volcanic eruption occurs.
3. Building codes and infrastructure design: Building codes and infrastructure design should be developed with volcanic eruptions in mind, incorporating features such as ash-resistant construction.
4. Disaster preparedness and emergency response planning: Emergency response teams and relief organizations should be well-prepared and equipped to respond quickly and effectively to volcanic disasters.
5. Land-use planning: Land-use planning can help reduce the risk of volcanic eruptions by ensuring that critical infrastructure and buildings are not located in high-risk areas.
6. Education and public awareness: Communities and individuals should be educated on volcanic hazards, including how to evacuate safely and how to respond in the aftermath of a volcanic eruption.

63

Tsunamis

Tsunamis, or large ocean waves triggered by earthquakes, landslides, or volcanic eruptions, pose a significant risk to coastal communities around the world. While tsunamis have occurred throughout history, the risk of these devastating events is expected to increase in the future due to several factors.

One significant factor is climate change, which is causing sea levels to rise and making coastal areas more vulnerable to tsunamis. As sea levels continue to rise, even relatively small tsunamis can cause significant damage and displacement.

Another factor is the increasing frequency and intensity of natural disasters such as earthquakes and volcanic eruptions, which can trigger tsunamis. As populations grow and more people live in coastal areas, the potential impact of these events is increasing.

To address the risk of tsunamis in the future, a comprehensive and coordinated approach is needed. This includes:

1. Early warning systems: Early warning systems can provide critical time for people to evacuate and take protective measures before a tsunami occurs.

2. Evacuation planning: Communities in high-risk areas should have evacuation plans in place and regularly practice drills to ensure that

everyone knows what to do in the event of a tsunami.

3. Building codes and infrastructure design: Building codes and infrastructure design should be developed with tsunamis in mind, incorporating features such as elevated foundations, flood-resistant materials, and emergency shelters.

4. Land-use planning: Land-use planning can help reduce the risk of tsunamis by ensuring that critical infrastructure and buildings are not located in high-risk areas.

5. Education and public awareness: Communities and individuals should be educated on tsunami hazards, including how to evacuate safely and how to respond in the aftermath of a tsunami.

In summary, tsunamis pose a significant risk to coastal communities in the future. However, by investing in resilient infrastructure, early warning systems, and emergency response capabilities, we can work to minimize the impact of tsunamis and build a more resilient future.

64

Hurricanes

Hurricanes, also known as typhoons or cyclones, are powerful and destructive storms that can cause extensive damage to communities along coastlines and in low-lying areas. With climate change and rising sea levels, the risk of hurricanes is expected to increase in the future.

Hurricanes are created when warm ocean water evaporates, leading to the formation of clouds and intense storms. The warming of the oceans due to climate change is leading to the creation of more frequent and more intense hurricanes. In addition, rising sea levels make coastal areas more vulnerable to storm surge, which can cause significant damage and loss of life.

To address the risk of hurricanes in the future, a comprehensive approach is needed. This includes:

1. Early warning systems: Early warning systems can provide critical time for people to evacuate and take protective measures before a hurricane hits.
2. Preparedness planning: Communities in high-risk areas should have preparedness plans in place and regularly practice drills to ensure that everyone knows what to do in the event of a hurricane.
3. Building codes and infrastructure design: Building codes and infrastructure design should be developed with hurricanes in mind, incorporating features such as elevated foundations, wind-resistant

materials, and emergency shelters.

4. Land-use planning: Land-use planning can help reduce the risk of hurricanes by ensuring that critical infrastructure and buildings are not located in high-risk areas.

5. Climate change mitigation: Addressing the root causes of climate change, such as reducing greenhouse gas emissions, can help reduce the frequency and intensity of hurricanes in the future.

In summary, hurricanes pose a significant risk to coastal communities in the future. However, by investing in resilient infrastructure, early warning systems, and emergency response capabilities, we can work to minimize the impact of hurricanes and build a more resilient future. Addressing the root causes of climate change is also critical to reducing the risk of hurricanes in the long term.

65

Tornadoes

Tornadoes are one of the most destructive natural disasters that can strike with little to no warning. They are often unpredictable and can cause extensive damage to homes, businesses, and communities. With climate change, the risk of tornadoes is expected to increase in the future.

Tornadoes are formed by a combination of warm, moist air and cool, dry air. Climate change can lead to changes in atmospheric conditions, which can result in more frequent and intense tornadoes. In addition, changes in land use, such as urbanization and deforestation, can also affect tornado formation and intensity.

To address the risk of tornadoes in the future, it is important to take a comprehensive approach. This includes:

1. Early warning systems: Early warning systems can provide critical time for people to take shelter and protect themselves before a tornado hits.
2. Preparedness planning: Communities in high-risk areas should have preparedness plans in place and regularly practice drills to ensure that everyone knows what to do in the event of a tornado.
3. Building codes and infrastructure design: Building codes and infrastructure design should be developed with tornadoes in mind, incorporating features such as safe rooms, reinforced roofs, and wind-resistant materials.

4. Land-use planning: Land-use planning can help reduce the risk of tornadoes by ensuring that critical infrastructure and buildings are not located in high-risk areas.

5. Climate change mitigation: Addressing the root causes of climate change, such as reducing greenhouse gas emissions, can help reduce the frequency and intensity of tornadoes in the future.

In summary, tornadoes pose a significant risk to communities in the future. However, by investing in resilient infrastructure, early warning systems, and emergency response capabilities, we can work to minimize the impact of tornadoes and build a more resilient future. Addressing the root causes of climate change is also critical to reducing the risk of tornadoes in the long term.

66

Landslides

Landslides are a serious natural disaster that can cause significant damage to infrastructure, homes, and communities. They are often triggered by heavy rainfall or seismic activity and can be exacerbated by human activities such as deforestation and urbanization.

With climate change, the risk of landslides is expected to increase in many parts of the world. This is due to the increased frequency and intensity of extreme weather events, such as heavy rainfall and floods, which can trigger landslides.

To address the risk of landslides, it is important to take a comprehensive approach that includes:

1. Early warning systems: Early warning systems can help provide critical time for people to evacuate before a landslide occurs. This can be especially important in areas where landslides are common or in high-risk areas.

2. Land-use planning: Land-use planning can help reduce the risk of landslides by avoiding development in high-risk areas, such as steep slopes or areas prone to erosion.

3. Slope stabilization and erosion control: Slope stabilization and erosion control measures can help prevent landslides by stabilizing slopes and reducing erosion.

4. Emergency response planning: Communities in high-risk areas should have emergency response plans in place that include evacuation routes, emergency shelters, and supplies.
5. Climate change adaptation: Adaptation measures, such as improved drainage systems and more resilient infrastructure, can help reduce the risk of landslides in the face of changing weather patterns.

In summary, landslides are a significant risk to communities, particularly in areas prone to heavy rainfall, seismic activity, and human activities such as deforestation and urbanization. By implementing early warning systems, effective land-use planning, slope stabilization measures, and emergency response planning, we can work to reduce the risk of landslides and build more resilient communities. Addressing the root causes of climate change through mitigation and adaptation measures is also critical to reducing the risk of landslides in the long term.

67

Wildfires

Wildfires are a growing risk around the world, as changing weather patterns and human activities contribute to an increased frequency and intensity of wildfires. Climate change, drought, and human-caused ignition sources are among the key drivers of wildfires, which can have devastating effects on communities and ecosystems.

As temperatures continue to rise and drought conditions become more frequent and severe, the risk of wildfires is expected to increase in many parts of the world. In addition, human activities such as land use change and urbanization can also contribute to the risk of wildfires.

To address the risk of wildfires, it is important to take a comprehensive approach that includes:

1. Prevention: Prevention efforts can help reduce the risk of wildfires by addressing human-caused ignition sources, such as campfires and discarded cigarettes, and promoting responsible land use practices.
2. Early warning systems: Early warning systems can help provide critical time for people to evacuate and for firefighters to respond to wildfires.
3. Effective suppression and containment efforts: Rapid and effective suppression and containment efforts are essential to limiting the spread and damage caused by wildfires.
4. Climate change mitigation: Addressing the root causes of climate

change through mitigation measures such as reducing greenhouse gas emissions can help reduce the risk of wildfires in the long term.

5. Ecosystem management: Managing ecosystems through practices such as prescribed burning and forest thinning can help reduce the risk of wildfires and promote healthy ecosystems.

In summary, wildfires are a growing risk around the world due to climate change, drought, and human activities. By implementing prevention measures, early warning systems, effective suppression and containment efforts, and addressing the root causes of climate change through mitigation measures, we can work to reduce the risk of wildfires and build more resilient communities and ecosystems. Effective ecosystem management practices can also play a critical role in reducing the risk of wildfires and promoting healthy ecosystems.

68

Avalanches

Avalanches pose a significant risk to people living or visiting mountainous areas, particularly during the winter months. An avalanche occurs when snowpack becomes unstable and slides downhill, gathering momentum and mass as it goes. This can cause destruction to infrastructure, properties, and most importantly, human life.

Several factors contribute to the risk of avalanches, including weather conditions, slope angle and steepness, and the type and thickness of snowpack. Unstable snow can easily be triggered by a person, snowmobile or even the weight of snowfall, resulting in an avalanche.

The effects of avalanches can be catastrophic, including severe injury or even death. In addition, avalanches can disrupt transportation routes, cause power outages and damage buildings and infrastructure.

To reduce the risk of avalanches, people living or visiting mountainous areas should take precautions and follow safety guidelines. Some measures include:

1. Stay informed: Check the avalanche forecast and weather conditions before venturing into mountainous areas.
2. Practice safe travel techniques: Avoid traveling alone in avalanche-prone areas and travel with experienced individuals. Stay on designated trails or established routes, and avoid steep slopes.

3. Carry avalanche safety equipment: This includes an avalanche beacon, shovel, and probe.

4. Take an avalanche safety course: This can help people learn how to recognize avalanche terrain, identify signs of instability, and how to respond in case of an avalanche.

5. Respect closed areas: Always heed warnings and avoid closed areas during avalanche season.

6. Report avalanches: If you observe an avalanche or see signs of instability, report it to the appropriate authorities.

Avalanches are a significant risk to those living or visiting mountainous areas, particularly during the winter months. By taking precautions and following safety guidelines, people can reduce the risk of avalanches and minimize the impact of potential disasters. Avalanche safety courses, carrying safety equipment, respecting closed areas, staying informed, and reporting any signs of instability are some of the measures that people can take to stay safe in avalanche-prone areas.

69

Heat waves

Heat waves are prolonged periods of hot and humid weather, where the temperature rises above average levels and can cause severe health problems for humans and animals. Heat waves have become more frequent and intense due to climate change, and they are expected to continue to increase in the future.

During a heat wave, people can experience dehydration, heat exhaustion, and even heat stroke. These conditions can be fatal if left untreated, particularly in vulnerable populations, such as the elderly, infants, and those with pre-existing medical conditions.

Heat waves can also have significant impacts on agriculture, livestock, and natural ecosystems. They can cause crops to fail, reduce crop yields, and increase the risk of wildfires.

To mitigate the risk of heat waves, there are several measures that individuals and communities can take, including:

1. Stay hydrated: Drink plenty of water and avoid alcohol, caffeine, and sugary drinks.
2. Stay cool: Stay indoors in air-conditioned environments, or seek shade and cool spaces when outside. Wear lightweight, loose-fitting clothing, and use a fan or air conditioning when possible.
3. Check on vulnerable populations: Check on the elderly, infants, and

those with pre-existing medical conditions to ensure they are staying cool and hydrated.

4. Reduce energy use: During a heat wave, electricity demand can increase significantly. By reducing energy use, such as by turning off lights and unplugging electronics, individuals can help reduce the strain on the power grid.

5. Prepare for emergencies: Have an emergency plan in place, including knowing the signs of heat-related illness and how to respond in case of an emergency.

6. Climate action: Taking action to reduce greenhouse gas emissions and combat climate change can help prevent future heat waves from becoming more severe and frequent.

Heat waves pose a significant risk to human health, agriculture, and natural ecosystems. To mitigate the risk, individuals and communities can take several measures, including staying hydrated and cool, checking on vulnerable populations, reducing energy use, and preparing for emergencies. Long-term solutions such as climate action are also necessary to reduce the risk of heat waves in the future.

70

Cold snaps

In the future, there is a risk of cold snaps that could bring severe weather conditions and endanger human lives. A cold snap is a sudden and intense period of cold weather, often accompanied by strong winds and heavy snowfall. This extreme weather can cause transportation disruptions, power outages, and damage to infrastructure. In addition, exposure to cold temperatures for prolonged periods can lead to hypothermia, frostbite, and other health problems.

Climate change is believed to be a factor in the increasing frequency and intensity of cold snaps. As global temperatures rise, the temperature difference between the poles and the equator decreases, causing a weakening of the jet stream. This can lead to pockets of frigid Arctic air being pushed further south than usual, resulting in cold snaps in regions that are not used to such extreme weather.

To address the risk of cold snaps, it is crucial to prioritize measures that can help mitigate the impacts of climate change. This includes reducing greenhouse gas emissions and investing in renewable energy sources. In addition, preparations should be made to ensure that communities are equipped to handle extreme cold weather conditions, such as having adequate heating systems and emergency supplies. Public education campaigns can also help raise awareness about the dangers of cold snaps and how to stay safe during extreme weather events.

Overall, it is essential to recognize the potential risks of cold snaps in the future and take proactive steps to address them. By working together, we can help ensure the safety and well-being of our communities in the face of these challenges.

VIII

Resource Depletion

Resource depletion refers to the loss or exhaustion of natural resources such as oil, gas, minerals, and water. The overconsumption of these resources by human activities, combined with population growth and urbanization, has led to concerns about their finite availability and the long-term sustainability of our planet.

71

Water scarcity

Water is a vital resource for life, and its scarcity is a significant concern for the future. The demand for freshwater is increasing due to population growth, urbanization, and industrialization, while the supply of freshwater is limited and unevenly distributed around the world. Climate change is exacerbating this problem by altering rainfall patterns and increasing the frequency and intensity of droughts.

Water scarcity can have severe consequences, including reduced agricultural productivity, health risks, social and economic disruption, and even conflict. This risk is particularly acute in regions with poor water management practices, inadequate infrastructure, and limited access to safe and clean drinking water.

Addressing water scarcity requires a comprehensive approach that includes conservation efforts, water reuse and recycling, the development of new water sources, and the promotion of sustainable water management practices. These efforts should be supported by increased investment in water infrastructure, research and development of new technologies, and international cooperation to ensure equitable access to water resources.

In addition, individuals can also play a role by adopting water-efficient behaviors such as fixing leaky faucets, reducing water consumption in households and businesses, and supporting policies that promote sustainable water management. By working together, we can mitigate the risk of water scarcity and ensure that this vital resource is available for generations to come.

Addressing water scarcity requires a multifaceted approach that includes the following solutions:

1. Conservation: Water conservation efforts can help reduce water usage by promoting more efficient water use and reducing waste. This can include things like fixing leaky faucets, using water-efficient appliances, and practicing water-wise landscaping.
2. Water Reuse and Recycling: Recycled water can be used for non-potable purposes like landscaping, industrial processes, and agriculture, thereby reducing demand on freshwater sources.
3. Developing New Water Sources: Desalination, rainwater harvesting, and wastewater treatment can provide additional sources of freshwater.
4. Sustainable Water Management: Promoting sustainable water management practices, such as watershed management and water-use planning, can help ensure equitable access to water resources.
5. Increased Investment in Water Infrastructure: Investing in water infrastructure, such as water treatment plants, pipelines, and storage facilities, can improve water access and supply.
6. Research and Development of New Technologies: Research and development of new technologies, such as water-efficient crops, water sensors, and nanofiltration membranes, can help improve water management and usage.
7. International Cooperation: International cooperation can help ensure equitable access to water resources and promote sustainable water management practices. This can include agreements on water-sharing, technical assistance, and financial support for developing countries.

By implementing these solutions, we can address water scarcity and ensure that this vital resource is available for generations to come.

233

72

Energy depletion

The increasing demand for energy, along with the depletion of non-renewable sources of energy, poses a significant risk of energy depletion in the future. The continued reliance on fossil fuels, such as coal, oil, and natural gas, contributes to climate change and environmental degradation. This, in turn, further exacerbates the depletion of energy resources.

The risks associated with energy depletion include increased energy prices, supply shortages, and geopolitical conflicts over energy resources. These risks can have significant economic, social, and environmental impacts.

To mitigate the risks of energy depletion, it is essential to adopt sustainable energy sources and reduce energy consumption. Here are some solutions that can help address the risk of energy depletion:

1. Renewable Energy Sources: Transitioning to renewable energy sources, such as solar, wind, geothermal, and hydroelectric power, can help reduce the reliance on non-renewable energy sources.
2. Energy Efficiency: Promoting energy-efficient technologies, such as LED lighting and energy-efficient appliances, can help reduce energy consumption.
3. Energy Storage: Developing energy storage technologies, such as batteries and pumped hydro storage, can help address the intermittent nature of renewable energy sources and provide a reliable source of

energy.

4. Energy Conservation: Promoting energy conservation practices, such as using public transportation, carpooling, and reducing unnecessary energy consumption, can help reduce energy demand.

5. Research and Development: Investing in research and development of new technologies, such as fusion energy and advanced battery storage, can help develop new sustainable energy sources and improve energy efficiency.

6. International Cooperation: International cooperation and agreements can help ensure equitable access to energy resources and promote sustainable energy management practices.

By adopting these solutions, we can mitigate the risks of energy depletion and transition to a more sustainable energy future.

73

Oil depletion

Oil is a finite resource, and as global demand continues to rise, the risk of oil depletion becomes increasingly concerning. As oil reserves are depleted, there may be a shortage of supply, which could cause prices to skyrocket and lead to economic instability. Additionally, many countries rely heavily on oil exports to fuel their economies, so a decline in production could have significant geopolitical consequences.

Furthermore, the burning of fossil fuels, including oil, is a major contributor to climate change, which poses its own risks and challenges. To address the risk of oil depletion, countries need to shift towards more sustainable and renewable sources of energy, such as wind and solar power. This requires significant investment in new infrastructure and technologies, as well as changes in consumer behavior and government policies.

In addition, there needs to be greater emphasis on energy efficiency and conservation measures to reduce overall energy consumption. This could include building design that prioritizes natural lighting and ventilation, as well as transportation policies that encourage public transit and cycling.

Overall, addressing the risk of oil depletion requires a concerted effort from governments, businesses, and individuals to transition towards cleaner and more sustainable forms of energy, while also promoting greater efficiency and conservation.

To address the risk of oil depletion, there are several potential solutions:

1. Transition to renewable energy sources: Investing in renewable energy sources such as wind, solar, geothermal, and hydroelectric power can reduce dependence on oil and other fossil fuels.

2. Develop new technologies: Developing new technologies for extracting oil from unconventional sources such as shale or for reducing the environmental impact of oil production can help to extend the life of oil reserves.

3. Increase energy efficiency: Improving energy efficiency in transportation, buildings, and industry can reduce overall energy consumption, which in turn reduces demand for oil.

4. Promote alternative transportation: Encouraging the use of public transportation, electric vehicles, and bicycles can help reduce the demand for oil in transportation.

5. mplement government policies: Governments can implement policies such as carbon taxes, subsidies for renewable energy, and regulations on energy efficiency to encourage the transition away from oil.

6. Increase awareness: Raising public awareness about the risks of oil depletion and the benefits of transitioning to renewable energy can help to build support for these solutions.

74

Mineral depletion

The world's population is growing rapidly, and as the demand for goods and services increases, so does the need for minerals. Unfortunately, many of the minerals we rely on for technology and infrastructure are finite resources that are becoming increasingly scarce. As the world's population continues to grow, the demand for minerals will only increase, putting pressure on mining companies to find new sources of these resources.

The depletion of minerals poses a significant risk to the global economy, as many industries rely on these resources to manufacture products. Additionally, the depletion of minerals can have significant environmental consequences, as mining activities can lead to soil erosion, water pollution, and habitat destruction.

To address the risk of mineral depletion, governments and industries need to work together to find new sources of minerals and to reduce our reliance on non-renewable resources. One solution is to focus on recycling and reusing minerals that have already been extracted. Another solution is to develop new technologies that can extract minerals more efficiently and with less environmental impact.

In addition to these technological solutions, there is also a need for more sustainable mining practices. This includes reducing the amount of waste generated during the mining process, minimizing the use of hazardous chemicals, and ensuring that mining operations are conducted in an environmentally responsible manner.

Ultimately, addressing the risk of mineral depletion requires a concerted effort from governments, industries, and individuals to reduce our reliance on non-renewable resources and to develop more sustainable practices for mining and resource extraction. By working together, we can ensure that future generations have access to the minerals and resources they need to thrive.

Mineral depletion is a serious risk that needs to be addressed urgently. To mitigate this risk, there are several solutions that can be implemented. First, there needs to be more investment in research and development of new, sustainable technologies that can reduce our reliance on mineral resources. This can include developing alternatives to minerals that are in short supply or finding new and innovative ways to extract minerals that are less damaging to the environment.

Second, we can focus on recycling and reuse of minerals. Many minerals can be recycled and reused, which reduces the need for new mining and extraction. Governments and businesses can encourage recycling by offering incentives for recycling and promoting the use of recycled materials.

Third, there can be better international cooperation to manage and conserve mineral resources. This can include the establishment of international agreements to protect and manage resources, and the development of programs to promote sustainable practices in the mining industry.

75

Acid Rain

Acid rain is a serious environmental problem that results from the release of pollutants such as sulfur dioxide and nitrogen oxides into the atmosphere. These pollutants can combine with water vapor to form acidic precipitation, which can have harmful effects on the environment and human health. Acid rain can damage crops, forests, and bodies of water, leading to declines in biodiversity and economic losses.

In the future, the risk of acid rain may increase due to factors such as continued industrialization, fossil fuel use, and climate change. However, there are steps that can be taken to mitigate this risk. One solution is to reduce the emissions of sulfur dioxide and nitrogen oxides through the use of cleaner fuels, technologies, and regulations. Another solution is to promote sustainable land use practices that can help to buffer and protect sensitive ecosystems from the impacts of acid rain. Additionally, increasing public awareness and education about the causes and effects of acid rain can encourage individuals and businesses to take action to reduce their contribution to this problem. By working together and taking proactive steps to address the risk of acid rain, we can help to protect our planet and promote a healthier, more sustainable future for all.

Acid rain is a serious environmental issue that can cause harm to the ecosystem and human health. It is caused by the emission of sulfur dioxide and nitrogen oxide gases, which react with the water, oxygen, and other chemicals in the atmosphere to form acids. These acids then fall back to the earth as acid rain, which can damage forests, lakes, and crops, as well as corrode buildings and monuments.

To address the risk of acid rain in the future, a number of solutions can be implemented. One approach is to reduce the amount of sulfur dioxide and nitrogen oxide emissions by enforcing stricter regulations on factories and power plants. The use of cleaner energy sources, such as renewable energy, can also reduce emissions. Additionally, individuals can reduce their own carbon footprint by conserving energy, using public transportation, and choosing environmentally friendly products.

Another solution is to implement measures to neutralize the effects of acid rain, such as adding lime or other alkaline substances to lakes and rivers to neutralize the acidity. Planting trees and other vegetation can also help to absorb the excess acid and reduce its harmful effects on the environment.

Education and awareness campaigns can also be effective in addressing the risk of acid rain. By educating people about the causes and effects of acid rain, individuals can take steps to reduce their own carbon footprint and become more environmentally conscious. Through these efforts, we can work to mitigate the risk of acid rain and protect our planet for future generations.

76

Soil erosion

Soil erosion is a major environmental challenge that is expected to increase in the future due to various factors such as climate change, deforestation, and unsustainable land use practices. Soil erosion not only leads to the loss of fertile soil but also contributes to water pollution, reduced agricultural productivity, and increased frequency and severity of floods and landslides. Moreover, it can have long-term impacts on the ecosystem and the livelihoods of people who depend on agriculture and other natural resources.

To address the risk of soil erosion, there is a need for sustainable land use practices that promote soil conservation and restoration. This includes measures such as afforestation, crop rotation, contour farming, terracing, and conservation tillage. In addition, it is important to promote sustainable land use policies and regulations that promote soil conservation, such as promoting soil-friendly farming practices and prohibiting deforestation and other activities that contribute to soil erosion. Finally, raising public awareness and providing education on the importance of soil conservation and restoration can help to encourage individuals and communities to take action to protect and preserve soil resources. By adopting these solutions, we can mitigate the risk of soil erosion and promote sustainable land use practices for a healthier and more resilient future.

Soil erosion can have significant negative impacts on the environment and the society as a whole. Here are some solutions to address the risk of soil erosion:

1. Planting trees and vegetation: Trees and vegetation can help to stabilize the soil and reduce erosion by slowing down water runoff.
2. Reducing tillage: Tillage can increase the risk of soil erosion by breaking up soil aggregates and exposing the soil to the elements. Reducing tillage can help to preserve soil structure and reduce the risk of erosion.
3. Cover crops: Planting cover crops can help to maintain soil health and reduce erosion by providing cover and preventing soil from being exposed to the elements.
4. Conservation tillage: Conservation tillage involves tilling the soil less frequently, leaving crop residues on the soil surface, and using specialized equipment to plant crops. This method helps to maintain soil health and reduce erosion.
5. Terracing: Terracing involves building steps or terraces into steep slopes to slow down water runoff and prevent soil from being washed away.
6. Soil conservation practices: Adopting soil conservation practices, such as crop rotation, contour farming, and nutrient management, can help to reduce soil erosion by preserving soil structure and improving soil health.

It is important to prioritize sustainable land use practices and soil conservation efforts to mitigate the risk of soil erosion and maintain the health and productivity of our soils.

77

Overfishing

Overfishing is a growing concern as the demand for seafood increases worldwide. The depletion of fish stocks can have a significant impact on the health of oceans and coastal communities. Overfishing can cause ecological imbalances, disrupt food chains, and harm the livelihoods of fishermen and their families. Moreover, it can lead to the extinction of certain fish species, which can have a domino effect on the entire ecosystem. The depletion of fish stocks also makes it difficult for the fish population to recover, leading to long-term economic and ecological problems.

To address the risk of overfishing, several solutions have been proposed, such as establishing marine protected areas, implementing sustainable fishing practices, and regulating fishing quotas. Additionally, raising awareness about the importance of sustainable fishing practices can help reduce the demand for seafood from overfished areas. By adopting sustainable fishing practices and reducing the demand for seafood from overfished areas, we can ensure that fish stocks remain healthy and available for future generations.

Overfishing is a serious threat to the world's oceans and the communities that depend on them. Here are some solutions to tackle this risk:

1. Enforce fishing regulations: Governments can put in place regulations that limit the amount and size of fish that can be caught. These

regulations must be enforced strictly to ensure that fish populations can replenish.

2. Promote sustainable fishing practices: Encouraging sustainable fishing practices, such as the use of selective fishing gear and avoiding fishing in sensitive areas, can help reduce the impact of fishing on the marine ecosystem.

3. Create marine protected areas: Designating areas in the ocean where fishing is prohibited can help fish populations to recover and create a healthier marine environment.

4. Support small-scale fishing communities: Small-scale fishing communities often rely on fishing as their primary source of livelihoods. Supporting them with alternative livelihood options can reduce the pressure on fish stocks.

5. Raise public awareness: Educating the public about the importance of sustainable fishing practices and the impact of overfishing can create a demand for sustainable seafood and help reduce the demand for overfished species.

78

Water pollution

Water pollution is a significant risk for the future, as it threatens the health and well-being of both humans and the environment. As the world's population continues to grow, so does the demand for resources, including water. Unfortunately, the increase in human activity and industrialization has led to an increase in water pollution. This pollution can come from a variety of sources, including agricultural runoff, sewage, oil spills, and industrial waste. These pollutants can harm aquatic ecosystems and make water unsafe for human consumption.

Furthermore, water pollution can have long-term effects on the environment and the economy. The degradation of aquatic ecosystems can lead to the loss of important fish and wildlife habitats, which can have a significant impact on the food chain. It can also lead to a decline in the availability of clean water, which can increase the costs of water treatment and decrease the availability of water for irrigation and other uses.

To mitigate the risks of water pollution, there must be a concerted effort to reduce pollution sources and improve water treatment methods. Governments and industries can enact and enforce regulations to limit pollution from factories, farms, and other sources. Additionally, investments in technology and infrastructure can improve water treatment methods and ensure that clean water is accessible to all. Finally, individual actions, such as reducing the use of single-use plastics and properly disposing of hazardous waste, can also make a significant impact in reducing water pollution. By working together, we can ensure that water remains a valuable resource for future generations.

To address the risk of water pollution, there are several solutions that can be implemented:

1. Proper waste disposal: One of the main causes of water pollution is improper waste disposal. To prevent this, communities should have designated waste disposal sites and proper trash collection methods.
2. Reducing the use of chemicals: Chemicals like pesticides and fertilizers can contaminate water sources. Reducing their use can help minimize the risk of water pollution.
3. Wastewater treatment: Wastewater should be properly treated before being released back into water sources. This can be achieved through the use of treatment plants or natural treatment methods like constructed wetlands.
4. Encouraging sustainable farming practices: Sustainable farming practices like crop rotation, organic farming, and conservation tillage can help minimize soil erosion and prevent pollutants from entering water sources.
5. Promoting eco-friendly products: Businesses and individuals can opt for eco-friendly products like biodegradable soaps and detergents to reduce the risk of water pollution.
6. Increasing public awareness: Educating the public about the importance of water conservation and proper waste disposal practices can help create a culture of responsible water use and reduce the risk of pollution.

Here is a list of tips and recommendations for clean water:

1. Boil water before drinking it to kill any harmful bacteria and parasites that may be present.
2. Use a water filter or purifier to remove impurities and contaminants

from your drinking water.

3. Store water in clean, covered containers to prevent contamination.
4. Avoid using pesticides and chemicals near water sources to prevent contamination.
5. Test your water regularly for contaminants and impurities.
6. Keep water treatment systems well-maintained and up-to-date to ensure they are functioning properly.
7. Dispose of hazardous materials and chemicals properly to prevent contamination of water sources.
8. Use water-conserving devices and practices to reduce water usage and waste.
9. Support efforts to protect and conserve water sources, such as wetlands and aquifers.
10. Educate yourself and others about the importance of clean water and the actions we can take to protect it.

By following these tips and recommendations, we can help to ensure that our water is safe, clean, and healthy for ourselves and future generations.

79

Land degradation

Land degradation is a serious environmental problem that has been exacerbated by human activities. It is the deterioration or loss of the productive capacity of the land, resulting from natural or anthropogenic causes. Soil erosion, desertification, deforestation, and pollution are some of the major factors contributing to land degradation. As a result, the soil loses its fertility and becomes less productive, leading to reduced crop yields, loss of biodiversity, and even desertification in extreme cases.

The impact of land degradation is felt worldwide, affecting the livelihoods of millions of people who depend on the land for their survival. It poses a threat to food security, water resources, and biodiversity. Moreover, land degradation exacerbates climate change by releasing carbon into the atmosphere and reducing the land's capacity to store carbon.

To address this problem, there is a need for concerted efforts from governments, non-governmental organizations, and individuals. One approach is to promote sustainable land management practices such as conservation agriculture, agroforestry, and crop rotation. These practices help to improve soil health, reduce soil erosion, and increase the land's productivity.

Another solution is to promote reforestation and afforestation. Trees play a critical role in preventing soil erosion and degradation by stabilizing the soil and providing shade that helps to reduce water loss from the soil surface. Planting trees also helps to sequester carbon from the atmosphere, mitigating climate change.

Finally, reducing pollution from industrial activities and agriculture is critical to protecting the land and mitigating land degradation. Governments and industries can adopt environmentally friendly practices and regulations to limit the release of harmful pollutants into the environment.

Land degradation is a serious risk that must be addressed to ensure sustainable development and protect the environment. By promoting sustainable land management practices, reforestation and afforestation, and reducing pollution, we can work towards a healthier and more productive planet.

Land degradation is a serious issue that threatens the productivity and sustainability of our planet's natural resources. It is caused by various factors such as deforestation, overgrazing, soil erosion, and urbanization. However, there are solutions that can help mitigate this risk and prevent further land degradation.

1. Sustainable land use practices: Implementing sustainable land use practices such as agroforestry, crop rotation, and conservation tillage can help to maintain soil fertility and prevent soil erosion.

2. Reforestation and afforestation: Planting trees in degraded areas can help to prevent soil erosion, restore soil fertility, and provide habitat for wildlife.

3. Conservation of wetlands and grasslands: Wetlands and grasslands play a critical role in maintaining soil fertility and preventing soil erosion. Conservation of these areas can help to prevent further land degradation.

4. Land-use planning and management: Effective land-use planning and management can help to prevent soil degradation by regulating land use, promoting sustainable practices, and protecting critical ecosystems.

5. Investment in sustainable agriculture: Investing in sustainable agriculture practices can help to reduce pressure on land resources and

promote sustainable land use.

6. Education and awareness-raising: Education and awareness-raising campaigns can help to promote sustainable land use practices and encourage individuals and communities to take action to prevent land degradation.

80

Fossil fuel dependency

As the world continues to rely heavily on fossil fuels, the risk of fossil fuel dependency looms large in the future. Fossil fuels, including coal, oil, and natural gas, provide a significant portion of the world's energy needs, but they are finite resources that are being rapidly depleted. The continued use of these fuels also contributes to the growing problem of climate change, which has far-reaching consequences for the planet.

One major risk of fossil fuel dependency is the volatility of fuel prices. As reserves become depleted, the cost of extracting fossil fuels becomes increasingly expensive, which can lead to sudden spikes in energy prices. This can have a major impact on the global economy, particularly for countries heavily reliant on fossil fuel exports. In addition, political instability in regions where fossil fuels are extracted can disrupt supply chains and lead to further price fluctuations.

Another risk of fossil fuel dependency is the environmental damage caused by extraction and use. Fossil fuel extraction methods can lead to pollution of air, water, and soil, as well as habitat destruction and other environmental impacts. The burning of fossil fuels also contributes to greenhouse gas emissions, which trap heat in the atmosphere and contribute to global warming.

To address the risks of fossil fuel dependency, it is crucial to shift towards renewable energy sources such as solar, wind, hydro, and geothermal power.

Governments and industry leaders must invest in research and development to improve the efficiency and affordability of these technologies. In addition, policies such as carbon taxes and emissions trading schemes can incentivize the transition away from fossil fuels and towards renewable energy.

Individuals can also play a role in reducing fossil fuel dependency by adopting more sustainable habits, such as reducing energy consumption at home and choosing low-carbon transportation options. By working together, we can mitigate the risks of fossil fuel dependency and create a more sustainable future for ourselves and future generations

The world has been heavily reliant on fossil fuels for energy for several decades now. However, the use of fossil fuels has several negative consequences for the environment, including air pollution and greenhouse gas emissions. To reduce the risk of over-dependency on fossil fuels, several solutions can be implemented:

1. Alternative Energy Sources: Governments and private entities should invest in alternative energy sources such as solar, wind, geothermal, and hydro power to reduce reliance on fossil fuels.
2. Energy Efficiency: It's important to increase energy efficiency by using energy-saving technologies and equipment in homes, businesses, and industries to decrease energy consumption.
3. Carbon Capture and Storage: The technology to capture carbon dioxide emissions from power plants and industries and store them underground is available, and its adoption should be encouraged.
4. Transition to Electric Vehicles: Governments can incentivize the adoption of electric vehicles by providing subsidies and installing charging infrastructure.
5. Investment in Research and Development: Investment in research and development of new energy technologies can help develop solutions to the world's energy challenges.
6. Fossil Fuel Subsidies: Governments can reduce subsidies for fossil

fuel companies and redirect those funds towards renewable energy development.

By implementing these solutions, it's possible to reduce the risk of fossil fuel dependency and transition to a cleaner and more sustainable energy future.

IX

Political Risks

Political risks can have a significant impact on individuals, businesses, and communities around the world. These risks can include political instability, authoritarianism, dictatorship, and human rights abuses. They can also include risks related to censorship, militarization, and nuclear accidents.Addressing political risks requires a range of solutions, including promoting transparency, accountability, and the rule of law,investing in renewable energy and sustainable development and diplomacy

81

Authoritarianism

Authoritarianism refers to a form of government where power is concentrated in the hands of a small group of individuals or a single individual. While authoritarianism has been present throughout history, it poses significant risks in the modern world.

One of the most significant risks associated with authoritarianism is the potential for abuse of power. In authoritarian regimes, power is concentrated in the hands of a few individuals, which can create an environment that is conducive to corruption, human rights abuses, and other forms of oppression. Authoritarian regimes can also limit freedom of speech, limit access to information, and restrict individual rights and freedoms.

Another risk of authoritarianism is the potential for stifling innovation and progress. Authoritarian regimes can limit access to new ideas and perspectives, which can limit innovation and progress. This can lead to economic stagnation, social and cultural isolation, and the decline of the society as a whole.

Additionally, authoritarianism can also pose risks to regional and global stability. Authoritarian regimes can create an environment that is conducive to conflict and instability, which can threaten regional and global security. Authoritarian regimes may also engage in aggressive behavior towards other nations, which can lead to regional and global tensions.

Addressing the risks associated with authoritarianism requires a range of solutions. Promoting democracy and human rights can help to prevent the risks associated with authoritarianism. This can involve measures such as investing in democratic institutions, promoting civic education, and supporting civil society organizations.

Fostering greater transparency and accountability can also help to prevent the risks associated with authoritarianism. This can involve measures such as promoting open and transparent governance, increasing citizen participation in decision-making processes, and investing in initiatives that promote accountability and transparency.

There are a number of potential risks associated with authoritarianism in the future. Here are some key considerations:

1. Populist movements: Populist movements that play on fears and grievances can pave the way for authoritarian leaders to take power. This is particularly true in times of economic uncertainty, social unrest, or political polarization.
2. Weak institutions: In countries with weak institutions, such as a lack of independent media, judiciary, or civil society, it can be easier for authoritarian leaders to consolidate power and suppress opposition. This can lead to a lack of accountability and the erosion of democratic norms and values.
3. Technological advances: Advances in technology, such as surveillance tools or social media algorithms, can be used to monitor, manipulate, and control populations. This can create a fertile ground for authoritarianism to take hold, particularly in countries with weak data privacy protections.
4. International trends: The rise of authoritarianism in other countries can embolden leaders in other countries to follow suit. This can create a domino effect where authoritarianism becomes more normalized and accepted around the world.
5. Economic factors: Economic factors, such as inequality, poverty, or corruption, can fuel popular resentment towards democratic institu-

tions and leaders. This can create an opening for authoritarian leaders to exploit and consolidate power.

Overall, the risk of authoritarianism in the future will depend on a complex set of factors, including political, social, economic, and technological trends. It will be important for societies around the world to remain vigilant and committed to defending democratic institutions and norms, while also addressing the underlying factors that can lead to authoritarianism in the first place.

Addressing authoritarianism is a complex and multifaceted challenge that requires a range of solutions. Here are some potential approaches:

1. Strengthen democratic institutions: Building strong democratic institutions, such as independent media, an impartial judiciary, and robust civil society organizations, can help to create a system of checks and balances that can prevent authoritarian leaders from consolidating power.
2. Promote transparency and accountability: Promoting transparency and accountability in government and other key institutions can help to prevent corruption and abuses of power, which can undermine trust in democratic institutions and pave the way for authoritarianism.
3. Invest in education and civic engagement: Investing in education and civic engagement can help to promote democratic values and norms, and empower citizens to hold their leaders accountable. This can help to build a strong and active civil society that is resistant to authoritarianism.
4. Support economic development: Addressing economic inequality and promoting inclusive economic growth can help to reduce the factors that can fuel support for authoritarian leaders. This can help to promote greater social stability and build a stronger foundation for democracy.

5. Foster international cooperation: Working with other countries and international organizations to promote democratic values and norms can help to create a more supportive international environment for democracy. This can help to build a global network of support that can resist authoritarianism and promote democratic governance.

82

Political instability

Political instability is a condition that occurs when the government of a country is unable to maintain stability and order. Political instability can be caused by a variety of factors, including economic instability, social unrest, corruption, and weak governance. Political instability poses significant risks to countries and their populations.

One of the most significant risks associated with political instability is the potential for violence and conflict. Political instability can create an environment that is conducive to violence and conflict, which can threaten the safety and well-being of the population. Violence and conflict can also have significant economic and social impacts, including increased poverty and social dislocation.

Another risk of political instability is the potential for economic instability. Political instability can create an uncertain business environment, which can negatively impact investment and trade. This can lead to economic stagnation, high unemployment rates, and a decline in living standards.

Additionally, political instability can also pose risks to regional and global stability. Political instability can create a ripple effect, which can spread beyond national borders and impact regional and global security. Political instability can also create an environment that is conducive to extremist ideologies, which can threaten regional and global security.

Addressing the risks associated with political instability requires a range of solutions. Promoting stability and security can help to prevent the risks associated with political instability. This can involve measures such as investing in security and stability initiatives, promoting democratic institutions, and supporting civil society organizations.

Fostering greater transparency and accountability can also help to prevent the risks associated with political instability. This can involve measures such as promoting open and transparent governance, increasing citizen participation in decision-making processes, and investing in initiatives that promote accountability and transparency.

There are a number of potential risks associated with political instability in the future. Here are some key considerations:

1. Economic factors: Economic instability, such as high unemployment, inflation, or inequality, can lead to political instability as citizens become disillusioned with their leaders and institutions. This can create an environment of social unrest and protests.

2. Social divisions: Social divisions, such as ethnic or religious tensions, can also contribute to political instability. When groups feel marginalized or discriminated against, they may turn to violence or other forms of resistance to push for change.

3. Climate change: Climate change can exacerbate political instability by contributing to resource scarcity, displacement, and conflicts over land and water. This can lead to increased migration, social tensions, and conflicts.

4. Cybersecurity threats: Cybersecurity threats, such as cyberattacks or disinformation campaigns, can undermine trust in democratic institutions and create uncertainty in the political system. This can lead to a lack of confidence in the ability of governments to protect citizens and respond to crises.

5. International tensions: International tensions, such as conflicts between major powers or geopolitical rivalries, can also contribute to political instability. When countries feel threatened or insecure, they

may become more aggressive or engage in actions that destabilize other countries or regions.

Overall, the risk of political instability in the future will depend on a complex set of factors, including political, social, economic, environmental, and technological trends. It will be important for leaders to address these challenges proactively, while also promoting greater transparency, accountability, and inclusivity in governance. By working together to build more stable and resilient political systems, we can help to create a more peaceful and prosperous future for all.

Addressing political instability is a complex challenge that requires a range of solutions. Here are some potential approaches:

1. Promote inclusive governance: Building inclusive political systems that are responsive to the needs and concerns of all citizens can help to promote stability and reduce the risk of political unrest. This can involve ensuring that all groups have equal access to political partici-pation and decision-making, and that leaders are held accountable for their actions.
2. Invest in economic development: Addressing economic inequality and promoting inclusive economic growth can help to reduce the factors that can fuel support for instability. This can involve promoting job creation, reducing poverty, and providing access to basic services.
3. Address social divisions: Addressing social divisions, such as ethnic or religious tensions, can help to reduce the risk of conflict and instability. This can involve promoting intergroup dialogue, fostering social cohesion, and addressing grievances in a peaceful and constructive manner.
4. Address environmental challenges: Addressing environmental chal-lenges, such as climate change or resource scarcity, can help to reduce the risk of instability by promoting sustainable development and

reducing competition over resources.

5. Foster international cooperation: Working with other countries and international organizations to promote stability and address global challenges can help to create a more supportive international environment for stability. This can involve promoting conflict resolution, supporting peacebuilding efforts, and promoting greater international solidarity.

83

Dictatorship

Dictatorship is a form of government where an individual or a small group holds absolute power over a country or a region. Under a dictatorship, the government operates without the consent of the people, and there are no meaningful checks and balances on the exercise of power. While dictatorships have been a part of human history for thousands of years, the modern era has seen significant efforts to promote and protect democracy, which emphasizes the rule of law, the protection of individual rights, and the involvement of citizens in the political process.

Despite these efforts, dictatorship continues to be a challenge in many parts of the world. Rising nationalism and populism in many countries can create an environment where authoritarian leaders can gain support by playing on fears and grievances. Technological advances have also created new challenges for democracy. Advances in surveillance tools, social media algorithms, and other technologies can be used to monitor, manipulate, and control populations, leading to violations of privacy, freedom of expression, and other fundamental rights.

Dictatorships can have serious consequences for individuals and societies. Under a dictatorship, there is no meaningful protection for basic human rights, such as the right to freedom of speech, freedom of assembly, or freedom of the press. Dissent and opposition to the regime are often met with violence, torture, or imprisonment. Dictatorships can also lead to significant economic and social inequalities, with the ruling elite controlling the country's resources and denying basic services to the majority of the population.

Addressing dictatorship requires a range of solutions. Strengthening democratic institutions, such as independent media, an impartial judiciary, and robust civil society organizations, can help to create a system of checks and balances that can prevent authoritarian leaders from consolidating power. Promoting transparency and accountability in government and other key institutions can help to prevent corruption and abuses of power, which can undermine trust in democratic institutions and pave the way for dictatorship.

Investing in education and civic engagement can help to promote democratic values and norms and empower citizens to hold their leaders accountable. Addressing economic inequality and promoting inclusive economic growth can help to reduce the factors that can fuel support for dictatorship leaders. Finally, fostering international cooperation and support can help to create a more supportive international environment for democracy.

In conclusion, dictatorship remains a significant challenge facing societies around the world. While progress has been made in promoting and protecting democracy, much work remains to be done. By working together across sectors and across borders, we can build a more just and equitable world where democracy and human rights are respected and protected for all.

There are a number of potential risks associated with dictatorship in the future for the world. Here are some key considerations:

1. Rising nationalism: Rising nationalism and populism in many countries can create an environment where authoritarian leaders can gain support by playing on fears and grievances. This can lead to a

consolidation of power and erosion of democratic norms and values.

2. Technological advances: Advances in technology, such as surveillance tools or social media algorithms, can be used to monitor, manipulate, and control populations. This can create a fertile ground for dictatorship to take hold, particularly in countries with weak data privacy protections.

3. Weakening of democratic institutions: In countries where democratic institutions, such as an independent judiciary and free press, are weakened or dismantled, it can be easier for dictatorship to take hold. This can lead to a lack of accountability and the erosion of democratic norms and values.

4. Economic inequality: Economic inequality, poverty, or corruption can fuel popular resentment towards democratic institutions and leaders. This can create an opening for dictatorship leaders to exploit and consolidate power.

5. International trends: The rise of dictatorship in other countries can embolden leaders in other countries to follow suit. This can create a domino effect where dictatorship becomes more normalized and accepted around the world.

The risk of dictatorship in the future will depend on a complex set of factors, including political, social, economic, and technological trends. It will be important for societies around the world to remain vigilant and committed to defending democratic institutions and norms, while also addressing the underlying factors that can lead to dictatorship in the first place.

dictatorship is a complex and multifaceted challenge that requires a range of solutions. Here are some potential approaches:

1. Strengthen democratic institutions: Building strong democratic institutions, such as independent media, an impartial judiciary, and robust civil society organizations, can help to create a system of checks and balances that can prevent dictatorship leaders from consolidating power.

2. Promote transparency and accountability: Promoting transparency and accountability in government and other key institutions can help to prevent corruption and abuses of power, which can undermine trust in democratic institutions and pave the way for dictatorship.

3. Invest in education and civic engagement: Investing in education and civic engagement can help to promote democratic values and norms, and empower citizens to hold their leaders accountable. This can help to build a strong and active civil society that is resistant to dictatorship.

4. Support economic development: Addressing economic inequality and promoting inclusive economic growth can help to reduce the factors that can fuel support for dictatorship leaders. This can help to promote greater social stability and build a stronger foundation for democracy.

5. Foster international cooperation: Working with other countries and international organizations to promote democratic values and norms can help to create a more supportive international environment for democracy. This can help to build a global network of support that can resist dictatorship and promote democratic governance.

6. Sanctions and pressure: International actors, including governments and civil society organizations, can exert pressure on dictatorships through diplomatic means and economic sanctions. This can limit the regime's access to resources and weaken its ability to maintain power.

84

Human rights abuses

Human rights abuses are a widespread and pressing challenge facing societies around the world. From discrimination and inequality to violence and torture, human rights abuses take many forms and can affect individuals and communities in profound ways. While human rights abuses have long been a part of human history, the modern era has seen significant efforts to promote and protect human rights, including the establishment of international human rights laws and institutions.

Despite these efforts, human rights abuses continue to occur in many parts of the world. Discrimination and inequality based on factors such as race, gender, religion, or sexuality are still common, and can lead to violations of basic human rights such as the right to education, work, and healthcare. Political instability, conflict, and authoritarianism can also create an environment where human rights abuses are more likely to occur. This can lead to situations where basic human rights, such as the right to life, freedom from torture, or freedom of speech, are violated.

Technological advances have also created new challenges for human rights. Advances in surveillance tools, artificial intelligence, and social media algorithms can be used to monitor, manipulate, and control populations, leading to violations of privacy, freedom of expression, and other human rights. In addition, climate change can exacerbate human rights abuses by contributing to resource scarcity, displacement, and conflicts over land and water. This can lead to increased migration, social tensions, and violations of basic human rights.

Addressing human rights abuses requires a range of solutions. Promoting human rights education can help to raise awareness of the importance of human rights and empower individuals to stand up for their own rights and those of others. Strengthening legal frameworks, such as international human rights law and domestic legislation, can help to ensure that human rights are protected and enforced. Supporting civil society organizations, such as human rights groups and advocacy organizations, can help to create a strong and active community that is committed to promoting and defending human rights.

Promoting transparency and accountability in government and other key institutions can help to prevent human rights abuses and undermine trust in democratic institutions, and pave the way for authoritarianism. Addressing discrimination and inequality can help to reduce the risk of human rights abuses, and promoting greater inclusion and diversity in all aspects of society. Finally, fostering international cooperation and support can help to create a more supportive international environment for human rights.

In conclusion, human rights abuses remain a significant challenge facing societies around the world. While progress has been made in promoting and protecting human rights, much work remains to be done. By working together across sectors and across borders, we can build a more just and equitable world where human rights are respected and protected for all.

Addressing human rights abuses is a complex challenge that requires a range of solutions. Here are some potential approaches:

1. Promote human rights education: Promoting human rights education can help to raise awareness of the importance of human rights, and empower individuals to stand up for their own rights and those of

others.

2. Strengthen legal frameworks: Strengthening legal frameworks, such as international human rights law and domestic legislation, can help to ensure that human rights are protected and enforced.

3. Foster civil society: Supporting civil society organizations, such as human rights groups and advocacy organizations, can help to create a strong and active community that is committed to promoting and defending human rights.

4. Promote transparency and accountability: Promoting transparency and accountability in government and other key institutions can help to prevent human rights abuses, which can undermine trust in democratic institutions and pave the way for authoritarianism.

5. Address discrimination and inequality: Addressing discrimination and inequality, based on factors such as race, gender, religion, or sexuality, can help to reduce the risk of human rights abuses. This can involve promoting greater inclusion and diversity in all aspects of society.

6. Foster international cooperation: Working with other countries and international organizations to promote and defend human rights can help to create a more supportive international environment for human rights. This can involve promoting greater cooperation on human rights issues, and supporting international institutions that are committed to human rights.

85

Censorship

Censorship is the suppression or prohibition of any parts of books, films, news, speech, or other forms of communication that are considered obscene, politically unacceptable, or a threat to national security. Censorship has been practiced by governments, religious organizations, and other groups throughout history, with varying degrees of severity and justification.

Censorship can take many forms, from government restrictions on the media to self-censorship by individuals or organizations. The reasons for censorship can also vary widely, from protecting public morality to preventing the spread of false information. However, censorship can also be used as a tool for suppressing dissent, limiting freedom of expression, and promoting political agendas.

One of the most common forms of censorship is government censorship, where governments control or regulate the content of media and communication platforms. This can be done through laws, regulations, and restrictions on access to information. In some cases, governments use censorship to prevent the spread of information that is critical of the government, while in other cases, censorship is used to protect national security or public safety.

Censorship can also be practiced by private organizations and individuals, including social media platforms and publishers. These entities may censor content that is deemed offensive or harmful to their users, or to comply with local laws and regulations. While private censorship may not involve direct government intervention, it can still have significant implications for freedom of expression and access to information.

Censorship can have a range of consequences, both positive and negative. On the one hand, censorship can help to protect vulnerable populations from harmful content, such as hate speech, violent imagery, or pornography. Censorship can also be used to protect national security and prevent the spread of false information.

On the other hand, censorship can also be used to suppress dissent, limit freedom of expression, and promote political agendas. Censorship can prevent citizens from accessing important information about their government, society, or the world at large. Censorship can also have a chilling effect on free speech, making individuals hesitant to express their opinions or engage in open debate.

Addressing censorship requires a range of solutions. Promoting transparency and accountability in government and other key institutions can help to prevent censorship and ensure that citizens have access to accurate and reliable information. Strengthening legal frameworks, such as international human rights law and domestic legislation, can help to ensure that freedom of expression and access to information are protected and enforced.

Investing in education and civic engagement can help to promote democratic values and norms and empower citizens to stand up for their own rights and those of others. Finally, fostering international cooperation and support can help to create a more supportive international environment for freedom of expression and access to information.

Censorship remains a significant challenge facing societies around the world. While censorship can have positive effects, such as protecting vulnerable populations or preventing the spread of false information, it can also have negative consequences, such as limiting freedom of expression and suppressing dissent. By working together across sectors and across borders, we can build a more just and equitable world where freedom of expression and access to information are respected and protected for all.

Censorship is a complex challenge that requires a range of solutions. Here are some potential approaches:

1. Promote transparency and accountability: Promoting transparency and accountability in government and other key institutions can help to prevent censorship and ensure that citizens have access to accurate and reliable information. This can involve measures such as freedom of information laws and independent media watchdogs.

2. Strengthen legal frameworks: Strengthening legal frameworks, such as international human rights law and domestic legislation, can help to ensure that freedom of expression and access to information are protected and enforced. This can involve measures such as establishing clear standards for censorship and providing avenues for legal recourse.

3. Foster civil society: Supporting civil society organizations, such as free speech groups and media watchdogs, can help to create a strong and active community that is committed to promoting and defending freedom of expression and access to information.

4. Promote technological solutions: Developing and promoting technological solutions, such as secure communication tools and encryption software, can help to ensure that individuals and organizations can communicate freely and without fear of censorship or surveillance.

5. Educate citizens: Promoting education and awareness of the importance of freedom of expression and access to information can help to build a more informed and engaged citizenry. This can involve measures such as media literacy programs and public education campaigns.

6. Foster international cooperation: Working with other countries and international organizations to promote and defend freedom of expression and access to information can help to create a more supportive international environment for these values. This can involve promoting greater cooperation on internet governance and supporting international institutions that are committed to freedom of expression and access to information.

86

Militarization

Militarization is the process of increasing the role of military forces and values in society. It can take many forms, from the expansion of military budgets and the deployment of troops in domestic settings to the promotion of military culture and values in education and media. While militarization can have some positive effects, such as ensuring national security and protecting against external threats, it can also have negative consequences for society and individuals.

One of the most significant consequences of militarization is the erosion of democratic values and institutions. When the military becomes more involved in domestic affairs, there is a risk that it will become a dominant force in society, and that civil liberties and democratic institutions will be undermined. This can lead to the suppression of dissent, the erosion of human rights, and the suppression of free speech.

Militarization can also have significant social and economic consequences. Military spending can divert resources away from social welfare programs and other essential services, leading to increased poverty and inequality. Military values, such as obedience, discipline, and conformity, can also be promoted at the expense of individual creativity and innovation.

Furthermore, militarization can have serious environmental consequences. Military activities, such as the development and testing of weapons, can cause significant environmental damage, including pollution and destruction of ecosystems. The use of military force in conflicts can also lead to the displacement of communities and destruction of cultural heritage sites.

Addressing militarization requires a range of solutions. Promoting transparency and accountability in military spending and decision-making can help to prevent the militarization of society and ensure that military activities are conducted in a manner that is consistent with democratic values and human rights. Investing in social welfare programs and other essential services can help to ensure that resources are allocated in a way that benefits all members of society.

Promoting education and civic engagement can help to promote democratic values and norms and empower citizens to hold their leaders accountable. Finally, fostering international cooperation and support can help to create a more peaceful and secure international environment, where the use of military force is less necessary.

Militarization can have significant negative consequences for society and individuals, including the erosion of democratic values, social and economic inequality, and environmental damage. Addressing militarization requires a range of solutions that promote transparency and accountability, invest in social welfare programs, promote education and civic engagement, and foster international cooperation and support. By working together across sectors and across borders, we can build a more just and equitable world where militarization is minimized, and democratic values and human rights are respected and protected for all.

militarization is a complex challenge that requires a range of solutions. Here are some potential approaches:

1. Promote transparency and accountability: Promoting transparency and accountability in military spending and decision-making can help to prevent the militarization of society and ensure that military activities are conducted in a manner that is consistent with democratic

values and human rights. This can involve measures such as freedom of information laws, independent media watchdogs, and oversight committees.

2. Invest in social welfare programs: Investing in social welfare programs and other essential services can help to ensure that resources are allocated in a way that benefits all members of society. This can help to reduce the risk of economic and social inequality, which can contribute to the rise of militarization.

3. Promote education and civic engagement: Promoting education and civic engagement can help to promote democratic values and norms and empower citizens to hold their leaders accountable. This can involve measures such as media literacy programs, public education campaigns, and the promotion of civil society organizations.

4. Foster international cooperation: Working with other countries and international organizations to promote peace and security can help to create a more peaceful and secure international environment, where the use of military force is less necessary. This can involve promoting greater cooperation on disarmament, conflict prevention, and peace-building.

5. Strengthen legal frameworks: Strengthening legal frameworks, such as international humanitarian law and domestic legislation, can help to ensure that the use of military force is consistent with human rights and international law. This can involve measures such as establishing clear standards for the use of force, promoting accountability for human rights violations, and providing avenues for legal recourse.

6. Promote environmental sustainability: Promoting environmental sustainability can help to reduce the environmental impact of military activities, such as the development and testing of weapons, and promote a more peaceful and sustainable world. This can involve measures such as promoting renewable energy, reducing waste and pollution, and protecting ecosystems and biodiversity.

87

Nuclear accidents

Nuclear power has been a source of energy for several decades, providing reliable, clean energy to communities around the world. However, nuclear power plants are also a source of risk, as accidents can lead to significant environmental damage and loss of life. Despite significant advances in nuclear technology and safety, the risk of nuclear accidents remains a major concern for many individuals and communities.

One of the most significant risks of nuclear accidents is the potential for radiation exposure. Radiation can cause a range of health problems, including cancer, birth defects, and other serious illnesses. In the event of a nuclear accident, the release of radiation can lead to significant health risks for individuals in the surrounding area, as well as those who may be exposed to radiation through food, water, or other sources.

Nuclear accidents can also have significant environmental consequences. In addition to the immediate effects of radiation exposure, nuclear accidents can lead to long-term environmental damage, including contamination of soil and water, destruction of ecosystems, and damage to agriculture and other industries.

Finally, nuclear accidents can also have significant economic consequences. In addition to the cost of cleanup and recovery efforts, nuclear accidents can also lead to significant economic disruption, as communities and industries may be forced to shut down or relocate in the aftermath of an accident.

Addressing the risk of nuclear accidents requires a range of solutions. Ensuring the safety of nuclear power plants requires ongoing monitoring, maintenance, and investment in safety systems and protocols. Additionally, promoting greater transparency and accountability in the nuclear industry can help to ensure that risks are identified and addressed in a timely and effective manner.

Investing in renewable energy sources, such as wind and solar power, can help to reduce the demand for nuclear power and minimize the risks associated with nuclear energy. Promoting greater international cooperation on nuclear safety can also help to ensure that best practices are shared and that countries are held accountable for meeting safety standards.

Finally, promoting education and awareness of the risks of nuclear accidents can help to build a more informed and engaged citizenry, which is better equipped to advocate for safer and more sustainable energy policies.

The risk of nuclear accidents remains a significant concern for individuals and communities around the world. While there are no easy solutions to this problem, addressing the risks of nuclear accidents requires a range of approaches that prioritize safety, transparency, and accountability in the nuclear industry, promote renewable energy sources, and foster greater international cooperation. By working together across sectors and across borders, we can build a more just and equitable world where the risks associated with nuclear power are minimized, and where individuals and communities are protected from the potentially devastating effects of nuclear accidents.

Here is a list of some of the most significant nuclear accidents in history, along with their dates, locations, and consequences:

1. Chernobyl, Ukraine (1986) - On April 26, 1986, an explosion at the Chernobyl nuclear power plant released a massive amount of radiation into the environment. The accident caused the deaths of at least 31 people, and led to the evacuation of over 100,000 people from the

surrounding area.

2. Fukushima, Japan (2011) – On March 11, 2011, a massive earthquake and tsunami struck the Fukushima Daiichi nuclear power plant in Japan, causing a meltdown and release of radioactive material. The accident led to the evacuation of over 100,000 people and has had significant environmental and economic consequences.

3. Three Mile Island, USA (1979) – On March 28, 1979, a partial meltdown occurred at the Three Mile Island nuclear power plant in Pennsylvania. The accident led to the release of a small amount of radioactive material and raised concerns about the safety of nuclear power.

4. Kyshtym, Russia (1957) – On September 29, 1957, a storage tank containing nuclear waste exploded at the Mayak nuclear reprocessing plant in Kyshtym, Russia. The accident released significant amounts of radioactive material into the environment and led to the evacuation of thousands of people.

5. Tokaimura, Japan (1999) – On September 30, 1999, a criticality accident occurred at a nuclear fuel processing plant in Tokaimura, Japan. The accident exposed several workers to high levels of radiation and led to the evacuation of thousands of people.

6. Windscale, UK (1957) – On October 10, 1957, a fire broke out at the Windscale nuclear reactor in the UK. The accident released significant amounts of radioactive material into the environment and raised concerns about the safety of nuclear power.

7. Goiânia, Brazil (1987) – On September 13, 1987, a radiation accident occurred in Goiânia, Brazil, when a container of radioactive material was stolen and opened. The accident exposed over 200 people to high levels of radiation and led to several deaths.

8. Sellafield, UK (2014) – On April 19, 2014, a leak of radioactive material occurred at the Sellafield nuclear reprocessing plant in the UK. The accident led to the evacuation of several workers and raised concerns about the safety of nuclear power.

9. SL–1, USA (1961) – On January 3, 1961, a criticality accident occurred at the SL–1 experimental nuclear reactor in Idaho. The accident led to the

deaths of three workers and raised concerns about the safety of nuclear power.

10. Church Rock, USA (1979) - On July 16, 1979, a tailings dam at the Church Rock uranium mill in New Mexico broke, releasing significant amounts of radioactive material into the environment. The accident was one of the largest releases of radioactive material in US history.

These accidents demonstrate the potential risks and consequences associated with nuclear power, highlighting the need for continued efforts to promote safety, transparency, and accountability in the nuclear industry.

Preventing nuclear accidents is a complex challenge that requires a range of solutions. Here are some potential approaches:

1. Promote safety and accountability: Promoting safety and accountability in the nuclear industry can help to prevent nuclear accidents and ensure that the risks associated with nuclear power are minimized. This can involve measures such as investing in safety systems and protocols, ensuring regulatory compliance, and promoting transparency and accountability in decision-making.

2. Develop and promote new technologies: Developing and promoting new technologies, such as advanced nuclear reactors and renewable energy sources, can help to reduce the demand for traditional nuclear power and minimize the risks associated with nuclear energy. This can involve measures such as investing in research and development, promoting innovation and entrepreneurship, and supporting startups in the energy sector.

3. Strengthen emergency response capacity: Strengthening emergency response capacity can help to ensure that the risks associated with nuclear accidents are minimized and that communities are better prepared to respond in the event of an emergency. This can involve measures such as investing in emergency response training and equipment, establishing effective communication networks, and building strong partnerships between government, industry, and civil society

organizations.

4. Promote international cooperation: Promoting greater international cooperation on nuclear safety can help to ensure that best practices are shared and that countries are held accountable for meeting safety standards. This can involve measures such as promoting greater collaboration between national nuclear regulators, supporting international treaties and agreements on nuclear safety, and sharing information and expertise across borders.

5. Promote education and awareness: Promoting education and awareness of the risks and benefits of nuclear power can help to build a more informed and engaged citizenry, which is better equipped to advocate for safer and more sustainable energy policies. This can involve measures such as media literacy programs, public education campaigns, and the promotion of civil society organizations.

88

Terrorism financing

Terrorism financing is the process of providing financial support to individuals or groups who carry out terrorist activities. The risks associated with terrorism financing are significant and can have far-reaching consequences for individuals, communities, and society as a whole.

One of the most significant risks associated with terrorism financing is the potential for terrorist groups to carry out attacks against civilians and critical infrastructure. These attacks can lead to loss of life, destruction of property, and significant economic disruption. The funding provided to terrorist groups can also enable them to expand their operations, recruit new members, and increase their influence in vulnerable communities.

Terrorism financing can also have significant consequences for global security. The funds provided to terrorist groups can be used to support transnational terrorist networks, which can have a destabilizing effect on regions and countries around the world. In addition, the use of financial institutions and money laundering techniques can make it difficult to track and disrupt terrorist financing networks.

Furthermore, terrorism financing can have a negative impact on the global economy. The diversion of funds from legitimate economic activities to support terrorist groups can lead to reduced economic growth and increased poverty, particularly in countries that are already vulnerable to economic instability.

Addressing the risk of terrorism financing requires a range of solutions. Governments and financial institutions can play a key role in disrupting terrorist financing networks by implementing and enforcing laws and regulations that target the financing of terrorism. This can involve measures such as freezing assets, imposing sanctions, and strengthening anti-money laundering laws.

Promoting greater international cooperation and information-sharing can also help to disrupt terrorist financing networks and prevent the flow of funds to terrorist groups. This can involve measures such as sharing financial intelligence, coordinating investigations and prosecutions, and supporting international efforts to combat terrorist financing.

Finally, promoting economic development and financial inclusion can help to reduce the vulnerability of individuals and communities to terrorist financing. This can involve measures such as promoting access to financial services, supporting small and medium-sized enterprises, and investing in education and training to promote financial literacy.

Terrorism financing is a significant risk that requires a range of solutions to address. By implementing and enforcing laws and regulations, promoting greater international cooperation and information-sharing, and supporting economic development and financial inclusion, we can work to disrupt terrorist financing networks and prevent the flow of funds to terrorist groups. By working together across sectors and across borders, we can build a more just and secure world where the risks associated with terrorism financing are minimized, and individuals and communities are protected from the devastating effects of terrorism.

terrorism financing requires a range of solutions. Here are some potential approaches:

1. Strengthen laws and regulations: Strengthening laws and regulations related to terrorism financing can help to disrupt the flow of funds to terrorist groups. This can involve measures such as freezing assets, imposing sanctions, and strengthening anti-money laundering laws.

2. Promote international cooperation: Promoting greater international cooperation and information-sharing can help to disrupt terrorist financing networks and prevent the flow of funds to terrorist groups. This can involve measures such as sharing financial intelligence, coordinating investigations and prosecutions, and supporting international efforts to combat terrorism financing.

3. Enhance financial institution measures: Financial institutions can play a key role in preventing terrorism financing by implementing and enforcing strong measures to detect and prevent suspicious transactions. This can involve measures such as monitoring for unusual transactions, conducting customer due diligence, and implementing anti-money laundering programs.

4. Promote financial inclusion: Promoting financial inclusion can help to reduce the vulnerability of individuals and communities to terrorism financing. This can involve measures such as promoting access to financial services, supporting small and medium-sized enterprises, and investing in education and training to promote financial literacy.

5. Disrupt the financing of extremist ideology: Disrupting the financing of extremist ideology can help to reduce the appeal of terrorism to vulnerable individuals and communities. This can involve measures such as promoting counter-narratives, working with social media companies to remove extremist content, and supporting education and awareness campaigns.

6. Strengthen law enforcement and intelligence agencies: Strengthening law enforcement and intelligence agencies can help to disrupt terrorist financing networks and prevent terrorist attacks. This can involve measures such as investing in training and equipment, enhancing international cooperation, and promoting a whole-of-government approach to countering terrorism financing.

Overall, addressing terrorism financing will require a range of approaches that prioritize strengthening laws and regulations, promoting international cooperation, enhancing financial institution measures, promoting financial inclusion, disrupting the financing of extremist ideology, and strengthening law enforcement and intelligence agencies. By working together across sectors and across borders, we can build a more just and secure world where the risks associated with terrorism financing are minimized, and individuals and communities are protected from the devastating effects of terrorism.

89

Political extremism

Political extremism has been a persistent challenge throughout history, and there are concerns that it could continue to be a significant risk in the future. Political extremism is characterized by a radical and uncompromising commitment to political ideals, often at the expense of democratic institutions and civil liberties.

One of the most significant risks of political extremism is the potential for violence and instability. Extremist groups may resort to violence to achieve their political goals, which can lead to loss of life, destruction of property, and significant economic disruption. In addition, political extremism can undermine democratic institutions and processes, leading to political instability and a breakdown in the rule of law.

Another risk of political extremism is the potential for discrimination and human rights abuses. Extremist groups may promote discriminatory and exclusionary policies that target specific groups based on their race, ethnicity, religion, or other characteristics. This can lead to a range of human rights abuses, including the denial of basic freedoms and opportunities.

Addressing the risk of political extremism requires a range of solutions. Promoting greater transparency, accountability, and the rule of law can help to strengthen democratic institutions and prevent the rise of extremist groups. This can involve measures such as promoting media literacy, fostering a culture of civil discourse, and supporting independent journalism and media outlets.

Investing in education and promoting intercultural dialogue can also help to reduce the appeal of political extremism and promote greater understanding and tolerance. This can involve measures such as promoting access to education and opportunities, supporting cultural exchange programs, and investing in community-based initiatives that promote diversity and inclusion.

Finally, promoting economic development and sustainable growth can help to reduce the social and economic factors that can contribute to the rise of political extremism. This can involve measures such as investing in infrastructure, supporting entrepreneurship and innovation, and promoting sustainable development practices.

The risk of political extremism remains a significant challenge for individuals, communities, and society as a whole. By promoting greater transparency, accountability, and the rule of law, investing in education and intercultural dialogue, and promoting economic development and sustainable growth, we can work to reduce the appeal of political extremism and build a more just and equitable world where democratic institutions and civil liberties are protected and valued.

Addressing political extremism requires a range of solutions. Here are some potential approaches:

1. Promote transparency and accountability: Promoting transparency and accountability in government and political processes can help to prevent the rise of extremist groups. This can involve measures such as promoting media literacy, fostering a culture of civil discourse, and supporting independent journalism and media outlets.

2. Invest in education: Investing in education can help to reduce the appeal of political extremism and promote greater understanding and tolerance. This can involve measures such as promoting access to education and opportunities, supporting cultural exchange programs, and investing in community-based initiatives that promote diversity

and inclusion.

3. Support intercultural dialogue: Supporting intercultural dialogue can help to reduce tensions between different communities and promote a sense of common identity. This can involve measures such as promoting cultural exchange programs, supporting community-based initiatives that promote diversity and inclusion, and fostering a culture of civil discourse.

4. Strengthen democratic institutions: Strengthening democratic institutions can help to prevent the rise of extremist groups and promote greater stability and security. This can involve measures such as investing in election security, promoting transparency and accountability in government, and supporting independent civil society organizations.

5. Promote economic development: Promoting economic development can help to reduce the social and economic factors that can contribute to the rise of political extremism. This can involve measures such as investing in infrastructure, supporting entrepreneurship and innovation, and promoting sustainable development practices.

6. Foster greater international cooperation: Promoting greater international cooperation can help to prevent the spread of extremist ideologies and promote a more stable and secure world. This can involve measures such as supporting international treaties and agreements, promoting cross-border collaboration on security issues, and investing in diplomatic and humanitarian initiatives.

90

Voter suppression

Voter suppression is a tactic used to prevent eligible voters from exercising their right to vote. This can take many forms, including voter ID laws, gerrymandering, and voter intimidation. The risks associated with voter suppression are significant and can have far-reaching consequences for individuals, communities, and society as a whole.

One of the most significant risks associated with voter suppression is the potential for a lack of representation. When eligible voters are prevented from exercising their right to vote, their voices are not heard in the democratic process. This can lead to a lack of representation for marginalized communities, as well as a lack of accountability for elected officials.

Another risk of voter suppression is the potential for the erosion of democratic institutions and processes. When individuals and communities are prevented from exercising their right to vote, it can undermine the legitimacy of democratic institutions and processes. This can lead to a breakdown in the rule of law and a lack of trust in government.

Addressing the risk of voter suppression requires a range of solutions. Promoting greater access to the ballot box can help to ensure that eligible voters are able to exercise their right to vote. This can involve measures such as expanding early voting, implementing same-day voter registration, and promoting absentee voting.

Strengthening election security can also help to prevent voter suppression. This can involve measures such as investing in cybersecurity, ensuring the accuracy of voter rolls, and promoting transparency in the voting process.

Fostering greater civic engagement can also help to prevent voter suppression. This can involve measures such as promoting media literacy, supporting community-based initiatives that promote voter participation, and investing in education and awareness campaigns.

Finally, promoting greater accountability for elected officials can help to prevent voter suppression. This can involve measures such as promoting transparency and accountability in government, supporting independent civil society organizations, and investing in efforts to combat corruption.

The risk of voter suppression is a significant challenge for individuals, communities, and society as a whole. By promoting greater access to the ballot box, strengthening election security, fostering greater civic engagement, and promoting greater accountability for elected officials, we can work to prevent voter suppression and ensure that the democratic process is fair, transparent, and inclusive. By working together across sectors and across borders, we can build a more just and equitable world where the right to vote is protected and valued.

Addressing voter suppression requires a range of solutions. Here are some potential approaches:

1. Promote greater access to the ballot box: Promoting greater access to the ballot box can help to ensure that eligible voters are able to exercise their right to vote. This can involve measures such as expanding early voting, implementing same-day voter registration, and promoting absentee voting.
2. Strengthen election security: Strengthening election security can help to prevent voter suppression. This can involve measures such as investing in cybersecurity, ensuring the accuracy of voter rolls, and promoting transparency in the voting process.
3. Foster greater civic engagement: Fostering greater civic engagement

can help to prevent voter suppression. This can involve measures such as promoting media literacy, supporting community-based initiatives that promote voter participation, and investing in education and awareness campaigns.

4. Promote greater accountability for elected officials: Promoting greater accountability for elected officials can help to prevent voter suppression. This can involve measures such as promoting transparency and accountability in government, supporting independent civil society organizations, and investing in efforts to combat corruption.

5. Challenge discriminatory policies and practices: Challenging discriminatory policies and practices can help to prevent voter suppression. This can involve measures such as challenging voter ID laws that disproportionately affect marginalized communities, advocating for fair and impartial redistricting processes, and addressing voter intimidation tactics.

6. Strengthen the legal framework: Strengthening the legal framework can help to prevent voter suppression. This can involve measures such as supporting organizations that provide legal support to individuals and communities affected by voter suppression, advocating for the enforcement of existing laws and regulations, and pushing for the adoption of new legislation that promotes greater access to the ballot box.

X

Cultural Risks

Cultural risks refer to the potential challenges and threats posed by cultural factors such as stereotypes, prejudices, and discrimination.These risks can include a lack of cultural awareness and understanding, the perpetuation of harmful stereotypes, and the marginalization of minority communities. Addressing cultural risks requires a range of solutions, including promoting diversity and inclusion, investing in education and awareness-raising initiatives, and challenging discriminatory policies

91

Cultural erosion

Cultural erosion refers to the loss or degradation of cultural traditions, practices, and beliefs over time. This can occur due to a range of factors, including globalization, urbanization, and the influence of dominant cultural forces. The risks associated with cultural erosion are significant and can have far-reaching consequences for individuals, communities, and society as a whole.

One of the most significant risks associated with cultural erosion is the potential loss of identity and heritage. When cultural traditions and practices are lost or degraded, individuals and communities may experience a loss of connection to their history, language, and customs. This can lead to a sense of dislocation and alienation, as well as a lack of understanding and appreciation for other cultures.

Another risk of cultural erosion is the potential for the loss of knowledge and wisdom. Many cultural traditions and practices are rooted in centuries-old knowledge and wisdom that have been passed down from generation to generation. When these traditions are lost or degraded, the knowledge and wisdom they contain may also be lost.

Addressing the risk of cultural erosion requires a range of solutions. Promoting cultural preservation can help to ensure that cultural traditions and practices are preserved for future generations. This can involve measures such as supporting cultural institutions and organizations, promoting cultural exchange programs, and investing in education and awareness-raising initiatives.

Fostering greater cultural awareness and understanding can also help to prevent cultural erosion. This can involve measures such as promoting intercultural dialogue, supporting cultural education programs, and investing in initiatives that promote cultural diversity and inclusion.

Finally, promoting sustainable development practices can help to prevent the negative impacts of globalization and urbanization on cultural traditions and practices. This can involve measures such as promoting community-based development initiatives, supporting local economies, and investing in sustainable tourism practices that respect and support local cultures.

The risk of cultural erosion is a significant challenge for individuals, communities, and society as a whole. By promoting cultural preservation, fostering greater cultural awareness and understanding, and promoting sustainable development practices, we can work to prevent cultural erosion and ensure that cultural traditions and practices are preserved and valued. By working together across sectors and across borders, we can build a more just and equitable world where the richness and diversity of cultural heritage is celebrated and protected.

Addressing cultural erosion requires a range of solutions. Here are some potential approaches:

1. Promote cultural preservation: Promoting cultural preservation can help to ensure that cultural traditions and practices are preserved for future generations. This can involve measures such as supporting cultural institutions and organizations, promoting cultural exchange programs, and investing in education and awareness-raising initiatives.
2. Foster greater cultural awareness and understanding: Fostering greater cultural awareness and understanding can help to prevent cultural erosion. This can involve measures such as promoting intercultural dialogue, supporting cultural education programs, and investing in initiatives that promote cultural diversity and inclusion.
3. Encourage the sharing of cultural knowledge: Encouraging the sharing

of cultural knowledge can help to prevent the loss of knowledge and wisdom associated with cultural erosion. This can involve measures such as supporting community-based initiatives that promote the sharing of traditional knowledge, investing in cultural education programs, and promoting cultural exchange programs.

4. Support community-based development initiatives: Supporting community-based development initiatives can help to prevent the negative impacts of globalization and urbanization on cultural traditions and practices. This can involve measures such as supporting local economies, promoting sustainable tourism practices that respect and support local cultures, and investing in community-based initiatives that promote cultural diversity and inclusion.

5. Challenge discriminatory policies and practices: Challenging discriminatory policies and practices can help to prevent cultural erosion. This can involve measures such as advocating for the recognition of cultural diversity and promoting policies that support cultural preservation and diversity.

92

Language extinction

Language extinction refers to the phenomenon of languages disappearing over time as fewer and fewer people speak them. The risk of language extinction is significant and can have far-reaching consequences for individuals, communities, and society as a whole.

One of the most significant risks associated with language extinction is the loss of cultural heritage. Languages are often closely tied to cultural traditions, practices, and beliefs. When a language becomes extinct, the knowledge and wisdom contained within that language may also be lost, leading to a loss of cultural identity and heritage.

Another risk of language extinction is the potential for a lack of diversity and representation. Languages reflect the unique perspectives and experiences of the communities that speak them. When a language becomes extinct, the diversity of human experience is diminished, leading to a lack of representation for minority communities.

Addressing the risk of language extinction requires a range of solutions. Promoting language preservation can help to ensure that languages are preserved for future generations. This can involve measures such as supporting language learning programs, investing in language documentation and revitalization efforts, and promoting multilingualism and language education.

Fostering greater cultural awareness and understanding can also help to prevent language extinction. This can involve measures such as promoting intercultural dialogue, supporting cultural education programs, and investing in initiatives that promote cultural diversity and inclusion.

Finally, supporting community-based initiatives that promote the use and preservation of endangered languages can also help to prevent language extinction. This can involve measures such as supporting local language revitalization projects, promoting multilingualism in communities, and investing in language preservation efforts.

the risk of language extinction is a significant challenge for individuals, communities, and society as a whole. By promoting language preservation, fostering greater cultural awareness and understanding, and supporting community-based initiatives that promote the use and preservation of endangered languages, we can work to prevent language extinction and ensure that the diversity and richness of human experience is celebrated and protected. By working together across sectors and across borders, we can build a more just and equitable world where the unique perspectives and experiences of all communities are valued and preserved.

There are numerous languages that are currently endangered or have gone extinct over the years. Here are some examples:

1. Eyak - This indigenous language was spoken in Alaska, but the last native speaker passed away in 2008.
2. Livonian - This Finno-Ugric language was once spoken in Latvia, but it is now considered extinct as the last native speaker passed away in 2013.
3. Manx - This Celtic language was once spoken on the Isle of Man, but it went extinct in the 20th century. However, efforts have been made to revive the language, and there are now a small number of fluent speakers.
4. Aka-Bo - This language was spoken by a small community in India, but it is now considered extinct as there are no known living speakers.
5. Kusunda - This language was spoken in Nepal, but it is now considered critically endangered as there are only a handful of known speakers

left.

6. Njerep - This language was spoken in Nigeria, but it is now considered extinct as the last known speaker passed away in 2009.
7. Pazeh - This indigenous language was spoken in Taiwan, but it is now considered extinct as there are no known living speakers.

These are just a few examples of the many languages that are at risk of extinction or have already gone extinct. The loss of these languages represents a significant loss of cultural heritage and diversity, and efforts are being made around the world to preserve and revitalize endangered languages.

the risk of language extinction requires a range of solutions. Here are some potential approaches:

1. Promote language preservation: Promoting language preservation can help to ensure that endangered languages are preserved for future generations. This can involve measures such as supporting language learning programs, investing in language documentation and revitalization efforts, and promoting multilingualism and language education.
2. Fostering greater cultural awareness and understanding: Fostering greater cultural awareness and understanding can help to prevent language extinction. This can involve measures such as promoting intercultural dialogue, supporting cultural education programs, and investing in initiatives that promote cultural diversity and inclusion.
3. Encourage the sharing of linguistic knowledge: Encouraging the sharing of linguistic knowledge can help to prevent the loss of knowledge and wisdom associated with language extinction. This can involve measures such as supporting community-based initiatives that promote the sharing of traditional knowledge, investing in linguistic education programs, and promoting linguistic exchange programs.

4. Support community-based initiatives: Supporting community-based initiatives that promote the use and preservation of endangered languages can help to prevent language extinction. This can involve measures such as supporting local language revitalization projects, promoting multilingualism in communities, and investing in language preservation efforts.

5. Document and archive endangered languages: Documenting and archiving endangered languages can help to preserve linguistic diversity and knowledge for future generations. This can involve measures such as creating language archives, investing in linguistic documentation projects, and supporting research into endangered languages.

6. Promote policy initiatives: Promoting policy initiatives that support language preservation can help to prevent language extinction. This can involve measures such as promoting multilingualism in education and government, advocating for the recognition of linguistic diversity, and supporting policies that preserve and promote endangered languages.

93

Religious conflict

Religious conflict refers to the phenomenon of conflicts and tensions that arise between different religious groups or communities. The risk of religious conflict is significant and can have far-reaching consequences for individuals, communities, and society as a whole.

One of the most significant risks associated with religious conflict is the potential for violence and destruction. Religious conflicts can lead to acts of violence, including terrorism, hate crimes, and sectarian violence. These acts can result in loss of life and property, as well as long-term social, economic, and political instability.

Another risk of religious conflict is the potential for the breakdown of social cohesion and trust. Religious conflicts can deepen divisions and mistrust between different religious communities, leading to a breakdown in social cohesion and a weakening of the bonds that hold society together.

Addressing the risk of religious conflict requires a range of solutions. Promoting interfaith dialogue and understanding can help to prevent religious conflict by fostering greater understanding and respect between different religious communities. This can involve measures such as promoting interfaith events and initiatives, supporting interfaith organizations and networks, and investing in interfaith education and awareness-raising initiatives.

Fostering greater social cohesion and trust can also help to prevent religious conflict. This can involve measures such as promoting inclusive policies and practices that support social cohesion, investing in community-based initiatives that promote intercultural dialogue, and promoting greater access to education and economic opportunities for marginalized communities.

Finally, supporting conflict prevention and resolution efforts can also help to prevent religious conflict. This can involve measures such as supporting mediation and conflict resolution initiatives, promoting dialogue and negotiation, and investing in efforts to address the root causes of conflict, such as inequality, poverty, and political instability.

The risk of religious conflict is a significant challenge for individuals, communities, and society as a whole. By promoting interfaith dialogue and understanding, fostering greater social cohesion and trust, and supporting conflict prevention and resolution efforts, we can work to prevent religious conflict and build a more just and peaceful world where the diversity of religious beliefs and practices is respected and valued. By working together across sectors and across borders, we can build a more inclusive and equitable world where religious differences are celebrated and conflicts are prevented.

Addressing the risk of religious conflict requires a range of solutions. Here are some potential approaches:

1. Promote interfaith dialogue and understanding: Promoting interfaith dialogue and understanding can help to prevent religious conflict by fostering greater understanding and respect between different religious communities. This can involve measures such as promoting interfaith events and initiatives, supporting interfaith organizations and networks, and investing in interfaith education and awareness-raising initiatives.

2. Foster greater social cohesion and trust: Fostering greater social cohesion and trust can also help to prevent religious conflict. This can involve measures such as promoting inclusive policies and practices

that support social cohesion, investing in community-based initiatives that promote intercultural dialogue, and promoting greater access to education and economic opportunities for marginalized communities.

3. Support conflict prevention and resolution efforts: Supporting conflict prevention and resolution efforts can help to prevent religious conflict. This can involve measures such as supporting mediation and conflict resolution initiatives, promoting dialogue and negotiation, and investing in efforts to address the root causes of conflict, such as inequality, poverty, and political instability.

4. Address structural inequality and discrimination: Addressing structural inequality and discrimination can help to prevent religious conflict by promoting greater equality and justice for all communities. This can involve measures such as advocating for policies that promote equality and justice, supporting organizations that work to address discrimination and prejudice, and investing in education and awareness-raising initiatives that promote diversity and inclusion.

5. Promote freedom of religion: Promoting freedom of religion can help to prevent religious conflict by ensuring that all individuals and communities are free to practice their religion without fear of persecution or discrimination. This can involve measures such as advocating for policies that promote freedom of religion, supporting organizations that work to protect religious minorities, and investing in education and awareness-raising initiatives that promote tolerance and understanding.

<h1 style="text-align:center">94</h1>

Globalization backlash

Globalization is the phenomenon of increased interconnectedness and interdependence between countries, facilitated by advancements in communication, transportation, and technology. While globalization has brought many benefits such as increased economic growth, improved access to goods and services, and greater cultural exchange, it has also led to a backlash in some communities.

The risk of globalization backlash refers to the tensions and conflicts that arise when individuals or communities perceive that the benefits of globalization are not being evenly distributed, or when globalization is seen as a threat to local cultures and traditions.

One of the most significant risks associated with globalization backlash is the potential for economic and political instability. As globalization has led to increased economic integration, it has also created winners and losers. Communities that are left behind by globalization may feel a sense of economic and political disenfranchisement, which can lead to social unrest and political instability.

Another risk of globalization backlash is the potential for the breakdown of social cohesion and trust. Globalization can lead to the homogenization of cultural practices and traditions, which can threaten the identity and sense of belonging of local communities. This can lead to social divisions and mistrust between different communities, which can further exacerbate tensions and conflicts.

Addressing the risk of globalization backlash requires a range of solutions. Promoting inclusive economic growth can help to ensure that the benefits of globalization are distributed more evenly. This can involve measures such as investing in education and training programs, promoting local economic development, and supporting small and medium-sized enterprises.

Fostering greater cultural awareness and understanding can also help to prevent globalization backlash. This can involve measures such as promoting cultural exchange programs, supporting local cultural initiatives, and investing in intercultural education and awareness-raising initiatives.

Finally, promoting greater democratic participation and transparency can also help to prevent globalization backlash. This can involve measures such as promoting open and transparent governance, increasing citizen participation in decision-making processes, and investing in initiatives that promote democratic values and practices.

The risk of globalization backlash is a significant challenge for individuals, communities, and society as a whole. By promoting inclusive economic growth, fostering greater cultural awareness and understanding, and promoting greater democratic participation and transparency, we can work to prevent globalization backlash and build a more just and equitable world where the benefits of globalization are shared by all. By working together across sectors and across borders, we can build a more inclusive and equitable world where cultural differences are celebrated and tensions are prevented.

Addressing the risk of globalization backlash requires a range of solutions. Here are some potential approaches:

1. Promote inclusive economic growth: Promoting inclusive economic growth can help to ensure that the benefits of globalization are distributed more evenly. This can involve measures such as investing in education and training programs, promoting local economic develop-

ment, and supporting small and medium-sized enterprises.

2. Foster greater cultural awareness and understanding: Fostering greater cultural awareness and understanding can help to prevent globalization backlash. This can involve measures such as promoting cultural exchange programs, supporting local cultural initiatives, and investing in intercultural education and awareness-raising initiatives.

3. Promote greater democratic participation and transparency: Promoting greater democratic participation and transparency can also help to prevent globalization backlash. This can involve measures such as promoting open and transparent governance, increasing citizen participation in decision-making processes, and investing in initiatives that promote democratic values and practices.

4. Address concerns about job displacement: Addressing concerns about job displacement can also help to prevent globalization backlash. This can involve measures such as investing in retraining and reskilling programs, supporting job creation initiatives in affected communities, and promoting policies that ensure fair labor standards and protections.

5. Support local communities and industries: Supporting local communities and industries can help to ensure that the benefits of globalization are felt at the local level. This can involve measures such as supporting local business initiatives, promoting local products and services, and investing in infrastructure and development programs that benefit local communities.

95

Urbanization

Urbanization is the process of increasing the proportion of the population living in urban areas, often resulting in the growth of cities and the expansion of urban infrastructure. While urbanization can bring many benefits such as increased economic growth, improved access to education, healthcare and other services, it also poses a number of risks.

One of the most significant risks associated with urbanization is the potential for environmental degradation. Urban areas often suffer from poor air quality, water pollution, and land degradation, which can have negative impacts on public health and the environment.

Another risk of urbanization is the potential for social and economic inequality. Urban areas often attract migrants seeking employment opportunities, but these migrants may struggle to find affordable housing, access to services, and social inclusion. This can lead to the development of informal settlements, where residents lack access to basic services and live in poor conditions.

Additionally, urbanization can lead to increased social isolation and decreased social cohesion. As cities grow, individuals may feel disconnected from their communities and experience a loss of social capital. This can lead to decreased trust and cooperation between individuals and groups, which can further exacerbate social and economic inequality.

Addressing the risks associated with urbanization requires a range of solutions. Promoting sustainable urban planning can help to mitigate the negative impacts of urbanization on the environment. This can involve measures such as promoting public transportation, investing in green spaces, and implementing waste management and recycling programs.

Fostering greater social inclusion and reducing inequality can also help to address the risks associated with urbanization. This can involve measures such as promoting affordable housing initiatives, investing in education and training programs, and supporting community-based initiatives that promote social cohesion and inclusion.

Finally, promoting greater citizen participation in urban planning and governance can also help to address the risks associated with urbanization. This can involve measures such as promoting public participation in decision-making processes, investing in initiatives that promote democratic values and practices, and supporting local government transparency and accountability.

The risks associated with urbanization are significant and require a range of solutions that prioritize promoting sustainable urban planning, fostering greater social inclusion and reducing inequality, and promoting greater citizen participation in urban planning and governance. By working together across sectors and across borders, we can build more just and equitable cities that are environmentally sustainable and promote social cohesion and inclusion.

urbanization requires a range of solutions. Here are some potential approaches:

1. Promote sustainable urban planning: Promoting sustainable urban planning can help to mitigate the negative impacts of urbanization on the environment. This can involve measures such as promoting public transportation, investing in green spaces, and implementing waste management and recycling programs.

2. Foster greater social inclusion and reduce inequality: Fostering greater

social inclusion and reducing inequality can also help to address the risks associated with urbanization. This can involve measures such as promoting affordable housing initiatives, investing in education and training programs, and supporting community-based initiatives that promote social cohesion and inclusion.

3. Promote citizen participation in urban planning and governance: Promoting greater citizen participation in urban planning and governance can also help to address the risks associated with urbanization. This can involve measures such as promoting public participation in decision-making processes, investing in initiatives that promote democratic values and practices, and supporting local government transparency and accountability.

4. Invest in infrastructure and services: Investing in infrastructure and services can help to support sustainable urbanization. This can involve measures such as investing in public transportation systems, water and sanitation systems, and waste management systems.

5. Support economic growth and job creation: Supporting economic growth and job creation can help to reduce inequality and promote social inclusion. This can involve measures such as promoting small business development, investing in education and training programs, and supporting innovation and entrepreneurship.

96

Migration

Migration refers to the movement of people from one location to another, often driven by economic, political, social, or environmental factors. While migration has been a fundamental aspect of human history, it also poses a number of risks in the modern world.

One of the most significant risks associated with migration is the potential for social and economic inequality. Migrants often face discrimination and may struggle to find affordable housing, access to services, and social inclusion. This can lead to the development of informal settlements, where residents lack access to basic services and live in poor conditions.

Another risk of migration is the potential for political instability and conflict. Migrants may face hostility and resentment from local communities, which can lead to social unrest and political instability. This can further exacerbate the social and economic inequality that migrants face, leading to a cycle of poverty and exclusion.

Additionally, migration can also pose risks to public health. Migrants may face barriers to accessing healthcare and may be more susceptible to infectious diseases due to poor living conditions and lack of access to healthcare.

Addressing the risks associated with migration requires a range of solutions. Promoting inclusive policies and practices can help to reduce the social and economic inequality faced by migrants. This can involve measures such as promoting affordable housing initiatives, investing in education and training programs, and supporting community-based initiatives that promote social cohesion and inclusion.

Fostering greater understanding and respect for diversity can also help to address the risks associated with migration. This can involve measures such as promoting intercultural dialogue, investing in language and cultural education programs, and supporting initiatives that promote social integration.

Finally, addressing the root causes of migration is also critical to mitigating its risks. This can involve measures such as investing in sustainable economic development, addressing political instability and conflict, and supporting initiatives that promote environmental sustainability.

The risks associated with migration are significant and require a range of solutions that prioritize promoting inclusive policies and practices, fostering greater understanding and respect for diversity, and addressing the root causes of migration. By working together across sectors and across borders, we can build more just and equitable societies that promote social inclusion, diversity, and sustainable development for all.

Addressing the risks associated with migration requires a range of solutions. Here are some potential approaches:

1. Promote inclusive policies and practices: Promoting inclusive policies and practices can help to reduce the social and economic inequality faced by migrants. This can involve measures such as promoting affordable housing initiatives, investing in education and training programs, and supporting community-based initiatives that promote social cohesion and inclusion.

2. Fostering greater understanding and respect for diversity: Fostering greater understanding and respect for diversity can also help to address the risks associated with migration. This can involve measures such as promoting intercultural dialogue, investing in language and cultural

education programs, and supporting initiatives that promote social integration.

3. Addressing the root causes of migration: Addressing the root causes of migration is critical to mitigating its risks. This can involve measures such as investing in sustainable economic development, addressing political instability and conflict, and supporting initiatives that promote environmental sustainability.

4. Supporting access to healthcare: Supporting access to healthcare can help to reduce the risks associated with migration to public health. This can involve measures such as investing in healthcare infrastructure, promoting awareness-raising initiatives about healthcare services, and supporting healthcare programs for migrants.

5. Promote legal and safe migration: Promoting legal and safe migration can help to reduce the risks associated with irregular migration. This can involve measures such as promoting legal migration channels, supporting international protection systems, and investing in border management policies that prioritize human rights.

97

Historical revisionism

Historical revisionism refers to the reinterpretation of historical events and facts with the aim of changing the historical narrative or promoting a particular political agenda. While historical revisionism can have legitimate and constructive purposes, such as correcting historical inaccuracies or re-evaluating past events, it also poses a number of risks in the future.

One of the most significant risks associated with historical revisionism is the potential for eroding social and cultural cohesion. Historical revisionism can promote a distorted and inaccurate understanding of history, which can lead to the development of conflicting and competing narratives that undermine social and cultural cohesion.

Another risk of historical revisionism is the potential for promoting extremist ideologies and radicalization. Historical revisionism can be used as a tool to promote extremist ideologies that are based on distorted or falsified historical narratives. This can lead to the radicalization of individuals and the development of extremist movements that threaten social and political stability.

Additionally, historical revisionism can also pose risks to the preservation of cultural heritage and diversity. By distorting or erasing aspects of history, historical revisionism can contribute to the loss of cultural heritage and diversity, which can have negative impacts on social cohesion and the preservation of cultural identity.

Addressing the risks associated with historical revisionism requires a range of solutions. Promoting critical thinking and media literacy can help to prevent the spread of false or misleading historical narratives. This can involve measures such as promoting media literacy education in schools, investing in fact-checking initiatives, and supporting media outlets that prioritize accuracy and objectivity.

Fostering greater respect for diversity and cultural heritage can also help to prevent the risks associated with historical revisionism. This can involve measures such as promoting cultural exchange programs, investing in cultural heritage preservation initiatives, and supporting intercultural dialogue and awareness-raising initiatives.

Finally, promoting democratic values and practices can also help to prevent the risks associated with historical revisionism. This can involve measures such as promoting open and transparent governance, increasing citizen participation in decision-making processes, and investing in initiatives that promote democratic values and practices.

The risks associated with historical revisionism are significant and require a range of solutions that prioritize promoting critical thinking and media literacy, fostering greater respect for diversity and cultural heritage, and promoting democratic values and practices. By working together across sectors and across borders, we can build a more just and equitable world where the preservation of accurate history, cultural heritage, and social cohesion are prioritized.

Addressing the risks associated with historical revisionism requires a range of solutions. Here are some potential approaches:

1. Promote critical thinking and media literacy: Promoting critical thinking and media literacy can help to prevent the spread of false or misleading historical narratives. This can involve measures such as promoting media literacy education in schools, investing in fact-checking initiatives, and supporting media outlets that prioritize accuracy and objectivity.

2. Foster greater respect for diversity and cultural heritage: Fostering greater respect for diversity and cultural heritage can also help to prevent the risks associated with historical revisionism. This can involve measures such as promoting cultural exchange programs, investing in cultural heritage preservation initiatives, and supporting intercultural dialogue and awareness-raising initiatives.

3. Promote democratic values and practices: Promoting democratic values and practices can also help to prevent the risks associated with historical revisionism. This can involve measures such as promoting open and transparent governance, increasing citizen participation in decision-making processes, and investing in initiatives that promote democratic values and practices.

4. Support independent research and scholarship: Supporting independent research and scholarship can help to promote accurate and objective historical narratives. This can involve measures such as investing in research and scholarship programs, supporting academic institutions and organizations that prioritize accuracy and objectivity, and promoting initiatives that support open access to information and data.

5. Encourage fact-checking and accountability: Encouraging fact-checking and accountability can also help to prevent the spread of false or misleading historical narratives. This can involve measures such as promoting independent fact-checking initiatives, investing in journalism and investigative reporting, and supporting initiatives that promote accountability and transparency in government and media.

Overall, addressing the risks associated with historical revisionism will require a range of approaches that prioritize promoting critical thinking and media literacy, fostering greater respect for diversity and cultural heritage, promoting democratic values and practices, supporting independent research and scholarship, and encouraging fact-checking and accountability. By working together across sectors and across borders, we can build a more just and equitable world where accurate history, cultural heritage, and social cohesion are prioritized.

98

Mass media manipulation

Mass media manipulation refers to the use of media channels such as television, newspapers, social media, and other digital platforms to manipulate public opinion, shape political outcomes, and influence social and cultural values. While mass media manipulation has been a concern for many years, it poses significant risks in the future.

One of the most significant risks associated with mass media manipulation is the potential for eroding democratic values and practices. Mass media manipulation can be used as a tool to manipulate public opinion, distort facts and promote misinformation, and undermine the democratic process. This can lead to a loss of public trust in government, media, and other institutions.

Another risk of mass media manipulation is the potential for promoting extremist ideologies and radicalization. Mass media manipulation can be used to promote extremist ideologies that are based on false or misleading information. This can lead to the radicalization of individuals and the development of extremist movements that threaten social and political stability.

Additionally, mass media manipulation can also pose risks to public health and safety. By promoting false or misleading information, mass media manipulation can contribute to the spread of misinformation and conspiracy theories, which can have negative impacts on public health and safety.

Addressing the risks associated with mass media manipulation requires a range of solutions. Promoting media literacy and critical thinking can help to prevent the spread of false or misleading information. This can involve measures such as promoting media literacy education in schools, investing in fact-checking initiatives, and supporting media outlets that prioritize accuracy and objectivity.

Fostering greater respect for diversity and pluralism can also help to prevent the risks associated with mass media manipulation. This can involve measures such as promoting intercultural dialogue, investing in language and cultural education programs, and supporting initiatives that promote social integration and cohesion.

Finally, promoting democratic values and practices can also help to prevent the risks associated with mass media manipulation. This can involve measures such as promoting open and transparent governance, increasing citizen participation in decision-making processes, and investing in initiatives that promote democratic values and practices.

The risks associated with mass media manipulation are significant and require a range of solutions that prioritize promoting media literacy and critical thinking, fostering greater respect for diversity and pluralism, and promoting democratic values and practices. By working together across sectors and across borders, we can build a more just and equitable world where the media serves the public interest and upholds democratic values and practices.

Addressing the risks associated with mass media manipulation requires a range of solutions. Here are some potential approaches:

1. Promote media literacy and critical thinking: Promoting media literacy and critical thinking can help to prevent the spread of false or misleading information. This can involve measures such as promoting media literacy education in schools, investing in fact-checking initiatives, and supporting media outlets that prioritize accuracy and objectivity.

2. Fostering greater respect for diversity and pluralism: Fostering greater respect for diversity and pluralism can also help to prevent the risks

associated with mass media manipulation. This can involve measures such as promoting intercultural dialogue, investing in language and cultural education programs, and supporting initiatives that promote social integration and cohesion.

3. Promote democratic values and practices: Promoting democratic values and practices can also help to prevent the risks associated with mass media manipulation. This can involve measures such as promoting open and transparent governance, increasing citizen participation in decision-making processes, and investing in initiatives that promote democratic values and practices.

4. Encourage fact-checking and accountability: Encouraging fact-checking and accountability can also help to prevent the spread of false or misleading information. This can involve measures such as promoting independent fact-checking initiatives, investing in journalism and investigative reporting, and supporting initiatives that promote accountability and transparency in government and media.

5. Support media diversity and plurality: Supporting media diversity and plurality can help to prevent mass media manipulation by promoting a range of perspectives and ideas. This can involve measures such as supporting independent media outlets, investing in public media, and promoting initiatives that prioritize diverse voices and perspectives.

99

Intolerance

Intolerance refers to the unwillingness to accept or respect beliefs, practices, or opinions that differ from one's own. While intolerance has been a persistent issue throughout history, it poses significant risks in the future.

One of the most significant risks associated with intolerance is the potential for social and cultural division. Intolerance can lead to the development of conflicting and competing narratives that undermine social and cultural cohesion. This can lead to discrimination, conflict, and violence.

Another risk of intolerance is the potential for promoting extremist ideologies and radicalization. Intolerance can be used as a tool to promote extremist ideologies that are based on a narrow and exclusionary worldview. This can lead to the radicalization of individuals and the development of extremist movements that threaten social and political stability.

Additionally, intolerance can also pose risks to public health and safety. By promoting discriminatory attitudes and behaviors, intolerance can contribute to the spread of disease, violence, and other forms of harm.

Addressing the risks associated with intolerance requires a range of solutions. Promoting respect for diversity and pluralism can help to prevent the development of conflicting and competing narratives. This can involve measures such as promoting intercultural dialogue, investing in language and cultural education programs, and supporting initiatives that promote social integration and cohesion.

Fostering greater understanding and empathy can also help to prevent the risks associated with intolerance. This can involve measures such as promoting empathy education in schools, investing in initiatives that promote emotional intelligence and conflict resolution, and supporting community-based initiatives that promote social cohesion and inclusion.

Finally, promoting democratic values and practices can also help to prevent the risks associated with intolerance. This can involve measures such as promoting open and transparent governance, increasing citizen participation in decision-making processes, and investing in initiatives that promote democratic values and practices.

The risks associated with intolerance are significant and require a range of solutions that prioritize promoting respect for diversity and pluralism, fostering greater understanding and empathy, and promoting democratic values and practices. By working together across sectors and across borders, we can build a more just and equitable world where the principles of respect, empathy, and inclusion are prioritized.

Addressing the risks associated with intolerance requires a range of solutions. Here are some potential approaches:

1. Promote respect for diversity and pluralism: Promoting respect for diversity and pluralism can help to prevent the development of conflicting and competing narratives. This can involve measures such as promoting intercultural dialogue, investing in language and cultural education programs, and supporting initiatives that promote social integration and cohesion.

2. Foster greater understanding and empathy: Fostering greater understanding and empathy can also help to prevent the risks associated with intolerance. This can involve measures such as promoting empathy education in schools, investing in initiatives that promote emotional intelligence and conflict resolution, and supporting community-based initiatives that promote social cohesion and inclusion.

3. Promote democratic values and practices: Promoting democratic

values and practices can also help to prevent the risks associated with intolerance. This can involve measures such as promoting open and transparent governance, increasing citizen participation in decision-making processes, and investing in initiatives that promote democratic values and practices.

4. Encourage fact-checking and accountability: Encouraging fact-checking and accountability can also help to prevent the spread of false or misleading information that can promote intolerance. This can involve measures such as promoting independent fact-checking initiatives, investing in journalism and investigative reporting, and supporting initiatives that promote accountability and transparency in government and media.

5. Support grassroots initiatives: Supporting grassroots initiatives can help to prevent intolerance by promoting community-based solutions that prioritize social inclusion and cohesion. This can involve measures such as supporting community-led initiatives that promote dialogue and understanding, investing in community-based organizations, and promoting initiatives that prioritize social justice and equality.

100

Cultural isolationism

Cultural isolationism refers to the practice of isolating oneself or one's culture from the rest of the world. While cultural isolationism has been practiced throughout history, it poses significant risks in the future.

One of the most significant risks associated with cultural isolationism is the potential for limiting access to new ideas and perspectives. Cultural isolationism can prevent individuals and communities from being exposed to diverse ideas and perspectives, which can limit innovation, progress, and social and economic development.

Another risk of cultural isolationism is the potential for promoting extremist ideologies and radicalization. Cultural isolationism can create an environment that is conducive to the development of extremist ideologies that are based on a narrow and exclusionary worldview. This can lead to the radicalization of individuals and the development of extremist movements that threaten social and political stability.

Additionally, cultural isolationism can also pose risks to public health and safety. By preventing access to new ideas and perspectives, cultural isolationism can contribute to the spread of disease, violence, and other forms of harm.

Addressing the risks associated with cultural isolationism requires a range of solutions. Promoting intercultural dialogue and exchange can help to prevent the risks associated with cultural isolationism. This can involve measures such as investing in cultural exchange programs, promoting language and cultural education, and supporting initiatives that promote social integration and cohesion.

Fostering greater understanding and empathy can also help to prevent the risks associated with cultural isolationism. This can involve measures such as promoting empathy education in schools, investing in initiatives that promote emotional intelligence and conflict resolution, and supporting community-based initiatives that promote social cohesion and inclusion.

Finally, promoting democratic values and practices can also help to prevent the risks associated with cultural isolationism. This can involve measures such as promoting open and transparent governance, increasing citizen participation in decision-making processes, and investing in initiatives that promote democratic values and practices.

In conclusion, the risks associated with cultural isolationism are significant and require a range of solutions that prioritize promoting intercultural dialogue and exchange, fostering greater understanding and empathy, and promoting democratic values and practices. By working together across sectors and across borders, we can build a more just and equitable world where the principles of respect, empathy, and inclusion are prioritized.

Addressing the risks associated with cultural isolationism requires a range of solutions. Here are some potential approaches:

1. Promote intercultural dialogue and exchange: Promoting intercultural dialogue and exchange can help to prevent the risks associated with cultural isolationism. This can involve measures such as investing in cultural exchange programs, promoting language and cultural education, and supporting initiatives that promote social integration and cohesion.

2. Fostering greater understanding and empathy: Fostering greater understanding and empathy can also help to prevent the risks associated with cultural isolationism. This can involve measures such as promoting empathy education in schools, investing in initiatives

that promote emotional intelligence and conflict resolution, and supporting community-based initiatives that promote social cohesion and inclusion.

3. Promote democratic values and practices: Promoting democratic values and practices can also help to prevent the risks associated with cultural isolationism. This can involve measures such as promoting open and transparent governance, increasing citizen participation in decision-making processes, and investing in initiatives that promote democratic values and practices.

4. Encourage cultural diversity and pluralism: Encouraging cultural diversity and pluralism can help to prevent cultural isolationism by promoting a range of perspectives and ideas. This can involve measures such as supporting independent media outlets, investing in public media, and promoting initiatives that prioritize diverse voices and perspectives.

5. Support initiatives that prioritize social justice and equality: Supporting initiatives that prioritize social justice and equality can help to prevent cultural isolationism by promoting an inclusive and equitable society. This can involve measures such as investing in initiatives that promote social justice and equality, supporting community-led initiatives that promote dialogue and understanding, and promoting initiatives that prioritize social inclusion and cohesion.

101

In Summary

Let's Make the World a Better Place

As we look around us, we can see many challenges and obstacles that we face as a society. But I believe that together, we can overcome these challenges and create a brighter future for ourselves and future generations.

The first step towards making the world a better place is to **embrace diversity.** Diversity is what makes our world a beautiful and unique place. By embracing diversity, we can create a more inclusive society where everyone is valued and respected.

The second step is to **promote sustainability.** We must prioritize sustainability to ensure that our planet remains habitable for future generations. This means reducing our carbon footprint, investing in renewable energy, supporting sustainable agriculture and resource management, and promoting environmental education and awareness.

The third step is to support **human rights.** Human rights are the foundation of a just and equitable society. We can work towards promoting human rights by supporting organizations that protect and defend human rights, advocating for policies that promote equality and justice, and standing up against human rights abuses and violations.

The fourth step is to practice **kindness and empathy.** Kindness and empathy can go a long way in making the world a better place. By practicing kindness and empathy in our daily lives, we can create a more compassionate and caring society.

The fifth step is to **invest in education.** Education is key to creating a better world. We can invest in education by supporting initiatives that promote access to education for all, investing in teacher training and development, and supporting educational research and innovation.

The sixth step is to support **community-building initiatives.** Strong communities are the foundation of a healthy and thriving society. We can support community-building initiatives by volunteering, donating to community-based organizations, and participating in local events and initiatives.

So, my friends, let's work together to make the world a better place. By embracing diversity, promoting sustainability, supporting human rights, practicing kindness and empathy, investing in education, and supporting community-building initiatives, we can create a brighter future for ourselves and future generations.

Let us all commit to doing our part, no matter how small, to make the world a better place. Together, we can create a more just, equitable, and sustainable world.

Thank you.

www.ingramcontent.com/pod-product-compliance
Lightning Source LLC
Chambersburg PA
CBHW061553250726
48657CB00021B/1135

Dedicación

En amorosa memoria de mi esposa,

Miriam Vassallo Nodar,

y su presencia siempre presente.

Siempre estás en mis pensamientos.

Para todo aquel que haya amado profundamente, su-frido
una pérdida total y aun así encontrado

el valor para volver a empezar.

Table of Contents

1

Gesto

Mientras los primeros rayos del amanecer pintaban suavemente la somnolienta localidad de Northport, Nueva Gales del Sur, Roebuck S. Cooke se encontraba posado junto a la ventana de su sala de conferencias, con vistas a la bulliciosa vía principal que se extendía abajo. Con un vistazo a su reloj, Roebuck S. Cooke, Roe para su personal y amigos cercanos, vio la hora: precisamente las 7:30 a.m.

Los lunes por la mañana eran siempre el presagio tanto de desafíos como de oportunidades, y hoy no era la excepción. Con mirada aguda, escudriñó el horizonte, a la espera de su equipo.

Investigaciones Alder y Finch se enorgullecía de su puntualidad y profesionalismo, virtudes legadas por los fundadores que le dieron nombre a la empresa, y puestas en práctica por el mismo Roebuck.

Poco se imaginaba Roe que un día él sería el dueño de Investigaciones Alder y Finch, cuando comenzó por primera vez en el negocio nada más graduarse de la universidad a la edad de 22 años.

Tanto el padre como la madre de Roe habían sido empleados del gobierno de Nueva Gales del Sur. El padre de Roe, Albert, era detective principal en el cuerpo de policía, y su madre, Mary, era subdirectora en la escuela secundaria local.

Siguiendo los pasos de su padre, Roe completó los requisitos para obtener un título en criminología, pero su madre no apoyó su decisión de unirse a la policía.

Roe también lo pensó cuando se graduó, y después de un pequeño comentario de su padre, en lugar de unirse a la policía, Roe se postuló y fue contratado como un investigador de menor rango en las oficinas de Alder y Finch en el distrito central de negocios en Sídney.

Eso fue en el año de 1973.

Investigaciones Alder y Finch era entonces, y lo sigue siendo ahora, la principal firma de investigación de seguros en Nueva Gales del Sur.

A lo largo de los años, Investigaciones Alder y Finch realizó muchos análisis detallados de reclamaciones de seguro, para verificar su legitimidad e identificar fraudes potenciales. Su especialidad comprendía desde la investigación de antecedentes, detección de fraudes, trabajo de campo y reportes detallados documentando los hallazgos, información que las compañías de seguros utilizaban para decidir sobre la aprobación de las reclamaciones, rechazos, o posibles acciones legales cuando se producía un potencial fraude.

Investigaciones Adler y Finch trabajó en varios tipos de seguros, incluyendo seguros de autos, de vida, de salud, de propiedad y compensación laboral.

Cuando los expertos de las compañías de seguros no pudieron detectar ningún fraude, pero los directivos tenían sospechas, Investigaciones Alder y Finch entró en acción. Roe había aprendido todos los aspectos de este negocio desde que él se unió a la empresa siendo muy joven.

Vaya, cómo pasa el tiempo, pensó Roe antes de permitirse otro momento de reflexión.

Su viaje desde sus humildes comienzos hasta el mando de una de las más estimadas agencias de investigación de seguros, fue la prueba de su perseverancia y determinación. Sin embargo, en medio de los elogios y los éxitos, él había permanecido con los pies en la tierra, guiado por una firme brújula moral que definió cada una de sus acciones. Una brújula que le inculcaron sus amados padres.

Roe cerró los ojos, recordando esa horrible noche hace años cuando recibió la noticia de la muerte de sus padres a manos de un conductor ebrio. A los 35 años de edad, ese había sido uno de los peores momentos de su vida.

Después de todos los trámites del funeral, Roe se había sentado en la oficina de su abogado, parecía como entumecido y apenas concentrado en las palabras del otro hombre. No fue hasta que él tuvo en sus manos el testamento de sus padres que él "despertó" ante el impacto de su contenido. Él se había quedado impresionado por la cantidad de fondos que ellos habían acumulado a lo largo de los años, sin mencionar sus seguros y varias propiedades. Sin embargo, la propiedad que más lo había sorprendido había sido este edificio de oficinas de dos niveles. ¡Ellos eran los dueños de su lugar de trabajo y él ni siquiera lo sabía! En conjunto, todas esas propiedades constituían una cartera de bienes muy sólida.

Pero lo que en verdad tomó por sorpresa a Roe, fue la carta maravillosamente escrita por sus padres para él.

En ella, sus padres le habían expresado su amor, pero lo más importante, ellos habían notado su amor por el trabajo de investigación que había estado realizando en Investigaciones Alder y Finch durante más de doce años en ese momento. Ellos mencionaron cuánto había aprendido él en ese tiempo y las relaciones que había construido con ambos fundadores.

En algún punto antes de su muerte, ellos se habían acercado a los fundadores con una propuesta para comprarles la empresa. Ellos habían aceptado y, al final del año, los fundadores se retirarían, facilitando la transición de la administración.

Ellos habían querido que ese fuera su regalo de cumpleaños número 35.

El accidente y choque fatal habían destruido el brillo del maravilloso gesto, pero al final, el trato se había llevado a cabo según lo planeado. Y el 31 de diciembre de 1985, Roebuck Cooke se había convertido en director y propietario de Investigaciones Alder y Finch.

Durante los siguientes dos años, él había hecho crecer aún más el negocio y decidió mudarse del Distrito Central de Negocios de Sídney a Northport, después de recibir la notificación de su agente de bienes raíces de que la actual compañía que alquilaba su edificio, lo estaba desocupando.

Mudarse a una pequeña localidad rural podría ser justo lo que necesita mi personal, fue lo que él se dijo a sí mismo y tomó la decisión.

Él planeó que su personal se encargara de la mudanza, permitiéndole a Agnes "Aggie" MacTavish, su leal administradora de oficina, estar a cargo de toda la mudanza, mientras él tomaba algún tiempo libre e iba a pescar a Crystal Cove.

De regreso al presente, Roe observó cómo el sol de la mañana proyectaba un brillo dorado sobre las calles, bañando la ciudad en un cálido abrazo. Detrás de él, podía oír las voces de su personal entrando en la sala de conferencias. Con una sensación de anticipación contenida, Roebuck volvió su atención a la sala de conferencias y vio a su equipo, todos con un café en la mano.

"Buenos días a todos". Él le sonrió a cada uno de ellos. "Vamos a empezar".

Y cuando su equipo se filtró en la sala, listo para embarcarse en otro día de trabajo, Roe sabía que juntos, eran imparables.

2

Contexto

Cuando los miembros del equipo llegaron y se acomodaron en sus sillas, Roe hizo un rápido resumen en su mente de la forma en que reclutó a cada uno de ellos.

En primer lugar, dos de ellos no habían sido reclutados.

Agnes, "Aggie" MacTavish, a sus 58 años de edad, era la mano firme dentro del guante de terciopelo que mantenía a Investigaciones Alder y Finch funcionando sin problemas. Aggie había sido la administradora de una oficina con doble mando desde el día en que entró en la oficina y ambos hombres, Mr. Alder y Mr. Finch, se enamoraron de ella y de la forma en que se manejaba en la oficina.

Su cabello entrecano estaba recogido en un moño sencillo y práctico, resaltando el brillo intenso de sus ojos color avellana. Años de tratar con detectives excéntricos y clientes exigentes, habían grabado algunas líneas alrededor de sus ojos, pero su sonrisa aún tenía un toque de picardía.

Su uniforme consistía en una blusa impecable metida dentro de una falda de corte a medida, con zapatos cómodos y discretos, necesarios para navegar en la, a veces, caótica oficina. Aunque proyectaba un aire profesional, llevaba una pequeña navaja de plata dentro de su bolsillo, lo cual servía como un sutil recordatorio de que la vida como administradora de una oficina de un investigador, no siempre se trataba de archivar documentos.

Bajo la apariencia severa, había una fuente de conocimiento acerca de la agencia y sus casos, a me-nudo, secretos. Aggie tenía un sexto sentido para de-tectar problemas, ya sea que se tratara de un cliente con una historia sospechosa, o un investigador a punto de incumplir con un plazo crucial. Aunque la reputación de Alder y Finch generó los nuevos nego-cios, Aggie se aseguró de que todo se hiciera, todo con un humor irónico y sutil y un toque de preocu-pación maternal por el personal de la empresa. Fue por ello que cuando Roe se convirtió en el propieta-rio, él no dudó en mantener a Aggie. Ella era su "right-hand man" pero en versión femenina.

Después estaba Liam O'Connor, su investigador principal. Liam era viudo, tenía más de cincuenta años. De aspecto rudo y atractivo, cabello rubio cenizo corto con matices grises, ojos color avellana, y una complexión física musculosa desarrollada en su época de militar en las Fuerzas de Defensa Australianas FDA. Por lo general, él vestía de manera casual con pantalones de mezclilla y camisas cómodas para pasar desapercibido en sus labores de vigilancia. Liam fue la persona que tomó a Roe bajo su ala cuando Roe se unió a la empresa, y le enseñó los conceptos básicos del negocio de investigación. A través del trabajo duro, Roe aprendió el resto. Lo que más aprendió Roe acerca de Liam, fue que era inteligente y leal.

Cerca de él estaba sentado Mateo Reyes, investigador auxiliar de Liam. Mateo era estadounidense de nacimiento, de ascendencia cubana, había conocido a su esposa Olivia Vassallo en línea, se enamoró y se mudó a Australia. Al recibir su residencia, Mateo ya había completado sus estudios y aprobado el certificado III en estudios de investigación y, actualmente, estaba estudiando con Liam. Él rondaba los treinta, era de complexión delgada, piel aceitunada, ojos oscuros y cabello negro corto. En el trabajo prefería usar pantalones y camisas de vestir.

A su izquierda, estaba Sophia Nguyen. Sophia era una investigadora con cinco años de experiencia y estaba a la mitad de sus treinta, pero lucía como si tuviera diecinueve años. Ella era vietnamita australiana, soltera, menuda, con cabello negro azabache hasta la barbilla y ojos cafés almendrados; ella tenía un físico ágil y atlético gracias a los años de entrenamiento de artes marciales. Con frecuencia vestía sacos y blusas, proyectaba un porte elegante, pero al mismo tiempo accesible.

Finalmente, Roe miró a Noah Peters, su investigador cibernético. Noah estaba a principios de sus treinta. Él era delgado, soltero y constantemente comía Twisties, lo cual hacía que tuviera un desastre alrededor de su computadora, escritorio y equipo. Noah tenía el cabello castaño claro y ligeramente despeinado, lo que contrastaba con su intensa mirada detrás de sus gafas de montura metálica. Por lo general, vestía de forma sencilla, con camisetas y sudaderas con capucha para sus largas sesiones de codificación.

Ese es mi equipo, pensó Roe con una sonrisa cariñosa en su rostro. Dirigiéndose hacia Aggie, él preguntó: "Entonces, ¿cuál es el resultado de la semana?".

"Sólo un momento, Roe". Liam levantó la mano, interviniendo. "Acabas de regresar de vacaciones. Tómate un momento y compártenos. ¿Cómo estuvo la pesca?".

El grupo se rió un poco ante la improvisada pregunta, pero Roe explicó cómo pasó los diez días relajándose y pescando cada vez que tenía oportunidad.

"¿Hay algo emocionante para compartir, jefe?". Preguntó Mateo.

"De hecho, sí, Mateo, algo digno de mención sucedió justo en el momento en el que me estaba registrando en el Poplar Inn. La policía estaba ahí haciendo un arresto por lo que más tarde me enteré era un robo cometido por uno de los huéspedes de la posada".

"¡Guau!, ¿hubo acción?". Soltó Liam sin pensarlo.

"No, el individuo arrestado era un caballero de edad avanzada. Fue atrapado por una cámara escondida colocada allí por otro huésped".

"Ah, ¿no es un detective del hotel?", preguntó Aggie.

"No, más tarde me enteré de que este huésped del hotel, su nombre es Daniel Monk, es propietario de una librería aquí en Northport llamada Village Books & Stuff, y tiene participación en varias empresas de la zona. Un individuo muy interesante". Roe soltó una risita suave. "Su socio de negocios también estaba ahí, un Mr. Guzmán que dirige un salón llamado Locks & Loaded. Él era un tipo extravagante, vestido de forma llamativa".

Sophia levantó las cejas, sorprendida. "¿Estás bromeando? ¿Conociste a Albert?".

Asombrado, Roe respondió: "¿Conoces a este tipo Sophia?".

"Si, esa es la peluquería a la que tienes que ir en todo Sidney. Él es un artista. Aunque ahora él es propietario del lugar y ha hecho todo el entrenamiento de su equipo. Ellos son caros, pero hacen un maravilloso trabajo. Yo me arreglé el cabello allí para la boda de mi prima el año pasado y tengo que decir que yo lucía mejor que ella en su boda".

Esto provocó una risita entre el grupo.

"¿Vas a reclutarlo jefe? Ya sabes, a este Daniel Monk".

"Por supuesto que no". Roe descartó la idea con un gesto de la mano. "Fue solo uno de esos momentos en la vida en los que sucede algo inesperado y tú estás allí, y conoces a un par de personas. Ahora, suficiente charla; vamos a nuestra reunión de personal. Aggie, ¿qué es lo primero en la agenda?".

"Liam está al día con la actualización sobre su investigación de Mythical Menagerie Insurance Company de Nueva Gales del Sur y su reclamo por el robo del galgo, Wackines Rogue".

"OK, Liam; un resumen rápido por favor", agregó Roe.

"Si miras su ficha, creo que Wackiness Rogue ha ganado más de $153,000 en premios y fue asegurado para fines de cría por $1 millón. El perro ganó previamente la Champion Stakes y la Queen's Stakes, y fue uno de los favoritos el año pasado del Connolly Stamford Memorial Puppy Stake antes de que fuera robado. Él es propiedad del Midtown Syndicate, encabezado por Joe Cahill. El perro fue sacado a punta de pistola de la granja Valley Stud en Dapto, el 8 de diciembre de 2023. La policía trató, pero no pudo recuperarlo. Pero…" Liam hizo una pausa para conseguir un efecto dramático. "Un servidor, y gracias a Mateo, quien hizo mucho del trabajo de campo y Noah, quien hizo todo el rastreo de la web oscura, fue localizado y recuperado la semana pasada. Ahora está en el veterinario siendo examinado antes de regresar a casa con sus legítimos dueños".

Roe asintió con la cabeza en señal de agradecimiento mientras Liam se sentaba de nuevo. "Así que, Aggie, ¿cómo nos fue en el departamento de contabilidad con este caso?".

"Después de los gastos, hemos ganado $65,000— lo que nos dejó con un margen favorable".

"Bien, excelente trabajo ustedes tres. Ahora Sophia, eres la próxima. Por favor infórmanos cómo va tu trabajo".

Tomando un sorbo de su café y aclarando su garganta, Sophia puso al tanto al equipo.

"Centaur Insurance nos contrató nuevamente el 17 de enero para recuperar varias motocicletas de alto rendimiento de Velocity Motohaus. Eran cinco Ducati Dessert X valuadas en $80,000, seis BMW R 1250 GS Adventures en $30,000 cada una, y tres Harley Davidson Pan America 2018, cada una con menos de cien kilómetros recorridos, se cotizaba en un precio superior a $50,000 cada una. Colaborando con la policía local— y con Noah otra vez, quien es un salvavidas aquí—, pude organizar una reunión con la pandilla que se llevó las máquinas bajo la premisa de que un coleccionista estaba interesado en adquirir una de las Harley Davidson Pan America. Llegué al lugar, vi la motocicleta y con mi micrófono de la policía oculto, ellos arrestaron a la pandilla. Las motos fueron entregadas en la tienda la semana pasada mientras estabas de vacaciones".

"Impresionante Sophia. Espero que no hayas corrido ningún riesgo"

"¿Riesgo? Esos tipos tuvieron suerte de que no tuve que mostrarles mi técnica de kung fu".

Eso hizo reír a todos.

Antes de que Roe pudiera preguntar, Aggie intervino. "Para seguir con Sophia, después de los gastos, Centaur Insurance nos hará un pago de $43,000. Debería estar en la cuenta esta semana".

"Mateo, tienes la palabra", declaró Roe.

El joven aclaró su garganta. "En los últimos dos meses, bajo la guía de Liam, he estado trabajando en tres investigaciones sobre relaciones y dos de ellas han dado fruto, mientras que la tercera debería estar concluida a finales de la siguiente semana. Tengo mucha información para compartir con el cliente. Todas las horas facturables por las dos primeras investigaciones se le han entregado a Aggie, y solo estoy esperando a terminar con la tercera".

Roe echó un vistazo a Aggie, y todo lo que ella dijo fue: "A la Ms. Billings se le facturaron cincuenta y tres horas a $125, mientras que a Mr. Rollins se le facturaron setenta y cuatro horas también a $125. La facturación combinada del mes pasado para Mateo fue de $15,875".

"Una vez más, excelente Mateo. Ahora, no es para ponerte en aprietos, pero ¿cómo te está tratando Liam?".

Una gran sonrisa se dibujó en el rostro de Mateo y él dijo, "Ya sabes, para ser un hombre mayor, él lo hace muy bien".

Liam le arrojó un trozo de papel arrugado, trayendo más risas a la sala.

"Finalmente, Noah; cuéntanos sobre tu semana".

"Agitada, jefe. Como Sophia y Liam mencionaron, pude obtener información, que les ayudó con su investigación y, por supuesto, hay un par de otros pequeños casos en los que tú me pediste que trabajara. Y me preguntaba si podría entregarte esta propuesta para que la leas". Él le entregó una pila de papeles para que su jefe las tomara.

Tomando la propuesta, Roe preguntó, "¿Qué tipo de propuesta?".

"Bueno, me gustaría crear un pequeño departamento; una unidad forense digital, la cual investigará únicamente informática forense, enfocándose en identificar, adquirir, procesar, analizar e informar sobre los datos almacenados electrónicamente. Como sabes, el fraude y su evidencia electrónica, son un componente de todas las actividades criminales, y el apoyo de la informática forense es fundamental para todas las investigaciones policiales. Aquí hay una mina de oro de oportunidades que aún no hemos aprovechado. Mi propuesta muestra dónde se encuentran esas oportunidades y cuántas ganancias potenciales pueden generar a tu empresa con costos adicionales mínimos. ¿Te tomarías algún tiempo para pensar sobre ello?".

Roe hojeó el reporte rápidamente y encontró la página que mostraba los resultados finales y sus cejas se levantaron un poco.

"¿Son correctos estos números, Noah?".

"Sí, señor, lo son. Estoy cien por ciento seguro".

"OK, déjame leer esto y me pondré en contacto contigo. ¿Está bien?".

"Excelente, Roe. Te agradezco la oportunidad de presentarte esta propuesta. Es algo que creo que será bueno para tu empresa".

"Y yo te agradezco el esfuerzo, Noah". Él miró a los demás. "¿Hay algo más, equipo?".

Un rápido vistazo alrededor de la mesa mostró que todos habían tenido la oportunidad de hablar y estaban contentos. "OK, entonces vamos a comenzar el día. Aggie y Liam, por favor, quédense un segundo".

El grupo se dispersó y dejó la sala de conferencias para los tres miembros de mayor antigüedad de la empresa.

"Bueno Liam, primero, ¿qué piensas de Mateo? Un elemento valioso, creo".

"En efecto, es un elemento que vale la pena conservar en el equipo. En su primer año, ha hecho un excelente trabajo y está aprendiendo rápidamente todas las técnicas adecuadas. Es un elemento valioso, seguro".

"Y Aggie, ¿tú qué opinas?".

"Lo mismo que Liam, estoy de acuerdo. Él sabe jugar en equipo, trabaja duro, hace su papeleo y es puntual con sus informes. Me agrada y creo que él puede crecer y convertirse en algo bueno para la empresa".

"Ahora, Liam. ¿Sabías acerca de esta propuesta de Noah?".

"Sí y no. Él ha estado haciendo muchas preguntas sobre algunos aspectos del trabajo y buscando información. No he leído la propuesta, pero Noah es inteligente y astuto. Creo que deberías leer la propuesta. O si tú quieres, puedo leerla y luego darte un resumen rápido con mi opinión".

Roe murmuró pensativo. "Aggie, ¿qué hay de ti? Noah compartió esto contigo?".

"No, no lo hizo, pero al igual que con Liam, él hizo muchas preguntas sobre salarios, compensaciones, etc., entonces estoy segura de que él hizo su tarea. Yo también podría echarle un vistazo a la propuesta desde la perspectiva de la empresa y darte mi opinión para ver su viabilidad".

"OK, está arreglado. Liam, tú lo revisas primero para detectar algún conflicto en la empresa y si crees que esto es algo que Noah puede supervisar basado en lo que él ha hecho en estos últimos años, y luego se lo pasas a Aggie. Aggie, tú mira los números e infórmame si parecen tan buenos como Noah considera que son".

Aggie asintió con la cabeza. "¿En cuánto tiempo quieres nuestro punto de vista Roe? Digamos, ¿una semana para que la revisemos y te demos una respuesta?".

"Una semana está bien. Si los números son buenos, entonces necesitamos actuar rápido sobre esta oportunidad y si no, necesitaré hacérselo saber a Noah".

Aggie y Liam solo asintieron, entonces Aggie agregó: "¿Quieres revisar ahora tu agenda de la semana?".

"Claro. Liam, ¿algo más?".

"Todo en orden. Te dejo continuar. Hablamos más tarde". Él se fue con la propuesta de Noah en la mano.

"Entonces, ¿qué hay para esta semana Aggie?".

"Hoy a las 10 am tienes una reunión con Elizabeth Armstrong, vicepresidente ejecutivo de Odyssey Insurance, para hablar acerca de dos casos en los que creen que se trata de un fraude de seguro de vida. Te reservé una hora y media solo en caso de que necesites tiempo".

"OK. Tenemos alguna información previa antes de que me reúna con ella?".

"No. Cuando ella llamó, dijo que discutiría todo en privado contigo".

"OK, ¿qué más?".

"Tu hora de almuerzo está libre, entonces puedes invitarme a almorzar si quieres, y tu próxima cita es a la 1.30 p.m. con Roland Jamieson, director de Aegis Arts, y él envió por correo electrónico "alguna" información que imprimí para que la leas en esta carpeta. Sin embargo, no es mucho".

"¿La leíste? ¿Alguna opinión sobre que la empresa acepte este caso?".

"Creo que deberías leer la información y escucharlo, pero sí, la leí, pero como dije, no hay mucho ahí".

"¿Qué les pasa a estas personas que no comparten información por adelantado?". Roe negó con la cabeza con un suspiro. "OK, entonces almorcemos, así al menos puedo recompensarte por hacer la mudanza sin mí. El lugar luce encantador. Buen trabajo".

"Ah, una cosa más, una muy interesante. Un Mr. J.F. Nodar, un autor local en el área de Northport, está haciendo algunas investigaciones sobre los investigadores de seguros privados y un Mr. Alan Garrett lo refirió de una firma privada en Manhattan Beach, California, con el nombre Gumshoe & Fox. ¿Has oído de él?".

Roe hizo un recordatorio rápido y en efecto, recordó haber conocido a Mr. Garrett en el malecón durante una caminata mañanera mientras él estaba de vacaciones en California.

"Pues sí, recuerdo haber conocido a Mr. Garrett. Él me dijo que era un oficial retirado de la Fuerza Aérea de Estados Unidos, de la Oficina de Investigación Especial, ahora es un investigador privado en ejercicio. ¿Entonces Mr. Nodar quiere entrevistarme y está haciendo algunas investigaciones? ¿Eso es todo?".

"Es correcto. Él fue muy encantador y persuasivo, y creo que deberías darle algo de tiempo, así que lo reservé para las 4.30 esta tarde. Espero que esté bien. Hazme saber si necesito llamarlo para cancelar, pero espero que no lo hagas. Como dije, es un personaje bastante interesante".

Roe pensó por un momento: ¿Por qué no? Podría ser interesante. Roe le dijo a Aggie que dejara la cita en el calendario.

Con una gran sonrisa, Aggie dejó la carpeta de Aegis Art sobre la mesa y se fue, dándole a Roe un momento para sentarse y relajarse.

Sí, este es un gran equipo, él pensó.

3

Odyssey Insurance

Después de tomarse unos minutos para ordenar sus pensamientos, Roe tomó la carpeta de Aegis Art y fue a su oficina. Revisando el tiempo, él tenía al menos una hora antes de reunirse con Elizabeth Armstrong de Odyssey Insurance, así él tenía mucho tiempo para ponerse al día con sus correos electrónicos. Aggie ya había eliminado los que no eran importantes y le dejó revisar y responder aproximadamente treinta de ellos.

Antes de que se diera cuenta, sonó su teléfono: "Mr. Cooke, Elizabeth Armstrong de Odyssey Insurance está aquí. ¿Puedo pasarla?".

Dándole a Aggie una rápida respuesta afirmativa, Roe terminó con sus correos electrónicos y rodeó su escritorio para saludar a Ms. Armstrong cuando se abrió la puerta.

"Ms. Armstrong, él es Mr. Cooke, director de Investigaciones Alder y Finch. Mr. Cooke, ella es Elizabeth Armstrong de Odyssey Insurance". Aggie cerró la puerta detrás de ella.

"Ms. Armstrong, un placer". Roe extendió su mano. "Por favor, llámeme Roe".

"Llámeme Liz. Un placer conocerlo también, señor".

Indicando hacia la sala de estar, Roe se tomó un momento para echar un vistazo rápido a Liz.

Ella parecía estar en sus cuarentas, de baja estatura y complexión robusta, proyectaba una actitud tranquila y profesional. Su tez era morena clara debido a un bronceado reciente, lo que le daba un tono cálido a sus rasgos y armonizaba perfectamente con su cabello corto y ondulado de color castaño, enmarcando su rostro con suave elegancia.

Sus ojos de color avellana oscuro, mostraban una expresión de inteligencia y discernimiento, reflejando su experiencia en la industria de los seguros. Para su atuendo profesional, ella había escogido un elegante saco azul marino a juego con una blusa blanca impecablemente planchada y pantalones confeccionados a la medida, lo cual se ajustaba perfectamente a su papel.

Un par de zapatos clásicos negros de tacón bajo, completaban el atuendo combinando comodidad con una estética refinada. Este atuendo no solo realzaba su presencia con aire de autoridad, sino que, además, encajaba a la perfección con el entorno profesional y exclusivo de su sector.

"Tiene mi atención, Liz. ¿Cómo puede ayudar Investigaciones Alder y Finch a Odyssey Insurance?".

"Powers Insurance nos refirió a ustedes porque ellos quedaron extremadamente impresionados con el trabajo de su firma en un caso reciente. Por eso estoy aquí, para discutir dos de nuestros casos. Nosotros hicimos una verificación de los antecedentes de usted y de su empresa, y creemos que podemos trabajar juntos al menos en un caso. Aunque también espero que usted pueda ayudarnos en el otro, o referirnos a otra firma si usted no tiene interés en el caso. ¿Puedo empezar?".

"Por supuesto Liz. Por favor, proceda".

"Nosotros creemos que tenemos un caso de fraude con uno de nuestros clientes, pero nuestro equipo de investigaciones internas está desconcertado y no parece poder determinar si hay o no hay fraude. Esto involucra a un concesionario de automóviles exóticos en Parramatta—LCU— propiedad conjunta de Mr. y Ms. James y Marybeth Saxon. El seguro cubría los vehículos por $47 millones. También aseguramos la casa particular de los Saxon en Parramatta. El edificio y los gastos fueron cubiertos por otra compañía y ya han llegado a un acuerdo con los propietarios".

"¿Por qué están ustedes retrasando el pago?".

"Nosotros creemos que el matrimonio está deteriorado y el divorcio es inminente, y el dinero es la razón. Los Saxon están en profundas deudas, tanto en sus negocios como en sus finanzas personales. Antes de este incidente ha habido dos reclamaciones sobre la vivienda que suman más de $278,000, los cuales pagamos. Pero ahora todo está conectado y, como dije, las conversaciones con el agente de seguros y nuestras investigaciones siempre parecen chocar contra un muro".

"¿Cuál fue el incidente en su casa?".

"Nosotros creemos que el incendio empezó en la sala de estar, en su chimenea, y entonces envolvió toda el área de la sala y los cuartos contiguos. Afortunadamente, el cuerpo de bomberos respondió rápidamente, salvando la casa, pero resultando casi en la destrucción total de la mitad inferior".

"¿Por qué la sospecha entonces? ¿Cree que fue un incendio provocado?".

"Como sabe, un incendio provocado es difícil de investigar por tres principales razones: 1) el incendiario puede planear el incendio con mucha anticipación y traer todas las herramientas que necesita para cometer el acto. 2) el incendiario no necesita estar presente en el momento del acto. Y 3) el mismo fuego destruye la evidencia que relaciona al incendiario con el crimen. El agente y nuestros investigadores revisaron todos los hechos reunidos por el departamento de bomberos y concluyeron que una brasa comenzó el incendio cuando cayó sobre la alfombra".

"¿Ellos tenían la chimenea encendida en verano? ¿No les pareció extraño?".

"En efecto, nos lo pareció, pero la gente hace cosas extrañas. ¿Qué puedo decir? Entonces, tres meses después, el incendio en el concesionario y, como mencioné, los mismos resultados de la investigación. Causa desconocida esta vez, aunque los investigadores creen que pudo haber sido una batería de litio, pero ellos no pudieron encontrar una. La magnitud del incendio fue tan intensa, que algunos coches parecían montones de ceniza".

"En conclusión, Liz; ¿Qué desean que haga Investigaciones Alder y Finch?".

"Simple. Probar que fue un incendio provocado en ambos casos, la reclamación de la casa y del concesionario. Entonces nosotros trataremos de recuperar nuestros $278,000 y no pagar el seguro del concesionario. Y mientras nosotros hacemos eso, ustedes descubren cómo y quién lo hizo. Y si realmente fue por el dinero".

Roe se tomó un momento para considerar sus opciones y, basándose en sus muchos años de experiencia, él decidió tomar una mirada más profunda a todo ello antes de asumir un compromiso.

"Liz, ambos casos parecen interesantes, pero me gustaría examinar todos los expedientes de ambos casos antes de decidir. ¿Sería posible obtener una copia? Si usted me da un día o dos, me pondré en contacto con usted con mi decisión".

"Por supuesto, no espero que usted se eche un clavado en esto sin conocer en detalle todos los hechos. Mi oficina le enviará toda la información esta tarde. Y si todo está bien para usted, podría enviarle también un pequeño caso pero bastante interesante por el que nosotros hicimos el pago. Se refiere a un reloj TAG Heuer Carrera. ¿Si eso está bien para usted?".

Liz se puso de pie y Roe le abrió la puerta de la oficina. Cuando ella pasó junto a él, él llamó a Aggie. "Aggie, por favor, dale a Ms. Armstrong toda nuestra información de contacto, ella proporcionará antecedentes de dos casos esta tarde. Una vez que los tengas, por favor repártelos entre el equipo, y agenda una reunión para discutirlos el miércoles en la tarde con todos". Él asintió a Liz mientras ella abría su boca para decir algo. "Sí, Ms. Armstrong, usted ha despertado mi interés. Por favor, envíeme ese archivo sobre el reloj TAG Heuer Carrera también".

"Sí, Mr. Cooke. Por aquí Ms. Armstrong; permítame obtener algunos detalles y ya no la entretengo más".

Roe cerró la puerta y volvió a sentarse en su escritorio. Otra mirada a su reloj mostró que eran las 11:30 a.m.

Solo unos minutos más y llevaré a Aggie a almorzar, pensó y continuó leyendo sus correos electrónicos, sabiendo que Aggie tocaría a su puerta al medio día en punto para el almuerzo.

4

Aggie MacTavish

Justo a tiempo, Aggie tocó a la puerta. "Listo para el almuerzo, jefe?"

Roe levantó la vista de la pantalla y le hizo un rápido gesto de aprobación con el pulgar y, con dos dedos, indicó dos minutos más.

"Esperaré en mi escritorio".

Roe terminó con su último correo electrónico del día. Él tenía suerte de tener a Aggie y a Liam como parte de su equipo estratégico. Ellos habían hecho un trabajo fantástico mientras él tomaba un descanso muy necesario. Liam había monitoreado al equipo y todos sus casos, mientras que Aggie supervisó la mudanza a las nuevas oficinas. Hoy llevaría a Aggie a almorzar y a darle una pequeña sorpresa. Él también había planeado ir a tomar algo con Liam más tarde, donde también expresaría su agradecimiento por los esfuerzos del hombre.

Tomando su saco, Roe se acercó a Aggie y le indicó que era el momento de irse. Con una gran sonrisa, Aggie dijo: "Ya era hora jefe, estoy *hambrienta*".

Abriendo la puerta para que ella pasara, él dijo: "Tú eliges Aggie. ¿Dónde te gustaría almorzar?".

"Bueno, tienes una cita a la 1:30 p.m. con Roland Jamieson, director de Aegis Arts, entonces vamos a algún lugar rápido y agradable. ¿Qué tal White Sheep?".

"Por supuesto, vamos ahí".

Llegar a White Sheep fue una caminata fácil, a solo una cuadra desde la oficina.

El menú era fácil de entender, pero al mismo tiempo, era bastante ecléctico. Ofrecía la comida típica de un pub, como hamburguesas y pechugas de pollo empanizadas, pero también hacía alarde de tres opciones diferentes de pescado en salsas extraordinarias.

Aggie se decidió por la hamburguesa Wagyu con una salsa alioli de mostaza, queso suizo, tomate, lechuga, cebolla blanca cruda y papas fritas. Roe se sintió aventurero y eligió un filete de atún perfectamente sellado. El exterior lucía una ligera costra crujiente de semillas de ajonjolí negras y blancas, cocinado hasta obtener un interior rosado que resaltaba la riqueza natural del atún y su textura mantecosa. El filete venía rociado con una salsa vibrante y exótica: una mezcla armoniosa de mango, maracuyá y un toque de chile, equilibrada con un toque de jugo de lima y jengibre. La salsa era al mismo tiempo dulce y ácida, con un toque picante sutil que realzaba el sabor del atún sin opacarlo.

Para complementar su plato, Roe recibió una guarnición de arroz jazmín infusionado con un toque de coco, que proporcionaba un fondo perfecto para los sabores intensos del atún y la salsa. Otros acompañamientos incluían una ensalada refrescante de papaya, pepino y zanahoria en juliana, mezclado con un aderezo ligero de miso y ajonjolí, lo que le añadía un contraste fresco y crujiente al sabor intenso del atún. Finalmente, Roe pidió una botella del vino favorito de Aggie, Gossips Rose. Era la botella más económica de la carta y demasiado dulce para Roe, pero si a Aggie le gustaba, bueno, Aggie la tenía que tener.

Mientras ellos esperaban a que llegara la comida, Aggie puso al corriente a Roe en algunos aspectos de la mudanza desde el Distrito Central de Negocios de Sídney a la nueva oficina. No había ocurrido nada importante; todos los archivos estaban completos y no había habido pérdidas en la mudanza. Todas las cajas habían llegado y fueron contabilizadas, y ahora se encontraban en sus nuevos archiveros.

"Aggie, tengo que decir que hiciste un trabajo excepcional en la mudanza, no solo gestionando el día a día, sino, además de eso, también la mudanza. Estoy bastante impresionado".

"¿Lo suficientemente impresionado como para un aumento espectacular?". Ella se rió.

"Oh, Aggie, estás arruinando el almuerzo hablando de dinero". Ambos se rieron mientras sus comidas eran colocadas en la mesa delante de ellos.

La comida era excelente, y cuando ambos empezaron a comer, su conversación se volvió casi inexistente. ¿Qué solía decir su padre? *No puedo hablar; estoy demasiado ocupado comiendo.*

Ah, él lo extrañaba mucho a él y a su madre.

Después de la comida, les ofrecieron el postre, pero ellos prefirieron optar por un café, Aggie pidió un capuchino ligero y Roe un expreso.

Mientras aguardaban a que llegaran sus cafés, Roe metió la mano en el bolsillo de su saco, extrajo un sobre, y lo deslizó sobre la mesa.

"Aggie MacTavish—un pequeño agradecimiento de mi parte".

El sobre lucía como una típica tarjeta de agradecimiento que puedes encontrar en las librerías locales. Aggie casi se cae al suelo cuando abrió el sobre y encontró un cheque en él. La cantidad era de seis meses de salario.

"Oh Roe, esto es demasiado. Yo…Yo no sé qué decir. Yo solo estaba bromeando acerca del aumento".

"Aggie, tú has sido una piedra angular para Investigaciones Alder y Finch y para mí, es lo menos que puedo hacer por encargarte de la oficina durante esos dos meses que estuve fuera".

El café llegó y lo disfrutaron, y entonces Aggie miró a Roe y simplemente dijo: "Jefe, eres el mejor, pero ahora tienes que trabajar. Es la 1:15 p.m. y no queremos llegar tarde para tu próxima cita".

Con eso, Roe pagó la cuenta y miró a Aggie salir por la puerta principal, todavía sosteniendo su sobre.

"Sabía que eso funcionaría". fue lo que pensó Roe al salir él también.

5

Aegis Arts

Roe y Aggie caminaron lentamente de regreso a la oficina, sintiendo los efectos del vino y la comida, pero llegaron allí con tiempo de sobra ya que el director de Aegis Arts aún no había llegado.

Al entrar en su oficina, Roe se sentó y tomó el expediente de Mr. Roland Jamieson. Aggie tenía razón. No había más que información general sobre Aegis Arts, no había nada más que indicara por qué era necesaria una reunión, ni de lo que se trataría en ella.

Fundada en 1905, Aegis Arts ascendió rápidamente al pináculo de la industria de seguros de arte, estableciéndose como un proveedor líder en soluciones de seguros personalizadas para piezas de arte raras y de gran valor, y colecciones de todo tipo. Con su sede central en Melbourne y filiales en la ciudad de Nueva York, Londres y Hong Kong, Aegis Arts había construido una formidable reputación por su experiencia incomparable en la tasación de obras de arte, evaluación de riesgos y servicio personalizado al cliente.

Tuvo ganancias en 2023 por $1.2 billones de dólares australianos y un ingreso neto de $300 millones, con 624 empleados en todo el mundo.

Además de eso, ellos conservaban una posición predominante en el mercado de nicho de seguros para piezas de arte raras, con un 25% de la cuota de mercado a nivel mundial. La compañía aseguraba la mayoría de las colecciones privadas más prestigiosas, museos y galerías alrededor del mundo.

Cerrando la carpeta del expediente, Roe murmuró para sí mismo: "Una lista de clientes bastante impresionante".

Con expertos internos proporcionando soluciones de seguro personalizadas—incluyendo seguro de piezas individuales, de colecciones, y seguro de exposiciones, servicios de tasación y gestión de riesgos—Aegis Arts era una compañía muy completa y bien establecida. ¿Por qué necesitarían los servicios de Investigaciones Alder y Finch?

A la 1:40 p.m. Aggie tocó la puerta y asomó la cabeza. "Mr. Cooke, Mr. Jamieson está aquí. ¿Puedo hacerlo pasar?".

"Por supuesto, Aggie, hazlo pasar por favor", dijo Roe mientras volvía a ponerse el saco. Al acomodarse de nuevo en su asiento, Jamieson entró.

Ronald Jamieson luce espectacular, pensó Roe.

Jamieson parecía estar rondando los treinta años, usaba un traje confeccionado a la medida de color azul marino y gris oscuro, a juego con una camisa blanca impecable y una elegante corbata roja. Cuando Jamieson entró, Roe notó que él además había complementado su atuendo con zapatos de cuero pulido y un reloj minimalista. Una actitud tranquila y serena caracterizaba los ademanes de Jamieson, que emanaba confianza, pero sin arrogancia.

No era la persona ni lo que pensé que conocería.

"Por favor, entre Mr. Jamieson. Tome asiento. ¿Puedo ofrecerle un café?".

"No, estoy bien por el momento. Gracias de todos modos, Mr. Cooke".

"Por favor, llámame Roe".

"Puedes llamarme Ronny, entonces. Ya que ahora nos tratamos por nuestro nombre, ¿puedo contarte mi dilema?".

Señalando hacia la sala de estar, Roe dijo: "Por supuesto Ronny, por favor, cuéntame ¿cómo puede Investigaciones Alder y Finch asistir a tu compañía el día de hoy? La información del archivo realmente no me ayudó a comprender cuáles pueden ser sus necesidades".

Ronny se acomodó en la sala y empezó.

"Roe, déjame darte un poco de contexto y verás por qué no había información en el archivo. Primero, soy el tataranieto del fundador de Aegis Art y me encuentro en una situación difícil. Me enfrento a un tema complejo que mis predecesores habrían manejado hábilmente. Una reclamación de seguro fue pagada bajo circunstancias que parecían, bueno, cómo debería decirlo, "inusuales" sería una palabra adecuada, y recuperar estos fondos ha sido una tarea difícil para mí. A pesar de mi distinguido linaje, carezco de la experiencia y los conocimientos necesarios del intrincado mundo de los seguros y recuperación de arte, lo que hace a este desafío aún más desalentador. Sí, tengo un personal que debería trabajar en esto para una conclusión exitosa, pero creo que el personal está disfrutando del hecho de que estoy dando tumbos aquí.

Básicamente Roe, estoy perdido. No hice nada más en la universidad que divertirme. Me aseguré de graduarme con las notas mínimas y pensé que simplemente conseguiría una oficina en algún lugar en la empresa, cobraría un salario decente y seguiría divirtiéndome. No pensé que mi padre realmente esperaría que hiciera algún trabajo. Quiero decir, trabajo real de seguros. Ahora, me estoy dirigiendo a Investigaciones Alder y Finch para que me ayuden a salir de este lío en el que estoy metido".

La reacción de Roe a la respuesta de Ronny fue una mezcla de incredulidad y frustración. Él cruzó los brazos, apoyando el peso de su cuerpo sobre un lado, y miró fijamente a Ronny por un momento, tratando de procesar la ridiculez de lo que acababa de escuchar. Sus labios se apretaron formando una delgada línea y un suspiro de exasperación escapó de él.

"No puedes hablar en serio", Roe murmuró finalmente.

La decepción de Roe era palpable. "Lo sé, lo sé, Roe; esto es totalmente inaceptable, pero es lo que es, y realmente necesito tu ayuda. Pagaré cualquier tarifa que tú solicites, pero necesito que se solucione este lío".

Roe no estaba seguro, pero un trabajo es un trabajo, y aunque él no tenía intención de sacar ventaja del joven hombre, Roe iba a asegurarse de que todos sus gastos y honorarios de recuperación fueran generosos.

Él suspiró. "OK, así que, ¿cuál es la situación aquí respecto a esta reclamación?".

"Entonces, ¿tomarás el caso?".

"Tentativamente, sí. Ahora dame los antecedentes sobre el caso del seguro".

"Por supuesto, pero primero, Roe, ¿cuánto sabes sobre mariposas?".

Roe lo miró extrañado, pero lo complació. "A parte de que ellas empiezan como una oruga, comen hojas hasta que están listas para convertirse en crisálidas y posteriormente emergen como una mariposa adulta, no sé nada más. ¿Qué tiene que ver tu caso con las mariposas?".

"Todo, desafortunadamente. En el año 2021, uno de los museos de Sídney pidió una cotización de seguro sobre su extensa colección de mariposas, ya que ellos querían llevar a cabo una exposición. No solo querían el seguro de la exposición, sino también querían el seguro de su colección de mariposas. Pensé que iba a ser una prima de seguro sencilla, entonces hice un pequeño análisis, envié una propuesta para ambos, la exposición y la colección, y ellos la aceptaron. Aegis Art obtuvo su pago y yo recibí el pago por mi comisión".

"Entonces, ¿qué sucedió Ronny? ¿Por qué estás aquí?".

"Un día antes de que la exposición empezara, recibí una llamada frenética del museo. Alguien había robado alrededor de medio millón de sus mariposas, y las que se llevaron eran las más raras de todas".

"¿Medio millón de mariposas? ¿Qué tan grande es la colección, Ronny?".

"Alrededor de siete millones de especímenes únicos de todo el mundo".

"Entonces, ¿alguien robó casi el 10% de la colección del museo y nadie lo notó hasta el día anterior en que se suponía que daría inicio la exposición?".

"Correcto. Por supuesto, la policía llegó y hubo un sospechoso inmediato. Un entomólogo que estaba de visita de Nueva Zelanda—él se había acercado al personal del museo en múltiples ocasiones, pero después de extensas conversaciones con la policía, él fue descartado como sospechoso".

"¿Ellos tenían otros sospechosos?".

"Sí, todo el personal del museo, particularmente aquellos involucrados en la sección que presentaría las mariposas. Después de semanas de interrogatorios y seguimiento, la policía no pudo averiguar nada. Nadie en el departamento podría haberlo hecho".

Roe ahora entendía por qué el joven Jamieson estaba allí, entonces él fue directamente a la pregunta: "¿Cuánto tendrá que pagar Aegis Art al museo por la reclamación?".

Ronny se tomó un momento para responder. Roe pudo ver que él estaba incómodo proporcionando la respuesta, pero si Roe iba a tomar el caso, él debía saber cuál sería el posible reembolso para su empresa.

Finalmente Ronny respondió: "Bueno, es un pago por dos conceptos. Primero, está el seguro de la exposición, que ascendería a $1.2 millones, basado en las experiencias previas de los museos al hacer exposiciones similares. Luego, las

500,000 mariposas robadas, dado que ellas reflejan casi el 10% de la colección, fueron valuadas en $1,000,000, pero nosotros acordamos $1.5 millones, entonces Aegis Arts tiene que cubrir $2.7 millones".

Roe tomó un momento para hacer algunos cálculos mentales antes de ofrecer una propuesta.

"Ronny, ¿tienes todos los expedientes de la policía? ¿Todos sus reportes, todos los nombres de los detectives de la policía asignados al caso? Me refiero a todo".

"Sí, lo tengo, pero si me falta algo, estoy seguro de que podemos conseguir la información".

"OK, mándame toda la información cuando regreses a tu oficina". Roe se levantó del sofá, fue a su escritorio y levantó el teléfono para pedirle a Aggie que entrara. Cuando ella lo hizo, él le dijo: "Aggie, quiero que lleves a Mr. Jamieson a la sala de conferencias y que firme nuestro contrato estándar. Ronny, habrá un ligero cambio en este contrato. En lugar de nuestros honorarios normales de recuperación del 20% más gastos, será modificado para que sea del 40% de honorarios de recuperación más gastos. ¿Te parece bien?".

"Oh, sí Roe, por supuesto. 40% o—" Roe pudo ver a Ronny haciendo números en su cabeza, "alrededor de $1,080,000 por la recuperación, correcto?".

"Correcto, más gastos. ¿Está bien?".

"Lo está. ¿Y tú empezarás de inmediato?".

"Tan pronto como firmes el contrato y envíes los archivos, haré que mi equipo empiece a trabajar en esto".

Satisfecho, Ronny se levantó y extendió su mano. "Yo sabía que estaba en lo correcto al venir aquí. Tú eres un salvavidas, Roe Cooke".

"Ya veremos cuando terminemos el caso, Ronny".

Comprendiendo la mirada que Roe le lanzó, Aggie señaló hacia la puerta. "Por aquí Mr. Jamieson. Déjeme llevarlo a la sala de conferencias. ¿Puedo ofrecerle un café?".

"¿Tiene algo más fuerte?".

Aggie miró a Roe, quien asintió.

"Si, lo tenemos Mr. Jamieson, lo tenemos".

6

Contrataciones

Roe se sentó en su escritorio, pensando en los casos recientes que había decidido que Investigaciones Alder y Finch investigara.

Mientras estuvo en Crystal Cove relajándose y pescando, él había pensado en contratar más personal, ya fuera por contrato o como personal permanente. Ambas opciones tenían sus pros y sus contras, por lo que pensó que lo mejor era involucrar a su investigador principal, para que no lo tomara por sorpresa.

Roe levantó el teléfono. "Liam, ¿tienes un minuto? Hay un asunto que me gustaría consultarte". OK, ven cuando tengas un momento. Ah, tengo una reunión a las 4:30 p.m. entonces tenemos como una hora".

Mientras esperaba, Roe pensó en la próxima cita. Seguramente iba a ser interesante.

Él recordó conocer a Alan Garrett mientras estaba en California, y le había parecido un tipo honesto, que conocía bien su trabajo. Quizás, si Roe alguna vez necesitara ayuda en los Estados Unidos, se pondría en contacto con él. Hasta el momento, Roe había visitado Europa, Malasia, y otros países en el área de Asia Pacífico, así que él estaba seguro de que tarde o temprano Investigaciones de Alder y Finch tendría un caso relacionado con Estados Unidos.

Tocaron la puerta y Liam asomó la cabeza. "¿Listo?".

"Por supuesto, pasa Liam y siéntate".

Sentándose en la silla frente al escritorio de Roe, Liam preguntó: "Entonces, ¿qué pasa Roe?".

"Primero, ¿has revisado la propuesta de Noah?".

"Sí, la leí un poco por encima y miré los números en detalle. Aunque es preliminar, Noah ha hecho un excelente trabajo en presentar esta oportunidad a la empresa, y estaré listo para darle un pulgar arriba en nuestra reunión del miércoles. ¿Por qué? ¿estás listo para seguir adelante con esto ya?".

"En cierto modo, sí, pero lo discutiremos más a fondo el miércoles. Hablemos acerca de tu carga de trabajo. ¿En cuántos casos están trabajando tú y el equipo?".

"Bueno, Mateo tiene seis casos y Sophia ocho. Noah está colaborando con ellos dos en esas tareas y él tiene algunos otros por su cuenta. Personalmente yo estoy supervisando cuatro. ¿Por qué?".

Roe había querido esperar para darle a Liam su sorpresa tomando una copa, pero esta oportunidad se presentó sola y él pensó, ¿por qué no? Roe metió la mano en el cajón superior de su escritorio y sacó un sobre. Se lo pasó a Liam. "Aquí está algo de mí para ti por todo el trabajo que has estado haciendo".

Con un tono sarcástico, Liam dice: "Oh Roe, no tenías que hacerlo. ¿Son boletos para la temporada de los Rabbitohs?". Sin embargo, al abrir el sobre, a Liam casi se le cae la mandíbula.

"Maldición, Roe, esto es demasiado. Quiero decir, maldición, tú realmente no tenías que hacerlo. Qué generoso de tu parte".

"Liam, tú eres una pieza importante en este negocio, y quería que lo supieras. Espero que esto te muestre cuán apreciadas son tus contribuciones a la empresa. Ahora déjame contarte el verdadero motivo por el que te llamé".

"Mientras estaba en Crystal Cove, me tomé tiempo para reflexionar y para hacer planes para el negocio al mismo tiempo. Estoy pensando, como tú, que la propuesta de Noah es viable, pero nosotros también necesitamos gente trabajando en el terreno, al estilo tradicional. De hecho, estoy buscando contratar a cuatro investigadores, ya sea en régimen de subcontratación o como empleados fijos. Esto ayudará a crecer la empresa. Nos permitirá tomar más clientes, liberarte de parte del trabajo real de investigación y hacerte más un director de investigadores. ¿Es algo en lo que estarías interesado?".

Liam miró a Roe e iba a hablar, pero se detuvo.

"Dudaste. ¿Qué pasa?".

"Roe, ¿estás seguro de que tengo madera de gerente? Quiero decir, sé cómo entrenar a los principiantes y me aseguro de que se sigan todos los procesos correctos, pero en lo que respecta a las tareas reales de un director de recursos humanos, nunca lo he hecho. Me las he arreglado sobre la marcha todos estos años. ¿Qué pasa si digo algo equivocado o hago algo mal? Podría perjudicar a tu empresa".

"Tonterías. Lo harás muy bien. Continuarás haciendo lo que has estado haciendo desde que te hice investigador principal: asegurarte de que todos los casos avancen con rapidez, entrenar a cualquier persona nueva y asegurarte de que todos los investigadores con experiencia se mantengan al día con sus casos. Nada diferente. El título de 'director' será entre tú y yo. Tú eres aún el investigador principal de Investigaciones Alder y Finch. Ahora, ¿tienes alguna otra preocupación?".

Con la simple explicación de Roe, Liam pareció satisfecho. "No, creo que puedo trabajar dentro de estos parámetros. Ahora, dijiste que querías contratar a cuatro investigadores adicionales. ¿Estás buscando principiantes como Mateo, o unos con experiencia?".

Roe abrió una carpeta enfrente de él, sacó varias hojas y le dio una a Liam. "Liam he estado pensando en contratar a cuatro de esta lista. No me importa el género en tanto que su experiencia complemente nuestras necesidades. Toma un momento para revisar los nombres y podemos hablar acerca de ellos".

Liam leyó:

Jack Stone: Un expolicía directo y sin rodeos, con diez años de experiencia que se volvió investigador privado.

Lena Graves: Seis años de experiencia en psicología.

Max Ryder: Investigador privado con cuatro años de experiencia, experto en tecnología, combina técnicas de investigación tradicionales con tecnología innovadora.

Evelyn Drake: Experiodista con tres años de experiencia que se volvió investigadora privada.

Sam Carter: Un investigador altamente calificado, con 20 años de experiencia en la Policía Federal Australiana.

Nina Hart: Una investigadora privada independiente con seis años de experiencia.

Aloysius Black: Solo tiene cuatro años de experiencia como investigador privado, pero se presenta a sí mismo como un veterano. Le llaman Al.

Isabella "Izzy" Knight: Una antigua oficial de inteligencia militar con diez años de experiencia, convertida en investigadora privada.

Luke Cross: Otro investigador privado tranquilo pero muy observador, con solo dos años de experiencia y amante de las computadoras.

Maya Rivers: Empezó como trabajadora social para Centrelink y entró al mundo de la investigación privada con la firma Whittle and Sons. Lleva allí 14 años.

Jack Malone: Antiguo detective de policía. Se retiró después de 20 años. Se rumora que él quiere volver a la acción.

Ethan Carter: Antiguo militar de inteligencia con cinco años de experiencia.

Andrew (Andy) O'Reilly: Un experto en ciberseguridad y experto investigador en tecnología. Podría formar parte del equipo de Noah.

Miguel Álvarez: 15 años como reportero investigador para el Sidney Morning Herald.

David Kim: Lleva ocho años como psicólogo forense.

Sarah Blake: Exagente del FBI con 12 años de experiencia. Trabaja como contratista/freelancer desde que se mudó a Australia.

Nina Patel: Seis años como consultora legal. Nina también es una freelancer que hizo la transición de una carrera en consultoría jurídica a la investigación privada.

Alicia Torres: Una exagente encubierta de la Policía Federal Australiana, con 18 años de experiencia en operaciones encubiertas.

Emily Chen: Siete años como investigadora de fraudes de seguros para Carmichael, Strong y Weathers.

Rebecca Lawson: 14 años como investigadora privada para Carmichael, Strong y Weathers. Ha trabajado con Emily. Rebeca empezó como aprendiz en la misma empresa, pero no está feliz con su posición actual allí.

Liam levantó la vista hacia Roe y lanzó un silbido de admiración.

"Vaya Roe, ¿cómo y cuándo conseguiste toda esta información sobre estas personas?".

"Como dije Liam, estuve pensando en expandirnos mientras estaba en Crystal Cove, y contraté a Pathway Professional Services para iniciar la búsqueda mientras estuve allí. Ellos me enviaron el archivo que tienes en tus manos el día anterior a que dejara Crystal Cove. No tenía ni idea de que tendría que actuar sobre la lista tan pronto. ¿Qué opinas? Sin pensarlo mucho, sin análisis. Liam, escucha a tu intuición, eso es todo".

"Tú estás buscando a cuatro, ¿correcto?".

"Sí, cuatro, pero dime qué piensas".

"¿Ya has leído la propuesta de Noah?".

"No, ¿por qué?".

"Bueno, reconocí a Max Ryder's y Andrew O'Reilly de su lista. Ellos eran tecnológicos de acuerdo a la propuesta de Noah y de acuerdo a lo que leí en ella, ellos deberían colaborar muy bien con él así como dentro de tu empresa. Entonces yo no los consideraría como parte de los cuatro que estás buscando, si eso está bien contigo, Roe".

"Tiene sentido. Vamos a considerarlos para el grupo de Noah. Entonces ¿cuáles cuatro te llaman la atención?".

"En realidad Roe, seis de ellos me llaman la atención, como has dicho. Ellos son, sin un orden en particular: Aloysius Black, Emily Chen, Alicia Torres, David Kim, Sarah Blake y Ethan Carter. Todos se ven muy bien, pero creo que estos seis traerán lo que necesitas para Investigaciones Alder y Finch y, por supuesto, Max Ryder y Andrew O'Reilly para el equipo de Noah".

Roe se tomó un momento para asimilar los comentarios de Liam.

Recogiendo la carpeta, él se la entregó a Liam y le dijo: "Liam, confío en tu intuición. Dale los seis nombres —mejor dicho, los ocho nombres— a Aggie y que ella programe las citas con ellos a través de Pathway Professional Services, y tu comienza el proceso de las entrevistas. Escoge los mejores cuatro para trabajar sobre el terreno y los dos para el nuevo departamento de Noah. Eso hará un total de seis, y cuando hayas hecho tu selección, nos reuniremos otra vez para revisar tus notas y recomendaciones".

"Recogiendo la carpeta, Liam asintió y sonrió. "Claro jefe. Aggie y yo los entrevistaremos".

"¿Aggie?".

"Por supuesto". Liam sonrió. "Si tú no la dejas participar en el proceso de las entrevistas, lo pagarás caro".

7

Una Persona Interesante

Después de que Liam había dejado la oficina, Roe se tomó unos minutos antes de salir detrás de él. Dirigiéndose al baño, él se detuvo en el escritorio de Aggie para hacerle una pregunta.

"Has recibido alguno de los archivos de Odyssey Insurance?".

"Aún no. Pero conseguí que Ronald Jamieson firmara el contrato antes de que se fuera. Él dijo que trataría el asunto con su equipo legal si surgía algún problema. Mencionó que tendríamos toda la información a más tardar mañana en la tarde". Ella respondió agitando el contrato firmado.

"Excelente, esperemos recibir todos los archivos mañana para tener una rápida lectura y entonces discutirlo en nuestra reunión del miércoles con Liam. Hablando de Liam, ¿ha hablado contigo acerca de las posibles contrataciones?".

"Sí, lo ha hecho y te agradezco por incluirme en el proceso. Creo que será emocionante para la empresa y para su crecimiento. ¿Estás seguro de que quieres avanzar en esta dirección?".

"Sí, lo estoy".

"Qué bueno escuchar eso. En términos de dinero, no debería ser un problema. Por otro lado, chequé la propuesta de Noah y parece sólida. ¿Quieres escuchar mi opinión?".

"Hagámoslo en la reunión del miércoles, Aggie".

"OK, ahora, lo que fuera que ibas a hacer, necesitas hacerlo rápido porque solo tienes 10 minutos antes de tu próxima cita".

"Sí, jefa", contestó Roe mientras se dirigía al baño de hombres.

Mientras caminaba de regreso a su oficina pocos minutos después, él vio a un caballero llamativo hablando con Aggie. Él parecía estar a la mitad de sus setentas, mostrando una presencia distinguida, con cabello abundante y bien peinado que se había convertido en una elegante mezcla de canas y tonos oscuros. Esto complementaba su aspecto general saludable y en forma, lo que indicaba que se ocupaba de sí mismo con dedicación. Él usaba gafas elegantes de montura fina que agregaban un toque de sofisticación intelectual a su aspecto.

Roe asumió que esta era su cita de las 4:30 p.m.—Mr. J. F. Nodar. Si era correcto, Mr. Nodar estaba vestido de una manera semicasual, optando por un atuendo cómodo pero elegante. El entrevistador/autor llevaba una camisa de corte impecable y unos pantalones de vestir. Su atuendo estaba acompañado de un par de mocasines pulidos y una chaqueta casual, insinuando un estilo relajado pero refinado.

Sí, él luce como un autor, pensó Roe, porque desprende un aire de creatividad.

Roe miró de reojo el cuaderno forrado en cuero bajo su brazo, listo para tomar notas de los pensamientos e inspiraciones de Roe en cualquier momento durante la entrevista. Su actitud parecía tranquila y accesible mientras hablaba con Aggie, entonces Roe esperaba que fuera una entrevista fácil.

"Mr. Nodar, supongo". Él se acercó a la pareja y le tendió la mano al caballero para saludarlo. "Mi nombre es Roebuck S. Cooke— su entrevista de las 4:30 p.m. Por favor, entre a mi oficina".

Mr. Nodar respondió con una sonrisa tranquila y un firme apretón de manos. "Un placer conocerlo, Mr. Cooke, y le agradezco por tomarse un tiempo de su ocupada agenda para reunirse conmigo".

"No hay problema. Usted fue capaz de convencer a mi jefa de oficina, Aggie, y eso es toda una hazaña en sí mismo. Por favor llámeme Roe".

Sonriendo y haciéndole un guiño rápido a Aggie, Mr. Nodar respondió: "Bueno, fue un placer conectar con Ms. MacTavish y ella fue tan generosa con su tiempo. Me alegro que usted también haya estado de acuerdo para esta entrevista. Le prometo que no le quitaré mucho tiempo. También, llámeme José, por favor".

Entrando en la oficina de Roe, los ojos de José miraban a la izquierda y a la derecha, como si absorbiera la energía del lugar.

"No es lo que esperaba de la oficina de un investigador, Roe" él dijo.

"¿En serio? ¿Qué esperaba?".

"No estoy seguro, pero esperaba un escritorio más desordenado, montones de archivos sobre el escritorio de cualquier caso en el que se esté trabajando actualmente. Y un aroma a cigarros y café. Estoy pensando en Lew Archer, J.J. 'Jake' Gittes, Philip Marlowe, and Mike Hammer, por nombrar algunos. Leí muchas historias de detectives cuando era joven".

"Estoy seguro de que usted aún encontrará algunos así, pero estos días usamos ciencia forense, computadoras y métodos más modernos—y Aggie se ha asegurado de que Investigaciones Alder y Finch sea una oficina donde no se permite fumar, entonces, lo siento mucho si nosotros arruinamos la ilusión que usted tenía de un investigador privado".

José rió discretamente. "Bueno, esa es la razón de la entrevista. Si me lo permite, quiero disculparme con usted por no enviar estas preguntas por adelantado para que pudiera estar preparado. ¿puedo compartirlas ahora con usted, Roe?".

José le entregó una hoja de papel extraída de su cuaderno forrado en cuero. Tomando la hoja, Roe le echó un vistazo.

"No hay nada aquí que no pueda responder, pero primero, ¿cómo conoció usted a Alan Garrett de Gumshoe & Fox?".

José se tomó su tiempo para relatar cómo conoció al propietario de Gumshoe & Fox, y cómo la reunión le había dado, como escritor, inspiración para producir una secuela de su última novela: "Reparando Corazones en Crystal Cove".

"Es interesante cómo llega la inspiración a un autor. Gracias por compartir eso conmigo José. Ahora, ¿qué le gustaría saber?".

Los siguientes treinta y cinco minutos fueron un rápido intercambio de información, por un lado, José siguiendo la lista con las preguntas que llevaba y, por el otro, Roe, respondiendo a todo con el mayor entusiasmo y tan honestamente como pudo.

Con la última respuesta, José cerró su cuaderno. "Roe, esto es fantástico. Yo simplemente no sabía lo que se necesitaba para hacer su trabajo. Muchas gracias por su tiempo y si no le importa, ¿puedo llamarlo en el futuro si necesito clarificar algo más que pueda necesitar?".

"Estoy a sus órdenes, José. Llame y pídale a Aggie que agende un momento para reunirnos en persona, o si no, para hablar por teléfono".

Levantándose y preparándose para irse, José extendió su mano a Roe. "Eso es muy amable de su parte. Llamaré a la adorable Ms. MacTavish cuando tenga una pregunta. Que tenga buen día, Roe".

"Buen día José". En lugar de dejarlo ir por su cuenta, como Roe lo había hecho con todas sus citas de hoy, Roe acompañó a José afuera, agradeciéndole una vez más.

Regresando a su escritorio, Aggie preguntó: "Bueno, ¿cómo te fue? ¿la entrevista fue lo que tú esperabas?".

"Lo fue, Aggie. No puedo creer lo interesante que soy como persona".

Con una carcajada, Aggie negó con la cabeza. "Apuesto que lo eres Roe. Apuesto que lo eres".

Cerrando la puerta de su oficina, Roe se recostó en su asiento y se preguntó si él o José obtendrían nuevas perspectivas sobre sus carreras personales a partir de esa entrevista. Mirando su reloj, Roe notó la hora: eran las 5:20 p.m. y era momento de cerrar la oficina.

Ha sido un día interesante. Pensó Roe mientras se dirigía a casa.

8

Nuevas Oportunidades

Exactamente a las 7:00 a.m. del miércoles, Roe, Liam y Aggie se sentaron alrededor de la mesa de la sala de conferencias, cada uno con una taza de café.

Roe tomó un último sorbo antes de empezar. "Buenos días a todos. Vamos a empezar discutiendo los seis posibles candidatos; quiero escuchar lo que piensan ustedes dos acerca de ellos. Quiero avanzar rápidamente en esto y tomar una decisión hoy, pero primero necesito su opinión. Me gustaría que cada uno hiciera un resumen de sus entrevistas con ellos y que me dieran sus recomendaciones. Liam empecemos con Max Ryder. ¿Qué opinas?".

"Bueno, Roe, mi impresión de él durante la entrevista fue que parece increíblemente experto en tecnología y puede combinar técnicas tradicionales de investigación con tecnología innovadora. Él habló de su dominio de diversos programas y dispositivos de investigación. Conoce bien su trabajo, y su conocimiento sería de gran valor para la empresa".

Aggie asintió con la cabeza. "Estoy de acuerdo con Liam. El acercamiento de Max a las investigaciones es moderna y efectiva. Él nos mostró algunos casos donde sus habilidades tecnológicas hicieron una diferencia significativa. Creo que él realmente podría mejorar las capacidades de nuestro equipo tecnológico".

"Suena prometedor. Pasemos a Aloysius Black, o Al, como él prefiere. Aggie, ¿Qué opinas de él?".

"Al fue bastante carismático. Él solo tiene cuatro años de experiencia, pero se presenta a sí mismo como un veterano experimentado. Su entrevista fue intrigante—es seguro de sí mismo, casi al punto de ser arrogante, pero eso podría ser una ventaja en nuestro ámbito de trabajo. Parece tener un don para conseguir que la gente se abra con él. Funcionó conmigo. A veces él estaba entrevistándome".

"Yo tuve una impresión similar", agregó Liam. "Pero Roe, él es joven. Su confianza es tanto una fortaleza como una debilidad potencial. Aunque sus habilidades interpersonales son excelentes, necesitamos verificar sus afirmaciones sobre su experiencia. En fin, esa es mi opinión sobre él".

Mirando sus notas, Roe asintió. "Ustedes dos tienen buenos puntos. Le daremos seguimiento a sus afirmaciones sobre su experiencia. OK, vamos a hablar acerca de Andrew O'Reilly—también conocido como Andy. Liam ¿qué piensas de él?".

"Andy es un experto en ciberseguridad e investigador con conocimientos sólidos en tecnología, especializado en delitos cibernéticos y análisis forense digital. Él realmente será un gran recurso para ayudar al equipo de Noah. Su formación académica es excelente. Él soltó tantos términos técnicos que yo simplemente no sabía lo que estaba diciendo, entonces los anoté y hablé con Noah quien confirmó que él "sabe de lo que habla" como se dice por ahí. Basado en la impresión de Noah de la jerga que Andy usó y sus credenciales, creo que él encajará bien en la nueva unidad que Noah está recomendando".

"Sí, me gustó desde el primer momento". Admitió Aggie. "Los aspectos técnicos también estuvieron mucho más allá de mi comprensión, pero después de comparar notas con Liam, creo que lo hará muy bien en la nueva unidad cibernética. Roe, él se mostró bastante meticuloso, tranquilo, con la cabeza bien puesta".

"OK, excelente". Roe asintió en señal de aprobación. "Vamos a discutir el próximo, David Kim. Aggie ¿cómo estuvo tu entrevista con él?".

Mirando sus notas un momento, Aggie expuso sus argumentos: "David es un psicólogo forense con ocho años de experiencia. Su dominio en la elaboración de perfiles y entendimiento de la conducta delictiva, es excepcional. Él es tranquilo, analítico y tiene un enfoque muy metódico. Su perspectiva podría ser invaluable para nuestros casos más complejos".

Asintiendo con la cabeza, Liam agregó: "Estoy de acuerdo. La actitud tranquila de David y su mente analítica son sus mayores fortalezas. De nuevo, él parece muy perspicaz en leer personas y situaciones, lo cual puede ayudarnos en la elaboración de perfiles y análisis de sospechosos".

"OK, estamos de acuerdo hasta ahora y avanzamos rápidamente, lo cual es genial. Ahora Liam, hablemos de Sarah Blake. ¿Qué opinas?".

"Bueno, Sarah es una ex agente del FBI con doce años de experiencia. Ella está trabajando ahora como freelancer en Australia. Su trayectoria y su historial hablan por sí mismos, y basado en todo lo que leí en su expediente, ella es altamente organizada y eficiente. Vale la pena tenerla en el equipo".

"¿Tu opinión Aggie?".

"La experiencia de Sarah en el FBI realmente destacó. Ella posee un vasto conocimiento e historia probada en la gestión de casos sensibles. Su expediente contiene varias notas sobre cómo manejó algunos casos, lo cual fue crucial en resolver algunos de los más importantes. Las notas estaban muy censuradas, pero pude leer lo suficiente para entender la idea. Ella parece trabajar bien bajo presión y, además, mantener la discreción es crucial para nuestro equipo".

"Genial Aggie. Parece que en efecto ella sería una adquisición valiosa. La siguiente es Alicia Torres. Aggie tú primero. Dime cómo te fue en la entrevista con ella".

"Ella es una persona extraordinariamente interesante. Alicia es una antigua oficial de policía encubierta de la AFP, con dieciocho años de experiencia. Ella es increíblemente intrépida e ingeniosa. Su habilidad para integrarse y recopilar información desapercibida es notable. Sin nombres o lugares, ella ha aceptado misiones peligrosas y sobresale en situaciones de alto riesgo".

"Bien. Entonces, ella sabe el valor de la confidencialidad. Liam ¿qué opinas?".

"El fuerte de Alicia es su amplia experiencia encubierta. Me gusta la forma elocuente en la que habló, pero al mismo tiempo mostraba gran experiencia sobre el terreno. Además de eso, ella parece una persona intrépida que no teme ensuciarse las manos en un caso. Me recuerda a Mateo un poco. Ellos trabajarían muy bien juntos. Dos gotas de agua en cuanto a habilidades muy similares. Ella sería una excelente incorporación a nuestro equipo".

"Esa es una manera inteligente de explicarme a Alicia. OK. Gracias a ambos por su tiempo y sus opiniones sobre cada candidato hasta este momento. Ahora el último: Ethan Carter. Liam, una vez más, ¿compartes tu opinión?".

Ethan tiene una trayectoria en inteligencia militar con cinco años de experiencia. Es el clásico perfil militar, yo diría. Parece ser disciplinado y sumamente competente, estoy seguro de que su experiencia militar y entrenamiento ayudará en cualquier situación de alto riesgo".

Aggie rápidamente agregó: "Bueno, Roe, él parecía tener un aire rígido, pero su pensamiento estratégico y disciplina fueron claras durante la entrevista. Es muy metódico y tiene habilidades avanzadas de vigilancia. Su experiencia militar lo hace muy adecuado para manejar escenarios desafiantes, pero me sentí incómoda con él. No estoy segura por qué".

"Genial. Parece que tenemos algunos candidatos fuertes y un 'tal vez'", dijo mirando a Aggie. "Vamos a tomar un momento para revisar nuestras recomendaciones. Parece que

Max Ryder, Andrew O'Reilly, David Kim, Sarah Blake, Alicia Torres, e incluso Ethan Carter, todos tienen sólidas recomendaciones y experiencia. Necesitamos verificar todas sus referencias para estar seguros de que nada se le escape a la agencia de empleos, pero todos son prometedores. Aunque, en cuanto a Carter, Aggie tiene reservas. ¿Algún comentario final antes de tomar nuestra decisión?".

"Creo que tenemos una alineación sólida. Solo tenemos que ser cautelosos con la experiencia de Al y asegurarnos de que se ajusta a lo que necesitamos. Y aunque no tuve ninguna mala impresión acerca de Carter, voy a confiar en la experiencia y sabiduría de Aggie en lo que concierne a él Roe, si no te importa". Declaró Liam.

"Gracias por eso Liam, yo asumo la responsabilidad", Aggie respondió con una sonrisa en su cara para suavizar el impacto de sus palabras. Pero entonces ella se volvió hacia Roe, seria, una vez más. "Confío en que estos candidatos pueden traer mucho al equipo, pero yo realmente no estuve cómoda con Carter. Yo recomiendo que no vayamos con él y, antes de que preguntes, no puedo darte una respuesta sólida y lógica. Atribúyelo a la intuición femenina.

Roe se quedó allí sentado un rato, considerando las recomendaciones de su equipo. Él no entrevistó a ninguna de las personas. Él no necesitaba hacerlo. Él confiaba en ellos dos para su negocio.

Mi trabajo es atraer negocios y cultivar relaciones. Él pensó para sí mismo.

Aunque él había hecho muchas investigaciones por su cuenta, ya casi nunca salía a hacer trabajo de campo. Roe dejó su pluma sobre la mesa y miró a Aggie y a Liam.

"Está bien. Vamos a seguir adelante con el proceso de contratación de Max, Andy, David, Sarah y Alicia. Vamos a esperar un poco con Ethan con base en la intuición femenina de Aggie. ¿Estás de acuerdo con solo tres nuevos investigadores, Liam y los dos nuevos de tecnología?".

"Sí, lo estoy. Tú eres el jefe, Roe".

"Aggie, algún otro comentario que quieras agregar?".

"No. Esta es la mejor forma de proceder y, además, reducirá el monto de la nómina por si alguna vez pasamos por tiempos difíciles".

"OK. Gracias a ambos por hacer esto posible, háganle saber a Noah que pronto tendrá el personal para su nuevo departamento. Aggie contacta a la agencia e infórmales sobre nuestra decisión. Y asegúrate de que me avisen cuando necesitemos que el nuevo personal venga a la oficina, después de que compres el mobiliario adicional y el equipo de cómputo".

"Lo haré".

"Liam ¿quieres que los tres nuevos empiecen al mismo tiempo? ¿o prefieres escalonarlos? Así les puedes asignar sus casos y monitorearlos antes de que el próximo llegue".

"No, Roe, todos de una vez. Todos ellos son profesionales experimentados y deberían empezar a trabajar de inmediato".

"OK, Aggie entonces que se presenten el mismo día y se reporten con Liam. Me reuniré con ellos más tarde ese día.

Ahora los dos nuevos de tecnología. ¿Qué piensas Aggie? ¿Cuándo los traemos?".

"Yo creo que al mismo tiempo Roe. Puedo repasar todos los procedimientos de la oficina con los cinco el mismo día y confío en que Noah tendrá todo preparado para ellos. Ordenar todas las computadoras extra y configurarlas no debería ser un problema para Noah y él estará emocionado de que su propuesta despegó".

Liam se recostó en su silla. "Jefe, nosotros realmente no discutimos la propuesta de Noah, ¿o lo hicimos?".

"Ustedes dos me dieron suficientes pistas de que la propuesta era sólida. Miré la última línea de lo que Noah proyectó como ingreso potencial. No hay que pensarlo. De nuevo, háganle saber a Noah que sus tecnológicos están en camino. Me pondré al día con él también más tarde".

Asintiendo y sintiéndose bien de saber que su jefe confiaba en ellos, Aggie y Liam se levantaron de la mesa y salieron de la sala de conferencias, dejando a Roe reflexionando sobre cómo atraer más oportunidades de negocio.

9

La Confusión de Roe

En las siguientes semanas ocurrieron muchas cosas. Roe no solo aceptó los casos de Odyssey Insurance y Aegis Art, sino además, consiguió tres nuevos clientes por recomendación, lo que le impulsó aún más a incrementar el número de contrataciones. Aggie y Liam habían hecho un trabajo fantástico en su selección y Aggie superó todas las expectativas remodelando la oficina para acomodar a todo el personal nuevo.

En lugar de seis nuevas contrataciones, Roe terminó haciendo diez. Tres serían asignadas al nuevo equipo tecnológico de Noah, y los otros siete harían trabajo de campo para todo el trabajo adicional que llegara gracias a contactos directos o a clientes recomendados.

Las cosas pintan bien para Investigaciones Alder y Finch, él pensó.

Roe había hablado con Noah, quien estaba encantado de que Roe hubiera aceptado su propuesta, y él prometió que su nuevo equipo cumpliría con los resultados en cada caso. Y con tres nuevos empleados que guiar, Noah adoptó una actitud más profesional en la oficina. Él dejó de usar camisetas y ahora prefería las camisas sin corbata.

"Me hace más respetable ante las tropas" le había dicho a Roe.

Roe había convocado a una reunión a las 10:00 a.m. con todo el equipo para obtener una actualización sobre los varios casos que ellos habían tomado recientemente, así como de aquellos en los que ya se estaba trabajando.

Roe miró la nueva sala de conferencias.

Aggie se había superado a sí misma.

La sala de conferencias recién remodelada de Investigaciones Alder y Finch irradiaba un ambiente elegante y profesional, con guiños sutiles al mundo de la investigación.

En la sala se sentaban cómodamente 20 personas, con sillas ergonómicas de cuero dispuestas alrededor de una mesa ovalada hecha a medida con madera de nogal oscuro. La mesa tenía enchufes y puertos USB integrados, asegurando que todos los participantes pudieran conectar fácilmente sus dispositivos.

Las paredes fueron adornadas con papel tapiz color gris mate, dándole a la sala un aspecto moderno y sofisticado. Una pared fue dedicada enteramente a un pizarrón blanco de vidrio de gran tamaño, perfecto para sesiones de lluvia de ideas y para trazar casos complejos. Junto a él, se instaló un monitor de 75 pulgadas de ultra- alta definición para presentaciones, videoconferencias, o para visualización de evidencias digitales.

La iluminación fue colocada estratégicamente, con luces LED empotradas que proporcionaban una amplia iluminación sin causar deslumbramiento. Del centro de la mesa colgaban lámparas con un diseño vintage tipo bombilla de Edison, agregando un toque que evocaba el estilo de los detectives clásicos.

Para mejorar la acústica y la privacidad de la sala, se integraron discretamente paneles insonorizantes en el techo y las paredes. Una alfombra sutil con diseño de espiga de color gris carbón cubría el piso, suavizaba el sonido y agregaba a la sala una atmósfera refinada.

En un guiño a las raíces investigativas de la empresa, la sala exhibía fotografías en blanco y negro enmarcadas del personal de Investigaciones Alder y Finch, tomadas a lo largo de los años.

Le da un toque más humano, pensó Roe.

Aggie había gastado su presupuesto sabiamente y, al final, cuando ella se lo presentó a Roe, ella estuvo por debajo por $343.27. Roe se rió para sí mismo cuando Aggie le presentó la factura, junto con las computadoras adicionales, los muebles de oficina para los nuevos empleados, y la ampliación de la oficina mediante el derribo de una pared en la parte posterior.

Roe estaba orgulloso de su equipo. Hay que gastar dinero para ganar dinero, él pensó de nuevo. Pero con los casos en curso y estos nuevos, si se resuelven todos, Investigaciones Alder y Finch estará posicionada muy por delante.

Roe miró alrededor, notando que 16 sillas estaban ocupadas, entonces, exactamente a las 10:00 a.m. él dio inicio a la reunión.

"OK, Liam, vamos a empezar con tu equipo. Por favor ilústranos con tus avances".

Liam se aclaró la garganta.

"Roe, he asignado a Aloysius Black, Emily Chen y yo mismo, los casos de Odyssey Insurance concernientes a los incendios provocados tanto del negocio comercial como el de la casa. Noah está trabajando con Luke Cross en la parte técnica, y hemos hecho algunos progresos. Aquí están mis reportes por escrito de ambos casos, los cuales creo que estamos listos para concluir".

Roe hojeó las carpetas mientras Liam se sentaba al otro lado de la mesa. "OK, Liam, comparte tus hallazgos con el grupo".

"Bueno, Roe, permíteme resumirlo rápidamente para ustedes. En la noche del 5 de agosto de 2024, aproximadamente a las 11:45 p.m., se produjo un incendio en LCU Ltd Pty, un concesionario de automóviles exóticos bien establecido en Parramatta, propiedad de Mr. y Mrs. James y Marybeth Saxon. El fuego causó daños extensos a la sala de exposición y a los espacios de oficinas, destruyendo todos los vehículos de alta gama y provocando pérdidas financieras significativas. El departamento de bomberos llegó puntualmente y contuvo el fuego previniendo que se extendiera a los negocios vecinos. La brigada inicial de incendios provocados de la policía investigó y concluyó que el incendio fue provocado deliberadamente. Sin embargo, debido a la falta de evidencia concluyente y testigos, no se identificó a ningún sospechoso. La policía notó que las cámaras de seguridad habían sido manipuladas y los puntos de entrada mostraban señales de haber sido forzados, sugiriendo la participación de incendiarios profesionales. A pesar de sus esfuerzos, el caso permaneció sin resolver".

"Pero no por mucho tiempo, ¿correcto Liam?". Roe preguntó, sonriendo.

Sonriendo también, Liam agregó: "Correcto. No por mucho tiempo".

"Ahora, tras ser contratados por la empresa aseguradora, nos hicimos cargo del caso. Revisamos meticulosamente la evidencia, incluyendo el punto de origen del incendio, grabaciones de seguridad, y declaraciones de los testigos—muy pocas, a propósito—mientras la policía se enfocaba en las cámaras de seguridad manipuladas y la entrada forzada, nuestro equipo descubrió un descuido crítico, un pequeño detalle aparentemente sin importancia que había pasado desapercibido".

Parecía que todo el grupo se inclinaba hacia adelante de sus cómodas sillas para escuchar lo que Liam, Al y Emily habían descubierto.

"Los incendiarios habían usado una marca específica de acelerante para encender el fuego, el cual fue identificado como un disolvente de grado industrial poco común. Durante nuestra investigación—aquí es donde ambos investigadores en campo, y Noah y Luke Cross trabajaron tan bien juntos—, nosotros descubrimos que un proveedor local vendió este disolvente exclusivamente a un puñado de clientes en el área. Tras una investigación más profunda, encontramos que uno de los compradores recientes era una empresa de construcción subcontratada por Mr. Saxon para renovaciones en su residencia personal.

Nuestro equipo vinculó la compra a un socio conocido de Mr. Saxon, un hombre con una historia de participación en actividades ilegales, incluyendo incendios provocados por encargo. Un seguimiento adicional y el análisis de las finanzas, revelaron una serie de pagos inexplicables de Mr. Saxon a esta persona, justo en el momento del incendio". Liam asintió a Noah y Luke, reconociendo su invaluable ayuda en esta área.

"Esta conexión crucial que pasó por alto la policía, nos llevó a concluir que Mr. Saxon había contratado a personas externas para provocar el incendio, esperando reclamar una gran indemnización del seguro". Liam se sentó de nuevo para dar su conclusión.

"Basados en nuestros hallazgos, presentamos la evidencia a la policía de NSW, lo que llevó al arresto de ambos: Mr. Saxon y el incendiario contratado. El plan de Mr. Lawson para disfrazar el incendio provocado como un acto criminal no relacionado, falló por el descuido crítico del uso de un acelerante rastreable que nuestra agencia identificó y relacionó con él. Estamos listos para compartir nuestros hallazgos con Odyssey Insurance cuando nos des el visto bueno, Roe".

"Excelente trabajo, Liam, y el resto de ustedes. ¿Qué pasó con el incendio de la casa?".

"Dejaré que Al y Emily lo resuman para ti. Al, empieza tú".

Aloysius se levantó. "Claro. No había duda de que tenía que haber una conexión entre el incendio del concesionario de autos y la casa propiedad de los Saxon. Esta vez, al mismo incendiario profesional se le ocurrió una forma interesante para producir el incendio.

Durante nuestra investigación, descubrimos un error crítico que había pasado desapercibido tanto para la policía como para los incendiarios. El fuego empezó en el sótano, donde un deshumidificador viejo, pero todavía en funcionamiento, había sido colocado. Nuestro equipo forense encontró que había sido manipulado para causar un corto circuito, encendiendo materiales cercanos. Este montaje tenía como propósito hacer que el incendio pareciera accidental.

Sin embargo, tras examinar el cableado, nuestro equipo descubrió una anomalía inusual: el cable de alimentación del deshumidificador había sido reemplazado por uno de un modelo diferente. Este cable no era compatible con el cableado original del deshumidificador, lo que provocó una conexión eléctrica inestable. Una investigación más detallada reveló que el cable de repuesto era de una marca específica utilizada solo por una pequeña tienda local de reparación de aparatos electrónicos".

"Me gusta lo que estoy escuchando", interrumpió Roe. "Por favor, continúa Al—¿puedo llamarte All?".

"Sí señor, adelante, pero me gustaría que Emily lo resumiera para nosotros". Él la miró y ella se puso de pie mientras él se sentaba.

Emily miró alrededor de la mesa y percibió que todos estaban listos para la conclusión, así que empezó: "Rastreando los registros de compra de esta tienda, identificamos a la persona que compró el cable solo días antes del incendio—otro socio de Mr. Saxon. Una investigación más profunda reveló que este socio había recibido recientemente un pago sustancial de Mrs. Saxon, no de Mr. Saxon, similar al patrón observado en el concesionario de automóviles incendiado. Nosotros concluimos que, o Mr. Saxon le había dado instrucciones a Ms. Saxon para que realizara el pago y ella no era consciente del propósito de éste, o ella estaba involucrada en el fraude. Al final, resultó que ella estaba involucrada. Ella quería remodelar la casa pero no quería gastar el dinero.

El error crítico—usar un cable de alimentación no compatible—llevó a desentrañar su plan. Descubrimos que Mrs. Saxon se enteró de que Mr. Saxon había contratado a alguien para que incendiara la concesionaria de automóviles sin que ella lo supiera, pero una vez que ella confrontó a su esposo, él le contó lo que hizo. Entonces ella le pidió hacer lo mismo con la casa y así es como ella se involucró en el segundo caso, pero no en el primero. Nosotros presentamos nuestros hallazgos a la policía, lo que resultó en la imputación de cargos adicionales contra Mrs. Saxon y el cómplice de Mr. Saxon.

Al igual que Liam en el caso previo, nosotros también estamos listos para compartir estos hallazgos con Odyssey Insurance cuando tú nos des luz verde para proceder, Roe".

Con eso, ella se sentó, satisfecha con su reporte.

Ahora era el turno de Roe de ponerse de pie.

"Gracias al trabajo meticuloso de nuestro equipo de investigación, nosotros conectamos exitosamente los dos casos del incendio intencional, exponiendo el plan orquestado por los Saxon y ahorrando a nuestro cliente una gran cantidad de dinero en pagos por reclamaciones. ¡Gracias al equipo!". Él aplaudió, como todos los demás.

Una vez que Roe se sentó, Liam dijo: "Roe, le pedimos a la policía de NSW no contactar a Ms. Elizabeth Armstrong de Odyssey Insurance y permitirte hacer ese honor. ¿Espero que esté bien?".

"Sí, buena decisión de tu parte, Liam. Tal vez podemos ofrecerle a Odyssey Insurance un contrato de servicios permanentes para el futuro. Sin duda puedo abordar el tema. ¿Qué opinas Aggie?".

"Un buen punto. Tendrás que pensar en el costo/análisis de tal arreglo, pero tengo algunas ideas que puedo compartir contigo más tarde, antes de que contactes a Ms. Armstrong".

"Excelente. Por favor llámala después de que terminemos esta reunión. ¿Ahora qué sigue Liam?".

Liam se levantó, caminó alrededor de la mesa y le entregó a Roe la carpeta del siguiente caso. Él leyó el número del caso y miró a Liam, quien sonreía como el gato de Cheshire.

"OK, Liam, cuéntame. ¿Qué pasó con este caso?".

"Un caso realmente extraordinario, Roe. Tuve a Jack Stone, Evelyn Drake y David Kim trabajando en él, y decir que este fue un caso inusual es quedarse corto. Dejaré que David lo explique".

David también se puso de pie y empezó: "Para refrescar la memoria de todos, déjenme recapitular. En un atraco que dejó a la ciudad entera desconcertada, 500,000 mariposas fueron robadas del Museum of Natural Oddities. La colección—promocionada como la colección más grande y diversa de mariposas del mundo—estaba valuada en $4.7 millones. La preciada exposición del museo 'Wings of the World', presentando mariposas de cada rincón del mundo, desapareció de la noche a la mañana. Lo más asombroso era el hecho de que los sistemas de seguridad del museo no mostraban signos de una entrada forzada, llevando a las autoridades a sospechar de un atraco tan meticulosamente planeado que rayaba en lo absurdo".

David miró alrededor del cuarto, detectando que el grupo esperaba más detalles extraños, entonces él continuó: "La Unidad de robo de Arte y Antigüedades del departamento de NSW acudió al lugar de los hechos. Ellos investigaron, enfocándose en los puntos posibles de entrada, revisando las imágenes de seguridad y entrevistando al personal del museo. La investigación se centró inicialmente en la posibilidad de un trabajo externo, puesto que el sistema de seguridad del museo no había sido violado, y no había signos de entrada forzada. Sin embargo, la policía se encontró en un callejón sin salida. Las imágenes de seguridad no mostraban nada inusual, y todas las puertas y ventanas estaban cerradas. La investigación era aún más complicada porque las mariposas se almacenaron en una sala con control climático, al que se tenía acceso limitado, monitoreado por un sistema de última generación. Sin pistas claras, la policía concluyó que el robo debió haber sido un trabajo interno, pero no pudo identificar un sospechoso".

Con una gran sonrisa en su cara, David continuó: "Frustrados por la falta de progreso, la compañía de seguros del museo nos contrató para tomar el control del caso. Nuestro equipo comenzó revisando toda la evidencia disponible y entrevistando a los empleados del museo con una perspectiva fresca".

"¿Qué encontraron, David?". Preguntó Aggie.

David miró a Evelyn, quien se puso de pie para tomar el control de la presentación.

"Gran pregunta, MacTavish. En realidad, una pregunta brillante. Primero examinamos los registros de acceso a la sala con control climático donde fueron almacenadas las mariposas. Aunque la policía había revisado los registros y no encontró nada sospechoso, nuestro equipo notó un patrón sutil, pero revelador. Un miembro del personal, un conserje llamado—¿están listos para esto? Reginald "Reggie" Flutters—tuvo acceso a esa sala a altas horas de la noche, solo horas antes de que el robo fuera descubierto. Aunque los conserjes tenían acceso para limpiar, el acceso de Reggie se registró a una hora inusual—alrededor de las 2:00 a.m. un momento en el que la limpieza ya suele estar terminada".

"¿Ese es el nombre del conserje? ¿Reginald "Reggie" Flutters?".

"Sí, en efecto, ese es".

Aggie miró a Evelyn por un segundo o dos más, entonces preguntó, "¿Y cómo sabes esto?".

"Por todos los registros de los años anteriores. Resultaba bastante inusual que alguien hiciera la limpieza a esa hora. Por lo tanto, nuestro equipo inspeccionó minuciosamente la sala con control climático y descubrió una pequeña y discreta rejilla de ventilación cerca del techo. Si bien se suponía que era parte del sistema HVAC, notamos que los tornillos de la cubierta de ventilación habían sido alterados recientemente. Las investigaciones posteriores revelaron que la ventilación era lo suficientemente grande como para que una persona pasara a través de ella o para sacar cajas pequeñas. Este descubrimiento sugería que podrían haber sacado las mariposas a través de la rejilla de ventilación sin activar el sistema de seguridad".

"¿Así es como entraron?".

Evelyn asintió. "Sí, eso creemos. Entonces nosotros revisamos los registros de mantenimiento y descubrimos que Reggie había presentado varias solicitudes de mantenimiento para reparaciones menores cerca del almacén de las mariposas, semanas previas al robo. Estas solicitudes eran aparentemente benignas, pero coincidían con momentos en los que el sistema de seguridad del museo estaba temporalmente desactivado, permitiéndole a Reggie explorar posibles debilidades sin levantar sospechas. Ahora permítanme pasarle la palabra a Jack para terminar".

Jack sonrió pero permaneció en su silla, aparentemente cómodo, haciendo el resto de la presentación sentado.

"Ahora, aquí es donde se pone un poco raro. La primera cosa que notó nuestro equipo fue la presencia de un conserje que había sido empleado del museo alrededor de 20 años. Reggie era conocido por sus excentricidades, incluyendo su amor por las mariposas—tanto, que había memorizado los nombres en latín de cada especie de la colección. La policía había entrevistado a Reggie, pero lo desestimaron debido a su sólida coartada: afirmó haber estado..." y aquí Jack hizo comillas con las manos, "'en casa cuidando su colección de mariposas' durante la hora del robo.

Quiero señalar aquí que nuestro equipo consideró esto absurdo y sospechoso".

Una rápida carcajada recorrió la sala, pero se apagó cuando Roe dijo: "Continúa, Jack".

Asintiendo, Jack continuó. "La coartada de Reggie quedó aún más debilitada cuando descubrimos un peculiar historial de pedidos en su cuenta de compras en línea, gracias a la búsqueda de Noah y Max. Reggie había comprado recientemente varios cientos de metros de malla fina, junto con una gran cantidad de miel—una sustancia conocida por atraer mariposas. Esto nos llevó a investigar la posibilidad de que, de alguna manera, Reggie había atraído a las mariposas fuera del museo. Pero ¿cómo podría haberlo hecho sin ser detectado?".

El grupo murmuró entre sí por un momento cuando Liam interrumpió: "Sigue adelante, Jack. No dejes al grupo en suspenso".

Sonriendo, Jack continuó.

"Nuestro gran avance vino cuando revisamos los registros de mantenimiento del museo, como señaló Evelyn. Reggie había reportado 'un problema de ventilación' en la exposición de mariposas justo días antes del robo. El sistema HVAC del museo se ajustó para aumentar el flujo de aire, y nadie le dio mayor importancia. De lo que nadie se dio cuenta fue que Reggie había cambiado los ductos de ventilación para crear una suave brisa que esparcía el aroma de la miel por toda la exposición. Durante varias noches Reggie liberó lentamente las mariposas dentro del sistema de ventilación abriendo los discretos paneles de acceso. Reggie atrajo a las mariposas con el aroma dulce de la miel y la promesa de libertad, haciendo que siguieran el flujo de aire a través de los ductos. Finalmente, las fue guiando hacia una serie de grandes bolsas de malla hechas a la medida que él había ocultado en el almacén del museo".

Ahora el grupo estaba realmente emocionado.

"Sigue, Jack. ¡Cuéntanos!", casi gritó Sophia. Ella rápidamente se sintió avergonzada por su arrebato, antes de que ella se diera cuenta de que Roe también sonreía.

"Muy bien, una vez que habíamos reconstruido este extraño método, necesitábamos encontrar dónde había llevado Reggie las mariposas. Reggie vivía en una pequeña casa a las afueras de la ciudad, conocida por su jardín descuidado y su 'santuario de mariposas'. Pero era lo que yacía debajo de ese jardín lo que nos llamó la atención—¡un búnker subterráneo oculto! Tras un examen más detallado, descubrimos que Reggie había transformado el búnker en un hábitat improvisado para mariposas, completo, con control de temperatura y filas de espacios cercados con malla. Las quinientas mil mariposas fueron encontradas vivas y en buen estado, revoloteando felices en su nuevo hogar subterráneo. Parecía que el amor de Reggie por las mariposas lo había llevado a cometer uno de los atracos más absurdos, pero meticulosamente planeados, en la historia de la policía de NSW".

Jack dijo: "Liam, tú haz los honores de terminar nuestro gran relato".

Encantado de ayudarle y reportar sus conclusiones, Liam afirmó: "El error crítico de "Reginald "Reggie" Flutter, fue subestimar lo absurdo de su propio plan—algo que nosotros aquí en Investigaciones Alder y Finch estamos especialmente equipados para detectar y desentrañar. Reggie fue arrestado y acusado de robo mayor, aunque él insistió en que él sólo había querido 'darles a las mariposas un hogar mejor'. Las mariposas fueron devueltas de manera segura al museo, y se evitó la reclamación del seguro por los $4.7 millones, para gran alivio del museo y de sus patrocinadores".

Liam se sentó para hacer su última declaración. "Roe, una vez más le pedí a la policía de NSW no contactar a Mr. Roland Jamieson de la compañía de seguros y dejarte hacer ese honor. Espero no estar presionando nuestra amistad con el departamento de policía sobre esto, pero pensé que era tal el caso que tú debías informarle a Mr. Jamieson todos los detalles personalmente".

Roe tomó unos minutos para pensar en las últimas palabras de Liam antes de que, sin una razón, él empezara a reírse y entonces estalló en una carcajada estruendosa. El resto de la sala se le unió. Después de un minuto, él se dirigió al grupo, tratando de reprimir su risa.

"Bueno, el caso de la desaparición de las mariposas quedará registrado en nuestros libros de récords como uno de los atracos más extraños, pero curiosamente creíbles, jamás descubiertos. Gracias a la diligencia y creatividad del equipo aquí reunido, se hizo justicia, y las mariposas fueron salvadas de una vida bajo tierra. ¡Excelente!".

El equipo respondió a la celebración ruidosamente, y riendo aún.

"OK, OK, vamos a calmarnos y a regresar al trabajo. Esta fue una gran reunión. Liam, Aggie, por favor quédense. Todos tomen una pausa para el café y regresen a sus casos", dijo Roe con la sonrisa más grande que Liam y Aggie habían visto jamás en el hombre.

Cuando la sala de conferencias se había quedado vacía, excepto por los tres, Roe se dirigió a su personal de mayor antigüedad.

"¿Cómo les fue a ellos en estas tareas?".

Ambos, Aggie y Liam se miraron el uno al otro y ella asintió con la cabeza a Liam como diciendo: "la pelota está en tu cancha".

"Roe, todos ellos lo hicieron maravillosamente. Estos casos nos permitieron conocer mejor a tu nuevo personal y ver sus habilidades en acción".

"OK, respondió Roe, "Aggie, dime tus impresiones".

Aggie sacó una hoja de papel y se la entregó a Roe. "Refresca tu memoria sobre las nuevas contrataciones antes de que te responda".

Una vez más, Roe miró el papel que le entregó y lo leyó por encima.

Andrew (Andy) O'Reilly —Un experto en ciberseguridad y experto investigador en tecnología, que se especializa en ciberdelincuencia e informática forense. Formará parte del equipo de Noah.

Max Ryder —Investigador privado con cuatro años de experiencia, experto en tecnología, quien combina técnicas de investigación tradicionales con tecnología innovadora para descubrir la verdad. Formará parte del equipo de Noha.

Luke Cross —Un investigador privado tranquilo pero muy observador (dos años de experiencia) que resuelve casos con una combinación de intuición y atención meticulosa al detalle. Le encantan las computadoras. Formará parte del equipo de Noah.

Jack Stone: Un expolicía sensato y robusto con diez años de experiencia que se volvió investigador privado, conocido por su agudo ingenio y búsqueda incansable de justicia.

Evelyn Drake —Una experiodista con tres años de experiencia, se volvió investigadora privada por su tenacidad e ingenio para descubrir historias y secretos ocultos.

Nina Hart —Una investigadora privada ferozmente independiente e inteligente, con seis años de experiencia, con frecuencia va encubierta para resolver casos que otros consideran demasiado peligrosos o complejos.

Aloysius Black —Investigador carismático y astuto con habilidad especial para conseguir que la gente revele sus secretos. Solo tiene cuatro años de experiencia, pero se presenta a sí mismo como un veterano. Se hace llamar Al.

Jack Malone —Antiguo detective de policía. Se retiró después de 20 años. Él tiene una habilidad especial para resolver casos complejos, con frecuencia confiando en su extensa red de contactos y su profundo conocimiento de la psicología criminal.

David Kim —Ocho años de ser psicólogo forense. Su experiencia en psicología y trabajo de investigación, lo hace excepcionalmente bueno para hacer perfiles de sospechosos y comprender su comportamiento delictivo. Su comportamiento tranquilo y mente analítica son sus mayores fortalezas.

Emily Chen —Siete años como investigadora de fraudes de seguros para Carmichael, Strong, y Weathers. En búsqueda de nuevos retos. Ella se especializa en detección de fraude y tiene un ojo agudo para detectar inconsistencias. Su enfoque metódico y diligencia la hacen altamente efectiva para descubrir estafas y actividades fraudulentas.

No le tomó mucho tiempo entender lo que Aggie estaba insinuando; estos eran los mejores de los mejores. Y aunque Malone y Hart no estuvieron involucrados en estos casos, Roe estaba seguro de que Liam los tenía trabajando en algo más.

"Liam, ¿qué tal Nina Hart y Jack Malone? Ellos no estuvieron en estos casos. ¿En qué están trabajando?".

"Tengo a Nina y a Jack trabajando en el caso del suicidio. Ellos están haciendo progresos sustanciales".

Ahora Roe llevaba las de perder. ¿Qué caso de suicidio? "Refresca mi memoria, Liam. ¿De qué caso estás hablando?".

Aggie y Liam intercambiaron una mirada, sorprendidos de que él no pudiera recordarlo.

"¿El de Southern Cross Life Assurance?", Aggie dijo tentativamente. "Y su preocupación acerca del fraude de un suicidio simulado".

Roe estaba avergonzado. ¿Cómo pudo haber olvidado el caso de Southern Cross Life Assurance y a Ms. Emily Dickson?

"Por supuesto—Ms. Dickson de Southern Cross Life Assurance. Yo solo no la relacioné con el caso del suicidio. Eso es todo. ¿Dices que el caso va bien?".

"Es cierto, y deberíamos terminarlo en breve".

Aggie miró a Roe y dijo: "¿Estás bien Roe? Parecías un poco perdido allí por un momento".

"Estoy bien, Aggie. Yo simplemente no relacioné el suicidio con Southern Cross Life Assurance", él repitió, forzando una sonrisa. "Ahora, ¿cuál es tu opinión del equipo de nuevos empleados?".

"Excelentes elecciones, sinceramente. Ellos ya han pagado todo su salario con estos dos casos, y todavía nos quedan nueve meses para que termine este año fiscal".

"Gracias a ustedes dos. Ahora déjenme leer los expedientes una vez más y llamaré a Ms. Armstrong y Mr. Jamieson para contarles las buenas noticias".

Aggie y Liam asintieron en señal de aproba-ción, pero les extrañó la confusión de Roe. ¿Todo es-taba realmente bien?

10

Emily Dickson

Después de que Liam y Aggie dejaron la sala de conferencias, la intención de Roe realmente era leer los expedientes y hacerles a ambos clientes una llamada rápida con las buenas noticias. En lugar de eso, él tomó las carpetas, las llevó a su oficina, tomó su saco y le dijo a Aggie que iba a ir caminando al pub White Horse para un almuerzo temprano. Él necesitaba salir, despejarse.

Habían pasado un par de meses desde que Roe le había dado a Liam el expediente de Southern Cross Life Assurance para trabajar en él después de haberlo discutido con Ms. Emily Dickson.

Emily Dickson, investigadora principal de reclamaciones en Southern Cross Life Assurance, fue la razón de que él se hubiera tomado un descanso y fuera a Crystal Cove por un par de semanas.

El año pasado Roe se había reunido con Mr. Jason Betancourt de Heritage Shield Insurance, cuando Investigaciones Alder y Finch tenía sus oficinas en el Distrito Central de Negocios de Sídney. Mr. Betancourt les había llamado para que les ayudaran en el caso de un fraude con un libro antiguo. Mr. Betancourt había asignado a Emily para colaborar con Investigaciones Alder y Finch.

Durante la investigación, Roe y Emily habían estado en constante contacto y, lo que empezó como una colaboración profesional, rápidamente se convirtió en algo más. Roe se descubrió a sí mismo esperando con interés cada reunión, cada llamada de teléfono. Emily era aguda, perspicaz y tenía un sentido del humor irónico que coincidía con el de él. Ella tenía una forma de hacerlo olvidar el estrés del trabajo, aunque solo fuera por un momento. Pero había más que eso — una innegable química que ninguno de los dos podía ignorar.

Mientras trabajaron juntos, Roe notó pequeñas cosas: la forma en que los ojos de Emily brillaban cuando ella encontraba una pequeña pieza de evidencia, la forma que mordía su labio cuando estaba absorta en sus pensamientos, y las miradas sutiles que ellos intercambiaban cuando sus manos se rozaban mientras revisaban minuciosamente los documentos.

Cuanto más cerca estaban de resolver el caso, Roe estaba más envuelto en pensamientos sobre Emily. No era solo su inteligencia o su belleza; era la conexión que ellos compartían, una conexión que se sentía natural e intensa, todo al mismo tiempo.

Pero Emily estaba casada, y Roe respetó ese límite, a pesar de la creciente tensión entre ellos.

Después de que el caso fuera exitosamente cerrado, ellos salieron a tomar unas bebidas para celebrar con el resto del equipo. A medida que avanzaba la noche, y los demás se retiraban, Roe y Emily de repente se quedaron solos, sentados en el bar. La conversación se volvió más personal, la risa más íntima. Emily le confió a Roe sobre su matrimonio en crisis, su infelicidad y su incertidumbre acerca del futuro. Roe escuchó ofreciéndole apoyo, pero luchaba internamente con sus propios sentimientos por ella.

Esa noche, mientras salían al aire fresco del puerto de Sídney, la atracción entre ellos era palpable. Ellos se quedaron cerca, demasiado cerca, como si fueran atraídos por una fuerza invisible. Por un momento, se sentía como si algo pudiera pasar, algo inevitable; algo que él no podría detener, no querría detener. Pero Emily se apartó, había una mirada de arrepentimiento en sus ojos.

"No puedo, Roe", ella había murmurado, con su voz cargada de emoción. "Yo estoy casada. Necesito resolver esto por mi cuenta".

Roe había asentido con la cabeza, comprendiendo, pero estaba en conflicto. Él la había visto alejarse, desapareciendo en la noche, y le costó un gran esfuerzo no seguirla.

Ahora, sentado en el pub White Horse con una cerveza frente a él, esperando que llegara su almuerzo, Roe no se pudo sacudir los pensamientos de Emily. Había pasado más de un año desde la última vez que la vio. Él había tomado tiempo libre para relajarse un poco, aclarar su cabeza, prepararse para la nueva oficina y, durante su tiempo en Crystal Cove, su mente había seguido divagando pensando en Emily.

Y entonces, justo cuando él estaba a punto de tomar un sorbo de su bebida, su teléfono vibró y, no reconociendo el número, él contestó.

Era Emily. Y todo lo que ella dijo fue: "¿Podemos hablar?".

Él rápidamente respondió: "Sí".

Emily explicó que ahora ella era vicepresidente en Stonebridge Insurance Group en Parramatta y necesitaba las habilidades de un experto como Investigaciones Alder y Finch, ella quería discutir un caso con él y otro asunto en persona. Roe estuvo de acuerdo inmediatamente y sugirió una reunión en el restaurante Petit Maison en Northport y, sin dudar ni hacer preguntas, ella estuvo de acuerdo en reunirse para una cena de trabajo.

Después de colgar, Roe solo se sentó ahí, preguntándose cuál era el caso con el que Emily quería ayuda, y cuál podría ser el "otro asunto" que ella quería discutir.

En ese momento, Roe permitió que sus emociones afloraran mientras los pensamientos sobre Emily seguían invadiendo su mente, pero se percató de que ella le había llamado para una oportunidad de trabajo para Alder y Finch. Fuera cual fuera el "otro asunto", él no tenía ni idea, y decidió solo esperar y ver lo que Emily tenía que decir sobre eso.

11

Juntos

Roe se vio atrapado en un torbellino de emociones, incluso un poco confundido por lo que sentía. Él se preguntó si sería capaz de trabajar en otro caso con Emily.

Su último caso juntos los había acercado tanto que cambió todo entre ellos. Ahora, con Emily pidiendo la ayuda de Alder y Finch una vez más, Roe no estaba seguro de si estaba listo para volver a la esfera profesional con ella, especialmente con tanto sin resolver entre ellos.

Pero no era solo el caso lo que ocupaba su mente. ¿Qué era el "otro asunto" que Emily quería discutir? Esto era lo que realmente dejó a Roe desconcertado. Él no pudo evitar preguntarse qué era.

¿Es algo personal? ¿Es algo acerca de su matrimonio, su vida? ¿O podría ser algo acerca de nosotros? Él pensó.

Ellos habían tenido algunos momentos en el pasado en los que él había sentido una creciente tensión. ¿Acaso Emily también sentía que había algo entre ellos, algo que ninguno de los dos se atrevía a decir?

Para su reunión, Roe había escogido un restaurante con un menú de inspiración francesa a donde él había llevado a muchos clientes para discutir algún caso. Él llegó temprano, no queriendo arriesgarse a llegar tarde y le mostraron un asiento en una mesa en un rincón apartado. El ambiente era cálido, con iluminación suave y el gentil murmullo de conversaciones alrededor de él, pero Roe apenas lo notó. Estaba cada vez más y más preocupado por esta reunión con Emily.

"Cálmate viejo amigo. Ella está aquí para discutir el caso y probablemente algún otro asunto menor", se dijo a sí mismo.

Cuando finalmente entró Emily, se quedó sin aliento. Ella lucía impresionante, más de lo que nunca antes la había visto.

Había algo diferente en ella. Ella caminaba con una confianza que la hacía parecer incluso más cautivadora. Mientras el mesero la conducía a la mesa, el corazón de Roe latía con fuerza en su pecho. Por supuesto, él había estado tan enfocado en la próxima discusión acerca del caso, que no estaba completamente preparado para la forma en que ella podría hacerlo sentir con solo una mirada.

Roe se puso de pie. "Emily. Es tan agradable verte de nuevo", fue lo único que se le ocurrió decir.

"Lo mismo digo, Roe. Es bueno verte, también".

Ellos se sentaron e intercambiaron frases de cortesía antes de continuar y, finalmente, discutieron el caso. Era un asunto que involucraba otro posible fraude de seguro que el equipo de Emily había estado investigando.

"Sin éxito", ella agregó antes de hacer una pausa. Ella miró sus manos por un momento, entones volvió a mirar a

Roe; su expresión era seria pero suave. "Roe, ¿tienes alguna pregunta más sobre el caso?".

No, Emily, lo explicaste bien. Yo solo necesitaría el expediente del caso para revisarlo en la oficina. ¿Podrías enviarme el expediente por mensajería en la mañana?".

"Por supuesto. Considéralo hecho". Emily dijo. Ella dudó un momento. "Roe, hay algo más de lo que necesito hablar contigo", ella dijo, con voz firme, pero llena de emoción.

OK. Aquí viene, pensó Roe.

"Es acerca de nosotros", ella continuó, sus ojos se encontraron con los de él. "He estado pensando mucho, y no puedo seguir fingiendo que nada ha cambiado entre nosotros. Roe, necesito ser honesta contigo acerca de cómo me siento".

El corazón de Roe se aceleró mientras escuchaba sus palabras, cada una golpeándolo como una ola.

Emily tomó una respiración profunda, su mirada era inquebrantable. "Yo no puedo parar de pensar en ti, en nosotros. Sé que esto no es fácil, y tú sabes que aún estoy casada, pero mi matrimonio ha terminado en todos los aspectos importantes. En muchos, muchos sentidos, Roe. Estoy haciéndolo oficial, y quería decírtelo antes de que sigamos con el caso. Me estoy… divorciando".

Roe estaba atónito. Él siempre había tenido sentimientos intensos por Emily y había tratado de no mostrarlos por respeto a ella y a su matrimonio, pero él sabía que se le habían notado un par de veces en el pasado. Él también sentía que Emily, en su momento, le había dejado entrever lo que sentía, pero ninguno de los dos había cruzado la línea.

Pero escuchar a Emily hablar tan abiertamente acerca de sus sentimientos, lo dejó todo claro.

Roe extendió la mano por encima de la mesa y tomó la suya. "Emily, quiero que sepas que he me estado sintiendo de la misma forma desde hace mucho tiempo y no quería complicar las cosas para ti, especialmente con todo lo que estás pasando. Sigo sin querer complicar la situación al involucrarnos mientras tú estás decidiendo qué vas a hacer. No puedo negar lo que hay entre nosotros, pero esperaré todo el tiempo que sea necesario para que tomes todas tus decisiones. Entonces, y solo entonces, nosotros podemos seguir adelante con, vamos a llamarlo, una nueva relación. ¿Qué opinas?".

Emily sonrió, una mezcla de alivio y felicidad inundaba sus rasgos. "Me alegra que te sientas de la misma forma, Roe. He estado tan asustada de lo que esto podría significar, pero ya no quiero huir de ello".

La conversación que siguió estuvo llena de honestidad y vulnerabilidad conforme ambos se sinceraban sobre sus sentimientos y los desafíos que sabían que enfrentarían. No sería fácil, y los dos sabían eso, pero estaban listos para afrontarlo juntos.

Saliendo de Petite Maison, ellos caminaron juntos lado a lado, sus manos rozándose, ninguno de los dos estaba dispuesto a dejar ir este momento. Y cuando ellos llegaron a la esquina, Roe se detuvo, volviéndose hacia Emily.

"Este es solo el comienzo, ¿verdad?", él pregunto suavemente.

Emily asintió, sus ojos brillaban con una mezcla de esperanza y certeza. "Sí, lo es".

Y con eso, Roe se inclinó, acortando la distancia entre ellos, y le dio un beso en la mejilla derecha. Emily sonrió y se tocó la mejilla como si quisiera atrapar el beso, entonces, con la misma mano, posó su dedo índice sobre los labios de Roe y murmuró: "Pronto, Roe. Pronto".

Roe sintió ese dedo en sus labios como si fuera un beso. Un beso que marcaba el comienzo de algo nuevo y desconocido. Mientras ellos estaban ahí, de pie bajo el brillo de los faroles, ambos supieron que este era el comienzo de un viaje que estaban listos para emprender juntos sin importar a donde los llevara.

Roe interrumpió el momento y, en un tono serio, hizo una declaración.

Emily, ahora puedo asegurarte completamente que Investigaciones Alder y Finch puede tomar tu caso, pero yo no puedo estar involucrado más que como consultor de mi equipo. TrueBlue Life Insurance tendrá que tratar directamente con mi investigador principal, Mr. Liam O'Connor. ¿Esto te parece bien?".

La sonrisa de Emily vaciló ligeramente mientras ella asimilaba lo que Roe había dicho, la calidez del momento se enfrió bajo el peso de su seriedad. Ella lo miró a los ojos, intentando entender el cambio de tono y la repentina distancia que él estaba poniendo entre los dos.

"Roe", ella comenzó, su voz era firme pero teñida de preocupación, "estoy de acuerdo".

Roe respiró profundamente, su mano ahora sostenía la de ella, y dijo: "Necesitamos establecer límites, mantener el enfoque en el trabajo, y asegurarnos de manejar esto profesionalmente. Pero no me distanciaré de ti", él prometió, "ni cuando me necesites ni cuando yo quiera estar a tu lado".

Roe hizo una pausa, sus ojos buscaban en los de ella alguna señal que le diera seguridad. "Lo afrontaremos juntos, Emily, tanto en el caso como en lo que sea que se nos presente en el camino de manera personal. Pero debemos prometernos que seremos honestos, nos comunicaremos abiertamente, y mantendremos nuestras prioridades claras. Si podemos hacer eso, entonces creo que podemos manejar cualquier cosa".

Él sonrió entonces, una sonrisa genuina y cálida que llegaba a sus ojos. "Entonces sí, Emily, estaré contigo en esto, en cada paso del camino. Encontraremos la manera juntos".

Una vez más, Emily se inclinó hacia Roe y le dio un cálido beso.

"Roe, haré que mi oficina te envíe todos los archivos del caso para que tu equipo pueda empezar de inmediato. Acepto que manejemos este caso profesionalmente. Mientras tanto, continuaré con mis procedimientos personales y te mantendré al tanto de lo que pasa. ¿OK?".

Roe asintió y le abrió la puerta del coche.

Emily subió y se alejó, dejando a Roe lleno de expectación y esperanza por primera vez en mucho tiempo.

12

Stonebridge Insurance Group

Roe empujó la puerta de vidrio de la oficina de Investigaciones Alder y Finch haciendo una ligera mueca cuando esta chirrió. Él sabía que llegaba tarde y a juzgar por el suave murmullo de voces del fondo, Liam y Aggie ya habían empezado su día. Roe tomó nota mental para recordarse conseguir a alguien que engrasara las bisagras ya que él no quería que todos se enteraran de que había llegado tarde.

Él colgó su abrigo en el perchero y respiró hondo antes de dirigirse a su escritorio. Sus ojos se entrecerraron a la vista de una carpeta gruesa colocada justo en el centro, con letras grandes estampadas al frente estaba el inconfundible logo de Stonebridge Insurance Group. Debajo de la carpeta asomaba una pequeña nota cuidadosamente doblada dirigida a él con letra compacta y elegante.

Roe se hundió en su silla, tomó la nota, y la desdobló. Sus ojos recorrieron las líneas escritas: *Nosotros creemos que ha habido un evento fraudulento que involucra a uno de nuestros asegurados. Sin embargo, no contamos con pruebas sólidas para seguir adelante con esto. Valoramos su pericia y nos gustaría que nos ayudara a investigar más a fondo y nos proporcionara la evidencia necesaria para proceder.*

La vicepresidenta, Emily Dickson, la había firmado.

Roe dejó la nota, abriendo la carpeta. Dentro, él encontró una serie de documentos: formularios de reclamación de seguro, y unas cuantas fotografías borrosas. Él frunció el ceño mientras ojeaba los papeles. Si Stonebridge sospechaba de fraude, pero no podía probarlo, eso significaba que había algo particularmente sutil en juego.

Él agarró la carpeta y se dirigió a la oficina del fondo, donde encontró a Liam y a Aggie inclinados sobre una computadora portátil, murmurando acerca del último cliente que había insistido en pagar en pagos pequeños.

"Días", Roe habló en voz alta, llamando su atención. "Tengo algo aquí que requiere que usen ambos ojos".

Liam levantó la vista frunciendo el ceño. "Llegas tarde".

"Sí, lo sé", Roe respondió secamente, levantando la carpeta. "Stonebridge Insurance Group nos acaba de entregar un rompecabezas".

Aggie se animó, empujando su silla hacia atrás. "¿Dices un rompecabezas?". Ella se dirigió a Roe, mirando la carpeta en sus manos. "¿De qué clase de rompecabezas estamos hablando aquí?".

"Fraude", dijo Roe simplemente. "O eso creen ellos. Sin embargo, no pueden demostrarlo". Él arrojó la carpeta sobre la mesa redonda en el centro de la sala, haciéndoles un gesto para que miraran.

Liam y Aggie intercambiaron una mirada antes de dar un paso adelante. Liam levantó la hoja superior, sus ojos se movían rápidamente de un lado a otro mientras revisaba el contenido.

"Entonces, ¿qué esperan que hagamos nosotros?", murmuró Liam. "Si la compañía de seguros, con todos sus recursos, no puede probarlo…".

Aggie lo interrumpió, hojeando las fotografías. "Entonces significa que quienquiera que esté detrás es inteligente y cuidadoso. Nosotros solo necesitamos ser más inteligentes y más cuidadosos".

Roe asintió. "Exactamente. Ellos nos están pidiendo tener una mirada fresca. Hay algo ahí. Ellos pueden sentirlo, pero necesitan que nosotros veamos lo que ellos no pueden".

Liam entrecerró los ojos para mirar uno de los documentos. "De acuerdo con esto, alguien presentó la reclamación hace solo un mes. ¿Qué tiene de sospechoso?".

Roe cruzó los brazos, apoyado en la mesa. "Buena pregunta, por eso estamos aquí, para averiguarlo. Empezaremos por los detalles de la reclamación, cotejarlos con otra información, y ver si podemos detectar cualquier discrepancia que ellos hayan pasado por alto".

Aggie asintió, recogiendo una fotografía de un edificio dañado. "Ya sabes lo que dicen, 'el diablo está en los detalles'. Y nosotros somos sorprendentemente buenos encontrando al diablo".

Liam sonrió, dejando el papel sobre la mesa. "Bien, entonces. ¿Dónde empezamos? ¿Entrevistando a los testigos? ¿localizando al asegurado?".

Roe se frotó la barbilla pensativamente. "No nos adelantemos. Primero, revisemos esta carpeta con lupa. Haremos una lista de todo lo que parezca estar un poco fuera de lugar. Entonces partiremos de ahí para seguir las pistas".

Aggie ya estaba acercando una silla a la mesa, despejando el espacio para el contenido de la carpeta. "Suena como un buen plan. Voy a preparar el café. Va a ser un largo día, ¿verdad?".

Roe se rió suavemente entre dientes. "¿No es así siempre?". Él echó un vistazo a la carpeta, su mente ya corría a toda velocidad imaginando diferentes escenarios. Si Stonebridge estaba en lo correcto, entonces alguien había hecho un gran esfuerzo para lograrlo. Era su trabajo asegurarse de que esa persona no se saliera con la suya.

En los días previos a su reunión con Emily, Roe se vio atrapado en un torbellino de emociones. Sus pensamientos eran una maraña confusa, mientras él se preguntaba si podría manejar el trabajar en otro caso con ella. Su último caso juntos los había unido tanto que cambió todo entre ellos. Ahora, con Emily pidiendo la ayuda de Alder y Finch nuevamente, Roe no estaba seguro si él estaba listo para compartir con sus empleados de confianza su historia con ella. Bueno, al menos, no todavía.

Veamos qué descubren primero, pensó Roe.

"OK, chicos, dejaré esto en sus competentes manos, y nos volveremos a reunir cuando ustedes estén listos para ponerme al día", agregó Roe mientras se alejaba. De repente, él se giró y se dirigió a Aggie. "Llama al mantenimiento del edificio y haz que le pongan un poco de aceite a la puerta principal para que ese viejo trasto no me haga ver mal si llego tarde otra vez".

"Claro, jefe, de inmediato".

Una vez más, Roe se dirigió a su oficina para empezar el día, pero los recuerdos de Emily permanecieron en su mente.

13

Pinnacle Property Assurance

Roe empujó la puerta de su oficina y entró, se quitó el saco y casi se dejó caer en su silla.

La reunión de anoche con Emily aún pesaba profundamente en su mente, pero él necesitaba sacársela de la cabeza y concentrarse en el negocio que tenía entre manos.

Dirigiéndose a su credenza, metió una cápsula de Lavazza "Oro", su favorita, en la cafetera y se preparó un expreso. Con la taza en su mano, regresó a su escritorio, encendió su computadora y echó un vistazo a la actualización de los reportes de todos los casos. Cuando lo hizo, tomó nota de los casos pendientes, los ya concluidos y esos donde el pago había sido recibido.

Entonces echó un segundo vistazo al notar que el caso de Pinnacle Property Assurance había sido resuelto completamente, la factura había sido enviada y todo, pero el pago no había sido recibido.

Justo cuando él estaba a punto de llamar a Aggie para un "por favor, explícame", ella entró en la oficina y dijo: "Roe, necesitas ver esto".

Ella se acercó, se apoderó de su computadora y abrió su correo electrónico. "No creerás esto. Tómate un momento para leer este correo de Pinacle".

Roe se detuvo a la mitad de su sorbo, con una ceja levantada con curiosidad preguntó: "¿Qué te tiene tan alterada?".

"Es acerca del caso de Pinnacle Property Assurance", ella dijo, sonriendo burlonamente. "Ya sabes, el que cerramos la semana pasada. Ellos acaban de responder a nuestra factura".

"Ah, sí. Esa hermosa factura", dijo Roe, sonriendo. "Ochenta y ocho mil y algo de cambio. ¿Nos enviaron una nota de agradecimiento con un cheque gordo?".

Aggie resopló, sacudiendo la cabeza. "No del todo. Ellos están preguntando si pueden pagarlo en doce cuotas mensuales".

Roe parpadeó, mirándola fijamente. "Espera…¿qué? ¿Cuotas? ¿Como si estuvieran pagando un sofá?".

"Sip. Doce pagos mensuales", Aggie continúa, apenas conteniendo la risa. "Y ve esto—ellos están insistiendo en que no se les cobren intereses".

Roe dejó su café, soltando una risita. "Entonces, ellos quieren que seamos su banco ahora. ¿Qué sigue? ¿Deberíamos ofrecerles una tarjeta de lealtad también?".

"Oh, por supuesto", Aggie respondió acariciando su barbilla pensativamente. "Un pago atrasado y obtienen el doble de puntos en su próximo caso con nosotros. Quizás podríamos agregar un paraguas de cortesía con nuestro logo en él".

"¿Tenemos ese tipo de paraguas?".

"Nooo", respondió Aggie, sorprendida por la pregunta de Roe.

Roe se rió, sacudiendo la cabeza de incredulidad. "En serio, son una compañía de seguros. ¿No se supone que son buenos con el dinero? Es todo su modelo de negocio".

"Tú lo pensarías, ¿verdad?", respondió Aggie, fingiendo sorpresa. "Pero aquí estamos, ochenta y ocho mil dólares y ellos actúan como si estuviéramos tratando de venderles un coche.

Podemos incluir un tostador gratis". Roe suspiró, rascándose la cabeza. "Es decir, ¿ahora qué sigue? ¿Quieren que les demos una tasa del cero por ciento anual por ser tan buenos clientes? Quizá hasta podríamos incluir un tostador de regalo".

Aggie sonrió aplaudiendo. "Oooh, ¡eso me agrada! '¡Firme con Alder y Finch, y su próximo caso estará libre de intereses con un tostador gratis!' Podemos hacerlo nuestro nuevo eslogan de marketing".

Roe negó con la cabeza, aún con una leve risita. "Está bien, está bien. Vamos a ponernos serios. Los llamaré, pero si ellos mencionan los pagos mensuales otra vez, les pediré una garantía. Tal vez ese vestíbulo elegante de su oficina".

Aggie dio una palmada en el escritorio, riendo. "¡Sí! Y si se retrasan con un pago, ¡el vestíbulo se queda vacío porque nos llevamos todos los muebles! Construiremos un pequeño fuerte aquí en la esquina con sus plantas en maceta y sus sofás".

Roe por fin recuperó el aliento. "Trato hecho, me encargaré de la llamada. Tú solo mantén esa factura a la mano. Tal vez tengamos que explicárselas en partes bien sencillas para que la entiendan".

Mientras Aggie se alejaba, Roe gritó: "Ah, y no olvides incluir en la factura si quieren nuestro plan extendido de protección de pagos. Solo $9.99 al mes!".

Aggie le hizo un saludo burlón. "Entendido jefe. Un plan de pago libre de intereses está encamino".

Aggie dejó la oficina de Roe y se dirigió a su cubículo aun negando con la cabeza, incrédula, mientras Roe tomaba el teléfono para llamar al presidente de Pinnacle, incapaz de borrar la sonrisa de su rostro.

Ya nada me sorprende de la gente él pensó, y por primera vez en 24 horas, Emily Dickson no estaba en su mente.

14

Flinch y Sadler

Roe se recostó en su silla, respiró profundo, y marcó el número de Pinnacle Property Assurance. El presidente de la compañía, un Mr. Edwin Clark, contestó el teléfono después de un par de timbrazos.

"Habla Edwin Clark", se oyó una voz suave, casi demasiado encantadora.

"Mr. Clark, ¡buen día! Soy Roebuck Cooke de Investigaciones Alder y Finch", comenzó Roe, poniendo su mejor tono profesional. "Quería hablar con usted acerca de las condiciones de pago del caso que nosotros resolvimos recientemente para su compañía".

"Ah, sí, Alder y Finch", Clark contestó cálidamente. "Agradezco que se haya puesto en contacto conmigo. Yo supongo que recibió nuestro correo electrónico acerca del calendario de pagos. Nos gustaría pagar esa factura en cuotas de doce meses".

"Bueno, ese es el tema, Mr. Clark. La política de mi empresa es el pago total al finalizar nuestros servicios. Estoy seguro de que usted puede comprender eso".

"Lo entiendo, Mr. Roe, pero usted debe ver las cosas desde mi lado. Nosotros estamos hablando acerca de una cantidad considerable. Mi esposa tomó una decisión sobre algo que nosotros no habíamos discutido, y ahora recibo esta factura, y yo pensé que podríamos hacer un plan de pagos sencillo, algo como esos planes de apartado de Kmart. Algo que nos beneficie a ambos".

"Entiendo, pero nosotros proporcionamos un servicio que requirió una cantidad considerable de tiempo y recursos…Espere. ¿Qué quiere decir con como un plan de apartado de Kmart? ¿Qué clase de compañía de seguros está usted dirigiendo, Mr. Clark?".

Hubo un breve silencio del otro lado de la línea, seguido por un tono más seco de Clark. "Mr. Roe, estoy dirigiendo una compañía de seguros extraordinariamente exitosa, y eso no tiene nada que ver con los gastos o compras de mi esposa. Entonces, ahora, ¿Podemos acordar un plan de pago mensual para mi nuevo equipo de sonido? ¡Usted espera que le pague todo el dinero de una sola vez por algo tan frívolo!".

Roe se sintió completamente confundido. "Espere, ¿un sistema de sonido? Mr. Clark, creo que hay un malentendido aquí. Nosotros no estamos hablando acerca de un sistema de sonido; esto es por una investigación que nosotros realizamos para Pinnacle Property Assurance. El caso de fraude, ¿recuerda?".

"¿Caso de fraude?". Mr. Clark sonaba entre confundido y ofendido. "¿De qué está hablando? Mr. Roe, usted es de Flinch y Sadler, ¿no lo es? ¿La tienda de audio? ¡Mi esposa ordenó de ustedes un equipo de sonido doméstico escandalosamente caro, y ahora usted está exigiendo el pago total!".

Roe cubrió la bocina del teléfono mientras contenía la risa al darse cuenta de lo que había pasado. "No, Mr. Clark, llamo de Investigaciones Alder y Finch, no Flinch y Sadler. Nosotros ayudamos en investigaciones de seguros, no en ventas de audio. Deme un momento". Roe puso el teléfono en espera y tecleó alguna información en su computadora, abriendo el archivo del caso de Pinnacle Property Assurance. "Mr Clark, me estoy refiriendo al caso concerniente al fraude de la joyería cometido por Oceanview Jewellery en Coffs Harbour. La factura que nosotros le enviamos es por el caso del fraude resuelto para su compañía".

Hubo una densa pausa en la línea, seguida por el sonido lejano de papeles. "¡Oh...oh!" exclamó Clark, su voz ahora teñida de vergüenza. "Alder y Finch...correcto. Correcto. No Flinch y Sadler. Mis disculpas Mr. Roe. Yo, eh, se me hizo un lío aquí".

Roe no pudo evitar reírse esta vez, dejando que la tensión se disipara de la conversación. "No hay problema, Mr. Clark. Nos pasa a todos. Lo prometo, nosotros no instalamos ningún sistema de sonido de alta agama en su sala".

Clark soltó una risita avergonzada. "Bueno, eso es un alivio. Lamento la confusión—y por la idea de los pagos a plazos. Ya entiendo por qué eso fue un poco...ridículo".

"Sólo un poco", respondió Roe, aun sonriendo. "Entonces, acerca del pago..."

"El pago total, lo tendrá" Clark interrumpió. "Me aseguraré de que el departamento de finanzas se lo transfiera al final de la semana".

"Excelente", dijo Roe, sintiéndose triunfante. "Y por si sirve de algo, creo que usted debería hacerle una llamada a Flinch y Sadler. Sólo para asegurarse de que ellos saben que usted está planeando pagarles en plazos".

Clark rió a carcajadas esta vez. La tensión se disipó completamente. "Creo que usted tiene razón, Mr. Roe. Gracias por la llamada—y por aclarar las cosas".

"No ha problema en absoluto", Roe respondió. "Que tenga un gran día, Mr. Clark".

"Usted también", dijo Clark antes de colgar, dejando a Roe sentado en su silla, moviendo la cabeza con incredulidad ante lo absurdo de la conversación. Con una sonrisa de satisfacción, él levantó su café y tomó un sorbo de celebración, el cual estaba un poco frío, pero aún sabroso. Otro caso—bueno, una disputa de facturación—resuelto.

Quizá un plan de apartados también podría funcionar para Mrs Clark. Pensó Roe.

15

Una Capa Adicional

Dos semanas más tarde, Roe se encontraba garabateando notas en una libreta mientras revisaba los expedientes más recientes sobre su escritorio. La oficina estaba muy ocupada, como de costumbre, con papeles esparcidos por todas partes y el runrún de los coches que pasaban por las calles allá abajo. Liam tocó la puerta. "Roe, tienes un minuto?".

Levantando la vista, Roe vio a Liam flanqueado por Nina Hart y Jack Stone, dos de los nuevos empleados.

"Por supuesto, muchachos. ¿Qué pasa?". Él les hizo una señal para que entraran y se sentaran.

Señalando los archivos que Liam tenía en el regazo, Roe dijo: "Veo que trajiste refuerzos. ¿Qué pasa Liam?".

Liam sacó una carpeta de debajo de su brazo y la puso sobre el escritorio de Roe. "Tenemos cuatro casos para discutir contigo esta mañana. Hemos cerrado exitosamente dos de nuestros recientes casos. En primer lugar, está el caso de Cavanaugh Trust Fund. Gracias al ojo agudo de Nina, captamos las discrepancias en los trámites. Fue una situación de fraude interno y ellos ya nos han transferido el pago. Aggie no ha tenido la oportunidad de actualizar el sistema aún".

Nina le sonrió a Roe. "Este caso fue esencialmente pan comido. Ellos eran un grupo de aficionados. Ni siquiera trataron de borrar sus huellas correctamente".

Roe asintió agradecido. "Buen trabajo, Nina. ¿Qué hay del segundo caso?".

"Ese era el caso de Harper Reinsurance Group. Resultó ser un fraude, también", continuó Liam, mirando a Jack. "Jack, aquí presente, fue quien hizo el trabajo de campo en ese caso. Jack, ¿puedes explicarle a Roe?".

"Por supuesto. Obtuve declaraciones de tres testigos clave, se cotejaron los datos financieros, y se acorraló al sospechoso en un interrogatorio contundente. ¡Caramba!, no creerías lo rápido que admitieron el fraude. Este caso está claramente más que cerrado".

Roe soltó un silbido bajo. "Impresionante ustedes dos. Justo lo que quería escuchar. Espléndido trabajo".

Liam asintió sonriendo y aceptó: "Ellos son buenos en su trabajo de investigación. Ahora, sobre el tercer caso, es donde las cosas se ponen complicadas. Es Pinnacle Property Group".

La sonrisa de Roe se desvaneció ligeramente. "Ah, Pinnacle Property Assurance. Esta empresa es una caja de sorpresas. ¿Cuál es la actualización?".

"No Roe, esta es Pinnacle Property Group, no Pinnacle Property Assurance. No hay planes de pago mensual involucrados". Liam corrigió la confusión de nombre de Roe.

"OK, OK, tuve un despiste de adulto mayor. Cuéntame acerca de Pinnacle Property Group".

Liam abrió la carpeta y dispuso algunos documentos en frente de Roe. "Entonces, nosotros hemos estado haciendo un seguimiento de la reclamación. Está turbio, pero ahora tenemos algunas pistas. Nina ha estado revisando el historial de reclamaciones de Pinnacle. Resulta que Pinnacle ha realizado varios pagos en los últimos dos años bajo circunstancias notablemente similares. Los mismos tipos de 'accidentes', las mismas áreas. Todos edificios comerciales".

Nina intervino, su voz era aguda y confiada. "Huele a trampa. O ellos se enfrentan a un estafador en serie, o alguien, y podría ser más de una persona dentro, está orquestando estos reclamos".

Jack se tronó los nudillos y agregó su comentario. "Yo hice algunas investigaciones sobre los asegurados. Hay algunos de ellos que tienen conexiones con una empresa contratista privada, una que casualmente Pinnacle usa para reparaciones de sus propiedades".

Los ojos de Roe se agrandaron. "Bueno, ese es un punto interesante. ¿Entonces estamos ante un posible trabajo interno?".

"Potencialmente", dijo Liam, asintiendo con la cabeza. "Pero es demasiado pronto para decirlo con seguridad. La buena noticia es que tenemos suficiente para garantizar una investigación más profunda. Ya he contactado a unas cuantas personas en Pinnacle—sutilmente, por supuesto. Ellos están dispuestos a dejarnos entrevistar a algunos de sus empleados".

Roe dio golpecitos con el bolígrafo sobre el escritorio, pensando. "Buen trabajo a todos. Parece que estamos sobre la pista de algo. Entonces, ¿qué sigue Liam?".

"Voy a pedirle a Nina y a Jack que saquen los registros sobre esa empresa contratista, y que los cotejen con cualquier reclamación anterior para ver si hay alguna coincidencia con los empleados de Pinnacle", él dijo, mirando a Nina y a Jack.

"De eso me encargo yo", respondió Nina, abriendo ya su cuaderno para tomar notas.

Jack asintió secamente. "Investigaré los antecedentes del contratista y veré si aparece alguna señal de alerta".

Liam, mirando a Roe, dijo: "Entonces, ¿estamos listos? ¿Se te ocurre algo más Roe?".

Roe sonrió, un destello de determinación en sus ojos. "No, ya lo tienes todo Liam. Y si alguien en Pinnacle está jugando juegos, ellos pronto se darán cuenta de que ellos han elegido meterse con las personas equivocadas. Chicos, vamos a cerrar esto con éxito. Entonces, ¿qué hay del cuarto caso?".

"Este involucra a Stonebridge Insurance Group", dijo Liam. "Tengo a ambos, Mateo y Sophia, trabajando en este, dame dos o máximo tres semanas y te entregaré un caso exitoso para llevar a Stonebridge. Tenemos varias capas que analizar para hacerlo bien".

"Eso también es fantástico, Liam. Agradece a los chicos por mí".

Al unísono, Liam, Nina y Jack se giraron para irse y Roe los miró, sintiendo una oleada de confianza con las recientes incorporaciones al equipo.

Reclinándose en su asiento, él decidió que era mejor que llamara a Emily para darle una breve actualización. Sonó dos veces antes de que ella contestara.

"Emily Dickson, ¿cómo puedo ayudarle?".

"Hola Emily, soy Roe".

"¡Hola, Roe!" Emily saludó y su tono cambió, haciéndose más dulce que su tono profesional. "Me alegra saber de ti".

"Igualmente Emily", respondió Roe. "Pensé en darte una actualización de ese caso del fraude en el que hemos estado trabajando para ti y Stonebridge. Va tomando buena forma y mi equipo me dice que tal vez en tres semanas o algo así, podemos terminar con esto".

"¿Ah, sí? Por favor cuéntame", ella respondió, eso despertó su interés.

"Bueno, mis investigadores han descubierto algunos detalles interesantes", comenzó Roe. "Stonebridge ha estado tratando con múltiples reclamaciones similares los dos últimos años. Mis investigadores encontraron un patrón en estas reclamaciones con 'accidentes' similares, sucediendo en áreas específicas, y siempre involucrando a la misma empresa contratista. Está apuntando hacia un posible trabajo interno".

"Eso es interesante Roe. Entonces, estás diciendo que puede ser alguien dentro de Stonebridge, o ¿tal vez este contratista es quien mueve los hilos? ¿por qué nuestro equipo no se dio cuenta de esto?".

"No estoy seguro, Emily, pero nosotros averiguaremos quién está involucrado". Roe confirmó. "Otro investigador está indagando en los antecedentes del contratista. Estamos buscando cualquier conexión entre tus empleados. Tenemos muchas pistas, pero las piezas encajan entre sí. Podría implicar a más de una persona dentro haciendo esto".

"Realmente te estás acercando" dijo Emily, con un tono de admiración en su voz. "Sabía que tú y tu equipo llegarían al fondo de esto".

Roe se rió entre dientes. "Bueno, aún no hemos llegado, pero nos estamos acercando. Como dije, esperamos tener todo concluido en tres semanas, más o menos".

Hubo un breve silencio en la línea antes de que Emily hablara de nuevo. "Sabes, de hecho yo misma tengo algunas noticias".

"¿Ah? Roe dijo, su curiosidad se despertó. "¿Qué está sucediendo?".

"Bueno, yo preferiría decírtelo en persona", Emily respondió. "¿Qué tal si nos reunimos para tomar una copa a finales de esta semana? Digamos, en el mismo restaurante acogedor en el que disfrutamos de la cena la última vez. En esta ocasión yo invito. Creo que esto es algo que se discute mejor tomando una copa de vino".

"Eso suena genial, Emily. Indica la hora y ahí estaré".

"¿Qué tal el viernes por la tarde? ¿7:30 p.m?

"Bien, el viernes a las 7:30 p.m.", Roe aceptó. "Te veré entonces".

"Estoy deseando que llegue", dijo Emily suavemente antes de colgar.

Roe colgó el teléfono y, aunque el caso de Stonebridge puede ser complejo, con múltiples capas, la idea de volver a ver a Emily otra vez, le había agregado una capa adicional a esta semana.

16

Que la Naturaleza Siga su Curso

El viernes por la tarde, Roe se dirigió a Petite Maison directamente desde el trabajo. Él se había quedado en la oficina y vio a su equipo irse para el fin de semana. Ellos habían estado trabajando duro en una gran cantidad de casos y él se estaba poniendo al corriente con todos los comentarios en línea de cada uno de los investigadores.

Este año voy a tener que hacer algo especial por estos chicos. Especialmente para Liam y Aggie, pensó Roe. Terminando, él apagó su computadora, caminó hasta la puerta principal, la abrió y miró alrededor. Sí, las cosas están yendo bien para Alder y Finch, él pensó mientras cerraba con llave para el fin de semana.

Él caminaba lentamente sabiendo que tenía mucho tiempo para llegar a Petite Maison. Como estaba a solo un par de cuadras de la oficina, Roe dejó su coche estacionado en el estacionamiento de esta. Mientras él pasaba por cada uno de los pequeños comercios, él no pudo evitar pensar en lo agradable que era Northport.

Roe tomó aire, se ajustó el cuello de la camisa y empujó la puerta para entrar. Dentro, el bar estaba tranquilo, con el leve murmullo de las conversaciones y el tintinear de las copas creando un entorno agradable y acogedor. Él miró a su alrededor y rápidamente vio a Emily sentada en una pequeña mesa cerca del fondo con una copa de vino tinto frente a ella. Ella levantó la vista, una sonrisa se extendió por su rostro y le hizo un pequeño gesto con la mano.

"Roe", ella lo saludó calurosamente, levantándose para darle un breve y suave abrazo. "Estoy tan contenta de que hayas venido".

"No me lo perdería", contestó Roe, sacando una silla para sentarse frente a ella. Un mesero se aproximó, y Roe ordenó una copa de vino tinto para él.

Después de unos momentos de charla ligera sobre el ambiente del bar y la típica charla para ponerse al día, Roe se inclinó hacia adelante, con la mirada fija en Emily. "Bien, me has mantenido en suspenso por suficiente tiempo. ¿Cuáles son esas noticias que quieres compartir?".

Emily, dijo con calma: "Solicité el divorcio. El papeleo está completo. Todo está hecho, firmado y está oficialmente terminado. Ahora soy soltera legalmente".

Roe sintió una oleada de emociones encontradas: alivio, emoción y un dejo de inquietud. "Vaya, Emily", logró decir, suavizando su voz. "Eso es…mucho. ¿Cómo te sientes?".

Ella tomó un sorbo de su vino, "Libre, en mayor parte, no fue fácil, pero era la decisión correcta. En realidad, nosotros habíamos terminado hacía mucho tiempo. Este fue solo el último paso". Emily miró a Roe y continuó: "Y, bueno, quería que lo supieras. Pensé que merecías escucharlo de mí en persona".

El silencio se apoderó de ellos por un momento, y entonces Emily se inclinó más cerca, su voz era apenas un susurro. "No estoy mirando atrás, Roe. Ahora estoy mirando hacia adelante y tú sabes cómo me siento acerca de ti".

Roe tomó gentilmente su mano entre las suyas. El calor de su piel en contacto con la suya le provocó un estremecimiento y, por un momento, él se permitió perderse en la posibilidad de lo que esta nueva libertad podría significar para ambos. Él podía sentir que la atracción entre ellos se hacía más intensa. Emily se acercó más y presionó sus labios contra los de él.

Roe no dudó y le devolvió el beso. Después de lo que pareció una eternidad, él se apartó, tomó un sorbo de su vino y suavemente dijo: "Emily", su voz tenía un leve toque de arrepentimiento. "Me importas. De verdad. Pero ahora…no es el momento correcto para involucrarnos en esto".

Los ojos de Emily parpadearon. "¿Qué quieres decir con que no es el momento correcto?".

Roe exhaló, luchando por encontrar las palabras correctas. "Este caso con Stonebridge, es más complejo de lo que dije por teléfono. Seguramente, nosotros lo tendremos resuelto en unas pocas semanas, pero estamos lidiando con una red de engaños y, honestamente, no sabemos quién puede estar involucrado. No puedo…no podemos cruzar esta línea mientras estoy enredado en todo eso. Podría comprometer todo, especialmente a ti".

"Entonces, ¿esperamos? ¿Eso es lo que estás diciendo?".

Él asintió lentamente, odiando cómo sonó, pero sabiendo que era la verdad. "Sí. Por ahora, nos enfocaremos en lo que está enfrente de nosotros. El trabajo, el caso. Una vez que dejemos eso atrás, nosotros podemos averiguar dónde estamos parados. Déjame repetírtelo, Emily, no puedo arriesgar vernos envueltos en algo mientras todo esto es aún tan incierto. No si después puede salirnos el tiro por la culata, por así decirlo".

"Está bien, Roe. No me gusta. No me gusta nada, pero comprendo. Tienes razón".

Él soltó una pequeña risa triste. "No siempre, créeme. Pero esta vez…esta vez, es la mejor forma de proceder con esta nueva relación".

Ellos se sentaron en silencio por un momento, la tensión dio paso a una aceptación agridulce. Emily extendió la mano, tocando ligeramente su mano otra vez. "Sólo prométeme, que cuando todo esto termine, tomaremos otra copa, y entonces podremos decidir qué pasará después".

Roe le dedicó una suave sonrisa. "De acuerdo. Cuando esto termine, tomaremos esa copa".

"Y dejaremos que la naturaleza siga su curso".

17

¡Oh, Mierda!

A medida que la noche fue tomando un ritmo más cómodo después de su conversación, Roe y Emily compartían sonrisas y risas, el peso de su conversación anterior daba paso a una sensación de tranquilidad. La luz suave del restaurante los bañaba en un cálido resplandor y, por un momento, el mundo exterior parecía lejano.

La puerta del restaurante se abrió, llamando la atención de Roe. Él miró sutilmente hacia allí y Emily siguió su mirada, curiosa.

Allí estaban dos hombres parados en la entrada, recorriendo el lugar con la mirada, Danny Monk y Albert Guzmán. Roe los reconoció instantáneamente. Él los había visto la última vez en el Poplar Inn, y su aparición repentina lo hizo pensar en lo pequeño que es el mundo.

Danny fue el primero en captar la mirada de Roe, entonces dio un empujoncito a Albert, quien puso la sonrisa más radiante que Danny jamás le había visto al hombre.

"Roe", dijo Danny, con un tono amistoso mientras caminaba hacia su mesa con Albert detrás de él. "No esperábamos verte aquí".

Roe se puso de pie y extendió su mano. "Danny. Albert. Qué pequeño es el mundo".

Emily, siempre tan diplomática, sonrió cálidamente. "Parece que todos ustedes se conocen. ¿Por qué no se nos unen?". Sus ojos se dirigieron rápidamente hacia Roe en busca de confirmación, y él asintió.

"Sí, tomen asiento. Acabamos de terminar de cenar y nos estábamos poniendo al día cuando los vi entrar".

La cara de Albert se iluminó por la invitación, y con una reverencia simulada, él sacó una silla. "¿No les importa si lo hacemos? Vamos Danny, hagamos de esto una fiesta".

"No pensé que esta noche se convertiría en una reunión". Danny murmuró, aunque había un brillo en sus ojos".

Antes de que Danny y Albert se sentaran, Emily se presentó. "Yo soy Emily. Gusto en conocerlos a ambos".

Danny como siempre, el de la labia fácil, se inclinó ligeramente hacia adelante sonriéndole. "El placer es todo nuestro, Emily. Soy Danny y este de aquí es Albert. Nosotros… nos cruzamos con Roe hace un tiempo en el Poplar Inn".

Roe tomó un sorbo de su bebida. "Sí, así fue".

La curiosidad de Emily se despertó. "¿Cómo se conocen todos?".

"Vaya, eso sí que es una historia", dijo Albert frotándose las manos. "Pero primero, Roe, ¿por qué no compartes una de tus historias sobre seguros? Apuesto a que Emily no ha oído hablar de algunos de tus grandes éxitos".

Roe se recostó en la silla, miró a Emily, quien levantó una ceja expectante. "Bueno, no sé nada de los grandes éxitos", él dijo, riendo entre dientes suavemente, "pero me ocupé de un caso de fraude recientemente. El tipo estaba haciendo una estafa fingiendo lesiones, y cobrando indemnizaciones de varias compañías. Se creía intocable".

Emily se inclinó hacia adelante, intrigada. "¿Cómo lo atrapaste?".

Los ojos de Roe brillaban mientras relataba el caso. "Uno de mis investigadores lo siguió por una semana. El tipo dijo que no podía caminar sin muletas, tenía su pierna en una férula. Una noche, lo atrapó en un gimnasio de boxeo entrenando fuerte, sin férula, sin nada. Tomó unas cuantas fotos, y ese fue el fin de eso. Las compañías de seguros estuvieron felices de atraparlo.

Albert resopló, claramente impresionado. "Querido, esa es una agradable y corta historia. ¿La mayoría de los casos que investigas son como estos?".

"Más o menos del mismo tipo. Ahora, Danny, ¿quién es este criminal al que ayudaste a atrapar en el Poplar Inn?".

Danny miró a Albert. "OK, cuéntale a Roe y a Emily nuestra historia".

Albert sonrió, pero primero le hizo señas al mesero. "Por favor, tráiganos a Danny y a mí los menús y dos mojitos. ¿puedo pedirles algo encantos?".

Roe miró a Emily y respondió por los dos. "No, gracias Albert, nosotros acabamos de cenar y nos íbamos cuando ustedes entraron".

"Oh, es una lástima". Mirando al mesero, él dijo: "Entonces tráiganos a Danny y a mí los mojitos y deje el menú. No voy a retener a estos dos encantos por mucho más tiempo. Estoy seguro de que ellos tienen un mejor lugar donde estar que con dos solteros. Pero, primero, mi historia".

"Les traeré los dos mojitos en un momento", respondió el mesero.

"Ahora, ¿por dónde empiezo?", dijo Albert. "Ah sí, el Poplar Inn. Fueron un par de días de locos". Él echó un vistazo a Danny antes de continuar. "Nosotros estábamos rastreando a este tipo, un auténtico delincuente. Nos dieron el dato de que se escondía en el Poplar. El lugar era un agujero lleno de gente, pero lo acorralamos en la parte de atrás".

Danny negó con la cabeza y casi reprendió a Albert.

"Roe, Emily, me disculpo por Albert, él tiende a exagerar. Me estaba hospedando en el Poplar Inn, Albert vino unos días después, y él me ayudó a armar una trampa para un hombre mayor que parecía haber sido un experto en abrir cerraduras, y le encantaba colarse en los cuartos y robar objetos de valor de todos los hoteles en los que se había hospedado en el pasado. Era un plan simple de cebo, en el que cayó el hombre mayor y fue atrapado por una cámara escondida. No hubo secretismo ni intrigas como Albert está intentando decir".

"Oh Danny, dulzura, tú eres un aguafiestas. Yo quería ver qué tan lejos podía ir con esta historia. Eres un aguafiestas, muchacho, un simple aguafiestas".

Roe se rió entre dientes, moviendo la cabeza. "Recuerdo leer acerca de eso en nuestro periódico local, pero no los mencionaba a ustedes dos, solo que la policía local recibió ayuda del público, entonces ya sé que 'el público' eran ustedes dos".

La mesa estalló en carcajadas mientras la conversación continuaba. Ellos intercambiaron más historias. Roe compartiendo más acerca de sus casos de seguros más tranquilos, y Danny y Albert compartiendo sus historias de negocios, Albert con su peluquería y Danny con su librería. La noche cambió a algo inesperadamente animado, y por un momento, el mundo fuera del restaurante parecía lejano, el futuro incierto, pero menos inquietante.

Los mojitos llegaron y Albert convenció a Emily y a Roe de tomar algunos, y ellos lo hicieron. Danny y Albert ordenaron su comida, y más tragos siguieron llegando.

Para cuando llegó el postre, el grupo estaba completamente relajado, intercambiando bromas como si ellos se conocieran de toda la vida y se podía percibir una extraña camaradería formándose entre ellos. Fue un momento de ligereza que ninguno de ellos había esperado.

Observando su reloj, Roe miró a Emily y dijo: "por mucho que nos gustaría quedarnos aquí más tiempo, Emily y yo tenemos trabajos a los que ir por la mañana, así que debemos desearles buenas noches".

"Oh, queridos, ¿deben irse ambos?", dijo Albert, haciendo pucheros.

"Albert, por lo que compartiste con nosotros esta noche, supongo que ambos tienen subgerentes para sus tiendas y pueden dormir hasta tarde. Roe y yo no. Gracias por una velada encantadora", Emily agregó poniéndose de pie.

"Oh, bueno, intenté que se quedaran Danny", Albert intervino.

"Sí, lo hiciste Albert", y Danny hizo una señal al mesero para que se acercara y le dijo: "Por favor, pongan su comida y bebidas por cuenta de la casa".

"Sí Mr. Monk", respondió el mesero, recogiendo algunos vasos y alejándose".

"¿Por cuenta de la casa?", preguntó Roe.

"Sí Roe—Albert y yo somos dueños de Petite Maison y algunos otros negocios en Northport, y nos alegra que también hayas elegido Northport como tu sede".

"¿Cómo sabes eso Danny?", preguntó Roe perplejo.

"Tú nos lo mencionaste en el Poplar Inn cuando nos conocimos".

Roe se tomó un momento para pensar y recordó la breve conversación con ambos, Danny y Albert. Él recuerda el extraño comentario de Albert cuando él dijo que estaba montando un negocio en Northport: "Oh mierda".

Mientras ellos se despedían y se daban la mano, Roe se preguntó por qué a Albert Guzmán se le habría ocurrido un comentario tan extraño.

18

Comida y Bebida Gratis

Roe se echó hacia atrás en su silla en la oficina, su mirada estaba fija en el expediente que tenía enfrente de él. Los últimos días habían sido más ajetreados de lo esperado, especialmente después de encontrarse con Danny Monk y Albert Guzmán. Él cogió su teléfono y llamó a Liam. Pocos minutos después, Liam entraba, su expresión era curiosa. "¿Qué pasa, Roe? ¿Querías verme?".

"Sí. Cierra la puerta". Él se hizo un gesto a Liam para que se sentara. "Hace unos días, me reencontré con un par de personas: Danny Monk y Albert Guzmán. Algo no me dio buena espina. Hay una fuerte posibilidad de que mis impresiones estén equivocadas, pero quiero saber tanto como sea posible acerca de ellos dos. ¿Puedes hacer esto lo más discretamente posible y de manera informal?".

Liam asintió, "Entiendo. Empezaré a indagar en el asunto. Roe, estas impresiones ¿son sobre algo que ellos dijeron, o fue algo que escuchaste acerca de ellos? ¿Piensas que están involucrados en algo, digamos, sospechoso?".

Roe dudó. "No estoy seguro. Quizás. No lo sé. Rayos, podría estar equivocado, ellos podrían ser solo tipos encantadores, y yo aquí pensando lo peor. Solo necesito saber si hay algo bajo la superficie. Investiga sus negocios, conexiones personales, lo que sea que puedas encontrar".

"OK, estoy en ello", Liam dijo, ya tomando notas. "Haré que Jack Malone y Evelyn Drake revisen primero sus negocios, y luego vean lo que ellos pueden encontrar en el ámbito personal".

"Discretamente Liam". Roe le recordó. "No quiero que estos dos huelan nada respecto a que estamos investigando en sus negocios o en su vida personal. ¿Entendido?".

Asintiendo, Liam dejó la oficina.

Un par de días después, Liam entró a la oficina de Roe, con una carpeta en la mano.

"Tengo cierta información sobre Monk y Guzmán", empezó Liam, abriendo de golpe la carpeta. "Jack se metió de lleno en sus negocios y Evelyn investigó sus vidas personales para ver si había conexiones sospechosas. Ambos, Monk y Guzmán se han inscrito como copropietarios de un restaurante y una florería. También, Monk es propietario de una librería, mientras que Guzmán tiene una peluquería".

Roe se inclinó hacia adelante. "Bueno, sabíamos acerca de Guzmán. Sophia lo mencionó en una junta de personal hace un tiempo. OK, ¿algo más de interés?".

Liam dio golpecitos en el expediente. "En el papel, todo parece estar bien con ambos. Ellos tienen registros limpios, sin antecedentes penales, y sus negocios son rentables. Ellos están llevando a cabo una operación en regla, al menos, desde el punto de vista legal. Pero…". Él hizo una pausa, mirando a

Roe de cerca. "Tuve una conversación, extraoficial, con un inspector jefe de policía, Malcom Cassell".

"Continúa".

"Este detective, los ha estado observando por un tiempo. Él cree que Danny y Albert han estado involucrados en algún asunto sospechoso que él no puede probar. De acuerdo con el detective, ha habido algunas actividades sospechosas conectadas a sus negocios. Algunos artefactos de arte fueron robados y hubo algunos otros robos, pero el detective no pudo encontrar ninguna evidencia concreta. El detective afirmó repetidamente que él no puede creer que ellos siempre van por delante de él".

La expresión de Roe se endureció. "Hurto y robo ¿eh? ¿Y él no puede inculparlos de nada?".

"No. De nada", dijo Liam. "Él preguntó que si Alder y Finch estaba trabajando en algo que implicara a Monk y a Guzmán. No le di nada, por supuesto".

"Bien", dijo Roe, su mente ya estaba dándole vueltas a las implicaciones. Él se reclinó en su asiento, frotándose la barbilla. "Nosotros no queremos involucrarnos con la policía en esto. No nos corresponde a nosotros resolver los casos del departamento de policía de NSW".

Liam asintió, mirando cuidadosamente a Roe. "Entonces, ¿qué quieres que haga?".

Roe pensó por un momento. "Por ahora, no te involucres con el detective. Mantén esta información bien guardada en la carpeta. ¿Noah ha borrado todo rastro de nuestras computadoras y servidores? y diles a Jack y Evelyn, que ellos nunca los investigaron. ¿Entendido?".

"Entendido", Liam respondió, cerrando la carpeta, "Y me mantendré alejado del detective".

"Bien", dijo Roe, con tono definitivo. "Nosotros no estamos haciendo ningún movimiento aún, pero siempre es bueno estar preparado. Si Danny y Albert están jugando un juego, quiero estar seguro de que no seamos sorprendidos".

Liam se levantó, haciendo a Roe un gesto de asentimiento. "Me mantendré al tanto de ello. Avísame si quieres que indague más o necesitas darle seguimiento a cualquier otra cosa. También me aseguraré de que Jack y Evelyn detengan cualquier trabajo adicional sobre ellos".

"De acuerdo", dijo Roe mientras él miraba a Liam irse, sus pensamientos daban vueltas. Danny y Albert eran tan agradables en la superficie, especialmente Danny. Él parecía tan abierto, honesto con su conversación, por tanto, Roe estaba confundido".

¿El inspector jefe está detrás de ellos por alguna razón desconocida e inventando cosas? Pensó Roe.

Cuanto más pensaba Roe acerca de eso, más se decidía a dejar que Liam continuara con sus oídos abiertos a cualquier noticia y no preocuparse acerca de Monk y Guzmán.

Después de todo, ellos pagaron la cena y las bebidas la otra noche.

"No hay nada de malo en eso, ¿verdad?", pensó Roe.

19

Picton

El lunes por la mañana empezó como siempre. Roe se preparó una taza de café, se reclinó en su silla, y empezó a revisar las notas de un caso. Mientras lo hacía, Liam, sosteniendo una taza de café y algunas carpetas de casos, tocó a la puerta. Roe levantó la vista y le hizo señas para que entrara.

"Muy bien Roe, acaban de llegar tres casos frescos. Parece que los casos de fraude de seguros están aumentando. ¿Crees que haya algo en el aire?".

"Vamos, Liam, te encantan esos casos. Es otra razón para levantarte en la mañana, charlar con Aggie y afilar ese sentido de justicia tuyo".

"No puedo evitar que el fraude me moleste, Roe. Ahora, escucha esto—el primer caso es de Monarch Marine Insurance. Ellos tienen a un tipo que afirma que su yate de lujo se hundió en Port Stephens. ¿El único problema? Los datos de su GPS muestran al yate moviéndose dos horas después del supuesto hundimiento".

Roe levantó una ceja. "Parece alguien no muy listo".

"Exactamente. El próximo, tenemos a Metropolitan Assurance persiguiendo un pago dudoso de seguro de vida. Una viuda afirma que su esposo murió de fiebre de dengue en el extranjero durante una caminata en Perú haciendo el "Camino Inca". Pero los registros de aduanas muestran que el sujeto volvió a ingresar a Sídney dos días después".

"Entonces, o es un milagro de resurrección, o él quería desaparecer", Roe dijo con una leve sonrisa.

Liam continuó: "El último caso es más complicado— Southern Pacific Insurance. Ellos tienen un tipo que dice que la granja de su familia en Cootamundra fue arrasada por un incendio forestal. Sin embargo, las imágenes de satélite no muestran rastros de daños por incendio. No se ha televisado nada sobre incendios forestales, al menos, no en las fechas que él indicó".

"Estos casos tienen potencial. ¿Cómo quieres repartirlos?". Preguntó Roe.

"Siendo el investigador principal de la empresa, tomaré el del yate—buena excusa para pasar un día en el agua, ¿eh? También llevaré a David y a Al conmigo. Le asignaré a Emily indagar ese sospechoso caso del 'esposo muerto'. Algo me dice que hay mucho más que eso". Y dejemos ese trabajo de la granja a Luke y Evelyn. ¿Estás de acuerdo con esas asignaciones?".

Roe sonrió. "De acuerdo. Solo asegúrate de que ellos no se encariñen demasiado con el ganado".

Liam se rió. "Les recordaré que somos investigadores, no veterinarios".

Liam dio un sorbo a su café, pareciendo satisfecho con el plan. Entonces cambió de actitud, y su expresión se volvió más seria.

"Una cosa más, Roe. El detective Cassell ha estado husmeando. Él me preguntó otra vez si estamos investigando a Danny y Albert".

"¿Danny y Albert? Sé que tú dejaste de investigar a esos dos. ¿De qué está hablando Cassell?".

"Aparentemente, hubo un robo armado en un restaurante en Picton. Se dice que Danny y Albert podrían estar involucrados. Cassell cree que ya tenemos algo entre manos con ellos".

Roe se recuesta en el asiento con una cara pensativa. "Bueno, no es así. Además, originalmente, Cassell dijo que él los tenía en la mira por hurto. Simplemente no veo a esos dos siendo involucrados en un robo armado. Tiene poco sentido".

"Sí. Cassell dijo que el robo fue brutal. Ellos limpiaron el lugar en minutos. Lastimaron a un cliente, lo golpearon con la culata de la pistola. Pero eso le encendió las alarmas y, por alguna razón, él dice que los vieron en Picton ese día".

"Está bien", dijo Roe. "Juguemos con inteligencia. Estaremos atentos, pero no hay necesidad de intervenir sin motivo. Si Monk y Guzmán están involucrados, no pasará mucho tiempo antes de que uno de ellos cometa algún error y Cassell salte sobre ellos".

"Entiendo. Cerraré estos casos de fraude, pero mantendré a Cassell al tanto. Es mejor si nosotros sabemos lo que él sabe—y estamos un paso adelante, como siempre".

Roe le dirigió una leve sonrisa burlona. "Un paso adelante. Eso es seguro".

Liam se dirigió a su escritorio, ya repasando mentalmente la forma de indagar en el caso del yate, Roe lo vio marcharse, archivando mentalmente la mención de Danny y Albert. Era como si viejos fantasmas regresaran para perseguirlos —y con el robo armado de por medio, seguro iba a ser un desastre.

Murmurando para sí mismo, Roe dijo: "Esperemos que no nos veamos envueltos en algo más grande".

20

Disparo

El viernes por la tarde Roe se sentó en su escritorio, rebuscando en una pila de carpetas. El ruido sordo de la oficina llenaba el aire mientras la luz del sol se filtraba a través de las persianas entreabiertas. Un golpe en la puerta sacó a Roe de sus pensamientos.

Alzando la vista, él dijo: "Entra, Liam".

Liam entró a la oficina, sosteniendo una carpeta con una sonrisa de satisfacción en su rostro. Roe lo vio, entonces le hizo un gesto con la mano hacia la silla que estaba frente a su escritorio.

Mientras daba toquecitos sobre la carpeta, Liam dijo: "Tengo buenas noticias. ¿El caso de Stonebridge Insurance? Está oficialmente terminado".

"Estás bromeando. Dime que finalmente los tienen".

Con una sonrisa en el rostro, Liam continuó: "No solo los tenemos, sino que también indagamos tan profundamente que incluso el departamento de bomberos de NSW tuvo que admitir que nosotros descubrimos lo que ellos pasaron por alto. Resulta que el dueño incendió su propio edificio—en una jugada desesperada. Él se estaba hundiendo y pensó que el pago del seguro lo salvaría".

"Entonces, fue un incendio provocado para cobrar el seguro".

"Sip. Nosotros encontramos el residuo del acelerante que ellos pasaron por alto. El departamento de bomberos no pudo conectar los puntos, pero nosotros sí lo hicimos. Una vez que entregamos el reporte, ellos lo llevaron a la policía. El dueño del edificio está siendo arrestado mientras hablamos".

"Liam, eres un maldito genio".

"Aceptaré eso. Pero fue un esfuerzo de equipo".

"En efecto, lo fue. Agradécele al equipo por mi".

Roe se puso de pie, se estiró, y dijo, "Asegúrate de pasarle el caso a Aggie para que ella pueda enviar la factura a última hora de la tarde". Lo suficientemente tarde para que Stonebridge Insurance Group no pueda actuar al respecto hasta el próximo lunes. Voy a llamar a Emily Dickson. A ella le va a encantar estuchar esto".

Liam sonrió y dejó la oficina, cerrando la puerta detrás de él mientras Roe tomaba su teléfono y llamaba a Emily.

"Oficina de Ms. Dickson, ¿cómo puedo ayudarle?", dijo la encantadora voz que contestó el teléfono.

"Con Ms. Dickson, por favor. Habla Roebuck Cooke".

Roe esperó unos segundos hasta que Emily contestó.

"Buenas tardes, Roe. Me alcanzaste. Me estaba preparando para terminar y salir de la oficina por el día de hoy. "¿Qué pasa?".

"¿Qué tal si cenamos hoy en la noche en Petite Maison?".

"¿Hoy en la noche?". Bueno, tienes suerte. No tengo nada planeado. ¿Te parece a las 7:30 p.m.? Tengo una reunión mañana temprano en la oficina".

"¿En sábado?".

"Cosas del trabajo, te reúnes cuando un cliente quiere reunirse".

"Bueno, a las 7:30 p.m. en Petite Maison. Haré la reservación. Te veo ahí, Emily".

"¡Excelente! Te veré ahí!".

Al colgar, Roe sonrió para sí mismo. Esta es la excusa perfecta para verla, pensó.

La calidez acogedora del restaurante era una bienvenida que contrastaba con el frío de la noche afuera. Roe miró su reloj: 6:30 p.m., perfecto. Había tiempo para tomar una copa en el bar antes de que Emily entrara. Cuando Roe entró, recorrió el lugar con la mirada, sus ojos se fijaron en Danny Monk y Albert Guzmán sentados en una mesa del rincón, riendo de alguna broma privada.

Acerándose a la mesa, Roe dijo: "Bueno, mira quién está aquí, Danny, Albert. Gracias de nuevo por pagar la cuenta la última vez. Permíteme cubrir esta por ustedes—yo invito".

"Eso es generoso, Roe. Está bien, no nos quejaremos", agregó Danny.

Interviniendo, Albert agregó: "Brindaré por eso. ¿Por qué no te sientas aquí para charlar?".

"Claro. Tengo tiempo antes de mi reunión".

Roe miró a Danny y a Albert. Él tenía a Liam investigándolos y aun así, ahí estaba, bastante amistoso con ellos. Danny parecía relajado, tenía unos ojos a los que no se les escapaba ningún detalle y daba la impresión de captar las cosas con rapidez. Albert era, bueno, Albert. Realmente no había una forma para describir a este hombre. Agradable, divertido, un todo terreno completo cuando se trataba de divertirse. Un gran contraste entre estos dos, pensó Roe.

Los tres tenían una maravillosa conversación acerca de sus negocios y Roe estaba tan interesado que se había olvidado de ordenar esa copa, y justo cuando Emily cruzó la entrada, llamó la atención de Roe inmediatamente. Ella lucía radiante, con una suave sonrisa asomándose en sus labios.

"Disculpen caballeros. Mi invitada a la reunión ha llegado", y Roe se levantó y caminó hacia Emily.

Emily dijo con calidez: "Noches, Roe".

Devolviéndole la sonrisa, Roe dijo: "Emily. Llegas en el momento perfecto".

Roe se tomó un momento para explicar a Emily lo que él podía compartir acerca de Monk y Guzmán cuando su mesero llegó y les entregó la carta de vinos y el menú. El mesero estaba explicando cuáles eran los platillos especiales de la noche cuando la puerta principal se abrió de golpe.

Dos hombres enmascarados irrumpieron en el interior, empuñando pistolas. Uno disparó un tiro de advertencia al techo, y el lugar estalló en caos—los clientes gritaron, agachándose debajo de las mesas.

El ladrón número uno gritó: "¡Todos al piso!" "¡Ahora!".

El ladrón número dos anunció con calma: "¡Entreguen sus billeteras, relojes y teléfonos, o empezaremos a disparar!".

El corazón de Roe se aceleró mientras evaluaba la situación. Emily lo miraba, con los ojos muy abiertos, pero aparentemente tranquila. La mano de Roe se movió instintivamente hacia su saco—él no estaba armado, pero tendría que hacer algo.

Tranquilamente le dijo a Emily: "Quédate abajo. No te muevas".

Él se levantó lentamente, haciendo contacto visual con Danny y Albert al otro lado del lugar. Danny le hizo a Roe un leve gesto con la cabeza.

Levantando sus manos, Danny se dirigió a los ladrones: "Está bien, tranquilos amigos. No hay necesidad de lastimar a nadie".

Al escuchar la voz de Danny, uno de los ladrones dirigió su atención hacia él. Roe dio un paso adelante, listo para lanzarse sobre el ladrón más cercano. De repente, el ladrón armado reaccionó, y se oyó un disparo.

Antes de que Roe pudiera moverse, Danny se lanzó hacia el otro lado del restaurante, empujando a Roe y apartándolo fuera del camino de la bala. Roe se tambaleó y cayó al suelo, aturdido. Sin embargo, Danny fue herido en el hombro, una pequeña salpicadura de sangre brotó de la herida.

Danny gritó. "Hijo de—".

Antes de que los ladrones tuvieran tiempo de hacer algo más, Albert se lanzó hacia adelante con una silla, golpeándolos en la cabeza y gritando a pleno pulmón: "Le disparaste a Danny, le disparaste a Danny", derribando al ladrón al suelo.

Roe se puso en pie rápidamente, tomando al segundo ladrón armado por sorpresa, derribándolo y tirándolo al suelo. Más clientes gritaron mientras la escena se sumía aún más en el caos.

Alguien gritó: "¡Llamen a la policía, llamen a la policía!".

Pareció una eternidad, pero momentos después, el sonido de las sirenas llenó el aire, y la policía irrumpió en el restaurante, con las armas desenfundadas. Los oficiales sometieron a los ladrones, y los paramédicos entraron corriendo en el restaurante y empezaron a atender a Danny y a los ladrones. El detective inspector Cassell entró marchando con paso firme, observando la escena con una mirada aguda y lanzando órdenes a gritos a los oficiales uniformados. Al ver a Danny, se dirigió hacia él para hablarle.

Cassell miró a Danny, quien se agarraba el hombro, con sangre filtrándose por su camisa. "Parece que tú realmente no puedes mantenerte alejado de los problemas, ¿verdad?".

"Ellos parecen encontrarme, Cassell".

El detective sonrió cuando él inspeccionó la herida. "Mala suerte, Monk. Vivirás".

"Sí, sí. Es sólo un rasguño".

"¿Un rasguño? Podrían haberte matado, Danny, cariño. ¿Qué haría sin mi mejor amigo?". Dijo Albert, llorando y apretando a Danny, lo que lo hizo gruñir un poco. El paramédico empujó a Albert fuera del camino con un leve ceño fruncido.

Mientras los oficiales arrastraban a los ladrones sometidos hacia la salida, Cassell notó algo. Él estudió a los hombres, entonces se volvió hacia Roe con una ceja levantada.

"Estos dos coinciden con la descripción de los ladrones del restaurante Picton".

Actuando sorprendido, Roe respondió: "Está bromeando".

Cassel negó con la cabeza. "En absoluto". La misma constitución, misma altura. Significa que Danny y Albert no pudieron haber hecho ese trabajo. Ellos han sido inocentes todo este tiempo".

Roe intercambió una mirada con Danny, quien esbozó una sonrisa dolorida pero triunfante.

Con una sonrisa burlona, Danny le dijo a Cassell: "Te dije que nosotros no éramos los chicos malos".

Cassell puso los ojos en blanco ante Danny y entonces siguió a los oficiales, que estaban sacando a los dos ladrones por la puerta.

El restaurante se tranquilizó, los clientes regresaron lentamente a sus asientos, todavía con la adrenalina a tope. Los médicos terminaron de atender a Danny, vendando su hombro.

Roe se arrodilló junto a Danny. "Tú no tenías que hacer eso, ¿sabes?".

"Bueno, si no lo hubiera hecho, ¿quién pagaría por la cena y las bebidas esta noche?".

Roe se rió entre dientes. "Te lo agradezco, amigo. Definitivamente, ahora la cena la pago yo. Escucha. Estoy agradecido por tu ayuda. ¿Cómo sabías que yo iba a actuar? Te vi asentir como si estuvieras de acuerdo en que algo tenía que hacerse".

"No estoy seguro Roe. Tu mirada me hizo actuar instintivamente, supongo".

"¿Instintivamente? No parecía que te movieras como un vendedor de libros cualquiera, al menos para mí".

"Oye, leo mucho. Algo se me tenía que quedar. Puede que fuera una de las novelas de acción. ¿Entonces ya estás listo para pagar la cena?".

Dirigiéndose a Danny, uno de los paramédicos afirmó: "Esta noche no hay cena ni bebidas para usted, señor. Usted viene al hospital con nosotros esta noche".

Albert estaba justo a su lado repitiendo: "Querido, estarás bien, estarás bien", mientras los sacaban del restaurante y los subían a la ambulancia que los esperaba.

Emily se acercó, colocando una mano sobre el hombro de Roe.

Suavemente, ella preguntó: "¿Estás bien? ¿Danny va a estar bien?".

"Sí, estoy bien, gracias a Danny, y él estará bien. Aunque estoy preocupado por Albert.

Emily soltó una pequeña risita. "Albert estará bien. Él pasará la noche diciéndole a todos en la sala de emergencias cómo salvo el día golpeando a uno de los ladrones armados con una silla".

"Tienes razón". Roe miró a Emily y le dedicó una pequeña y cansada sonrisa".

"Bueno, esta no era exactamente la noche tranquila que tenía en mente para nosotros". Ella bromeó.

"¿Qué puedo decir, Emily? Ciertamente no hice esto para impresionarte. ¿Qué tal si aún tenemos esa cena? Creo que nos la ganamos".

Emily asintió, y ellos regresaron a su mesa mientras la policía finalizaba el trabajo en la escena.

Durante el resto de la noche, Roe tuvo un pensamiento: que el disparo era para él, pero Danny lo recibió en su lugar.

Le debo mi vida a Danny, él pensó, y estaba agradecido de que esa noche pudiera seguir viviendo.

21

Deuda

El restaurante retornó lentamente a la normalidad. Las copas tintinearon suavemente otra vez, las conversaciones se reanudaron en voz baja, y el personal, ahora tranquilo, se movía alrededor con gracia. Roe y Emily se sentaron en su mesa, sus corazones seguían un poco acelerados por el caos. Roe sirvió un vaso de agua para los dos.

Roe exhaló profundamente, entonces le ofreció una pequeña sonrisa tranquilizadora. "Bueno, esa no era exactamente la noche que yo había planeado".

Con una suave sonrisa, Emily dijo: "No, pero tú lo manejaste muy bien. Aunque la próxima vez, no hagamos que esquivar balas sea parte de nuestra noche".

"Ambos rieron, tratando de dejar que la tensión del robo se disipara".

El mesero regresó y preguntó: "Entonces, ¿están listos para ordenar?".

"¿Qué te parece si intentamos disfrutar el resto de la velada?" propuso Roe.

Asintiendo, Emily sonrió y dijo: "Sí, hagámoslo".

Ellos ordenaron su comida—Roe escogió el ribeye con una guarnición de papas asadas, y Emily seleccionó el salmón a la plancha con verduras de temporada. Cada uno ordenó una copa de vino.

"Excelentes elecciones. Las tendré listas en breve".

El mesero se alejó, y Roe se inclinó hacia atrás, mirando a Emily por un momento antes de tomar un sorbo de agua.

Él aclaró su garganta. "Bien. Entonces, déjame llegar al verdadero motivo por el que estamos aquí esta noche—profesionalmente hablando".

Inclinando la cabeza con una sonrisa juguetona, Emily preguntó: "¿Profesionalmente eh?".

Sonriendo, Roe continuó, "Por ahora, sí. El caso de Stonebridge Insurance está oficialmente concluido. La investigación encontró que el dueño del edificio incendió el lugar para cobrar el seguro. Nosotros entregamos todo al departamento de bomberos y a la policía—pruebas sólidas que ni siquiera ellos podían rebatir. El culpable debería estar detenido en estos momentos".

"Esas son grandes noticias, Roe. Tú has estado trabajando en ese caso por semanas. Debe sentirse bien haberte quitado finalmente ese peso de encima".

"Así es. Enviaré todos los archivos a Stonebridge Insurance el lunes junto con la factura, por supuesto".

Ellos compartieron una sonrisa cómplice.

"Naturalmente".

Roe hizo una pausa, echando un vistazo alrededor del lugar, como si estuviera ordenando sus pensamientos. Él volvió a centrar su atención en Emily, su tono se suavizó.

"Emily...ahora que el caso está cerrado, he estado pensando. En nosotros".

Al encontrarse con su mirada, ella le preguntó con expresión curiosa: "¿Y nosotros qué?".

"Yo sé que las cosas entre nosotros empezaron...inesperadamente. Pero me importas, Emily, más de lo que jamás pensé. Y supongo— que lo que estoy tratando de preguntar es—", Roe inspiró profundamente. "¿Crees que podemos llevar esto al siguiente nivel? ¿Algo más que reuniones profesionales?".

Por un momento, el ruido del restaurante pareció desvanecerse. Emily sostuvo su mirada; una pequeña y sincera sonrisa se dibujó en sus labios.

"Sí, Roe. Lo creo". Ella respondió suavemente.

La expresión de Roe se transformó en una cálida sonrisa de alivio. Por un momento, ellos simplemente se miraron el uno al otro, el peso de todo—trabajo, casos, su secreto—finalmente se aligeró.

De manera juguetona, Emily continuó: "Pero solo para que lo sepas, tú aún tendrás que enviar esos archivos el lunes. Y la factura".

Roe rió: "Absolutamente. A primera hora de la mañana. Lo prometo".

Sus risas se fundieron en la atmósfera del restaurante, un raro momento de ligereza entre ellos. Su comida llegó, y ellos levantaron sus copas de vino.

"Por nosotros y para que no haya más robos, balas esquivadas o facturas vencidas".

Emily hizo chocar su copa contra la de él. "Brindo por eso".

El resto de la noche se desarrolló sin contratiempos, con comida deliciosa, buen vino, y una conversación sincera. Y mientras ellos reían por el giro más reciente de los acontecimientos, algo quedó claro: por una vez, todo parecía encajar en su lugar.

Roe pidió la cuenta, y cuando el mesero la trajo, él agregó una generosa propina y le dijo: "Por favor haga una segunda impresión de la tarjeta de crédito. Pero no le ponga fecha. La próxima vez que Mr. Monk y Mr. Guzmán vengan a cenar y a beber algo, dígales que yo invito". Y con una sonrisa enorme, le dijo al mesero: "Agregue un veinte por ciento de propina también para el futuro mesero que los atienda".

Esto provocó una inmensa sonrisa en el rostro del mesero, y él volvió a mirar la tarjeta de crédito. "Gracias Mr. Cooke. Muy generoso", él dijo.

Roe se levantó y se acercó a la silla de Emily. Él le ayudó a levantarse y le ofreció su brazo.

Al salir, Roe pensó en Danny y Albert.

Le debo mi vida a ese hombre. Necesito recordar eso. Es una deuda que pagaré sin importar lo que pase. Él pensó.

Él y Emily salieron por la puerta. Él la escoltó a su coche, donde él la hizo girar, la sostuvo entre sus brazos, y le dio un largo y profundo beso.

Emily le devolvió esa pasión, y cuando ellos se apartaron para tomar aire, ella pensó para sí misma: *Cada vez estoy más enamorada de este hombre. ¿A dónde me llevará esto?*

22

Camino a Casa

Mientras Roe conducía a casa, el sabor de los labios de Emily permanecía en los suyos. Sus manos se aferraron con fuerza el volante, la adrenalina de su beso todavía bombeaba a través de él. Cada canción que sonaba a todo volumen por los altavoces del radio, era simplemente perfecta, como si hubiera sido escrita para ellos. El universo estaba en sincronía, incluso después del caos de esta noche.

Su beso confirmó, al menos a Roe, que Emily significaba más para él de lo que había pensado. Si Danny no se hubiera interpuesto delante de esa bala, él no tendría vida, ni a Emily. Él había sido imprudente al gritarle a los hombres armados. ¿En qué estaba pensando? Pero el beso de Emily reforzó todo lo que él sabía en lo más profundo de su ser.

¿La amo porque la necesito, o la necesito porque la amo? Se preguntó a sí mismo.

Él aún podía ver la forma en la que Emily lo miraba en ese momento, cómo se sentía, cómo deseaba dejar atrás todas las reglas que había seguido toda su vida.

¿Ella siente lo que yo siento? Ella dijo que sí. La idea lo emocionaba y lo aterrorizaba al mismo tiempo. Él sabía lo

complicado que era. Ella estaba casada. ¿Estaría ella realmente lista para una relación importante tan pronto? Ellos acababan de adentrarse en un territorio desconocido, y no había un camino fácil por delante.

"¿Qué significa esto para nosotros?", Roe se preguntó una vez más.

Roe pensó fugazmente en Emily cuando llegó a casa.

¿Qué está pensando ella? Era lo que pensaba mientras salía del coche y entraba en su casa.

Mientras tanto, Emily agarró el volante con fuerza, su corazón aún latía aceleradamente por el beso. Ella conducía, pero su mente estaba a millas de distancia reviviendo una y otra vez cada detalle de las caricias de Roe. Sentía un hormigueo en los labios al recordarlo, ella sonrió, aunque la culpa la rondaba. Ella sabía que no debió haber dejado que aquello pasara con semejante pasión, pero cuando Roe se inclinó hacia ella, todo lo demás desapareció—los recuerdos de su matrimonio anterior, sus responsabilidades, su miedo.

Se sintió real. demasiado real.

Ella no era ingenua acerca de lo que esto significaba. Roe no era solo una aventura pasajera—él era diferente. Había una profundidad en él que la hacía sentir comprendida de formas que su exesposo nunca logró.

Pero ¿qué estoy haciendo? Ella tragó saliva con dificultad, sabía que estaba cruzando una línea en la que ya no había vuelta atrás. No fue solo el beso. Era lo que venía antes de él: las confesiones no dichas, la vulnerabilidad. Con Roe, no había necesidad de fingir.

Emily se preguntaba por cuánto tiempo podría mantener sus dos vidas sin entrar en conflicto. El trabajo, sus carreras…era lo primero para ambos, y Roe…Roe estaba esperando más que sólo momentos robados.

¿Es él?

Ella sabía que él se merecía más. Pero ese beso era otro vistazo a algo que ella había echado de menos durante demasiado tiempo—algo emocionante y aterrador a la vez.

¿De verdad puedo tener esto?

A medida que el camino se extendía por delante, ella murmuró dentro de la quietud del coche: "¿Qué estoy haciendo?".

Pero incluso cuando la pregunta permanecía en el aire, su corazón sabía la respuesta. Ella no se arrepentía. Ni siquiera un segundo. Lo que fuera que viniera después, ella ya estaba más involucrada de lo que había querido—y una parte de ella estaba contenta.

Emily llegó a casa, y ella se preguntaba si Roe estaba sintiendo lo que ella estaba sintiendo.

¿Qué estaba pensando él? era su pensamiento mientras salía de su coche y entraba en su casa.

23

El Recuerdo De Su Beso

Roe se inclinó hacia atrás en su silla, girando el cuello para sacudirse el dolor persistente del caos del fin de semana. Frente a él, Liam y Aggie revisaban notas sobre el caso del robo. Ellos estaban absortos en una conversación, pero la mente de Roe iba y venía, atrapada en la huella que le había dejado el beso de Emily.

"Entonces, ¿me estás diciendo que Danny Monk recibió una bala por ti?" dijo Aggie, cruzando los brazos, con un toque de incredulidad mezclada con preocupación en la voz.

"Sí", respondió Roe, en voz baja. "Todavía estoy tratando de entenderlo".

Liam asintió, golpeteando con un bolígrafo la carpeta abierta que tenía delante. "Eso es una locura, amigo. Pero hay más. Algo extraño sucedió este fin de semana".

La atención de Roe se agudizó. "¿Qué quieres decir?".

"El inspector detective Cassell pasó por mi casa temprano—antes de saber lo que pasó este fin de semana", Liam empezó, rascándose la barbilla. "Él me preguntó si tenía algo sobre Danny Monk o Albert —algo que él pudiera usar para algunos viejos casos. Ya sabes, cosas que él investigó antes pero que nunca resolvió".

Roe entornó sus ojos. "¿Encontraste algo?".

"Sí", Liam admitió a regañadientes. "Un par de transacciones bancarias interesantes—ambos, Danny y Albert enviando dinero al extranjero. No es exactamente impecable, pero…" él se encogió de hombros. "No puedo demostrar que los fondos fueran ilegales".

La mirada de Roe se endureció. "Tú no se lo dijiste a Cassell, ¿verdad?".

"Por supuesto que no", dijo Liam. "Pensé consultarlo contigo primero. No parecía el tipo de cosa que se pudiera entregar sin comprobar".

Roe dio golpecitos sobre la mesa con los dedos, aumentando la tensión. "Déjalo, Liam. No le digas nada a Cassell y no indagues más".

Liam levantó una ceja, sorprendido. "Roe, ¿estás seguro de eso?".

Aggie inclinó la cabeza. "¿Por qué el repentino enfoque de no intervención? Algo no está bien con esos dos, de acuerdo con Liam".

La expresión de Roe no vaciló. "Ambos me salvaron la vida. Yo no estaría sentado aquí justo ahora si no fuera por ellos". Su tono era firme, no admitía réplica. "Se los debo".

Aggie consideró esto por un momento, entonces ella suspiró. "Tienes razón. Les enviaré un paquete de vino—uno para Danny a *Village Books & Stuff* y otro para *Albert a Locks &*

Loaded". Ella anotó la idea en una nota adhesiva. "Nada dice 'gracias por recibir una bala' como un excelente vino".

Liam rió entre dientes, pero Roe permaneció serio, asintiendo con gratitud a ambos. "Lo digo en serio. No hay más que decir sobre esto. Caso cerrado".

La conversación cambió de tema cuando Liam y Aggie recogieron sus cosas y salieron, dejando solo a Roe en la oficina. Él se inclinó hacia adelante, abriendo sus notas del caso para revisarlas, pero las palabras se difuminaban en la página. Su mente divagaba, alejándose de los casos que tenía enfrente de él.

Él se pasó la mano por el pelo y suspiró, mirando fijamente las páginas. Por mucho que él intentara concentrarse, su mente seguía volviendo a Emily—su risa, la sensación de sus labios contra los suyos, la forma en la que ella lo miraba cuando nadie más estaba mirando. Lo que ellos se dijeron esa noche.

Fue más que solo un beso; era la promesa de algo aún por definir. Y sin embargo, él no podía parar de pensar en ello. Ella estaba entretejida en sus pensamientos como una canción que él no podía dejar de tararear, aflorando al borde de cada momento de silencio.

Él se echó hacia atrás en el asiento, frotándose la cara con ambas manos.

Esto se va a poner interesante entre nosotros, ¿no es así? Él pensó, pero la idea de mantenerse alejado de ella se sentía imposible.

Le emocionaba pensar en lo que compartían - una chispa de algo nuevo. Él conocía los riesgos, sabía que si se apresuraba, podría alejar a Emily.

¿Lo hará?

Pero no importaba. Ella estaba en su cabeza ahora, y no había forma de sacársela.

Inhalando profundamente, Roe se enfocó en el caso que tenía ante sí. Un segundo después, él lo cerró otra vez.

Él sabía que debía concentrarse en el trabajo, pero cada vez que él cerraba los ojos, todo lo que veía era a Emily—Emily, y la forma en la que ella lo hacía sentir—como si el suelo bajo sus pies se estuviera moviendo, y él no estaba seguro de si correr o lanzarse de cabeza.

Él tomó su bolígrafo y garabateó distraídamente en los márgenes del expediente.

Mañana, se dijo a sí mismo. Me sumergiré de nuevo en el trabajo mañana.

¿Pero por ahora? Por ahora, él se dejaría llevar por el recuerdo de su beso.

24

Permaneciendo en el Silencio

Emily se reclinó en su asiento, sus dedos repiqueteaban rápidamente sobre la carpeta marcada como Investigaciones Alder y Finch. Frente a ella, Elisabeth, su asistente, se sentó con un bloc de notas en la mano, tan impecable y atenta como siempre. La hermosa mañana soleada se filtraba a través de las grandes ventanas, proyectando un cálido resplandor por todo el lugar.

"Nosotros tuvimos suerte, muchísima suerte Elisabeth. Fuimos realmente bendecidos", ella dijo, su voz era firme pero reflexiva. "Cuando me reuní con Roe en Petite Maison, se suponía que íbamos a hablar del caso de fraude; mera rutina, o eso pensé yo. Pero entonces, ocurrió ese robo, y por un momento…" ella dejó la frase en el aire. "Si algo le hubiera pasado a Roe…" ella hizo una pausa. "No sé qué hubiera hecho. Profesionalmente hablando, claro".

Elisabeth levantó una ceja con aire cómplice, su expresión era cuidadosamente neutral. "Por supuesto".

Elisabeth había trabajado con Emily por seis años y estaba al tanto de todo lo que pasaba en su vida. Desde su reciente divorcio, ella había estado de un mejor humor. Más segura. El divorcio había ayudado a Emily, o eso pensó Elisabeth, pero este hombre, este Roe—bueno, sin duda él también tuvo algo que ver con su cambio de humor.

Emily continuó, "Y Danny Monk, él recibió una bala por Roe. Y Albert Guzmán también estuvo involucrado en ello, de alguna manera. Ambos lo salvaron. Me siento tan agradecida por eso".

Elisabeth dio golpecitos con su bolígrafo sobre el cuaderno de notas pensativamente. "Ellos se pusieron en la línea. Nosotros deberíamos mostrar nuestro agradecimiento, sabe, discretamente. Déjeme revisar algo".

Elisabeth sacó su teléfono y empezó a teclear antes de ofrecerle a su jefa una pequeña sonrisa. "¿Qué le parece esto Ms. Dickson? Encontré sus negocios haciendo una búsqueda en Internet. La fiesta de Navidad de la oficina es en tres meses. ¿Y si me pusiera en contacto con ellos? La tienda de Danny es Village Books & Stuff, y el lugar de Albert se llama Locks & Loaded, una peluquería. Estoy segura de que ellos tienen paquetes de regalo que podríamos adquirir para el personal".

El rostro de Emily se iluminó ante la idea. "Esa es una idea perfecta, una gran idea, Elisabeth. Asegúrate de que sea algo bien pensado. Hagamos un paquete de regalo de doscientos dólares de cada uno. Libros o artículos de la tienda de Danny para los hombres, y un tratamiento o paquete de productos de la peluquería de Albert".

Elisabeth asintió. "Yo me encargaré de eso".

"Gracias", dijo Emily, agradecida por su eficiencia.

Dando una última mirada a la carpeta de la investigación, ella la empujó por encima del escritorio. "Aquí está el expediente sobre el caso de fraude que Alder y Finch acaba de terminar. Todo parece en orden. ¿Puedes asegurarte de que el departamento de cuentas por pagar reciba esto hoy?".

"Por supuesto". Elisabeth tomó la carpeta con una sonrisa, mirando a Emily con curiosidad antes de salir silenciosamente de la oficina.

Emily se recostó en su silla, exhalando lentamente. Ella abrió su correo electrónico, pero las palabras parecían distorsionadas. No importaba cuánto intentara concentrarse, su mente seguía volviendo a Roe. Maldita sea Roe. Parece que hoy no puedo trabajar por tu culpa, ella pensó.

El recuerdo del beso emergió de nuevo. Su intensidad, la vulnerabilidad, y el cambio repentino en todo.

¿Y si algo le hubiera pasado a él?

Esa idea le oprimía el pecho; un dolor silencioso que ella no esperaba. Se dio cuenta, con una sacudida, de que Roe había traspasado los muros que tan cuidadosamente había construido y que había mantenido por años. Ellos apenas habían empezado a conocerse el uno al otro, y ella ya no podía imaginar no tenerlo en su vida.

La parte racional de su mente le advirtió ser cautelosa. Roe era una complicación que ella no se podía permitir. Pero la lógica se sentía distante, como un ancla que se deslizaba.

¿Y si esto fuera el comienzo de algo más?

¿Algo de largo plazo?

La idea la emocionaba y la aterrorizaba al mismo tiempo.

Ella se forzó a sí misma a desplazarse a través de sus correos, pero las palabras no tenían sentido. Sus pensamientos estaban con Roe—preguntándose qué estaría pensando y qué significaba esto para ellos.

Una pequeña sonrisa involuntaria asomó en sus labios.

¿Qué sigue para nosotros, Roe? Ella se pregun-tó, y la pregunta quedó flotando en el silencio.

25

Powerball

Roe se recostó en el lujoso sillón de cuero, dando ligeros golpecitos con los dedos en el reposabrazos, mientras Bill Tompkins ajustaba sus anteojos, estudiando detenidamente las últimas páginas de los reportes financieros. Ambos estaban sentados uno enfrente del otro en la oficina impecable de Bill, el sol se filtraba a través de las persianas y proyectaba tenues rayas sobre el escritorio.

Roe había construido Alder y Finch desde cero en el estilo y modelo que él quiso y, ahora, él estaba esperando que los años de trabajo finalmente le darían la libertad de vivir la vida en sus propios términos—preferiblemente lejos de todo, con Emily a su lado.

Su mente estaba puesta en Emily. Él no había hablado con ella sobre sus planes pues quería tener todos sus patitos en fila, bien organizados, como dice el dicho, antes incluso de que él sacara el tema.

Cuando Bill terminó su revisión, entrelazó las manos, y una pequeña sonrisa asomó en la comisura de sus labios. "Bien, Roe", Bill empezó, "Estás en buena forma, tanto personalmente como profesionalmente, pero me temo que si estás pensando en retirarte pronto y escapar a una playa en algún lugar, necesitamos hablar seriamente de números y planificar".

Roe miró a Bill y solo dijo, "Dímelo sin tapujos, Bill. ¿Qué me estás mostrando?".

"Okay. Déjame mostrarte la hoja de resumen. Justo ahora, entre las ganancias de tu negocio y tu portafolio personal, estás generando un flujo constante. Se ve bien si continúas trabajando, pero para marcharse por completo y mantener un estilo de vida que te permita beber margaritas en una isla exclusiva, sin preocupaciones, bueno, tú necesitarías unos cinco millones de dólares reinvertidos en Alder y Finch para que siga funcionando de forma independiente bajo la mirada de Aggie, con Liam como gerente general".

Los labios de Roe esbozaron una pequeña sonrisa, pensando brevemente en Liam, su amigo de confianza y colega, y en Aggie, cómo les encantaría el reto de dirigir la agencia por ellos mismos.

Diablos, ya la dirigen ahora, pensó Roe.

Bill continuó, "Entonces, para tu portafolio personal, necesitarías otros diez millones de dólares invertidos para asegurarte de que nunca tendrás que tocar el principal. Con ello, tú podrías vivir cómodamente de los rendimientos de forma indefinida".

Roe dejó escapar un silbido bajo. "¿Y cuánto tiempo tardaré en alcanzar esas cifras?".

Bill echó un vistazo a sus hojas de cálculo, entonces volvió a mirar a Roe. "Dieciocho años, más o menos. Eso asumiendo un crecimiento constante y sin sorpresas en ambos aspectos: tu negocio y tu vida personal".

Roe pensó, ¡dieciocho años!

Él siempre se había enorgullecido de sí mismo por planificar con anticipación, pero eso no era lo que él había querido escuchar.

"¿Cuál es el mejor escenario posible?" Roe preguntó, inclinándose una vez más sobre la hoja de resumen, esperaba encontrar alguna fisura en los números de Bill.

Bill negó suavemente con la cabeza. "Podrías intentar acelerar las cosas diversificando tus inversiones, quizás aceptar clientes más grandes o vender partes del negocio. Incluso realizar opciones de inversión más arriesgadas, pero incluso entonces, necesitarás tiempo Roe. No hay magia aquí. El tiempo es dinero, como se dice, y mientras tengas algún dinero, el tiempo es lo que más necesitas".

"Maldita sea Bill, realmente estaba esperando que pudiera hacer esto en un año o algo así", dijo Roe.

"Lo siento, Roe". Él señaló la hoja de resumen una vez más. "Los números no mienten".

Los sueños y pensamientos de Roe sobre Emily volvieron a ocupar su mente. Emily, con su brillante sonrisa y rápido ingenio, de pie en alguna playa tropical junto a él. Ellos se despertarían con el sol, nadarían en aguas claras, y dejarían atrás el desorden de sus vidas actuales.

Pero dieciocho años era mucho tiempo. E incluso, aunque a él aún le quedaban muchos años por delante, el pensamiento de esperar incluso un momento más, le atormentaba.

"Bueno, gracias por ser claro conmigo", él dijo con un suspiro.

"Cuando quieras. Y mira, Roe, lo estás haciendo excelente. Esto no es el fin, solo parte del viaje".

Roe forzó una sonrisa, se puso de pie, agradeció a Bill otra vez, y se colocó la carpeta bajo el brazo. De camino de regreso a su coche, la mirada de Roe recorrió las calles, perdido en sus pensamientos—hasta que un rostro familiar le llamó la atención: Danny Monk, él estaba entrando a un café de la esquina.

Roe echó un rápido vistazo a su reloj: 10:24 a.m. ¿Tal vez está yendo por un café?

La campana sobre la puerta del café tintineó suavemente cuando Roe entró, su mirada se fijó en Danny Monk sentado en un cubículo de la esquina, bebiendo lentamente un flat white. Danny alzó la vista justo cuando Roe se deslizaba en el asiento frente a él, su expresión era una mezcla de curiosidad y precaución.

"No esperaba verte aquí, Roe. ¿Qué tal si te invito un café?" dijo Danny, se movió en su asiento con una leve mueca de dolor.

Roe se inclinó hacia adelante, con una mirada que parecía entenderlo. "¿Estás seguro de que tu hombro está mejor? Parece que todavía te duele".

Danny estaba tratando de enrollar un porro con cuidado, aunque Roe captó un leve destello de incomodidad que se dibujó en su rostro. "Nah, está bien. Es solo una punzada a veces. Ese incidente en Petite Maison no fue nada". Él se encogió de hombros tratando de restarle importancia.

"Sí, nada", Roe repitió secamente, descansando sus brazos sobre la mesa. "¿Qué pasa con Albert? ¿Dónde está? ¿Se va a reunir contigo?".

Danny se rió, asintiendo con la cabeza. "Por supuesto. Albert llegará pronto. Siempre tarde, ya sabes— le encanta hacer una entrada triunfal. Es lo suyo".

En efecto, justo cuando Danny terminó su frase, la puerta de la cafetería se abrió de golpe y, con un gesto teatral, entró Albert, luciendo una bufanda llamativa de seda, con una sonrisa amplia y sin el menor asomo de culpa.

"¡Allí estás, Danny querido!". Albert declaró, caminando hacia ellos. "¡Y Roe! ¡Qué sorpresa tan deliciosa!". Antes de que Roe pudiera reaccionar, Albert se inclinó, plantándole un beso en la mejilla a Roe y a Danny.

Roe se congeló, tomado por sorpresa por el gesto. Danny, por otro lado, no se inmutó—claramente, esto era lo normal tratándose de Albert.

"Encantado de verte también", Roe murmuró, ajustando su saco.

Danny sonrió burlonamente, pero no dijo nada, divertido por la ligera incomodidad de Roe.

Después de unos minutos de charla ligera, principalmente por parte de Albert relatando alguna absurda aventura matutina, Albert se inclinó hacia atrás en el asiento y aplaudió de repente.

"Chicos, ¡tengo una idea!", él anunció con una sonrisa contagiosa. "Aportemos cada uno, digamos, sesenta y ocho dólares para jugar una jugada grande del Powerball. ¡Eso nos da 150 oportunidades! El premio mayor es de ciento veinte millones. ¡Cuarenta millones para cada uno si ganamos!".

Danny arqueó una ceja y le lanzó a Albert una mirada escéptica. "Sabes que las probabilidades de ganar son algo así como de una en 292 millones, ¿verdad?".

Albert desestimó el comentario con un gesto desdeñoso de su mano. "Oh, querido, no seas aburrido. Alguien debe ganar. ¿Por qué no nosotros?". Él miró a Roe esperando su respuesta.

Roe dudó, las palabras anteriores de Bill daban vueltas en su mente. Dieciocho años. El número lo perseguía, pesado e implacable. Pero ¿y si—solo y si—esta ridícula idea funcionaba?".

"¿Por qué no? Si siento que nos conocemos de toda la vida, aunque haya sido poco el tiempo. Además, ya me has contado bastante de ti…así que sé dónde encontrarte".

Roe dijo, encogiéndose de hombros, buscando su cartera. "Cuenta conmigo".

Danny suspiró con resignación, pero también sacó su billetera. "Saben, ustedes dos no tienen remedio y tú deberías poder encontrarnos, Roe. Tú eres un investigador de seguros, después de todo. Además, te contamos acerca de nuestros negocios, entonces sí, tú puedes encontrarnos sin problema".

Los dos hombres entregaron setenta dólares cada uno. Albert hizo una pequeña reverencia, como si aceptara una comisión real. "¡Fabuloso! Vuelvo en un santiamén".

Mientras Albert estaba fuera comprando los boletos, Roe y Danny fueron entrando en la conversación acerca de sus respectivos negocios; el tipo charla informal que fluye con naturalidad entre dos personas que son empresarias y que son bastante conscientes de los altibajos propios de un pequeño negocio.

Después de un rato, Albert regresó hecho un torbellino de energía y dramatismo. "¡Aquí estamos, queridos!" él anunció, deslizándose en el asiento. "Tres boletos y una fotocopia de todos los números en una página". Él extendió las copias como un mago realizando un truco. "Las hice en casa. Yo me quedo con los boletos, pero ustedes ya tienen los números".

Él les hizo a ambos un guiño juguetón, entonces ordenó su habitual café extravagante—algo demasiado dulce y cubierto con mucha crema. Roe y Danny intercambiaron una mirada, pero no cuestionaron las excentricidades de Albert.

El tiempo pasó rápidamente mientras los tres charlaban y reían, la presencia de Albert aligeraba el ambiente como una ráfaga de aire fresco llegada en el momento oportuno. En poco tiempo, el reloj se acercaba al medio día, y Roe miró su reloj.

"Bueno, caballeros, ha sido divertido", Roe dijo, de pie y sacudiéndose las migajas imaginarias del regazo. "Pero tengo que regresar al trabajo".

Albert hizo un puchero dramáticamente. "Siempre tan responsable, Roe".

"Danny sonrió burlonamente. "Es por eso que Alder y Finch sigue en pie".

Roe les dedicó una sonrisa irónica. "Alguien tiene que mantener las cosas en marcha".

Él metió la fotocopia de los boletos de Powerball dentro del bolsillo de su saco y asintió hacia ambos. Al salir del café, la ciudad lo recibió con el sonido del tráfico de la hora del almuerzo y el parloteo de los transeúntes.

Con la conversación de Bill aun haciendo eco en su mente, Roe se permitió entregarse a un breve pensamiento: ¿Y si realmente ganaran? Por ahora, era solo un sueño, pero al menos había algo—una remota posibilidad—que podría cambiar todo.

Y tan improbable como parecía, Roe sabía una cosa con certeza: si la vida le lanzaba una bola curva, él estaría listo para batearla.

Quizá esta lotería es una forma para acelerar las cosas después de todo.

26

No Hace Falta Decir Nada Más

Roe y Emily paseaban tranquilamente por el Narellan Shopping Centre, disfrutando el bullicio de la multitud. Él y Emily se estaban escapando del trabajo este viernes, haciéndolo un fin de semana largo. Las últimas semanas ellos habían pasado la mayoría de los fines de semana juntos haciendo, bueno, nada, el hecho de estar juntos era suficiente para ellos a medida que su relación se volvía más y más estrecha. A ellos les encantaba mirar escaparates, compartir bromas acerca de lo absurdamente caros que eran los bolsos de mano y riéndose de aparatos extraños. Emily decía que si no fuera porque Roe pagaba el almuerzo, ella sería una cita barata.

Al acercarse la hora del almuerzo, ellos se dirigieron a Luigi's Trattoria, un encantador restaurante italiano escondido en el rincón más tranquilo del centro comercial. Ellos ordenaron una botella de vino tinto; risotto, el especial de la casa, para Roe, y pasta Alfredo para Emily. De postre, ellos no pudieron resistir compartir un rico tiramisú, seguido por un café expreso. Su conversación fluyó con facilidad, hablando brevemente de las pequeñas alegrías de la vida, planes futuros, y recuerdos que los hacían reír.

La comida era buena, el vino, aún mejor, y todo parecía perfecto. Fue entonces cuando el teléfono de Roe vibró sobre la mesa.

Roe miró la pantalla, era un número desconocido. Él frunció el ceño. "Lo siento, necesito tomar esta llamada", él dijo, deslizando el teléfono en su mano. Emily puso los ojos en blanco de manera juguetona, pero sonrió, bebiendo su café mientras él se levantaba de la mesa.

Él encontró un rincón tranquilo cerca de los baños y contestó la llamada. "¿Hola?".

Una voz masculina tranquila, aunque emocionada, lo saludó. "Roe, amigo, soy Danny Monk".

"¿Danny? ¿Qué pasa? ¿Cómo conseguiste mi número?".

"Llamé a la oficina y un compañero tuyo de nombre Liam me dio tu número. Escucha, ¡no vas a creer esto!". Dijo Danny, su voz prácticamente vibraba con incredulidad. "Albert está conmigo, y…bueno, ganamos, Roe. Powerball. Ciento veinte millones de dólares".

El corazón de Roe se detuvo. "¿Qué?".

"Sí, amigo. Nosotros ganamos ¡$120 millones! Dividido en tres partes—eso es cuarenta millones cada uno. ¡No puede ser! Pensé que Albert me estaba tomando el pelo, pero lo revisé yo mismo. Es real".

"¿Hablas en serio? ¿No es una broma?".

"¡Es verdad, ganamos el premio gordo! Albert me mostró los números, amigo, y son nuestros. Nos queremos reunir el lunes en la oficina de mi abogado para determinar los siguientes pasos. Mantenlo en secreto, ¿sabes? Nosotros tenemos que hacer esto bien y evitar cualquier circo mediático que viene con ganar tanto dinero. ¿puedes hacerlo?".

"Sí, sí. Solo envíame los detalles por mensaje. Ahí estaré".

"Bien. Es el lunes. Hablamos pronto, Roe".

Roe se quedó mirando su teléfono con incredulidad. Cuarenta millones de dólares. Así, sin más.

Roe guardó su teléfono en el bolsillo y caminó de regreso a la mesa, tratando de recomponerse, pero su rostro debió delatar algo.

Emily levantó la vista hacia Roe: "¿Todo está bien? Parece que viste a un fantasma".

"Es…nada. Te diré cuando sea el momento correcto. Pero…solo digamos que es una buena noticia".

"Está bien. Pero después me debes una explicación completa", ella dijo con una sonrisa juguetona.

Ellos se fueron de Luigi's y deambularon por el centro comercial, la naturaleza surrealista de la llamada telefónica permanecía en la mente de Roe. A pesar de su distracción, ellos se divirtieron, incluso fueron juntos al cine. Al caer la tarde, ellos condujeron a Parramatta para cenar en un restaurante acogedor junto al río.

Después de la cena, Roe se estacionó afuera del edificio del departamento de Emily. Ella se inclinó hacia adelante, dándole un suave beso en la mejilla. "¿Quieres subir a tomar una copa antes de dormir?", ella preguntó en voz baja, llena de una invitación implícita.

"Sí, eso me gustaría".

Al abrir la puerta, Roe pudo ver las luces de la ciudad filtrándose por la ventana del departamento de Emily, parpadeando suavemente sobre las paredes mientras él entraba.

Emily sirvió las copas, y una cosa llevó a la otra, y la noche se desarrolló con naturalidad, sin esfuerzo. Ellos solo disfrutaban la alegría de su mutua compañía. Era un paso hacia algo real.

El ambiente, el escenario, Emily. Todo era perfecto.

Emily sintió que había llegado el momento y, tomando la mano de Roe, lo guio a su habitación susurrando: "Roe, tómame. Te deseo".

Mientras Roe yacía al lado de ella, con sus piernas entrelazadas bajo las sábanas, los corazones latían lentamente, sumidos en la tranquila comodidad de estar juntos. Los dedos de Emily dibujaban suaves trazos en el pecho de Roe y su contacto dejaba a su paso un leve rastro de calor.

Roe se volvió hacia ella, acariciando su mejilla con la mano, y sus miradas se encontraron, buscando, ambos, un significado, seguridad, y algo más profundo que sabían que estaban construyendo entre ellos. Su pulgar acariciaba lentamente la línea de su mandíbula, de manera deliberada.

"Quédate", murmuró ella, su aliento rozando su cuello.

"No voy a ir a ningún lado", susurró él en respuesta.

Emily sonrió, sus labios se curvaron en algo suave y secreto, como si hubiera esperado escuchar esas palabras durante mucho más tiempo del que admitiría. Se inclinó hacia él, rozando sus labios en un beso suave como una pluma. Roe respondió de la misma manera—primero suave, casi titubeante — pero pronto sus bocas se encontraron en un ritmo que se sentía tan natural como respirar.

Su mano se deslizó por su pecho, y Roe gimió suavemente contra sus labios. Él se giró de lado atrayéndola hacia sí, sus cuerpos encajando el uno con el otro, como dos piezas destinadas a encontrarse. La piel desnuda de Emily unida a la suya, suave y cálida. Roe la besó profundamente, sus dedos enredándose en su cabello como si no pudiera tenerla lo suficientemente cerca.

Ellos se movían despacio, disfrutando de cada caricia, cada suspiro susurrado, mientras las manos de Roe recorrían su espalda y sus caderas, explorando cada curva, cada lugar que conocía, haciendo que ella se estremeciera. Ella suspiró contra él, su cuerpo se arqueó instintivamente al encuentro de sus caricias. Los besos de ambos se hicieron más profundos, el calor entre ellos aumentó, pero no había urgencia—solo el deseo puro de conectar plena y completamente.

Las uñas de Emily rozaron sus hombros mientras él la giraba bajo su cuerpo, su aliento se entrecortó cuando sus miradas se encontraron de nuevo. Por un instante, permanecieron quietos, como absorbiendo el significado de ese momento, con las emociones crudas y reales entre ellos.

"¿Estás segura?" preguntó Roe, suavemente, su voz apenas más alta que un susurro.

Emily sonrió, su respuesta reflejada en la manera en que sus manos rodeaban su rostro, y lo atrajo hacia sí para darle otro beso.

"Nunca he estado más segura", ella susurró contra sus labios.

Ellos se movían juntos en un ritmo perfecto, cada caricia encendía chispas que bailaban entre ellos, cada beso era una promesa silenciosa. El mundo exterior se desvaneció, quedando solo los dos y la intimidad que ellos compartían—algo que ninguno de los dos había esperado, pero ambos sabían que deseaban.

Roe murmuraba su nombre suavemente, con reverencia, mientras sus movimientos se volvían más urgentes, más frenéticos. Emily jadeó, sus dedos aferrándose a sus brazos, anclándose a él. Sus cuerpos se fundían entre sí, encontrando un ritmo que hablaba de anhelo, confianza y el deseo no expresado de ser visto, verdaderamente visto.

Cuando ellos llegaron juntos al límite, fue como si todo lo demás desapareciera—tiempo, espacio, dudas—dejando solo el calor de los alientos compartidos y los cuerpos entrelazados.

Después de todo lo que habían compartido, yacían enredados en las sábanas, sus cuerpos aun vibrando con los vestigios de lo vivido. Roe besó su hombro, sus labios demorándose sobre su piel, y Emily sonreía somnolienta, su cabeza descansando sobre su pecho.

"Quédate", ella susurró de nuevo, no como una petición sino como una convicción.

Roe besó la parte superior de su cabeza, envolviéndola entre sus brazos, sabiendo que él ya había decidido.

"Estoy aquí mismo".

Y por primera vez en mucho tiempo, ninguno de los dos sintió la necesidad de decir nada más.

A la mañana siguiente, el aroma del café y el tocino se extendía por todo el departamento de Emily mientras Roe se despertaba con la luz de la mañana. Él la encontró en la cocina, descalza, sin llevar nada más que su camisa y una gran sonrisa, haciendo el desayuno.

"Buenos días", ella lo saludó cálidamente mientras él se le unía en la pequeña mesa del comedor.

Ellos comían tranquilamente, hablando acerca de nada y de todo. En un punto, la conversación cambió a asuntos más serios—hacia donde veían que iba esta relación.

"Si alguna vez nos mudamos juntos", Roe dijo cautelosamente, "necesitaremos ser claros acerca de nuestras finanzas. No es el tema más romántico, pero es importante".

Emily asintió. "Acordado. Creo que la transparencia es la única forma en que esto funcionará".

Ambos compartieron su situación financiera—ingresos, ahorros, deudas. Roe escuchó cuidadosamente, notando su honestidad. Se sentía bien tener esa clase de apertura entre ellos. Pero en lo que respecta a su recién ganada fortuna, Roe mantuvo esa parte para él mismo por ahora. No era el momento correcto para dejar caer una bomba como esa.

"Supongo que si esto se convierte en algo más profundo", dijo Emily pensativa, "nosotros al menos sabremos dónde estamos parados".

Roe sonrió, ignorando la ligera punzada en su pecho. "Exactamente".

Al medio día, ellos salieron para almorzar, disfrutando de la compañía del otro, como si el fin de semana nunca fuera a terminar. Cuando finalmente fue hora de llevar a Emily de regreso a su departamento, Roe se estacionó frente a su puerta y la besó profundamente.

"¿Te veo pronto?" ella le preguntó suavemente.

"Absolutamente", Roe susurró, apartándole un mechón de pelo de su rostro.

Con eso, ellos salieron del coche de Roe, tomados de la mano. Se besaron, un beso largo y dulce de despedida, y se dijeron adiós.

Roe se dirigió a casa, sabiendo que el lunes traería un capítulo enteramente nuevo a su vida y a su relación. Cuarenta millones de dólares. Y Emily. Ambos misterios esperando revelarse.

27

En la Dirección Correcta

Roe se despertó justo después de las 5 a.m., más temprano de lo habitual. Su mente bullía, repasando una y otra vez las decisiones que él necesitaba tomar después de la reunión de hoy con el abogado de Danny. El dinero del premio del Powerball cambió las reglas del juego, pero el rompecabezas real era qué hacer con Investigaciones Alder y Finch.

La idea de vender la empresa cruzó por su mente brevemente. Podría ser un simple retiro de efectivo y dejar que alguien más la manejara. Pero eso no le sentó bien. Él no estaba listo para cerrar las puertas a lo que él y el equipo habían construido.

La sugerencia de Bill Tompkins regresó a él—mantener el negocio, dejar a Liam y a Aggie dirigir las operaciones del día a día, y pasar a un segundo plano. Tal vez incluso crear una nueva empresa holding y hacerlos directores a los tres.

A Roe le gustó esa idea. No solo aseguraría la continuidad, sino también le daría seguridad al personal, y él todavía se beneficiaría de sus éxitos sin necesidad de manejar las cosas directamente.

"Quizás", pensó Roe con una sonrisa, "Iré aún más lejos—convertirla en una empresa pública, darles todas las acciones".

Sin embargo, su mente iba demasiado rápido. Él exhaló lentamente, decidiendo enfocarse en una cosa a la vez. El abogado lo explicaría todo muy pronto. No había por qué adelantarse.

A las 7:30 a.m. el teléfono de Roe vibró con un mensaje de Danny: *11 a.m., Murphy & Reed Solicitors. 57 Chisholm Ave., Mt. Annan.*

Eso le daba tiempo a Roe. Tiempo de pasar por la oficina, ponerse al día con Liam sobre los casos y con Aggie sobre las operaciones de la oficina, y aun así llegar con el abogado sin prisas.

Roe llegó a la agencia justo después de las ocho y fue recibido por el habitual murmullo de llamadas telefónicas y el papeleo. Liam ya estaba ahí, encorvado sobre su escritorio con el expediente de algún caso abierto y una taza de café humeante junto a su codo.

"Días, jefe", Liam gritó. "No te esperaba a tan temprano".

"Nos espera un gran día, Liam. Pensé tener una rápida actualización antes de salir. ¿Hay algo que necesite saber?".

Liam le dio un rápido resumen. Dos nuevos clientes, un viejo caso finalmente cerrado, y una investigación sobre fraude de seguro que parecía prometedor.

Sí, Liam está dirigiendo bien la oficina, pensó Roe.

Satisfecho, Roe se dirigió al escritorio de Aggie. Los lunes, ella normalmente estaba ocupada con la nómina, con la cabeza metida en hojas de asistencia y hojas de cálculo. Ella levantó la vista con una mirada curiosa cuando Roe se acercó.

"¿La oficina funciona sin problemas?", él preguntó.

"Estoy aquí, ¿no? entonces está funcionando como un sueño", respondió Aggie. "¿Tú estás bien Roe? Pareces…diferente".

Roe solo sonrió, evadiendo la pregunta con una ligera risa entre dientes. "Pronto los pondré al tanto a ambos. Por ahora, solo mantengan las cosas estables".

Él se quedó unas horas más y a las 10:30 a.m él se excusó. "Tengo una reunión a la que debo asistir". Nos vemos más tarde".

Cuando Roe se detuvo frente a Murphy & Reed, eran las 10:50 a.m. El edificio de oficinas era moderno, con elegantes ventanales de vidrio y un aire de discreto profesionalismo. Dentro, Danny y Albert ya estaban esperando en el área de la recepción, ambos luciendo ligeramente nerviosos, pero emocionados.

"¿Listos para esto?" Roe preguntó, dándole a Albert una palmadita en la espalda.

Albert solo se rió, sacudiendo su cabeza. "Aún no puedo creer que es real".

Un hombre de aspecto impecable, de unos cuarenta y tantos, salió de una oficina cercana extendiendo una mano. "Buenos días, Danny". Mirando a Albert y a Roe, él extendió su mano primero a Albert y dijo: "Caballeros. Soy Gavin Reed".

Albert, como siempre, contestó de manera extravagante: "Encantado, sin duda, guapo". Danny le lanzó una mirada, pero Albert lo ignoró.

"Y yo soy Roebuck S. Cooke; un placer conocerlo, Mr. Reed".

"Por favor llámenme Gavin, Danny lo hace. Entremos a mi oficina".

La reunión fue sencilla. Gavin les explicó los pasos legales necesarios para recoger el dinero del premio, enfatizando la importancia de la confidencialidad. "Generalmente, los fondos tardan entre tres y cuatro semanas en transferirse", él dijo. "Mientras tanto, pondremos todo el papeleo en orden. Cada uno de ustedes deberá proporcionarme su identificación y detalles bancarios".

El trío entregó sus documentos, firmó lo necesario, y agradeció a Gavin por su ayuda. Al salir de la oficina, se percibía una sensación de emoción en el ambiente. Ellos acababan de sentar las bases para que sus vidas cambiaran para siempre.

"Vamos a comer algo", sugirió Danny. "Vi el pub Mt Annan al llegar y parece decente".

Ellos estuvieron de acuerdo y, pronto, después de hacer su pedido en la barra, se sentaron en un rincón acogedor del pub, con cerveza en mano, esperando a que sus comidas llegaran.

"Entonces", Danny dijo con una sonrisa, "¿Qué hará cada uno con su parte?".

Albert se echó para atrás en su silla, había una mirada soñadora en sus ojos. "Yo voy a comprar un boleto de primera clase y a viajar por el mundo sin parar". Cada país, cada ciudad. Sin itinerario, solo libertad. Y hacer nuevos amigos", Albert terminó con un gran guiño.

Danny se rió entre dientes. "Parece un plan perfecto para ti, Albert". Él tomó un sorbo de su cerveza. "En cuanto a mí, mantendré la librería. No puedo venderla, pero me mudaré a Crystal Cove. Estoy cansado de la relación de larga distancia con Toni Webster. Ella es una mujer increíble, y no quiero perder esta oportunidad. Creo que ya es hora de proponerle matrimonio. ¡Diablos! Quizá hasta de casarme".

Roe sonrió ante la sinceridad de Danny. "Parece que lo has pensado bien".

Danny se encogió de hombros. "Cuarenta millones hace todo un poco más claro".

Ellos se rieron ante el comentario de Danny. La camaradería entre ellos, ahora consolidada, rebosaba de emoción y posibilidades.

"¿Qué hay de ti Roe, cariño?, preguntó Albert.

Roe se inclinó hacia atrás y pensó por un momento. "En cuanto a mí, reestructuraré el negocio. Dejaré que mis dos empleados clave tomen las riendas mientras yo me retiro un poco. Y, como tú, Danny, creo que es momento de que comparta las buenas noticias con alguien especial. Quizás incluso sea lo suficientemente valiente como para hacerle la gran pregunta, como tú, cuando llegue el momento adecuado".

Él no mencionó el nombre de Emily, pero el solo hecho de pensar en ella lo llenó de calidez.

El almuerzo en el pub continuó más tiempo de lo esperado, y para cuando Roe regresó a la oficina, ya casi era la hora de cierre. Tan pronto como entró, Aggie y Liam se abalanzaron sobre él.

"¿Qué está pasando, Roe?" demandó Aggie, con sus manos en las caderas.

"Tú has estado actuando de forma extraña todo el día", agregó Liam. "Algo está pasando".

Roe se rió entre dientes, levantando las manos en señal de rendición simulada. "A su debido tiempo, chicos. Todo a su debido tiempo".

Sus expresiones curiosas y exasperadas, solo lo hicieron sonreír aún más. Con una risa despreocupada, Roe les dio una palmadita a ambos en los hombros.

"Confíen en mi", él dijo. "Ustedes lo sabrán muy pronto".

Con eso, Roe se metió en su oficina, sintiendo cómo el cansancio del día empezaba a hacerse sentir. El lunes había sido largo—pero de la mejor manera. Aún había decisiones por tomar y conversaciones por tener. Pero por primera vez en mucho tiempo, todo estaba dirigiéndose exactamente en la dirección correcta.

28

Sondeando el Terreno

Las siguientes cuatro semanas transcurrieron como de costumbre en Investigaciones Alder y Finch, con la actividad incesante de teléfonos sonando, los investigadores entrando y saliendo, y los informes siendo entregados, pero bajo la superficie se estaban produciendo algunos cambios pequeños, pero intencionados, y la gente lo notó.

Roe transfirió silenciosamente más control a Liam y a Aggie, tanteando el terrero para ver cómo manejaban la responsabilidad adicional. Él se limitaba a observar durante las reuniones, dejándolos tomar el mando, interviniendo solo cuando era necesario. El equipo notó el cambio, pero nadie dijo nada directamente. Ellos confiaban lo suficiente en Roe como para saber que él tenía sus razones.

Las reuniones de personal se volvieron más colaborativas. Roe insistió en incluir a todo el equipo—Jack Malone, Nina Hart, Jack Stone, y Evelyn Drake—dándole a todos información sobre los casos en curso y los nuevos. Esto les permitió tomar la iniciativa y asumir la responsabilidad de sus tareas. Cada uno de ellos aceptó estos casos adicionales con entusiasmo porque sabían que se les estaba confiando una mayor parte de la carga de trabajo.

Uno de los cambios más grandes fue el ascenso de Noah Peters.

Roe llamó a Noah a su oficina una mañana y dijo: "Tú eres oficialmente nuestro Oficial de Ciberseguridad. Con un aumento de sueldo, por supuesto". Él le entregó a Noah una lista de nuevas responsabilidades, incluyendo la gestión de Luke Cross y la tarea de contratar a dos especialistas en tecnología adicionales para la empresa.

Noah estaba atónito. "¿Estás seguro?".

Roe le dio un simple: "Sí".

Cuando Liam escuchó la noticia, al principio se quedó desconcertado. "¿No pensaste en consultármelo primero?". Él le preguntó a Roe, medio en broma, pero claramente curioso.

"Ya tienes bastante con lo tuyo, Liam. Confía en mí. Noah es el hombre adecuado para esto. Simplemente confía en mí y sigue adelante".

Liam estudió a Roe por un momento, entonces asintió con la cabeza. Él sabía que no debía cuestionar a Roe cuando estaba ocupado con algo más importante. El plan de Roe aún no estaba del todo claro, pero Liam confiaba en él. Siempre lo había hecho.

Con la oficina funcionando sin problemas, la vida personal de Roe empezó a florecer en formas que él no había previsto. Durante las últimas semanas, él había invitado a Emily a pasar fines de semana largos con él. Algunos fines de semana eran solo de tres días, pero otros se extendían hasta cuatro, dándoles una oportunidad de escapar realmente y disfrutar de la compañía del otro.

En uno de esos fines de semana largos, ellos volaron a Cairns, donde se divirtieron tomando el sol tropical y nadando en las aguas cristalinas de la Gran Barrera de Coral. En otro fin de semana, ellos volaron en un jet a Tasmania, disfrutando de vinos locales y saboreando el aire fresco y limpio de los viñedos de la isla.

Uno de sus viajes favoritos los llevó a North Island de Nueva Zelanda, donde ellos exploraron las colinas verdes onduladas y las playas remotas. Roe alquiló un autobús turístico completo, con una caja de champaña y varios tipos de quesos neozelandeses. Ellos vieron paisajes impresionantes, cascadas, ríos, aguas termales, y, en medio de todo ello, profundizaron la conexión que empezaba a sentirse menos como un romance pasajero y más como algo permanente. Cada vez que ellos regresaban a casa, Roe, y Emily sentían una sensación de claridad que crecía dentro de ellos.

Roe sabía que él estaba listo para más, tanto en su vida personal con Emily como en el negocio; él estaba reorganizando cuidadosamente ambos aspectos entre bastidores.

Al final de una tarde, mientras Roe terminaba de escribir algunas notas de una reunión, su teléfono vibró. Era Gavin Reed; el abogado que estaba supervisando su premio de Powerball. Roe contestó inmediatamente.

"Roe, soy Gavin", se escuchó la voz refinada al otro lado del teléfono. "Tengo buenas noticias. Los documentos están listos para firmarse. Necesito que te reúnas con Danny y Albert en mi oficina este jueves. Lo revisaremos todo, nos aseguraremos de que esté en orden, y discutiremos los siguientes pasos para cobrar el premio".

"Suena bien. ¿A qué hora?".

"¿Puedes llegar a las 11 de la mañana?", preguntó Gavin. "Eso debería darnos tiempo suficiente".

"Perfecto. Allí estaré".

Cuando Roe colgó, se permitió un raro momento de quietud. $40 millones. Una nueva vida por delante, con infinidad de posibilidades.

Vaya, vaya, era todo lo que podía pensar.

Pero la mejor parte no era el dinero; era saber que, lentamente, pero con seguridad, todo estaba cayendo en su lugar. Su negocio iba a estar en manos capaces, su vida personal iba prosperando, y con la próxima reunión, las últimas piezas de su plan estaban a punto de encajar.

Todo lo que él tenía que hacer era presentarse el jueves y firmar con su nombre.

Y tal vez, solo tal vez, pronto llegaría el momento de decirle todo a Emily—y, cuando fuera el momento adecuado, tomar la decisión que podría cambiar la vida de ambos para siempre.

29

Un Paso a la Vez

Roe llegó a la oficina de Gavin Reed pocos minutos antes de las 11 a.m. Danny y Albert ya estaban de pie junto al mostrador de la recepción, bromeando con la recepcionista.

"Buenos días, Roe", Danny gritó, con una sonrisa cada vez más amplia. "¿Listo para hacerte rico?".

Albert resopló ruidosamente, poniéndose en ridículo, apenas podía contener su emoción. "Se siente como un sueño, ¿verdad, querido?".

Roe asintió, sintiendo cómo su contagioso entusiasmo influía en su propio estado de ánimo. "Sí", él admitió con una sonrisa. "Como un sueño".

Gavin apareció en la puerta de su oficina, mostrando todo su profesionalismo, pero había un asomo de sonrisa en su rostro cuando él los saludó. "Entren, caballeros".

Ellos entraron en la oficina y se sentaron a la mesa, cada uno sentado frente a una carpeta grande con su nombre impreso en ella. Gavin no perdió tiempo en guiarlos a través del papeleo con meticuloso detalle. Todo estaba en orden. Formularios bancarios, documentos legales, firmas requeridas en cada paso. Se sentía como una experiencia fuera de este mundo mientras ellos firmaban los papeles finales, cada trazo del bolígrafo los llevaba un paso más cerca de una riqueza que les cambiaría la vida.

"Y eso es todo", dijo Gavin. "En catorce días, aproximadamente, los fondos serán depositados en sus cuentas. Felicitaciones, caballeros".

El trío se dio la mano, sintiendo cómo una corriente de incredulidad y emoción pasaba entre ellos. Danny sonrió. "Dentro de dos semanas, celebraremos".

"Cuenten conmigo". Dijo Roe.

Con las despedidas finales, Danny y Albert se fueron, sus voces animadas se apagaron lentamente mientras desaparecían por el pasillo.

Después de que los otros se habían ido, Roe permaneció en la oficina de Gavin, moviéndose en su silla mientras el abogado lo miraba con curiosidad. "¿Tienes algo más en mente, Roe?".

Roe asintió. "Sí. Necesito que prepares dos documentos para mí".

Gavin se reclinó en su asiento, cruzando las manos. "Estoy escuchando".

"Primero", Roe empezó, "Quiero reestructurar Alder y Finch. Hacerlo oficial. Quiero tres directores: Liam, Aggie y yo. Necesitaré que supervises todo el papeleo, formularios bancarios, contratos, todo. Para asegurarme de que ambos tengan un voto en la dirección futura de la empresa y yo sea un socio silencioso pero con derecho a voto".

"Eso no debería ser un problema", dijo Gavin, tomando nota rápidamente. "¿Y el segundo documento?".

Roe dudó, pero entonces dijo: "Un acuerdo prenupcial. Entre Emily Dickson y yo".

Las cejas de Gavin se levantaron ligeramente, aunque mantenía su expresión neutral. "Ya veo".

"Quiero estar preparado", Roe explicó rápidamente. "Con el dinero entrando, necesito asegurarme de que todo esté en orden. La amo y sé que ella me ama, pero he visto que a muchos se les complican las cosas cuando surge el tema del dinero. Quiero ser inteligente al respecto".

Gavin asintió lentamente. "Puedo hacer un borrador del prenupcial, Roe. Pero déjame preguntar. ¿Crees que Emily se lo espera? ¿sabe ella siquiera cuánto dinero ganaste?".

"Aún no", él admitió. "Se lo diré pronto".

"Roe, escucha. He estado en este negocio por un largo tiempo, y he visto muchas relaciones chocar contra un muro cuando se involucran documentos legales, especialmente un acuerdo prenupcial. Algunas personas lo toman como una falta de confianza, aunque sea solo por cuestiones prácticas.

No estoy diciendo que no deberías hacerlo", continuó Gavin. "Pero ten cuidado en la forma en que lo abordas". Este no es solo un asunto legal; también es un asunto muy personal. Muchas relaciones se han desmoronado cuando la gente involucra a abogados demasiado pronto".

Las palabras permanecieron en el aire entre ellos durante un rato.

"Haré el borrador para ti", dijo Gavin. "Pero te sugiero pensar cuidadosamente acerca de cómo—y cuándo—le mencionas esto a Ms. Dickson. La forma en que lo presentes hará toda la diferencia".

Roe asintió, aunque la duda se había apoderado de su mente.

¿Él estaba dándole demasiadas vueltas al asunto?

¿Emily lo entendería, o se sentiría herida por la sugerencia de un acuerdo prenupcial?

"Tendré ambos documentos listos para ti en una semana".

"Gracias, Gavin. Te lo agradezco".

Al salir de la oficina, Roe estaba confundido. ¿Había hecho lo correcto? Gavin no lo desaconsejó. Él solo dijo que fuera cuidadoso cuando le diera la noticia. Esto dejó a Roe preguntándose—¿él estaba cometiendo un error?

Y lo más importante, ¿cómo lo tomaría Emily?

Roe condujo por las calles de la ciudad, sus pensamientos daban vueltas. Él sabía que estaba haciendo algo inteligente, planear para el futuro. Pero el amor no siempre se trataba de lógica y planeación. Emily era especial, y su relación era diferente a cualquier otra que él hubiera tenido antes.

Él golpeó suavemente el volante con los dedos, sintiendo sobre sus hombros el peso de la decisión.

¿El prenupcial protegería lo que ellos tenían, o crearía una brecha entre ellos?

Al acercarse a su casa, Roe decidió actuar con cautela. Él le diría todo a Emily. La lotería, el dinero, y el futuro que él veía para ellos dos. Pero el momento tenía que ser perfecto.

Por ahora, todo lo que él podía hacer era tomar las cosas un paso a la vez.

30

Un Amor Al Fin Declarado

De regreso a casa, Roe se paró junto a su maleta, cuidadosamente empacada para el largo fin de semana en Melbourne. Algunas camisas, pantalones, ropa casual para pasear por la ciudad, y algo más arreglado para la cena—él quería que todo estuviera perfecto. Emily ya había bromeado con él antes por mensaje de texto sobre cómo "probablemente ella estaba empacando de más", Roe sonrió al pensarlo.

Ellos habían acordado que sería más fácil tomar un Uber al aeropuerto de forma separada y encontrarse en la terminal, sin preocuparse por el estacionamiento ni por quién iba a conducir. Solo los dos, disfrutando cada momento.

En el aeropuerto, Roe fue el primero en ver a Emily. Ella lo saludó con la mano en el momento en que lo vio.

"Justo a tiempo, galán", ella bromeó mientras se abrazaban.

Ellos se registraron juntos y antes de que se dieran cuenta, estaban abordando su vuelo, charlando sobre sus planes mientras se acomodaban en sus asientos.

El vuelo a Melbourne fue fácil, lleno de conversación ligera y risas compartidas. Ellos hablaron de las cosas que querían hacer: tour de vinos, explorar los callejones de la ciudad y el Victoria Markets, e incluso, dar un paseo por el Royal Botanic Gardens. El resto del mundo se había quedado atrás, y solo ellos importaban.

Su primer parada después de registrarse en su hotel boutique, fue Southbank, donde ellos almorzaron con vistas a Yarra River. Roe pidió sus cocteles, y brindaron por el fin de semana.

A partir de ahí, ellos se convirtieron en exploradores, deambulando entre los callejones que le daban a Melbourne su carácter. Ellos se detuvieron en varias cafeterías para tomar un café y comer algo. Echaron un vistazo a las librerías, pero no compraron nada, solo molestaban a los dependientes con preguntas ridículas y actuando como adolescentes tontos. De vez en cuando, ellos se detenían y admiraban el arte callejero que adornaba los muros de la ciudad.

Ellos caminaron de la mano a lo largo de la playa en St Kilda, mirando la puesta de sol. Emily se inclinó hacia Roe, su cabeza descansando ligeramente sobre su hombro, y en ese momento de tranquilidad, él sintió que estaba exactamente donde debía estar.

Por las noches, cenaban en restaurantes elegantes. El dinero no era un problema, comida italiana una noche, francesa la siguiente. Caminaban de regreso a su hotel sin prisa, dejando que el aire nocturno de la ciudad los envolviera. Cuando regresaban a su cuarto, la intimidad entre ellos crecía naturalmente, sin esfuerzo. Hacían el amor con suavidad, despacio, saboreando cada caricia, cada suspiro murmurado, como si tejieran una promesa en el corazón del otro.

Cada noche, se quedaban dormidos entrelazados, sus cuerpos cálidos debajo de las sábanas, sus corazones, en silencio, encontraban su ritmo latiendo al unísono.

El lunes en la tarde, el fin de semana parecía como un sueño.

Acomodándose en la clase ejecutiva, Roe tomó la mano de Emily entre la suyas, sus dedos entrelazados sin esfuerzo. A una hora del vuelo, sin aviso, el avión sufrió una fuerte turbulencia. La cabina vibró y se sacudió violentamente, y el avión cayó varios cientos de pies de repente, lanzando a los pasajeros hacia adelante en sus asientos. Jadeos, gritos y chillidos llenaron la cabina mientras los compartimientos superiores vibraban y los auxiliares de vuelo eran arrojados por todo el avión.

Roe instintivamente apretó con fuerza la mano de Emily, su corazón se aceleró. El avión volvió a dar una sacudida hacia abajo un par de cientos de pies más y la caída repentina hizo que los pasajeros gritaran aún más.

Emily apretó su mano en respuesta. Ellos se miraron a los ojos, el miedo era evidente entre ambos, pero se mantuvieron serenos, como si se anclaran mutuamente en medio del caos.

Afortunadamente, sus cinturones de seguridad los sujetaban firmemente previniendo cualquier lesión. Después de lo que se sintió como una eternidad, la voz tranquila pero tensa del piloto se escuchó por el intercomunicador: "Damas y caballeros, nos hemos encontrado inesperadamente con una turbulencia. Nos disculpamos por el inconveniente. Por favor permanezcan sentados con sus cinturones de seguridad abrochados. Tenemos todo bajo control".

"¿Estás bien?" Roe susurró, apartándole un mechón de pelo de la cara.

Emily respondió: "Sí. ¿Y tú?".

"Sí", murmuró Roe.

Cuando el avión aterrizó sin incidentes en Sídney, los pasajeros estallaron en aplausos, pero Emily y Roe permanecieron en silencio mientras desabrochaban sus cinturones de seguridad y recogían sus cosas.

Afuera de la terminal del aeropuerto, permanecieron cerca, esperando a que llegaran sus respectivos Uber.

Roe se acercó un paso más a Emily, acariciándole la mejilla con el pulgar. "Emily", él susurró, "Te amo".

"Yo también te amo, Roe", ella susurró, con una voz llena de tranquila certeza.

Ellos se quedaron ahí un momento más, con la frente apoyada una contra la otra, dejando que el momento los envolviera. No fue un gesto grandioso ni dramático. Fue sencillo, sincero, y perfecto.

Justo entonces, el Uber de Roe se detuvo junto a la acera. El coche de Emily no estaba muy lejos.

"Te llamaré más tarde", Roe prometió, le dio un beso suave en los labios.

"Estaré esperando", Emily respondió susurrando.

Mientras Roe se subía a su Uber, él miró hacia atrás una última vez, mirando a Emily hacerle señas con la mano desde la acera antes de darse la vuelta y entrar en su propio coche.

Decirle que la amaba se había sentido tan natural, tan bien, y escucharla decir lo mismo, fue un momento que llevaría consigo para siempre.

¿Cómo reaccionaría ella cuando le contara lo de la lotería y el acuerdo prenupcial?

Él sabía que su relación había crecido fuerte en las últimas semanas, pero la conversación con Gavin aún hacía eco en su mente.

Cuando el Uber se detuvo frente a su casa, él quería aferrarse a ese sentimiento el mayor tiempo posible. Pero pronto, él sabía, comenzarían las verdaderas conversaciones—las que podrían cambiar todo.

Él solo esperaba que ellos estuvieran preparados para lo que fuera que viniera después.

31

Confeti

El teléfono móvil de Roe sonó. Viendo el nombre de Gavin en la pantalla, él entró en su oficina y cerró la puerta.

"Roe, soy Gavin. Los documentos están listos para que los revises y recojas. ¿Podrías venir mañana, digamos, alrededor del medio día?".

"Por supuesto, Gavin. Allí estaré".

Tras colgar el teléfono, Roe se acercó a Liam y a Aggie, quienes estaban junto a la máquina de café conversando. "Aggie, Liam—algo ha surgido. No estaré el jueves ni el viernes. Mantengan funcionando todo sin problemas".

Aggie levantó una ceja, "¿Otro fin de semana largo?".

"Algo así". Roe dijo con una sonrisa, pero no dio detalles.

Roe volvió a entrar en su oficina y llamó a Emily.

"Oye, cariño. ¿Puedes tomarte el viernes libre?". Él preguntó.

"Roe, ya me he tomado mucho tiempo libre últimamente. Mi jefe se pregunta si todavía estoy comprometida con Stonebridge".

Roe rió un poco. "Confía en mí, no te arrepentirás de esto. Solo encuéntrame en Petite Maison para almorzar al medio día en punto. ¿Sí?".

Intuyendo que él tramaba algo: "Bien", ella dijo a regañadientes. "Pero me debes una por esto".

"Te prometo que no te arrepentirás", dijo Roe, y sonrió para sí mismo.

El resto del día transcurrió sin complicaciones.

Al día siguiente, según lo previsto, Roe llegó a la oficina de Gavin Reed. Gavin le dio una cálida bienvenida, indicándole que se sentara.

"Roe, aquí están los dos documentos", Gavin comenzó. "El primero es la reestructuración de Alder y Finch, contigo, Liam y Aggie figurando como directores. Todo está en orden. Solo necesita tus firmas".

Roe recogió el documento, pasó un par de páginas, le hizo a Gavin una pregunta, asintió con la cabeza y, una vez satisfecho, firmó los documentos.

"Y el segundo..." Gavin vaciló ligeramente, "Todo está redactado según tus indicaciones, pero Roe, recuerda lo que hablamos. El momento y la entrega son importantes. Encuentra el momento correcto".

Roe le agradeció, tomó ambos documentos, y salió de la oficina sintiendo una extraña mezcla de anticipación y ansiedad.

Roe llegó temprano a Petite Maison, escogió una mesa tranquila junto al jardín donde ellos pudieran hablar en privado. Él ordenó una botella del mejor vino y esperó.

Pocos minutos después del mediodía, Emily entró, llevaba un vestido ligero de verano que la hacía lucir verdaderamente radiante. El mesero la condujo a la mesa, y Roe se levantó para saludarla con un beso.

"Te ves hermosa", él dijo, apartando ligeramente la silla para que se sentara.

"Gracias", Emily respondió con una sonrisa, sentándose con elegancia.

Ellos ordenaron, y Roe inició la conversación con una pregunta inesperada. "Emily, si tú no trabajaras en Stonebridge Insurance—si el dinero no fuera un problema— ¿qué harías?".

Los ojos de Emily se iluminaron. "Tres cosas en realidad", ella dijo, inclinándose ligeramente hacia él. "Primero, abriría una pequeña galería en algún lugar de la costa. Segundo, dirigiría una granja de rescate de perros—nada lujoso, solo lo suficiente para darles una segunda oportunidad. Y tercero, escribiría. Hay un autor local, J. F. Nodar, que es simplemente maravilloso con sus historias. Siempre he querido escribir así, ya sabes…simplemente nunca encontré el tiempo".

Roe sonrió. Le encantaba cada palabra. "Todo eso suena perfecto".

Cuando llegó el almuerzo, su conversación continuó fluyendo fácilmente. Ellos rieron, compartieron historias sobre el trabajo, y disfrutaron de una tarde de esas que los hacía olvidar el mundo exterior.

Después del postre y el café, Roe miró a Emily y dijo: "Emily…hay algo de lo que necesito hablar contigo", él empezó, y puso el prenupcial sobre la mesa. "Esto es…bueno, un acuerdo prenupcial. Quería que estuviéramos protegidos. Pensé que era lo correcto, pero…"

Emily miró a Roe, pero recogió el documento y lo leyó cuidadosamente. Entonces ella lo puso de nuevo sobre la mesa, su mirada se desvió hacia el jardín. Durante un largo momento, ella estuvo en silencio.

A Roe se le encogió el corazón. ¿Había cometido un terrible error?

Finalmente, Emily se volvió hacia él, su expresión era suave pero seria. "Nunca esperé un acuerdo prenupcial, Roe. De verdad, nunca lo esperé, pero si tú piensas que es necesario, lo firmaré. Quiero que sepas que te amo". Ella buscó en su bolso y sacó un bolígrafo.

Mientras ella firmaba con su nombre el documento, él notó que Emily se secaba una lágrima del rabillo del ojo. "Malditas alergias", ella murmuró con una débil sonrisa.

Eso no son alergias, pensó Roe.

Roe tomó el acuerdo prenupcial firmado y lo miró fijamente por un largo rato. Gavin había hecho un gran trabajo. El acuerdo era justo. Completamente balanceado y los protegía a ambos. Pero este simplemente no parecía lo correcto.

Maldita sea. Gavin tenía razón. Pensó Roe.

"Al diablo el acuerdo prenupcial", él susurró, antes de romper el documento en tantas piezas que podría ser usado ahora como confeti.

Los ojos de Emily se abrieron, incrédula.

"Emily, te amo, maldición. Desde el primer instante en que nos conocimos, me enamoré de ti. Este prenupcial fue una pésima idea y me advirtieron sobre ello, y aun así, te lo presenté", señalando el confeti sobre la mesa. "Todo lo que tengo es tuyo, Emily. Sin condiciones, sin trámites".

Emily quedó impactada por sus palabras y aún más por sus acciones. Entonces, con un grito de alegría, ella saltó de su silla y se abalanzó sobre Roe, cubriéndolo de besos.

"Yo me hubiera casado contigo con el prenupcial, pero ahora", mirando el confeti en el piso del restaurant, "Ahora sé que también me amas más que al dinero".

Roe se levantó de su silla y se arrodilló en medio del restaurante.

"Ms. Emily Dickson", él dijo, levantando la vista hacia ella, "¿Quieres casarte conmigo?".

"Sí", ella susurró, entonces en voz alta dijo: "¡Sí! ¡Me casaré contigo!".

Roe se puso de pie de un salto, la tomó en sus brazos, y la besó profundamente. Entonces, volviéndose hacia los pocos clientes y el personal que aún quedaban en el restaurante, gritó: "¡Ella dijo que sí! ¡Nos vamos a casar!".

El restaurante estalló en vítores y aplausos. Los meseros aplaudieron, los comensales levantaron sus copas, y el gerente incluso se acercó corriendo con una botella de champán de cortesía.

Después de que se calmó la emoción y de que se dieron unos cuantos besos más para celebrarlo, Roe se inclinó hacia

Emily y le susurró al oído: "Vamos. Hay una cosa más que necesito hacer".

Emily arqueó una ceja. "¿Ah sí? Y ¿qué es?".

Roe sonrió con picardía. "Necesito hacer un anuncio en la oficina".

32

Anuncio

Roe estacionó su coche frente a Alder y Finch y se bajó, tomándose un instante para asimilar el momento. Girando hacia Emily, él sonrió y le extendió su brazo.

"Vamos, belleza", él bromeó.

Emily puso los ojos en blanco. "Eres ridículo", ella dijo.

Cuando entraron en la oficina, los recibió el familiar murmullo de las conversaciones y los teléfonos sonando, pero todo pareció detenerse en el momento en que entraron.

Aggie levantó la vista de su escritorio, y se quedó boquiabierta. En todos los años que ella había trabajado para Roe, ella nunca había visto una sonrisa como la que se le dibujaba en el rostro.

Liam salió de su oficina, mirando curiosamente entre Roe y Emily. "Está bien, ¿qué está pasando?", él preguntó, cruzando sus brazos.

El resto del equipo empezó a reunirse, atraído por el repentino revuelo en el ambiente. Mateo y Sophia entraron justo cuando todos se estaban reuniendo, aun con las chaquetas puestas después de estar en el trabajo de campo.

Roe les dedicó a todos una sonrisa juguetona, de pie, erguido y con Emily del brazo, se detuvieron en el centro de la oficina. "Muy bien, amigos, acérquense. Tengo un anuncio que hacer".

Todos se reunieron, curiosos y listos.

Roe sonrió radiante, su sonrisa prácticamente iluminaba la sala. "Todos, me gustaría que conocieran a Emily Dickson".

Un coro de saludos y sonrisas corteses siguieron mientras el equipo asentía y ofrecía cálidas bienvenidas. Liam y Aggie la reconocieron de Stonebridge Insurance, pero los otros la habían visto solo brevemente.

Roe le dio a Emily un apretón juguetón y, con una sonrisa de oreja a oreja, agregó, "Ah, y a propósito…justo le propuse casarnos—¡y dijo que sí! ¡Nos vamos a casar!".

Por un momento, la sala quedó en silencio, pero luego todo se volvió un caos. Todos estallaron en vítores y aplausos, y Liam cruzó el lugar con una gran sonrisa.

"¡Felicitaciones, Roe!", exclamó Liam. "Has conseguido a una buena pareja".

Aggie siguió justo detrás de Liam, y ella le dio a Roe un fuerte abrazo. "Estoy tan feliz por ti Roebuck".

Entonces Aggie giró para mirar a Emily. Se percibía algo en la forma en que Aggie entrecerraba los ojos ligeramente, como probando su sinceridad. Entonces, una vez satisfecha, una gran sonrisa se dibujó en su rostro.

"¡Bienvenida a la familia!" Aggie exclamó, lanzándose sobre Emily y envolviéndola en un abrazo de oso. Emily sonrió y se dejó sofocar por Aggie.

Roe levantó su mano para acallar la charla animada, y el equipo se quedó en silencio. "Esperen, esperen, gente, como dice el comercial de TV: ¡'hay más'! Tengo otro anuncio que hacer".

Roe juntó sus manos y aclaró su garganta. "Entonces…yo recientemente gané algún dinero en el Powerball. Y después de pensarlo mucho y con detenimiento, he decidido no vender Alder y Finch". Él miró con cariño al grupo. "Todos ustedes son como una familia para mí, y quiero que la empresa siga adelante con fuerza. Entonces, esto es lo que he decidido".

Todas las miradas estaban fijas en Roe, expectantes.

"Estoy reestructurando la empresa", dijo Roe. "Liam y Aggie se convertirán en directores—directores en activo—responsables de dirigir las operaciones en el día a día, mientras tanto, daré un paso atrás y me convertiré en un director pasivo. Aun así, seguiré disponible para consultas y asistir a las reuniones de la junta, pero a partir de ahora, ustedes dos estarán a cargo".

Liam parpadeó atónito, y Aggie llevó su mano a la boca, sorprendida.

Roe sonrió. "Pensé en vender el negocio, pero me di cuenta de algo: este equipo construyó este lugar conmigo. Es tan suyo como mío. Así que, por su éxito—durante muchos años más".

Los aplausos estallaron de nuevo, más fuertes que antes, y los vítores resonaron por toda la oficina. Aggie desapareció en la cocina y reapareció con una variedad de cervezas y botellas de licor.

Liam levantó una cerveza. "¡Por Roe y Emily!" ¡Y por Alder y Finch!".

Mientras la celebración bullía a su alrededor, Emily gentilmente tiró del brazo de Roe, llevándolo aparte. Con una sonrisa juguetona, pero curiosa, ella preguntó: "¿Cuánto dinero ganaste exactamente?".

Roe se rió, sabiendo que este momento llegaría. "Bueno", él dijo, "Hace un mes, Danny, Albert y yo organizamos un pequeño grupo para el sorteo del Powerball de 120 millones de dólares. Y por suerte para nosotros, uno de nuestros boletos ganó".

Emily lo miró fijamente, con los ojos muy abiertos. "Roe...¿cuánto?".

Roe sonrió. "Mi parte es de $40 millones. Debería estar en mi cuenta en unas dos semanas".

Las piernas de Emily se doblaron por un segundo, obligando a Roe a extender la mano para sostenerla. "¿Estás bien?" él preguntó, preocupado.

"Ahora entiendo el acuerdo prenupcial, y saber que estuviste dispuesto a romperlo—eso significa más para mí que todo el dinero del mundo".

Roe sonrió: "Te amo, Emily Dickson de Stonebridge Insurance Group. ¡Tú eres mi todo!".

Roe abrazó a Emily con fuerza y le susurró al oído: "Sabes lo que eso significa, ¿verdad?".

Emily se echó ligeramente hacia atrás, mirándolo con curiosidad. "No, ¿Qué?".

"Stonebridge Insurance Group va a necesitar una nueva vicepresidenta porque la anterior pronto va a estar muy ocupada con su escritura, su nueva galería de arte, y su nueva granja de rescate de perros".

Emily rió, su corazón se sentía ligero por primera vez en mucho tiempo. "Tienes toda la razón".

Roe sonrió y miró alrededor de la oficina. Alder y Finch, y todas las personas que le importaban, iban a estar bien.

33

El Mayor Premio de Todos

El familiar murmullo de voces llenó la oficina de Investigaciones Alder y Finch y se hizo presente alrededor de ellos mientras Roe y Emily cruzaban las puertas. Su hijo de dos años, Ian Cooke, descansaba cómodamente en sus brazos.

Llegar a tiempo para la primera reunión anual de la junta directiva, era algo en lo que Roe siempre insistía. A Roe le encantaba traer a Emily a sus reuniones trimestrales, así que las reuniones anuales no deberían diferentes. Aunque Emily no tenía voto, su presencia, junto con la del pequeño Ian, hacía que la reunión se sintiera más como un reencuentro entre amigos que como una formalidad.

Mientras se reunían en el interior de la sala de conferencias, Liam, y Aggie le hicieron a Ian un gesto juguetón con la mano, lo que lo hizo reír y extender sus pequeños brazos hacia ellos.

Una vez que todos se habían sentado, Liam se aclaró la garganta y leyó las minutas de la reunión del año anterior. Se presentaron algunas mociones, y después de breves discusiones y votos unánimes, la reunión se relajó y se convirtió en una charla amistosa.

Aggie se inclinó hacia Emily e Ian, haciendo caras y jugando al escondite con el pequeño niño, provocando carcajadas. Roe se recostó en su asiento, mirando a su familia y al equipo interactuar con un sentido de profunda satisfacción, sabiendo que esto era todo lo que él había esperado.

"Entonces, Roe", Liam empezó casualmente, "¿Qué fue de Danny Monk y Albert Guzmán?".

"Bueno, Danny mantuvo su librería y finalmente se mudó a Crystal Cove. Él y Toni Webster—ahora Toni Webster Monk—vendieron la casa de ella y juntos compraron una casa en la playa. Y poco después de eso, ellos tuvieron gemelos".

"Gemelos, ¿eh? ¿Cómo los llamaron?".

"Daniel y Albert, por supuesto".

"Bueno, eso tiene sentido. ¿Y qué pasó con el otro tipo, Albert?".

"Albert está fuera, viviendo el sueño. Él ha estado viajando sin parar, nunca se queda en un lugar por más de un mes. Cada tarjeta postal que recibo de él viene de un país o ciudad diferente. Con él no hay descanso".

"Suena bien. Bueno, me alegra que ambos estén bien", dijo Liam.

"Sí", dijo Roe, sonrió para sí mismo. "Ellos están justo donde querían estar", resopló, divertido. "Déjame preguntarte algo, Liam. ¿Qué fue de ese detective, Cassell?".

"Hay una historia interesante aquí, Roe. Le pidieron que se jubilara, ya que su portafolio, tanto el actual como el anterior, tenía un gran rezago de casos sin resolver".

"¿En serio?".

"Sí, particularmente esos que involucraban algún tipo de hurto. Imagínate", dijo Liam con una sonrisa.

Liam se puso de pie y tomó otra cerveza del pequeño refrigerador en la esquina. Cuando regresó le dio a Roe una cerveza, Roe lo miró y dijo: "Oye, Liam, hazme un favor. Toma la carpeta que nosotros teníamos sobre Danny y Albert, ¿sí?".

Curioso, pero complaciente, Liam fue al archivo de documentos y sacó la carpeta marcada con sus nombres. Se la entregó a Roe, quien le echó un rápido vistazo y caminó hacia la trituradora. Sin dudarlo, Roe introdujo la carpeta dentro de la máquina, mirándola desaparecer en diminutas tiras ilegibles.

"Bueno", dijo Roe con firmeza, limpiándose las manos, "ese es el fin de la historia de Danny Monk y Albert Matthew Guzmán".

A medida que la reunión llegaba a su fin, Roe, Emily, e Ian se dirigieron a la puerta. Justo cuando estaban a punto de irse, Aggie se acercó rápidamente, con los ojos brillando de emoción.

"¡Roe, espera, espera un segundo!", ella llamó.

Roe se giró, alzando una ceja. "¿Qué pasa, Aggie? ¿Ocurre algo?".

"No, todo está bien. Yo quería pedirte algo. ¿Recuerdas a ese autor que te entrevistó hace tres años?", ella preguntó con entusiasmo.

Roe pensó por un momento y asintió. "Sí, recuerdo—J. F. Nodar. ¿Por qué?".

Aggie sonrió. "Bueno, resulta que él es el autor favorito de Emily".

"Sí, lo sé; Emily me lo dijo hace un tiempo".

El rostro de Emily se iluminó con sorpresa. "Sí, él es. ¿Él te entrevistó? Tú nunca mencionaste eso en todas nuestras conversaciones".

"Se me debe haber olvidado. Hay mucho que hacer". Dijo Roe, sonrió y señaló al pequeño Ian.

"Bueno", continuó Aggie, "él quería que te dijera que acaba de terminar su nueva novela. ¿Y adivina qué? Él quiere enviarte una copia firmada".

"¿De verdad? Eso me encantaría. Pídele que la envíe aquí a la oficina, y la recogeré".

"Ah", agregó Aggie, "y nunca adivinarás cómo la tituló".

Roe alzó una ceja. "OK, te escucho. ¿Cuál es el nombre de la novela?".

"Él la llamó: 'Un amor al fin declarado", contestó Aggie. "Creo que debería ganar un premio si tú estás en él, Roe".

El título tocó una fibra muy profunda en él, resonando no solo con su propio camino junto a Emily, sino también con el de Danny Monk y Albert Guzmán.

Él rió entre dientes en voz baja, bajando la vista hacia Ian, quien se aferraba felizmente a Emily. "Sí", dijo Roe, medio para sí mismo. "Un amor al fin declarado" …para mí, para Danny y Toni. Y Albert…Bueno, Albert está enamorado de sí mismo".

Emily rió, apoyando la cabeza sobre el hombro de Roe. "Suena bien", susurró.

Roe sonrió mientras ellos caminaban hacia la puerta. En un brazo él llevaba a Ian mientras que con el otro sostenía la mano de Emily y, en ese momento, Roe supo una cosa con seguridad: él ya había ganado el mayor premio de todos.

Notas del Autor para el Final

Mientras escribo estas últimas palabras, me siento lleno de una mezcla de alegría y tristeza que conlleva el hecho de decir adiós a mis viejos amigos. Porque eso es en lo que se han convertido estos personajes para mí; una forma de mostrar a los lectores un poco de mí mismo a lo largo de los años. Se dice que un individuo puede ser su mejor amigo y eso es lo que estos personajes han sido para mí. Amigos que han compartido sus triunfos y fracasos, sus amores y pérdidas, sus sueños y miedos.

Esta trilogía ha sido más que solo palabras en papel para mí. Ha sido un viaje de descubrimiento y de intercambio entre el lector y yo.

Ahora, al cerrar este capítulo final y este libro, espero que usted haya encontrado la que fue mi primera intención: compartir con usted muchos de mis momentos privados escondidos entre las páginas y sus personajes.

A aquellos que han estado aquí desde la primera página del primer libro: gracias por su paciencia, su dedicación y su disposición para creer en este mundo, y en mí.

A aquellos que se unieron a nosotros en algún momento del camino: gracias por ponerse al día y unirse a nuestra caravana literaria.

A todos: cada final es también un comienzo. Aunque este puede ser el último capítulo de esta saga, con suerte los ecos de estas historias resonarán en su imaginación mucho tiempo después de que haya pasado la última página.

Con gratitud.

José F. Nodar

Tres libros, tres viajes, tres historias; tres aventuras que finalmente han llegado a su fin.

Acerca del Autor

José F. Nodar

Lanzado a uno de los desafíos más abrumadores a la edad de 11 años, el viaje de José comenzó en la Habana, Cuba. La revolución cubana desarraigó a su familia, forzando a sus padres a tomar una decisión desgarradora: enviarlo lejos, solo, a un lugar seguro. José abordó un avión, con la incertidumbre de lo que tenía por delante, y aterrizó no en la comodidad de rostros familiares, sino en un orfanato en un pequeño pueblo de Georgia llamado Washington.

Durante los siguientes siete años, él navegó por la vida como un extraño en tierra extranjera. Las cartas eran pocas, y la esperanza de reunirse con sus padres se convirtió en un sueño lejano. Finalmente, a la edad de 18 años—ahora graduado de la escuela secundaria de Atlanta— él abrazó a su familia de nuevo. La reunión fue agridulce ya que José había crecido sin ellos, volviéndose un joven independiente mucho antes que la mayoría.

Determinado a labrarse un futuro por sí mismo, José cursó la carrera de Administración de Empresas en la Universidad Estatal de Georgia. Se adentró en el mundo de las finanzas, comenzando en el First National Bank de Atlanta (hoy Wells Fargo). Su talento natural para los números y el pensamiento estratégico, lo impulsaron a convertirse en gerente de proyectos en consultoría financiera, lo que lo llevó a participar en proyectos de alto riesgo. Su carrera lo llevó por todo el mundo, desde las ciudades bulliciosas en los Estados Unidos hasta los centros financieros en Europa, e incluso a las soleadas costas de Australia.

Fue en Camden, Nueva Gales del Sur, donde comenzó un nuevo capítulo la vida de José. Mientras exploraba los tranquilos ritmos de esta ciudad australiana, José tropezó con un grupo de escritores locales. Lo que comenzó como un interés casual, pronto se convirtió en una pasión insaciable. Las historias que se arremolinaban en su mente tomaron forma y, de esa chispa creativa, nació Danny Monk, su primer personaje importante, una figura traviesa e intrigante que captaba las complejidades que José había observado a lo largo de su vida. Escribir la historia de Danny fue una revelación, y con ello, José descubrió una nueva vocación.

Avanzando rápidamente hasta hoy, José no solo es un escritor, sino también un prolífico narrador, que compagina múltiples proyectos a la vez. Él está inmerso en su séptima colección de relatos cortos, al tiempo que elabora su última obra—una novela policiaca cuyo lanzamiento está previsto para el 2026. Sus libros, llenos de personajes cautivadores y narrativas complejas, reflejan una vida rica en experiencias, retos y triunfos.

Sin embargo, el mundo de José no se limita al teclado y la pantalla, la inspiración le llega de todas partes, y uno de sus pasatiempos favoritos es pasear por el centro comercial local, observando a la gente en silencio, tomando nota de sus peculiaridades, comportamientos y fragmentos de conversación que puedan inspirarle un nuevo personaje o un giro en la trama. Cuando él no está escribiendo o recopilando ideas, José se sumerge en la literatura, alimentando su mente con las palabras de otros.

Además de sus actividades creativas, José atesora los placeres sencillos la vida—especialmente los largos paseos con su esposa Miriam, por las pintorescas calles de Spring Farm. Sus tranquilos paseos son una rutina muy apreciada; momentos de reflexión en los que se entrelazan historias, recuerdos y sueños.

La vida de José es un tapiz tejido a partir de la adversidad, la perseverancia y la creatividad. Desde el orfanato en Georgia hasta los distritos financieros del mundo, y ahora hasta los rincones tranquilos de Spring Farm, donde nacen las historias, su trayectoria es un testimonio de la resiliencia del espíritu humano. Y con cada libro que escribe, José no solo cuenta historias, sino que también deja atrás pedazos de sí mismo, enriqueciendo la vida de los lectores de todo el mundo.

Otros libros de José F. Nodar

Inglés

- Books, Pens & Larceny
- Mending Hearts at Crystal Cove
- A Love Finally Spoken
- The Universe Between Us
- The Compass Legacy
- The Teacher's Assistant
- A Night of Love
- The Northport Coffee Group
- The Time Bus
- SEX
- The Ghost Detective's First Case
- The Last Light of Aurethis
- Stories to Share with My Partner Book 1
- Stories to Share with My Partner Book 2
- Stories to Share with My Partner Book 3
- Stories to Share with My Partner Book 4
- Stories to Share with My Partner Book 5
- Stories to Share with My Partner Book 6
- Stories to Share with My Partner Book 7

- Stories to Share with My Partner Book 8
- Stories to Share with My Partner Book 9
- Stories to Share with My Partner Book 10
- Stories to Share with My Partner Book 11
- Quick Stories & Poems Volume I
- Quick Stories & Poems Volume II
- Quick Stories & Poems Volume III

Español

- Cuentos Para Compartir con Mi Pareja Libro 1
- Cuentos Para Compartir con Mi Pareja Libro 2
- Cuentos Para Compartir con Mi Pareja Libro 3
- Libros, Bolígrafos y Hurto
- Reparando Corazones en Crystal Cove
- Un Amor Finalmente Declarado
- El Autobús del Tiempo